T0323320

The Community of Advantage

Praise for *The Community of Advantage*

'In this book, Sugden brings together his work over twenty years in experimental economics and economic/political philosophy to develop a defence of the liberal market order in terms of "advantage", understood not in terms of preference satisfaction nor in objective metrics of well-being (such as Rawls' primary goods) but rather in terms of expanded opportunity sets. Sugden is one of the most interesting and creative minds working at the interface between economics and ethics these days; and his engagement with this ambitious project is a contribution of major significance.'

—Geoffrey Brennan, Professor of Political Science and Moral and Political Philosophy, Australian National University, Australia

'For many years Robert Sugden has opened new pathways in economics and philosophy. This highly original monograph finally weaves together his views on rational decision, paternalism, freedom, and markets. Sugden's contractarian approach provides a much-needed alternative to libertarian paternalism, demonstrating that classic liberalism can be brought up-to-date with the latest research in behavioural economics. *The Community of Advantage* will become a compulsory reading for all philosophers and social scientists interested in the moral and political implications of economic science.'

—Francesco Guala, Professor of Philosophy and Economics, University of Milan, Italy

'Robert Sugden's *The Community of Advantage* is a daring response to the findings of behavioural economics that show that preferences that people reveal in their choices cannot serve as a foundation for normative economics. Instead of conjuring up rational preferences that supposedly hide beneath the flawed ones we observe, Sugden proposes a radical transformation of normative economics which assesses policies by the freedom they offer interacting individuals. Sugden's arguments are a serious challenge to normative economics as we know it, and his proposals offer a fascinating unexplored path toward a replacement.'

—Daniel M. Hausman, Herbert A. Simon and Hilldale Professor, Department of Philosophy, University of Wisconsin-Madison, USA

The Community of Advantage

A Behavioural Economist's Defence of the Market

Robert Sugden

OXFORD
UNIVERSITY PRESS

Great Clarendon Street, Oxford, OX2 6DP,
United Kingdom

Oxford University Press is a department of the University of Oxford.
It furthers the University's objective of excellence in research, scholarship,
and education by publishing worldwide. Oxford is a registered trade mark of
Oxford University Press in the UK and in certain other countries

© Robert Sugden 2018

The moral rights of the author have been asserted

First Edition published in 2018

Published in the United States of America by Oxford University Press
198 Madison Avenue, New York, NY 10016, United States of America

British Library Cataloguing in Publication Data

Data available

Library of Congress Control Number: 2017962346

ISBN 978–0–19–882514–2

Printed in Great Britain by
Clays Ltd, ElcografS.p.A

Preface

To explain why I wanted to write this book, I must go back to the year 2000.

By then, I was already an old hand in what was just beginning to be called 'behavioural economics'. Graham Loomes and I had been working together in this area (which we preferred to call 'experimental economics') for almost twenty years, alongside a growing number of like-minded economists and psychologists. Our own informal research group—which had expanded to include Chris Starmer, Judith Mehta, Robin Cubitt, and Alistair Munro—had carried out many experimental tests of received assumptions about rational individual choice. We had identified an array of so-called 'anomalies'—regularities in people's decision-making behaviour that were inconsistent with standard economic theory. We had developed and tested new, psychologically-based theories that went some way towards explaining these observations. We had also spent a lot of time investigating the problems that anomalies cause for surveys that are designed to elicit individuals' valuations of non-marketed goods, such as environmental quality and publicly financed health care. I think that by then we were—I know that I was—fairly sure that the failures of standard theory were not isolated epiphenomena. Nor were they (as some more mainstream economists still maintained) the result of errors that would disappear if decision-makers had sufficient incentives and experience. Rather, they were evidence that the mental processes that underlie normal human decision-making do not correspond very closely with models of rational choice. What we had found was that a typical individual's choices between given options often vary according to factors that seem irrelevant when viewed in the perspective of rational choice, but whose effects are both predictable and psychologically understandable. I could see no reason to suppose—indeed, no credible way of making sense of the idea—that 'true' preferences with the properties assumed in rational choice theory existed somewhere beneath the psychology of actual mental processing.

It seemed to me that the biggest outstanding challenge for behavioural economics was to find a way of doing normative analysis—for example, to answer questions about how far markets should be regulated, or about whether public goods should be supplied by government and if so, which goods in which quantities. Up to 2000, behavioural economics had barely begun to develop its own answers to such questions. Normative economics, as conventionally practised, assumed that individuals had well-articulated and rational preferences over all relevant options; it used the satisfaction of those preferences as its criterion. This criterion was generally seen as embodying the principle that economists' recommendations should not be paternalistic: it was for each individual to judge what mattered to him or her. But how could this criterion be used if individuals lacked well-defined preferences? The challenge, as I saw it, was to develop a form of normative economics that did not depend on untenable assumptions about preferences while still respecting individuals' choices about how to live their own lives.

My thinking about this problem was influenced by my still earlier experience of working in a different area of economics. Back in the 1970s, many economists and philosophers were struggling with the problem of how to represent the value of individual liberty within the formal framework of social choice theory. Amartya Sen had proved a theorem that purported to show the impossibility of combining respect for 'protected spheres' of individual liberty with acceptance of a very weak principle of preference-satisfaction—that if everyone prefers one state of affairs to another, the first state is better than the second. More worryingly, it turned out that if Sen's method of representing liberty was correct, respect for individual liberty could not be guaranteed—full stop. These results revolved around the possibility that people might have 'meddlesome' preferences about one another's private affairs. One of the most common responses to these results was to look for criteria for defining meddlesomeness and then to find some way of purifying preferences to remove this normatively unacceptable property. In the first paper I ever wrote that made any significant impression on my fellow economists, I argued that this literature was a misguided attempt to express ideas about individual liberty while viewing society from the perspective of an autocratic social planner who was entitled to decide what use to make of data about individuals' preferences. The whole problem dissolved if one forgot about preferences and defined each individual's protected sphere in terms of his opportunities for choice. How each individual chose to use these opportunities was up to him, and irrelevant for the definition of liberty.

Throughout the 1980s and 1990s, I had seen myself not only as an experimental economist drawing on ideas and research methods from psychology, but also as a philosophical economist, working in the liberal tradition of David Hume, Adam Smith, and John Stuart Mill. I had never thought that these two aspects of my work were in tension. On the contrary, I had come to see Hume's scepticism about human rationality and his clear-sighted investigation of actual human psychology as anticipating key insights of behavioural economics. When, in 2000 or thereabouts, I set about trying to find a form of normative economics that was compatible with behavioural findings, I followed the same broad strategy as I had done in responding to Sen's theorem. In place of the preference-satisfaction criterion of traditional welfare economics, I substituted a criterion of opportunity. By defining people's opportunities independently of their preferences, I hoped to cut through the problems caused by the inadequacy of the standard assumptions of rational choice theory. By attributing normative value to individuals' opportunities without taking any view about how those opportunities should be used, I saw myself as upholding the non-paternalistic traditions of liberal economics. The first finished product of this programme of work was a paper, 'The opportunity criterion', published in the *American Economic Review* in 2004. This paper showed how some of the classic theoretical results of welfare economics could be reformulated in terms of opportunity.

It turned out that I had not been the only person trying to reconcile normative and behavioural economics. In 2003, two important papers appeared in American law journals, proposing an approach to that reconciliation problem that was very different from the one I was developing. Each of these papers had a prominent legal scholar (Cass Sunstein in one case, Samuel Issacharoff in the other) as one of its authors. The other authors were a roll call of the great and the good of American behavioural economics: Richard Thaler (writing with Sunstein) and Colin Camerer, George Loewenstein, Ted O'Donaghue, and Matthew Rabin (all writing with Issacharoff). The titles of these papers were significant, and significantly similar: 'Libertarian paternalism' and 'Regulation for conservatives'. The implication was clear: the findings of behavioural economics provide justifications for paternalistic interventions in the economy, and these justifications are not vulnerable to traditional objections to paternalism. Both papers were written as manifestos for what can conveniently be called *behavioural welfare economics*.

According to these manifestos, behavioural economics shows not merely that people's choices are often inconsistent with rational choice theory, but also that these inconsistencies result from mistakes that people would prefer not to make. Fortunately (it is claimed) behavioural economics also shows how, without the need for heavy-handed restrictions of freedom of choice, people can be 'nudged' towards choices that avoid these mistakes. Both papers make an implicit distinction between the preferences that are revealed in an individual's actual choices and the latent preferences on which she would have acted in the absence of error. Although there are only sketchy accounts of how latent preferences are defined and how they might be identified, there is an implicit assumption that these preferences will turn out to be consistent with the axioms of rational choice theory. The satisfaction of latent preferences is treated as the normative criterion. These two manifestos, and Thaler and Sunstein's popularization of their ideas in their later book *Nudge*, have been hugely influential. Behavioural welfare economics, in broadly the form set out by Camerer et al. and Sunstein and Thaler in 2003, has become the standard approach used by behavioural economists when engaging with normative questions. This approach has been endorsed by policy-makers around the world and has become a staple of media discussion.

I have to say that I have been surprised by the readiness of behavioural economists to interpret contraventions of rational choice theory as evidence of decision-making error. In the pioneering era of the 1980s and 1990s, this was exactly the interpretation of anomalies that mainstream economists typically favoured, and that we behavioural economists disputed. As some of us used to say, it is as if decision-makers are held to be at fault for failing to behave as the received theory predicts, rather than that theory being faulted for failing to make correct predictions. I have been less surprised, but still disappointed, by the willingness of behavioural economists to embrace paternalism. And I have felt increasingly uneasy that, in public discourse, ideas from behavioural welfare economics are appealing to a sensibility that is hostile to principles of economic freedom—principles that, for two and a half centuries, have been central to the liberal tradition of economics.

This book is my attempt to show the viability of a different way in which, having recognized that people often fail to conform to the axioms of rational choice theory, economists can still have something to say about normative questions. My 'Opportunity criterion' paper of 2004 was the first in a series of papers, sometimes written with co-authors, in which I have developed different aspects of what I have believed to be a coherent approach to the problem of reconciling normative and behavioural economics. This approach deviates in significant ways from the main path taken by economists since our discipline embraced rational choice theory in the late nineteenth century. In some respects, I stray further from that path than do the adherents of behavioural welfare economics; but that, I believe, is because I take the psychological evidence more seriously. Nevertheless, my approach conserves core features of the liberal tradition that are jettisoned by behavioural welfare economics. Its guiding idea is encapsulated in John Stuart Mill's description of the market as a 'community of advantage'—the idea that economic life is, or should be, mutually beneficial cooperation.

To repeat, I have *believed* that the various arguments in this series of papers make up a coherent way of thinking about normative economics. But ideas that seem mutually consistent when thought about informally often prove not to be so when one tries to write them down, whether in plain words or in the formal language of mathematics. One of my purposes in writing this book has been to satisfy myself that these arguments *do* make up a coherent whole or, where necessary, to find ways of reformulating them so that they become such a whole.

The book weaves together four main strands of argument. The first strand, introduced in Chapters 2 and 3, concerns a question that economists rarely ask explicitly: To whom should normative economics be addressed? My answer to this question is deeply influenced by the ideas of James Buchanan, as indeed is the book as a whole. Buchanan was one of the first economists to support my critique of Sen's analysis of liberty. I learned from him how this critique fits into a 'contractarian' conception of normative economics as an analysis that is addressed to citizens, viewed as potential parties to mutually beneficial agreements. I do not claim that citizens *must* be the addressees of normative economics, but I explain why I find the contractarian perspective valuable and why I have chosen to use it.

The second strand, introduced in Chapter 4, is a critique of the concept of latent preference that is implicit in behavioural welfare economics. Most of this chapter is adapted from a paper that I wrote with Gerardo Infante and Guilhem Lecouteux. The central argument is that there are no good grounds for assuming that, in the absence of error, individuals' choices would reveal 'true' preferences satisfying the standard axioms of rational choice theory.

The third strand, developed over the course of Chapters 5, 6, 7, and 8, proposes an alternative form of normative economics that does not use the concept of preference. Chapter 5 looks for a normative criterion that citizens might reasonably want economists to use when making recommendations about public policy. I propose the principle that, as viewed by each citizen separately, more opportunity for that person is better than less. I argue that each citizen can endorse this principle without needing to believe that his own preferences are rationally consistent. Chapter 6, which builds on work I have done with Ben McQuillin, develops an opportunity-based criterion which (roughly speaking) says that individuals collectively should have as much opportunity as possible to carry out whatever voluntary transactions they might want to make. I show that this criterion is satisfied in the equilibrium state of a competitive market, defined without any reference to preferences. Chapter 7, which includes material from a paper I wrote with Judith Mehta, considers what forms of market regulation might be justified as ways of expanding opportunities for mutually beneficial transactions. Chapter 8 considers issues of distribution in a contractarian perspective. I argue that the opportunity-enhancing properties of markets are not compatible with the kind of fairness that can be built into the rules of a handicap race: in this sense, the market cannot be fair. But if the rules of the market are to be acceptable to everyone, each person must have a continuing expectation of being able to share in the gains that the market creates.

The final strand, developed in Chapters 9, 10, and 11, is concerned with the moral status of market relationships. Chapter 9, which includes sections adapted from a paper I wrote with Luigino Bruni, is a critical examination of the widely-held view that market relationships are based on self-interested and instrumental motivations, and in consequence are morally impoverished. On this view, there are moral limits to the scope of markets: allowing the market to extend beyond these limits is liable to corrupt the virtues of other domains of social life. For the most part, behavioural economists have not got involved in virtue ethics, but the supposed contrasts between self-interested and socially-oriented preferences and between extrinsic and intrinsic motivation have become important themes in behavioural economics. In Chapter 10, building on my previous work on 'team reasoning' and on ongoing work with Andrea Isoni, I show how individuals can act on intentions that are neither self-interested nor altruistic, but are directed at mutual benefit. I argue that such intentions can underlie cooperation in many forms of voluntary interaction, in civil society in general and in the market in particular. In the final chapter, I address my fellow citizens, as a contractarian should, and try to persuade them of the advantages of living in a society that upholds a morality of mutual benefit.

* * *

As I have explained, important parts of the book are derived from, or based on, joint work with Luigino Bruni, Gerardo Infante, Andrea Isoni, Guilhem Lecouteux, Ben McQuillin, and Judith Mehta. Each of these collaborators shares responsibility for some part of the book, but none of them should be assumed to endorse all the arguments I present. As I have been working on the ideas in the book, I have learned a lot from discussing them with other people. Those who have helped me in this way (whether or not they have agreed with my conclusions) include Michael Bacharach, Nicholas Bardsley, Jane Beattie, Sergio Beraldo, Ken Binmore, Geoffrey Brennan, Nick Chater, Robin Cubitt, David Gauthier, Natalie Gold, Francesco Guala, Benedetto Gui, Shaun Hargreaves Heap, Daniel Hausman, Daniel Kahneman, Hartmut Kliemt, Richard Layard, Julian Le Grand, George Loewenstein, Graham Loomes, Bruce Lyons, Alistair Munro, Adam Oliver, Mozaffar Qizilbash, Daniel Read, Christian Schubert, Alessandra Smerilli, Chris Starmer, Cass Sunstein, Joshua Teng, Richard Thaler, Christine Tiefensee, Peter Wakker, Mengjie Wang, Jiwei Zheng, and a cast of anonymous reviewers (some of whom are perhaps among the people I have already mentioned). I also thank Katie Bishop, my editor at Oxford University Press, and Kim Allen, my copy-editor.

My work on the book has been supported by the Economic and Social Research Council (ESRC), first through a Professorial Fellowship (2006–2008, award RES 051 27 0146) and then through the Network for Integrated Behavioural Science (2013–2017, award ES/K002201/1). More recently, it has been supported by the European Research Council under the European Union's Horizon 2020 research and innovation programme (from 2016, grant agreement

670103). The ESRC awards supported two international conferences on the problems of reconciling normative and behavioural economics, held at the University of East Anglia in 2008 (primarily organized by Ben McQuillin) and 2016 (primarily organized by Gerardo Infante). The intense and open-minded discussions at these events helped me to shape my ideas. Over the many years that I have been working on this book, my wife Christine has provided encouragement, support, and an intelligent outsider's perspective on economics and philosophy.

Contents

Contents

List of Figures

Sources of Material

Sections 1.3, 4.1–4.3, and 4.5–4.7 are derived in part from Gerardo Infante, Guilhem Lecouteux, and Robert Sugden, 'Preference purification and the inner rational agent: a critique of the conventional wisdom of behavioural welfare economics', *Journal of Economic Methodology* 23 (2016): 1–25, available with open access under the terms of the Creative Commons Attribution Licence: DOI 10.1080/1350178X.2015.1070527.

Sections 2.1, 2.2, 3.3, and 3.4 are derived in part from Robert Sugden, 'The behavioural economist and the social planner: to whom should behavioural welfare economics be addressed?', *Inquiry* 56 (2013): 519–38, © Taylor and Francis, available online: http://www.tandfonline.com, DOI 10.1080/0020174X.2013.806139.

Section 3.2 is derived in part from Robert Sugden, 'Can a Humean be a contractarian?', published in Michael Baurmann and Bernd Lahno, eds, *Perspectives in Moral Science: Contributions from Philosophy, Economics, and Politics in Honour of Hartmut Kliemt* (Frankfurt School Verlag, 2009), pp. 11–24, with permission of the publisher.

Section 3.4 is derived in part from Robert Sugden, 'Do people really want to be nudged towards healthy lifestyles?', *International Review of Economics* 64 (2017): 113–23, available with open access under the terms of the Creative Commons Attribution Licence: DOI 10.1007/s12232-016-0264-1.

Section 4.4 is derived in part from Robert Sugden, 'Looking for a psychology for the inner rational agent', *Social Theory and Practice* 41 (2015): 579–98, with permission of the Philosophy Documentation Center, available online: DOI 10.5840/soctheorpract201541432.

Section 5.6 is derived in part from Robert Sugden, 'Taking unconsidered preferences seriously', *Philosophy*, Supplement 59 (2006): 209–32, © The Royal Institute of Philosophy and the contributors 2006, reprinted with permission of the publisher, available online: DOI 10.1017/S1358246106059108.

Sections 6.2–6.6 are derived in part from Robert Sugden, 'Characterising competitive equilibrium in terms of opportunity', *Social Choice and Welfare* 48 (2017): 487–503, available with open access under the terms of the Creative Commons Attribution Licence: DO1 10.1007/s00355-016-1015-7.

Sections 7.2 and 7.4 are derived in part from Judith Mehta and Robert Sugden, 'Making sense of complex choice situations', co-authored with Judith Mehta, published in Judith Mehta, ed., *Behavioural Economics in Competition and Consumer Policy* (Norwich: Centre for Competition Policy, 2013), pp. 41–8, with permission of the Centre for Competition Policy.

Sections 8.1 and 8.2 are derived in part from Robert Sugden, 'Living with unfairness: the limits of equality of opportunity in a market economy', *Social Choice and Welfare* 22 (2004): 211–36, © Springer-Verlag 2004, with permission of Springer.

Sections 9.1 and 9.2 are derived in part from Luigino Bruni and Robert Sugden, 'Reclaiming virtue ethics for economics', *Journal of Economic Perspectives* 27 (2013): 141–64, © American Economic Association, reproduced with permission of the *Journal of Economic Perspectives*.

Section 11.6 is derived in part from Robert Sugden, 'Fellow feeling', in Benedetto Gui and Robert Sugden, eds, *Economics and Social Interaction* (Cambridge University Press, 2005), pp. 52–75, © Cambridge University Press 2005, reprinted with permission of the publisher.

1

The Liberal Tradition and the Challenge from Behavioural Economics

The title of this book is taken from a passage in John Stuart Mill's *Principles of Political Economy*. Mill's *Principles*, first published in 1848 and revised many times up to his death in 1873, was the most authoritative English-language text on economics throughout the second half of the nineteenth century. Writing with characteristically Victorian (if perhaps misplaced) confidence in continuing progress towards international peace and free trade, Mill contrasts the enlightened views of his own time with the mercantilism of the past. With perhaps a touch of snobbery, he says that mercantilism is the 'political economy of the selling classes'; it treats economic relations between countries as if they were relations between rival tradesmen trying to undersell one another. This obsolete way of thinking 'overruled for centuries all sense of the general community of advantage which all commercial countries derive from the prosperity of one another' (Mill, 1871/1909, Book 3, Chapter 25, §1). Mill is telling his readers that the market is a *community of advantage*. I will begin my book by explaining what I think Mill means by this expression and, by this indirect route, what *I* mean by taking it as my title.

1.1 Mill and the Community of Advantage

Mill is telling us that if we look beneath the surface features of competition between rival businesses, we can understand a competitive market as a network of mutually advantageous relationships. By calling this network of relationships a *community*, Mill must intend something more than that the overall effect of a market is to promote the private interests of those who take part in it. Another of Mill's remarks about mercantilism helps to explain what he has in mind:

[C]ommerce first taught nations to see with good will the wealth and prosperity of one another. Before, the patriot . . . wished all countries weak, poor, and ill-governed, but his own: now he sees in their wealth and progress a direct source of wealth and progress to his own country.   (Mill, 1871/1909, Book 2, Chapter 17, §5)

The idea here is that, by participating in relationships of mutual benefit, people come to see one another as cooperative partners rather than as rivals, and that this perception tends to support more general attitudes of social solidarity and good will.

Mill makes this argument more explicitly in another book, *Utilitarianism* (1861). Mill wants to persuade his readers that it is reasonable to hope for a society in which utilitarianism is not just the principle on which governments act, but also the morality of private individuals. He explains that the hope is not that everyone consults the Greatest Happiness Principle before making day-to-day decisions, but only that people's moral feelings direct them towards actions that (in fact, but not necessarily in intention) tend to promote total happiness. Even so, he has to explain how, given the facts of human psychology, the right kinds of moral feelings can be sustained in a utilitarian society. His answer is that human beings have some natural propensity for 'social feelings', and that the degree to which these feelings develop depends on the structure of society. In so far as social life is structured by voluntary cooperation, each person can get what he wants only by helping others to get what *they* want. In such a society, individuals learn the necessity of taking account of one another's interests. By participating in relationships of mutual benefit, they form positive mental associations between benefits to themselves and benefits to others. Thus, such relationships are a nursery for the 'social feelings of mankind'. Mill justifies his optimism about utilitarian morality by arguing that, in the broad sweep of economic history, humanity is moving away from a 'state of savage independence' and becoming more and more dependent on mutually advantageous cooperation (1861/1972, Chapter 3). Given what he has said about international trade in the *Principles*, it seems clear that for Mill, the market is an important part of the growing network of cooperation that can sustain the social feelings of mankind.

Mill was not only one of the great economists and philosophers of his time; he was also one of its leading feminist thinkers. In *The Subjection of Women* (1869/1988) he often uses analogies with markets to explain what he sees as proper relationships between the sexes. Drawing on the contrast between free labour and slavery, he condemns the legal status of married women in mid-Victorian Britain on the grounds that it makes the wife the 'actual bondservant' of the husband; in opposition to this, he holds up business partnership as a model of what the marriage contract should be. While not going so far as to say that self-sacrifice has no place in marriage, he sees it as a merit of a partnership-like contract between equals that it would 'abate the exaggerated self-abnegation which is the present artificial ideal of feminine character'. Married life, according to Mill, ought to be 'an exercise of those virtues which each requires to fit them for all other association'; mankind should 'practice in the family the same moral rule which is adapted to the normal constitution of human society' (1869/1988: 32–52). In other words, cooperation for mutual benefit goes (or should go) all the way down—from international trade and the institutions of civil society to the relationship between husband and wife.

It is integral to Mill's concept of 'advantage' that each person is the ultimate judge of what counts as advantage to him or her. His *On Liberty* (1859/1972) is a passionate defence of individual liberty against paternalism, asserting the principle that

> ... the only purpose for which power can be rightfully exercised over any member of a civilised community, against his will, is to prevent harm to others.... He cannot rightfully be compelled to do or forbear because it will be better for him to do so, because it will make him happier, because, in the opinions of others, to do so would be wise, or even right.   (Mill, 1859/1972: 73)

Mill does not claim that people always choose the things that best promote their real well-being, but rather that no one is accountable to others for decisions that affect only himself. Mill's own ideas about human well-being, it must be said, are those of a high-minded and intellectual humanist. (I cannot resist adding that they sometimes seem to rest on shaky foundations, such as the famous claim, supposedly supported by the reports of people who know both sides of the question, that it is better to be a human being dissatisfied than a pig satisfied [1861/1972: 9].) But he is scrupulous in not using his own judgements about well-being to justify paternalism. For example, he seems to accept as an established 'prudential truth' that drunkenness and gambling are 'injurious to happiness' and 'hindrance[s] to improvement', but he insists on each person's right to choose to drink and gamble to excess (1859/1972: 137–8). Since the market supplies these forms of consumption to those who are willing to pay for them, I think we must take Mill to be treating such transactions as part of the community of advantage.

Mill's concept of a community of advantage encapsulates what I see as three core components of a liberal tradition of economic thought. The first is the idea that, in a well-ordered society, cooperation for mutual benefit is a governing principle of social life. The second is the idea that a competitive market is a network of mutually beneficial transactions. For each market transaction considered independently, mutual benefit among the parties to that transaction provides the motivation for them to transact. For market transactions considered in their entirety, their overall tendency is mutually beneficial for market participants in general. Thus, competitive markets belong to the class of institutions in which individuals cooperate for mutual benefit. These institutions have moral value by virtue of the reciprocity they express and the mutual benefit they tend to create. The third component is a principle of non-paternalism with respect to such institutions: in cooperative relationships, it is for each individual to judge what counts as his or her benefit.

This liberal tradition has been an important strand of economics ever since the founding contributions of David Hume and Adam Smith in the eighteenth century. Over that period, the core ideas of this tradition have been developed with increasing theoretical rigour and have been subjected to constant critical appraisal. As new facts have been observed and new theories have emerged, new challenges to these ideas have been mounted and new defences have been offered. The present book is a contribution to that process. It is an attempt to maintain the liberal tradition against a new challenge—a challenge from behavioural economics.

1.2 Neoclassical Welfare Economics

To see why the findings of behavioural economics might be thought to pose a problem for the liberal tradition, one needs to understand how normative economics developed from the late nineteenth century. One of my reasons for choosing Mill as a spokesperson for this tradition is that his body of work is one of the final achievements of what economists now call *classical economics*. From the 1870s, there was a significant shift—often called the *marginal revolution*—in economics. The main lines of theoretical development since that time, at least until the late twentieth century, have been in what is now called *neoclassical* economics. There was a corresponding shift in the way the ideas of the liberal tradition were expressed. Over the course of this book, I will argue that behavioural findings pose serious problems for neoclassical forms of normative economics, but that these problems are not fatal for the liberal tradition itself. My strategy for integrating the findings of behavioural economics with the liberal tradition will be to avoid making the theoretical moves that characterize the marginal revolution.

Economists who read Mill are often amused by a rash remark at the beginning of Book 3 of *Principles of Political Economy*. The subject of that book is 'Exchange'; its first chapter is 'Of Value'. In the first section of this chapter, Mill says: 'Happily, there is nothing in the laws of value which remains for the present or any future writer to clear up; the theory of the subject is complete' (1871/1909: 436). In the conventional history of economic thought, the central achievement of the marginal revolution was a crucial advance in the theory of value—the demonstration that, for any pair of goods and for any consumer who maximizes utility, the ratio of the marginal utilities of those goods is equal to the ratio of their prices. The three classic statements of this result, by William Stanley Jevons (1871/1970), Carl Menger (1871/1950), and Léon Walras (1874/1954), appeared within a few years of Mill's last substantial revision of his *Principles*. Viewed in the light of this result, Mill's analysis of retail demand is primitive. He says that it would be possible to derive a 'law' of demand only on the assumption that consumers buy at the lowest available prices, but he treats even this assumption as implausible. Buying at the cheapest prices and selling at the dearest are reliable regularities *in business*, and these regularities lead to economic laws of price which apply to wholesale markets; but these laws do not extend to retail trade. Well-off consumers are often too indolent or careless to search for low prices, or 'think it fine to pay and ask no questions'; poorer consumers lack the knowledge, time, or judgement to search, or are subject to various forms of coercion (Mill, 1871/1909: 440–1). As far as one can tell from the text, it has never occurred to Mill that consumers might be maximizing utility functions subject to budget constraints.

But *ought* it to have occurred to him? That surely depends on whether consumers really do make their decisions in this way. It is interesting that many of the factors that Mill thinks influence consumer choice and which neoclassical theory assumed away are ones that modern behavioural economists have investigated.

It took some time for the nature of the marginal revolution to be understood and accepted by the economics profession as a whole. But after its effects had settled down, there was a general consensus about how normative economics should be conducted. In what is now the standard form of neoclassical economic theory, each individual is assumed to have well-articulated preferences over all economically relevant outcomes. These preferences are assumed to be *stable* (that is, not liable to sharp changes over short periods of time, and not subject to significant degrees of random variation), *context-independent* (not affected by variations in the 'framing' of what, in terms of economic theory, is the same decision problem), and *internally consistent* (satisfying conventional properties of consistency, such as completeness and transitivity). In most but not all applications, preferences are also assumed to be *non-tuistic*. That is, an individual's preferences take no account of the interests of other participants in the economic activities that the theory is intended to explain. (For example, an entrepreneur who runs his business to make as much profit as possible and then gives a large share of the profit to his favourite charity is non-tuistic in his business life.) Economic behaviour is explained by assuming that each individual always chooses the most preferred of the options that are available to him.

5

In neoclassical welfare economics, the main normative criterion is the satisfaction of individuals' preferences. That is, economic institutions and policies are judged to be good to the extent that their outcomes rank highly in individuals' preferences orderings. When neoclassical economists use concepts such as 'cost', 'benefit', 'willingness to pay', or 'economic efficiency', these are normally interpreted in terms of preference-satisfaction. Thus, an outcome of a public policy *benefits* an individual if the individual prefers having that outcome to not having it; the largest amount of money she would be willing to give up in return for receiving the outcome is the measure of that benefit. Conversely, an outcome of a policy imposes a *cost* on an individual if she prefers not having it to having it; the smallest amount of money she would be willing to accept in return for putting up with the outcome is the measure of that cost. To say that the total benefits of a proposed policy exceed the total costs—or, equivalently, that the policy increases *economic efficiency*—is to say that in principle it is possible to combine the policy with a set of monetary transfers such that some individuals prefer this combination to the status quo, and no individual has the opposite preference. Welfare economists often say that, in using preference-satisfaction as a normative criterion for assessing public policies, they are treating each individual as the best judge of his own welfare. In this sense, neoclassical welfare economics can claim to uphold the non-paternalism of the liberal tradition.

What neoclassical welfare economics can say about competitive markets in general is encapsulated in its two *fundamental theorems*. The First Fundamental Theorem states that every equilibrium state of a competitive market is economically efficient (or 'Pareto-optimal'). That is, starting from a competitive equilibrium, there is no feasible reallocation of resources that would increase preference-satisfaction for some individuals while reducing preference-satisfaction for none. The Second Fundamental Theorem states that, under suitable background assumptions about the structure of the economy, every economically efficient outcome can be reached as a competitive equilibrium from *some* initial allocation of property rights.[1]

How far, and in what sense, these theorems are informative about competitive markets in the real world has been a matter of dispute for as long as they have been widely known. If one treats the competitive equilibrium of the theoretical model as a stylized representation of the workings of real markets, the theorems can be interpreted as a theoretically rigorous formulation of Adam Smith's (1776/1976: 456) metaphor of the invisible hand that leads market participants to promote an end—the interest of 'society'—that forms no part of their intention. They can also be read in more abstract terms, as showing how, under specific conditions, market mechanisms are efficient in satisfying individuals' preferences. In this sense, the fundamental theorems support a presumption in favour of allocating resources through individual rather than collective choice, and through market-like mechanisms rather than deliberate planning.

This presumption, which I will interpret as part of the liberal tradition, underlies a great deal of applied economics, including work that is concerned with the regulation of markets. For example, economists who work on competition policy are constantly alert to the tendency for firms to seek and exploit market power; in designing regulations to counter this tendency, they normally treat competitive markets as normative benchmarks. In dealing with problems of public goods and externalities, economists have generally favoured the creation of new markets (such as carbon trading) rather than direct controls. Cost-benefit analysis is often interpreted as 'market simulation'—that is, as an attempt to simulate the efficiency properties of competitive markets in situations in which actual markets would fail. All of this work is underpinned by theories that use preference-satisfaction as their normative criterion.

The whole edifice of neoclassical welfare economics rests on the assumption that individuals act on preferences that are stable, context-independent and internally consistent—or, as I will say for short, preferences that are *integrated*. I use the term 'integrated' because I want to be able to say that a person whose behaviour contravenes the neoclassical theory of choice may still be acting on her preferences—that, at each moment at which she makes an act of choice, she chooses what she prefers. Contraventions of the theory occur when the choices she makes at different moments, in different contexts, or when facing different sets of alternative options cannot be rationalized as revealing components of a single system of preferences.[2] The assumption that individuals act on integrated preferences is being called into question by the findings of behavioural economics.

1.3 The Challenge from Behavioural Economics

Starting from the late 1970s, there has been an explosion of work in what is now called 'behavioural economics'—the application to economics of ideas and research methods that originated in cognitive psychology.[3] So much work has been done, and so much of this has become so well known, that a comprehensive survey of behavioural findings would be out of place in this book.[4] Instead I will give thumbnail sketches of four experiments that are characteristic of research in behavioural economics, and which cast doubt on the empirical validity of (what used to be) standard economic assumptions about preferences.

Loss aversion. In an experiment reported by Daniel Kahneman, Jack Knetsch, and Richard Thaler (1990: 1338–9), student subjects reported their valuations for coffee mugs. Subjects were randomly assigned to experimental treatments. In one treatment, each subject was asked to consider each of a range of amounts of money, and to say whether she would choose to have a mug or the money. In another treatment, each subject was first given the mug, free of charge, and then asked whether she would choose to sell it back to the experimenters at each of a range of prices (the same range of money amounts as in the first treatment). Notice that, defined in terms of what a subject can take away from the experiment, the problems faced by the two sets of subjects are exactly the same: the only difference is whether the problems are framed as *choosing* between the mug and money, or as *selling* the mug. However, the median valuation of the mug in the selling treatment ($7.12) was more than double that in the choosing treatment ($3.12). This effect can be explained by the hypothesis that losses have greater psychological salience than equal and opposite gains. (In the choosing treatment, subjects are thinking about *gaining* the mug, while in the selling treatment, they are thinking about *losing* it.) It would be very difficult to argue that the difference between being told that you have been given a coffee mug and being told that you can choose to be given one is a good reason for a two-fold difference in your valuation of the mug, and in this sense the effect seems irrational. Notice, however, that saying that does not answer the question of whether $7.12 is an irrationally high valuation or whether $3.12 is an irrationally low one. The experiment has revealed an apparent inconsistency between people's responses to two separate decision problems, but it has not identified a specific error in either case.

Attention. Daniel Read and Barbara van Leeuwen (1998) report a field experiment in which workers made choices between free snacks which would be delivered at a designated time a week later. The menu from which subjects could choose contained healthy options (such as apples) and unhealthy ones (such as Mars bars). There were four treatments, defined by two different times of day—'after lunch time' and 'in the late afternoon'—at which the choice was made and (independently) at which the snack would be delivered. The background assumption was that most workers would be hungrier at the later time. Read and van Leeuwen found that, holding constant the time of delivery, subjects were more likely to choose unhealthy snacks if they made the choice in the late afternoon. In broad terms, the psychological mechanism behind this result is easy to understand. The hungrier you feel, the more attention you give to cues that are directed towards the satisfaction of hunger, and the more vividly you can imagine experiencing feelings of hunger in other situations. Thus, the hunger-satisfying properties of the Mars bar are perceived more vividly in the late afternoon, irrespective of when it will actually be eaten. Given the familiarity of the snack options and the predictability of daily fluctuations in hunger and satiation, it would be implausible to claim that differences in the time of day at which the decision is made provide good reasons for different choices about what to eat at a given time seven days later. In this sense, the context-dependent preferences revealed in the experiment seem irrational. But that does not answer the question of whether, in any given situation, it is more rational to choose an apple or a Mars bar. Again, what has been revealed is an inconsistency between two choices, not a specific error.

The Allais Paradox. This paradox, or 'common consequence effect', was first discovered by Maurice Allais (1953). Experimental evidence of this effect was reported by Daniel Kahneman and Amos Tversky (1979) in what is probably the most famous paper in behavioural economics. The example I will consider is a version of the effect discussed by Leonard Savage (1954: 101–3), who was worried by its apparent inconsistency with the axioms of expected utility theory, as he had formulated them. Respondents are asked to imagine two different situations, in each of which there is a choice between two gambles. In Situation 1, the choice is between Gamble 1, which gives $500,000 with probability 1, and Gamble 2, which gives $2,500,000 with probability 10/100, $500,000 with probability 89/100, and nothing with probability 1/100. In Situation 2, the choice is between Gamble 3, which gives $500,000 with probability 11/100 and nothing with probability 89/100, and Gamble 4, which gives $2,500,000 with probability 10/100 and nothing with probability 90/100. Many people report strict preferences for Gamble 1 in Situation 1 and for Gamble 4 in Situation 2: this is an instance of the common consequence effect. Intuitively speaking, this combination of preferences seems entirely reasonable (and indeed Savage himself reported exactly these preferences when Allais first confronted him with these decision problems). As Savage puts it, people in Situation 1 'do not find the chance of winning a *very* large fortune in place of receiving a large fortune outright adequate compensation for even a small risk of being left in the status quo', while in Situation 2, 'the chance of winning is nearly the same in both gambles, so the one with the much larger prize seems preferable'. However, according to the axioms of expected utility theory, a person who prefers Gamble 1 in Situation 1 should prefer Gamble 3 in Situation 2, and a person who prefers Gamble 2 in Situation 1 should prefer Gamble 4 in Situation 2. (Readers who are willing to accept this claim on trust may skip the next paragraph.)

To see why the common consequence effect can be interpreted as an inconsistency in preferences, consider (as Savage does in trying to persuade himself of the validity of his axioms) a gamble which gives $2,500,000 with probability 10/11 and nothing with probability 1/11 (Gamble 5). Now suppose that there is some random event E which will occur with probability 11/100. If E occurs, you will either play Gamble 1 (i.e. receive $500,000 with certainty) or play Gamble 5; if E does not occur, you will receive some certain amount of money x. Before knowing whether E occurs, you have to choose which of the two gambles you will play in that event. Surely (one might argue) what you should choose should be independent of x, since if E occurs, receiving x will no longer be a possibility. But, viewed at the time you have to make this decision, opting for Gamble 1 gives you an 11/100 chance of $500,000 and an 89/100 chance of x; opting for Gamble 5 gives you a 1/100 chance of nothing, a 10/100 chance of $2,500,000, and an 89/100 chance of x. (The 89/100 chance of x is the 'common consequence' in the two options.) If $x = \$500,000$, you are effectively choosing between Gamble 1 and Gamble 2, as in Situation 1. If $x = 0$, you are effectively choosing between Gamble 3 and Gamble 4, as in Situation 2.

Notice that nothing in this argument tells you which gamble you should choose in either situation. Expected utility theory is silent on that question; it merely asserts that preferring Gamble 1 to Gamble 2 is inconsistent with preferring Gamble 4 to Gamble 3.

The three experimental findings I have described so far have a common structure. Each of them identifies a case in which a person's choices are predictably affected by some factor that works through well-understood psychological mechanisms but which seems to have little or no relevance to that person's well-being, interests, or goals. Some change in the decision environment induces a change in the person's preferences, but if one looks for a reasoned explanation of a corresponding change in what it is in his interests to choose, it is difficult to find an argument that will stand up to rational scrutiny.[5] But although there is a clear sense in which the preferences revealed by the person in the different contexts are inconsistent *with one another*, it is not at all obvious *which* (if any) of these choices is correct, or even how 'correctness' should be defined. As I will explain in Chapter 4, this general structure is common to many of the findings of behavioural economics that pose problems for neoclassical welfare economics.

The final experiment I describe illustrates a different branch of research in behavioural economics, and another type of finding that is often interpreted as a challenge to neoclassical economics.

Trust. The 'Trust Game' was first investigated experimentally by Joyce Berg, John Dickhaut, and Kevin McCabe (1995). However, it has a far longer history: versions of the game are discussed in Thomas Hobbes's *Leviathan* (1651/1962, Chapters 14–15) and in Hume's *Treatise of Human Nature* (1739—40/1978: 520–1). In Berg et al.'s game, two players (A and B) are in separate rooms and never know one another's identity. Each player is given $10 in one-dollar bills as a 'show up fee'. A puts any number of these bills, from zero to ten, in an envelope which will be sent to B; he keeps the rest of the money for himself. The experimenter supplements this transfer so that *B* receives three times what *A* chose to send. *B* then puts any number of the bills she has received into another envelope, which is returned to *A*; she keeps the rest of the money for herself. The game is played once only, and the experiment is set up so that no one (including the experimenter) can know what any other identifiable person chooses to do. The game is interesting to theorists of rational choice because it provides the two players with an opportunity for mutual gain, but if the players are rational and self-interested, and if each knows that this is true of the other, no money will be transferred. (It is rational for *B* to keep everything she is sent; knowing this, it is rational for *A* to send nothing.) Traditional discussions of this kind of game (including those written by Hobbes and Hume) conclude that the opportunity for mutual gain will not be taken up unless the game is embedded in some larger structure in which individuals can build reputations or in which conventions can emerge from repeated play—possibilities that Berg et al.'s experiment is designed to exclude. In fact, *A* players sent an average of $5.16; having received three times what was sent, the *B* players returned an average of $4.66. (By pocketing the remaining $10.82, the *B* players collectively appropriated slightly more than the whole surplus generated by the *A* players' willingness to trust them.)

What general inferences can be drawn from these experiments? If one interprets neoclassical theory as postulating that individuals' decisions reveal stable and context-independent preferences, the findings of the loss aversion and attention experiments are contrary to that theory. If the theory is taken to include the postulate that preferences over uncertain prospects are consistent with the expected utility axioms, it is also disconfirmed by the results of the Allais experiment. And if it is taken to include the postulate that preferences are non-tuistic, the results of the trust experiment are a further disconfirmation.

Many behavioural economists (including me on some occasions, I have to say) have viewed these failures of neoclassical theory with a certain amount of complacency. Behavioural economists enjoy contrasting their approach with that of 'conventional' or 'textbook' economics, and suggesting that conventional economics rests on assumptions whose absurdity ought to be obvious to anyone with an ounce of common sense. Here is a typical (if unusually colourful) example of this rhetorical strategy. It is taken from the introductory chapter of Richard Thaler and Cass Sunstein's influential book, *Nudge* (2008)—a book whose arguments I will discuss in more detail in Chapter 4. After declaring their intention to defend 'libertarian paternalism', Thaler and Sunstein say:

> Those who reject paternalism often claim that human beings do a terrific job of making choices, and if not terrific, certainly better than anyone else would do (especially if that someone else works for the government). Whether or not they

have ever studied economics, many people seem at least implicitly committed to the idea of *homo economicus*, or economic man—the notion that each of us thinks and chooses unfailingly well, and thus fits within the textbook picture of human beings offered by economics.

If you look at economics textbooks, you will learn that homo economicus can think like Albert Einstein, store as much memory as IBM's Big Blue [sic], and exercise the willpower of Mahatma Gandhi. Really. But the folks we know are not like that. Real people have trouble with long division if they don't have a calculator, sometimes forget their spouse's birthday, and have a hangover on New Year's Day. They are not homo economicus; they are homo sapiens.

(Thaler and Sunstein, 2008: 6–7)

The contrast between the species of *Homo economicus* and *Homo sapiens* (or 'Econs' and 'Humans', as Thaler and Sunstein prefer to call them), is one of the organizing themes of *Nudge*. Notice that Thaler and Sunstein's satire is targeted at economists *who reject paternalism*. The premise is that conventional economists oppose paternalism, and that they oppose it because they believe that individuals act in everyday economic life with the kind of rationality that is represented in the more abstract reaches of neoclassical theory. The reader is invited to agree that the folks *she* knows are not like that, and to conclude that economists' traditional opposition to paternalism is unjustified. Having reached this conclusion, she is unlikely to be persuaded that economic institutions and policies should be evaluated in terms of preference satisfaction. If, as Thaler and Sunstein maintain, individuals often 'make pretty bad decisions' (2008: 5), what is the value of theoretical analyses that purport to show that competitive markets are efficient in satisfying the preferences that are revealed in those decisions? Thaler and Sunstein are presenting the findings of behavioural research as a challenge both to neoclassical welfare economics and to the liberal tradition of economics.

Similarly, evidence that individuals act contrary to self-interest has been interpreted as damaging for conventional economics. For example, Berg et al. (1995: 122) introduce their experiment on trust with the claim: 'A fundamental assumption in economics is that individuals act in their own self interest'. They present their experiment as demonstrating the falsity of that assumption. Reporting another famous experiment that reveals non-selfish behaviour (the first version of the 'Dictator Game'), Kahneman, Knetsch, and Thaler (1986) give their results an explicitly ideological spin. They claim that in most economic analysis there is an assumption of 'nonfairness':

The economic agent is assumed to be law-abiding but not 'fair'—if fairness implies that some legal opportunities for gain are not exploited. This nonfairness assumption expresses a resistance to explanations of economic actions in moral terms that has deep roots in the history of the discipline. The central insight that gave rise to modern economics is that the common good is well served by the free actions of self-interested agents in a market. (Kahneman et al., 1986: S286)

The suggestion seems to be that behavioural research is revealing a fundamental flaw in the liberal tradition of economics. That tradition, we are being invited to think, normalizes or even applauds the pursuit of self-interest in economic life. But real human beings, unlike the rational agents of economic models, can be motivated to act morally, and (as in the case of the Trust Game) moral action can promote the common good.

1.4 Reconciling Normative and Behavioural Economics

There can be no doubt that the findings of behavioural research pose a serious problem for normative economics. Normative economics uses preference satisfaction as its criterion, on the assumption that individuals have integrated preferences over economic outcomes. But behavioural research suggests that this assumption often fails. The problem, then, is to reconcile normative and behavioural economics—to find a way of doing normative analysis in economics that is compatible with the instability and context-dependence of human preferences.

The reconciliation problem has been addressed by economists, philosophers, psychologists, and legal scholars. A broad consensus seems to be emerging about how this problem is best resolved. The consensus solution retains many of the features of neoclassical welfare economics, but the features that are jettisoned are those that do most to align neoclassical welfare economics with the liberal tradition. Like much of neoclassical welfare economics, that solution presupposes that normative analysis is concerned with assessing individual well-being, as viewed by a neutral observer. The reconciliation problem is resolved by dropping the assumption that an individual's choices reliably reveal his judgements about his well-being. Instead, the individual is assumed to have 'true', 'underlying' or 'latent' preferences that are sufficiently well-integrated to be used as a normative criterion, but which he does not always act on. Actual choices that deviate from these preferences are classified as 'anomalies' and attributed to error. Welfare economics then has the task of reconstructing the preferences that the individual would have revealed in the absence of error. In this book, I present a critique of this consensus and propose an alternative solution.

My critique, which I develop in Chapter 4, questions the validity of modelling human decision-making as an interaction between true preferences and psychologically-induced error. I argue that this model lacks adequate psychological foundations. Laplace is supposed to have told Napoleon that a theory of the solar system had no need for hypotheses about the actions of a Creator. In much the same way, psychological explanations of the mental processes that lie behind human choices have no need for the concepts of true preference and error. If that is right, the idea that scientific investigation can reconstruct individuals' true preferences is a mirage. Normative economics must adapt itself to human psychology as it really is.

My alternative approach is inspired by the work of James Buchanan, one of the most thoughtful defenders of the liberal tradition of economics in the second half of the twentieth century. His understanding of that tradition is set out in a short essay, 'What should economists do?' (Buchanan 1964). In that essay, Buchanan challenges Lionel Robbins's (1935) famous definition of economics as being about the allocation of scarce means among alternative ends. For Buchanan, that definition leads to the view that the purpose of normative economics is to provide tools that a rational social planner can use to maximize some aggregate measure of social welfare. Buchanan defends a different conception of economics in which the central concern is not with rational choice (whether by planners or by ordinary individuals) but with voluntary exchange:

> The 'market' or market organization is not a *means* toward the accomplishment of anything. It is, instead, the institutional embodiment of the voluntary exchange processes that are entered into by individuals in their several capacities. That is all there is to it.   (Buchanan, 1964: 219)

Buchanan's normative approach is *contractarian*. In contractarian theories, social arrangements are not assessed from the viewpoint of a benevolent social planner. Instead, they are assessed from the several viewpoints of individual members of society, considered as potential parties to an agreement or 'social contract'. In evaluating a social institution, a contractarian theorist does not ask whether aggregate welfare is maximized. Instead, he asks whether it is in the interest of each individual to accept the rules of that institution, on the condition that everyone else does the same. This will be my approach too. I explain and defend this approach in Chapters 2 and 3.

In some versions of contractarianism, the individuals who are parties to the social contract are modelled as rational agents with integrated preferences. Working out the terms of the contract that those individuals would agree then becomes an exercise in the theory of rational choice under uncertainty, or the theory of rational bargaining.[6] But this is not the kind of contractarianism that I can use if I am to reconcile normative and behavioural economics. When I consider individuals as potential parties to an agreement, I will allow them to have preferences that are just as unstable and context-dependent as those of ordinary human beings. I will not assume that these people are merely making errors, and that integrated preferences can somehow be found in the recesses of their supposed true selves. The challenge is to find economic institutions that can be recommended to individuals who do not know what they prefer.

Before going any further, let me say that the normative economics that I will present in this book is much thinner than neoclassical welfare economics. It can say much less about the world to which it is intended to apply than neoclassical welfare economics can say about a world in which individuals act on integrated preferences. But if my understanding of the findings of behavioural economics is correct, and if my critique of behavioural welfare economics is sound, the problems I am trying to address are not of my making. They are consequences of the way the world happens to be. If the truth is that preferences are often unstable and context-dependent, developing a liberal form of normative economics—one that does not merely impose a social planner's conception of what is good for people—is not going to be easy. I can only say that I have done my best to make a start on this research programme.

The first essential is to find a criterion of individual interest on which contractarian recommendations can be grounded. My proposal, presented in Chapters 5 and 6, starts from the idea that it is in each individual's interest to have more opportunity rather than less. I argue that each individual can recognize that interest, whether or not her choices reveal integrated preferences. I propose the principle that every group of individuals should have the collective opportunity to carry out any transaction among themselves that all members of that group might want to take part in. In Chapters 6, 7, and 8, I investigate the economic implications of this principle. I show that it supports many of the fundamental conclusions of the liberal tradition of economics. Specifically, it supports the general presumption in favour of markets that neoclassical economics expresses in the Fundamental Theorems. It supports the case for certain kinds of market regulation, and for certain kinds of procedures for supplying public goods. It does not require that markets are fair in the sense that an egalitarian might wish them to be, but if its implications are to be recommended to everyone (as, given the contractarian approach, they must be), there has to be a continuing expectation that each individual can benefit from the sum of everyone's voluntary transactions. That may require a collective commitment to redistributive policies.

In all of this, the guiding idea is that a well-ordered economy is an institutional framework that allows individuals to cooperate with one another in the pursuit of what they perceive as their common interests. If one understands a market economy in this way, it is not at all obvious that markets depend on self-interested motivations. Of course, as Adam Smith (1776/1976: 26–7) points out in *The Wealth of Nations*, we do not rely on the *benevolence* of shopkeepers to provide us with the goods we need. But benevolence—willingness to sacrifice one's own interests to confer benefits on others—is not the only alternative to self-interest. In Chapters 9 and 10, I explain how individuals can act with the intention of playing their parts in mutually beneficial practices. Such intentions can lead people to return trust, even when doing so is contrary to self-interest, but they can also underlie ordinary behaviour in markets.

As I have said, a contractarian recommends an institution by showing that it is in each individual's interest to accept its rules, on the condition that everyone else does the same. Since a code of morality is a social institution, moral rules can be the objects of contractarian recommendations. In the final chapter, I present a contractarian recommendation in favour of a moral principle of mutual benefit. When people uphold this principle, a market economy can truly be a community of advantage in Mill's sense.

2

The View from Nowhere

This book is a contribution to normative economics—that branch of economics that deals with questions about what properties of an economy are good or bad, right or wrong, fair or unfair, just or unjust. Normative economists variously describe their work as 'welfare economics', 'economics of well-being', 'economics of happiness', or the 'theory of economic justice'. But none of these labels gives an accurate description of the kind of analysis that I present in this book. The approach I will follow is very much a minority taste among economists and philosophers. In Chapter 3 I will explain and defend this approach. But in the present chapter, I describe the majority position. By highlighting some of its peculiar features, I hope to encourage the reader to wonder whether there might be merit in alternative approaches.

2.1 The Impartial Spectator

For most of the last hundred years, the main tradition of normative economics has been that of neoclassical welfare economics.[1] Welfare economics is in direct line of descent from the utilitarian philosophy espoused by many of the classical and neoclassical economists of the nineteenth century. It aims to evaluate alternative states of affairs for a society from an impartial point of view. It tries to answer the question: 'What is good for society, all things considered?' It takes the position that the good of society is made up of the good or welfare of each of the individuals who comprise that society. Thus, welfare economics has to assess what is good for each person, all things considered, and then aggregate those assessments. How assessments of individual welfare should be aggregated has been one of the core theoretical problems of welfare economics, for which there is still no universally accepted solution; but that problem is orthogonal to the present discussion. Since the marginal revolution, however, there has been general agreement on the criterion for assessing what is good for each individual, considered separately.

That criterion is preference-satisfaction: if some individual prefers one state of affairs to another, the former is deemed to be better for him than the latter.

As I explained in Chapter 1, this former consensus has been disturbed by recent developments in experimental and behavioural economics. As usually applied, the criterion of preference-satisfaction presupposes that each individual has integrated preferences over the social states that welfare economics needs to assess, and that these preferences are revealed in the individual's choices. By treating the individual as the best judge of what is good for him, and by interpreting his preferences as expressing those judgements, welfare economics can provide a reasonably persuasive justification for the preference-satisfaction criterion.[2] But that presupposition has been called into question by evidence that suggests that individuals often come to decision problems without well-defined preferences that pre-exist the particular problem they face; instead, whatever preferences they need to deal with that problem are constructed in the course of thinking about it. Such 'constructed' preferences can be influenced by features of the problem that seem to have no bearing on the individual's well-being.

Given the underlying logic of welfare economics, a natural response to this problem is to supplement the preference-satisfaction criterion with some other principle for assessing individual welfare, applicable where individuals lack well-formed preferences. To remain as faithful as possible to the spirit of neoclassical welfare economics, one might try to find some way of inferring or reconstructing an individual's underlying judgements about what is good for him from whatever evidence seems most relevant. This, in broad-brush terms, is the approach that most behavioural economists seem to favour. In different variants, it has been called *libertarian paternalism* (Sunstein and Thaler, 2003a, 2003b; Thaler and Sunstein, 2008), *asymmetric paternalism* (Camerer et al., 2003; Loewenstein and Ubel, 2008), and *behavioural welfare economics* (Bernheim and Rangel, 2007, 2009).

I will discuss this kind of normative economics in more detail in Chapter 4. For my present purposes, what matters is the viewpoint from which welfare economics, in both its neoclassical and behavioural versions, looks at society. Because welfare economists are so used to imagining themselves occupying this viewpoint, they tend not to notice just how peculiar it is.

What is peculiar about it? The first thing to notice is that the viewpoint is *synoptic*: it is the viewpoint of a single viewer, who is not any of the individual people who comprise the society that is being assessed. The viewer somehow stands outside society and makes judgements about its overall goodness. This is the kind of view that has traditionally been attributed to God, looking down on his creation. To use a phrase coined by Thomas Nagel (1986), it is a 'view from nowhere'. Nagel thinks that this is exactly the viewpoint that we *should* take when we try to engage in moral reasoning. The thought is that when a person thinks morally, she somehow rises above her ordinary self and assumes a viewpoint from which she can see that self as just one person among others. But I cannot resist borrowing Nagel's words and giving them a sceptical intonation. A view from nowhere is a peculiar sort of view.

In forming her judgements about the overall good of society, the person who takes the view from nowhere needs to make judgements about what is good for each member of society, considered separately. Are these judgements about individual welfare views from nowhere too, or are they the respective views of the individual members of society? As far as neoclassical welfare economics is concerned, the best answer—the answer that best reflects what economists actually do—is that they are supposed to be both at the same time. In the standard models of neoclassical economics, each individual has well-formed, context-independent preferences that are revealed in his choices and that can be interpreted as expressing *that person's* judgements about what is good for him. The viewer uses these preferences as inputs to her judgements about the overall good of society. In doing so, she implicitly endorses these preferences as expressing *her* synoptic judgements about what is good for that person. In behavioural welfare economics, however, the viewer often has to do more than simply endorse individuals' given preferences. If an individual's revealed preferences vary according to contextual features that have no plausible connection with well-being, the viewer needs to construct her own judgements about that individual's welfare, using whatever information is to hand.

The welfare economist's viewpoint, then, is that of a *spectator*—someone who views society from outside. Since the point of taking this viewpoint is to try to filter out one's private interests and biases, it is crucial that the imagined spectator is *impartial* with respect to the preferences and interests of the various individuals whose welfare she is assessing. And since the aim is to assess welfare, the spectator must be assumed to take an interest in the welfare of every individual who comes into her synoptic view. So the welfare economist has to imagine an *impartially benevolent spectator*.[3]

2.2 The Benevolent Autocrat

Suppose we accept the meaningfulness of the view from nowhere. Suppose we have found a method of assessing the good of society, all things considered, as viewed by an impartially benevolent spectator. What then? Who is supposed to use this assessment, and for what purpose?

One possible answer, sometimes proposed by utilitarian moral philosophers, is that every individual ought to act with the objective of maximizing the overall good of society (or, better, the overall good of the universe). I have to say that this is not an idea that appeals to me. My internal sense of morality is of particular obligations and commitments that arise out of particular relationships between me and the rest of the world. I do not feel an unconditional obligation to give just as much weight to anyone's interests as I give to my own, or to those of my own family, friends, and colleagues; and nor do I expect unrelated others to feel such obligations to me. But perhaps that just reveals my moral limitations. For the purposes of this chapter, there is no need to pursue this line of thought. What is at issue here is what welfare economists do with their assessments of the social good. Welfare economics, as it is normally practised, is not about the moral obligations of private individuals.

The traditional addressee of welfare economics is an entity variously known as 'the policy-maker', 'the government', or 'the social planner'. (An outsider might be surprised that social planners still have their place in the dramatis personae of economics, but they do.) In an alternative formulation of the same basic idea, applied economists often end their papers by drawing 'policy implications' from their analyses, these being the actions that the policy-maker is recommended to take. The implicit assumption is that this addressee is, or ought to be, motivated by concern for the overall good of society, as viewed by an impartially benevolent spectator.

This understanding of the purpose of normative economics has been carried over to behavioural welfare economics in its various guises. Thus, in their first presentations of libertarian paternalism, Cass Sunstein and Richard Thaler conceive of themselves as addressing a 'planner', defined as 'anyone who must design plans for others, from human resource directors to bureaucrats to kings' (2003a: 1190). More recently, perhaps recognizing the negative connotations of social planning, they have renamed their addressee a 'choice architect', but the job specification remains the same (Thaler and Sunstein, 2008). They focus on the role of the choice architect in designing the formats in which decision problems are presented to individuals. If, as the behavioural evidence suggests is often the case, individuals' choices are sensitive to variations in decision formats, Sunstein and Thaler's addressee has the power to influence what individuals choose.

Using the example of a cafeteria director deciding how to display different food items, knowing that different displays will induce different choices on the part of her customers, Sunstein and Thaler (2003a: 1164) interpret traditional welfare economics as recommending that she should 'give consumers what she thinks they would choose on their own'. (Notice how the concept of *giving* is being used here: I will come back to this.) But this recommendation cannot help the cafeteria director, because what the customers will choose 'on their own' can be defined only relative to the decision format, and the whole problem is to decide what this format should be. Sunstein and Thaler conclude that the director should choose the format that 'she thinks would make the customers best off, all things considered', subject to the constraint that freedom of choice is not restricted. By virtue of this constraint, Sunstein and Thaler's recommendation ensures that individuals get what they prefer whenever their preferences are independent of the decision format. Thus, libertarian paternalism agrees with traditional welfare economics whenever the well-formed preferences assumed by the latter exist; when they do not, it substitutes judgements about the welfare of the relevant individuals.

Douglas Bernheim and Antonio Rangel's (2007, 2009) version of behavioural welfare economics follows a similar logic. Bernheim and Rangel are explicit in invoking a planner. They interpret 'standard welfare analysis' as 'instruct[ing] the planner to respect the choices an individual would make for himself'. This normative principle is presented as 'an extension of the libertarian deference to freedom of choice, which takes the view that it is better to give a person the thing he would choose for himself rather than something that someone else would choose for him' (2007: 464). (Notice again the idea that individuals' freedom of choice can be represented in terms of what a planner *gives* them.) Like Sunstein and Thaler, Bernheim and Rangel see the findings of behavioural economics as revealing ambiguities in the concept of what a person would choose for himself. If an individual's behaviour shows a 'choice reversal'—that is, if she would choose object x over object y under some conditions, but y over x in others—then her choices 'fail to provide clear guidance' to the planner (2007: 465). What is required in such cases, therefore, is some set of criteria 'to officiate between conflicting choice data' (2007: 469); one of the objectives of Bernheim and Rangel's version of behavioural welfare economics is to provide such criteria.

In another contribution to behavioural welfare economics, Yuval Salant and Ariel Rubinstein (2008) develop a theoretical framework similar to Bernheim and Rangel's. In this framework, a decision problem for an individual is described by the combination of a set of alternative objects of choice and a 'frame' in which that set of objects is presented to the individual. Salant and Rubinstein imagine a 'social planner' who chooses the frame with the aim that the individual's choice should be consistent with her (assumed) 'underlying preferences' over objects (2008: 1294).

So welfare economics, in both its traditional and behavioural forms, is addressed to an imagined policy-maker. The presumption must be that this policy-maker will find some use for the welfare economics that is addressed to her. But what use?

As James Buchanan has often said, welfare economics is implicitly addressed to a benevolent autocrat (e.g. Buchanan, 1986: 23; 1987).[4] The imagined policy-maker must be impartially benevolent if she is to have the motivation to act on the policy implications she is being informed about. In her public role, she must treat the social good, impartially assessed, as her only objective.

She must give no weight to her private career interests, or (if she is an elected politician) to the interests of her political party. But impartial benevolence is not enough. If she is to be able to implement whatever policies maximize the overall good of society, we must imagine her to have the powers of an enlightened despot. We must imagine that she is not subject to the messy constraints that political leaders and civil servants have to face in real-world democracies. Having recognized that a certain policy is the best, she does not have to negotiate with other members of her cabinet or party who might disagree with her. She does not have to take the policy to a Parliament or Congress where it might be voted down. She simply gives the order that the policy is to be implemented, and moves on to the next problem in her in-tray.

There is a further sense in which the imagined policy-maker is unconstrained. Recall how, both for Sunstein and Thaler and for Bernheim and Rangel, the idea of respecting individuals' preferences is represented in terms of the policy-maker *giving* individuals what they prefer. This is not a wholly innocent figure of speech. The social planner to whom welfare economics is addressed is not assumed to be *constrained by* individuals' preferences, in the way that a public official entrusted with the task of counting votes in an election is constrained by the choices that voters have made. She may choose to *take account of* those preferences, and welfare economics advises her on how to do so; but whether she acts on this advice is up to her. And so whether individuals get what they prefer depends on how the planner uses her discretionary power. If they do get what they prefer, that is as a result of the planner's decisions, for which she takes responsibility. In this sense, she is deciding what individuals are to be given: they are not deciding for themselves what they are to have.

There is yet more to the fiction. Even if the imagined policy-maker were impartially benevolent and had the powers of an enlightened despot, she might still not want to act on the welfare economist's recommendations. Take the case of Sunstein and Thaler's cafeteria. In this case, Sunstein and Thaler are playing the role of the welfare economist, advising on the display of food items; the cafeteria director is the addressee of their advice. The problem, as Sunstein and Thaler formulate it, is to choose the display that maximizes the welfare of the cafeteria customers, all things considered. In assessing people's welfare, Sunstein and Thaler seem to want to use what philosophers call an 'informed desire' criterion—that is, they want to assess welfare by reference to what people would choose if they had 'complete information, unlimited cognitive abilities, and no lack of willpower' (2003a: 1162). (I will say more about this in Chapter 4.) Already, Sunstein and Thaler are taking a philosophical position that the policy-maker might not share. (She might favour a different conception of impartial benevolence, such as the maximization of happiness.) To specify what a person would choose in the light of 'complete information', one has to make scientific judgements about the best inferences to draw from the available evidence. In the cafeteria problem, judgements have to be made about how variations in diet affect health and life expectancy. On this issue, different scientists make different judgements. A welfare economist who is confident that one dietary theory is correct may find himself advising a policy-maker who is equally confident about a different theory.

When welfare economists talk about 'policy implications', they normally use *their own* best judgements about contestable normative and scientific questions. Although they imagine themselves as addressing policy-makers, they do not ask whether these judgements are shared by their addressees. The implicit thought is that if the welfare economist uses *his own* best judgements, he is entitled to assume that the policy-maker will accept these as *the* best judgements. So the imagined policy-maker is not just an impartially benevolent autocrat: she is an impartially benevolent autocrat who, on contestable normative and scientific questions, agrees with the welfare economist who is advising her. But if this is so, the conceptual distinction between adviser and policy-maker evaporates. We might as well say that the welfare economist is imagining that *he* is the benevolent autocrat. The content of a policy implication is: *If I were an impartially benevolent autocrat, this is what I would do.*

Of course, welfare economists do not *really* believe that their work is being read by impartially benevolent autocrats who think as they do on all controversial questions and who are eagerly waiting for their advice. Nor, typically, do they think of benevolent autocracy as an ideal political system, to which actual procedures of collective choice are imperfect approximations. Their recommendations are *not intended to be taken literally.*

Suppose that, in my capacity as a welfare economist, I have been commissioned to write a report for a government department, advising on some issue of economic policy. My report recommends some course of action—say, the compulsory metering of domestic water supplies—which makes good economic sense to me but to which, for what I believe to be mistaken reasons, many people object. The politician who heads the department tells me that she agrees with my analysis, but judges my proposal too unpopular to implement. In other words, if she were an impartially benevolent autocrat, she would act on my advice; but that is not what she is. That does not make my advice mistaken or useless: we might both think that it is useful to look at the problem from the perspective of conventional welfare economics, while recognizing that this is not the only perspective that is relevant for a democratic politician. But notice that I am not advising her to ignore the political constraints to which she is subject. In the literal sense, I am not advising her to implement the policy I am 'recommending'. I am merely telling her that this is a recommendation that I would act on, were I an impartially benevolent autocrat.

So the idea of the impartially benevolent autocrat as the addressee of welfare economics is not an assumption about the powers of any real person or institution. It is a framework for organizing thought, a literary device. In the language of economics, it is a *model*. For the present, that is all I need to say. It is sufficient to recognize that the impartially benevolent autocrat belongs in a model world, and that all model worlds are unrealistic. To understand the arguments I will develop later in this book, the reader must be able to step outside the traditional model and see that it is not the only way of thinking about normative economics. I will present an alternative model in which there is a different addressee (or as will become clear, addressees). I will ask the reader to consider the two models side by side, and not to criticize my approach on the grounds that it fails to give the right recommendations to the impartially benevolent autocrat that the traditional model imagines. Of course it fails to do this: it is not addressed to her.

2.3 Public Reasoning

The idea that normative analysis should be addressed to an imagined social planner is perhaps peculiar to economics, but the idea that it should be based on a view from nowhere is not. Indeed, the writer who develops this idea most directly, and who uses *The View from Nowhere* as the title of the book in which he develops it, is a political and moral philosopher (Nagel, 1986). When philosophers address issues in normative economics, they do not usually talk about social planners or policy implications. Typically, however, their perspective on these issues is a view from nowhere. This, I think, predisposes them to favour the kinds of arguments that are characteristic of behavioural welfare economics.

To illustrate how the view from nowhere can be used in philosophical argument, I focus on the work of one of the most influential critics of neoclassical welfare economics, Amartya Sen. As a starting point, I take the 'parable' with which Sen (1999: 54–8) introduces a wide-ranging analysis of freedom and justice. The story is of a woman hiring a labourer to work in her garden. There are three applicants, all currently unemployed, and each of whom would do much the same work for the same payment. '[B]eing a reflective person', the employer 'wonders who would be the right person to employ.' Sen imagines the employer asking herself how, in choosing between the applicants, she can do the most good. Should she choose Dinu, the poorest applicant (thus doing as much as she can to reduce poverty)? Or should she choose Bishanno, the applicant who would gain most happiness from being employed (thus doing as much as she can to increase happiness)? Or should she choose Rogini, the applicant for whom the job would make the biggest difference to 'the quality of life and freedom from illness'? The purpose of the story is to set out three apparently credible 'evaluative approaches' to normative economics, each of which has a different 'informational basis'. Sen sees each of these approaches as having its merits, and tries to find a normative framework that can encompass their different informational bases.

Clearly, Sen's view of normative analysis is much wider than that of conventional welfare economics, which he sees as having a particularly impoverished informational basis. But it is still a view from nowhere. Sen's story is about alternative ways of distributing a valuable resource between three needy individuals; the suggestion is that this is a miniature version of one of the central problems of normative economics. Significantly, he presents this problem through the eyes of a fourth person who, from a neutral position, 'reflectively' asks which solution would be best—not best from her private viewpoint as an employer, but best in some impartial sense.

Thus (Sen tells us), when the employer thinks about Dinu, she asks herself: 'What can be more important than helping the poorest?' Similarly, when she thinks about Bishanno, she tells herself: 'Surely removing unhappiness has to be the first priority'. One might ask: important *for whom*? First priority *for whom*? I take it that, for Sen, these questions would be superfluous. He is not talking about what is important *for* anyone in particular; he is talking about what just *is* important. This is a view from nowhere, the view as seen by some kind of impartial spectator.

It would perhaps be wrong to describe Sen's imagined spectator as impartially *benevolent*, since that might suggest that she takes the evaluative approach of classical utilitarianism, and Sen sees utilitarianism only as one eligible approach among others. But we must imagine the spectator to be sympathetically or morally engaged with the society on which she is looking, while not being part of it. She is concerned that the state of this society should be good rather than bad. From her impartial viewpoint, she recognizes that income equality, happiness, quality of life, and freedom all contribute to the good of society, all things considered. Her problem is to reach an impartial assessment of the relative importance of these different forms of goodness.

What, then, is the point of arriving at an impartial assessment of overall goodness? Who is supposed to use it, and for what purpose?

Unlike neoclassical and behavioural welfare economists, Sen does not imagine himself addressing a social planner. He addresses individuals *as citizens*, participating in public discussion—or, as he often says, in *public reasoning*—about the social good. In democratic societies, such discussions may influence and perhaps even determine collective choices, but Sen wants to be able to contribute to public reasoning about *any* society, democratic or undemocratic. Indeed, it is particularly important for Sen that the kind of normative discourse in which he is engaging can be used to diagnose injustice anywhere in the world, and so can be used to 'fight oppression..., or protest against systematic medical neglect..., or repudiate the permissibility of torture..., or reject the quiet acceptance of chronic hunger' (2009: xi–xii). Some of the alleged injustices on Sen's charge sheet (for example, the deficiencies of health care provision in the United States, and the persistence of hunger in India) occur in open and democratic societies, but when he attacks injustices committed by authoritarian regimes, the public discussion to which he is contributing is presumably one of opposition: it is certainly not the policy-making process.

For Sen (2009: 39–46), public reasoning involves debate about 'the demands of ethical objectivity'. The implication is that there can be objectivity in ethics, and that objectivity makes 'demands' on us as citizens which in some sense we are required to meet. But what does this mean?

On the most natural reading, objectivity in ethics requires that there are ethical *objects*, and that what these objects are is a matter of fact. But Sen is not using the concept of objectivity in this way. (I think he is wise not to do so, but I do not want to get side-tracked into matters of meta-ethics.) Drawing on the work of Adam Smith (1759/1976), John Rawls (1993), Jürgen Habermas (1995) and Hillary Putnam (2004), Sen locates objectivity *in* public reasoning. By this I mean that, for Sen, public reasoning is not to be understood as an attempt to *discover* objective truths about ethics that have an independent existence. Rather, ethical propositions are objective *by virtue of their being certified by* the right kind of public reasoning. Sen argues that, in the work of Smith, Rawls, and Habermas, 'objectivity is linked, directly or indirectly, to the ability to survive challenges from informed scrutiny coming from diverse quarters'. Similarly, Sen says of his own analysis of justice: 'I will take reasoned scrutiny from different perspectives to be an essential part of the demands of objectivity for ethical and political convictions' (2009: 45). How, one might ask, is *reasoned* scrutiny differentiated from *unreasoned*? Sen is not particularly explicit about the standards of reasoning he is invoking, but he is clear that these must include impartiality: 'The reasoning that is sought in analysing the requirements of justice will incorporate some basic demands of impartiality, which are integral parts of the idea of justice and injustice' (2009: 42).

So, for Sen, normative economic analysis is a contribution to a process of public reasoning in which citizens try to reach agreement on an impartial assessment of the social good. Sen's language of *demands* and *requirements* (the 'demands of objectivity' for ethical and political convictions, the 'requirements of justice', the 'demands of impartiality') seems to imply that engagement in public reasoning is not to be thought of as an optional activity, like joining a reading group or debating society. Rather, there is some kind of moral requirement on each of us, as citizens or as rational agents, to make impartial assessments of the social good, to defend these assessments by reasoned argument, and to expose these arguments to other people's scrutiny.

As a model of this conception of public reasoning, consider a jury which has to determine an issue of judgement when there is no dispute about facts. (Suppose the defendant has been charged with murder, having shot and killed an intruder to his house; he admits the killing but pleads self-defence. Given the facts of the case, the jury has to decide whether the defendant's use of force was reasonable.) For each member of the jury, participation in the judgement process is a duty of citizenship. She is expected to set aside her private interests, preferences, and prejudices and try to reach an impartial judgement about whether the defendant's action was reasonable. Collectively, the jury is expected to engage in reasoned discussion; each member is expected to take account of the others' arguments, while being individually responsible for his or her final decision. Because the twelve members of the jury have been selected at random, there is an expectation that the discussion will be informed by the varied experiences and insights of the members. There is a hope, but not a requirement, that this process will end in agreement.

Sen's account of public reasoning belongs to a tradition of political philosophy in which politics is interpreted on the model of the jury.[5] I do not want to claim that there is anything incoherent in this conception of politics. But it does have some troubling features.

Recall that the objective is to arrive at an impartial assessment of the social good, all things considered, and that the building blocks for this are impartial assessments of the good of each individual. So consider a specific individual: Robert Sugden. Suppose that what is at issue is some decision that I am about to make about how to live my own life—perhaps about how to balance work and leisure, or how to weigh immediate enjoyment against future health in choices about eating and drinking. I might acknowledge that, *were I trying to make an impartial assessment of what is good for me*, other people's judgements would be relevant. But why do I need an impartial assessment of what is good for me? What matters *to me* is my own assessment. In arriving at that assessment, it would perhaps be wise for me to listen to what other people have to say about what they think is good for me; but ultimately how I live my life is my business and not theirs. I am entitled to treat my own judgements as authoritative, not because I believe they would be endorsed by an impartial spectator, but because I am the author of my own life.

I cannot see why I am morally required to justify my private choices by reasoned arguments, and to expose those arguments to public scrutiny. Where could such a requirement come from? If a moral philosopher tells me that it is a demand of objectivity, and that what he means by the 'objectivity' of a proposition is its ability to survive reasoned scrutiny in public debate, I can reply that, when I take decisions about my own life, I am not interested in that kind of objectivity. Subjectivity is good enough for me. In saying that, I am *not* claiming that, from an impartial point of view and all things considered, it is good that each individual is free to make decisions about his own life, and hence that it is good that I am free to make decisions about my life. Were I to make such a claim, the philosopher might perhaps be entitled to expect me to defend it by reasoned argument. But I am not pretending to report any view from nowhere. What I am saying is much simpler than that: all I am saying is that my own view is what matters to me.

A similar argument can be made about the internal affairs of a political community or voluntary association. Sen's analysis of public reasoning emphasizes the importance of taking account of outsiders' judgements in arriving at impartial assessments of what is good in any particular society. He proposes a principle of *open impartiality*: 'Impartial views may come from far or from within a community, or a nation, or a culture' (2009: 123). Thus, he urges Americans to listen to public debate in Europe about whether capital punishment is justified (2009: 407). Given that Sen is trying to find a view from nowhere, this stress on open impartiality is entirely natural. If we are asking whether an impartial spectator would approve or disapprove of capital punishment, it is surely relevant to consider judgements made by the inhabitants of jurisdictions with and without the death penalty. But one might still ask whether political debate should be understood as an attempt to achieve the viewpoint of an impartial spectator. When a decision has to be made about the American criminal justice system, shouldn't the judgements that ultimately count be the judgements of Americans—not because their judgements are more likely to be right, but because it is *their* system? If the members of some community can agree among themselves on how to organize their internal affairs, why do they need to ask whether their decisions would meet the approval of an impartial spectator?

The concept of public reasoning, like that of the benevolent autocrat, provides a framework within which ideas about normative economics can be organized. Common to both frameworks is the attempt to find a view from nowhere. One of the aims of the present book is to develop a viable alternative to this approach.

3

The Contractarian Perspective

In Chapter 2, I argued that the viewpoint from which normative economics is usually written is a view from nowhere, and that in making recommendations, economists usually address themselves to an imagined benevolent autocrat. I said that I would take a different approach: the normative economics to be presented in the present book would be written from a different viewpoint, and would have a different addressee. In this chapter, I explain what this approach is, how it can be useful, and why I find it attractive.

Following James Buchanan, I will call this approach *contractarian*. Here is a typical expression of Buchanan's conception of the contractarian perspective:

> If politics is to be interpreted in any justificatory or legitimizing sense without the introduction of supra-individual value norms, it must be modelled as a process within which individuals, with separate and potentially different interests and values, interact for the purpose of securing individually valued benefits of cooperative effort. If this presupposition about the nature of politics is accepted, the ultimate model of politics is *contractarian*.   (Buchanan, 1986: 240)

Contrasting his preferred viewpoint with what I have called the view from nowhere, Buchanan says that most political theorists interpret politics as 'a generalization of the jury', but the contractarian approach interprets it as 'a generalization of the market' (1986: 65). The central idea is the pursuit of mutual benefit by individuals who are concerned with their own interests. The motif of *contract* draws attention to the analogy between mutual benefit in politics and mutual benefit in voluntary contracts.

The topic of this chapter is the contractarian *perspective*. I want to describe the general characteristics of contractarian theories, and how they differ from the theories that are more commonly used in normative economics. Contractarianism has many variant forms. At this stage, I will not try to discriminate between these. The particular form of contractarianism that I favour will emerge in later chapters. Although the contractarian approach is now a minority taste among normative economists and political philosophers, it has deep roots in the history of economic, political, and social thought. So I shall begin by looking at two classic texts which exemplify this approach—Thomas Hobbes's *Leviathan* (1651/1962) and David Hume's *Treatise of Human Nature* (1739–40/1978).

3.1 Hobbes's Contractarianism

Hobbes's *Leviathan* would be on just about any list of the greatest works of political theory of all time. In recent years it has been particularly admired for the rigour and consistency with which it develops a rational-choice model of politics. Few modern commentators have sympathized with the conclusion of Hobbes's central argument, and neither do I. For my purposes, what is important is the structure of the argument and, in particular, to whom it is addressed.

Hobbes (1651/1962) begins the argument by describing 'the natural condition of mankind', in which there is no 'civil state' or (which Hobbes treats as synonymous) no 'common power to keep them all in awe'. This natural condition, or state of nature, is a 'war of every one against every one'. Despite—or perhaps because of—the 'incommodities' of this state, men are roughly equal in those faculties of body and mind that are of use to them. (Hobbes refers only to 'men', but perhaps intends to include women too.) There is no call for the refined mental skills that are valued in civil society; what is needed is prudence, which 'is but experience; which equal time, equally bestows on all men, in those things they equally apply themselves unto'. And 'as to the strength of body, the weakest has strength enough to kill the strongest, either by secret machination, or by confederacy with others, that are in the same danger with himself' (Chapter 13: 98–102). In the state of nature, everyone has the right to use his own power as he sees fit, to preserve his own life and to anticipate potential threats. Thus 'every man has a right to every thing; even to one another's body' (Chapter 14: 103).

Hobbes then formulates nineteen 'laws of nature' that apply to men in their natural condition. It is crucial to understand that these laws are not moral constraints, limiting one individual's actions so that others benefit. They are principles of self-preservation that are rational for every individual independently:

> A LAW OF NATURE, *lex naturalis*, is a precept or general rule, found out by reason, by which a man is forbidden to do that, which is destructive of his life, or taketh away the means of preserving the same; and to omit that, by which he thinketh it may best be preserved.   (Hobbes, 1651/1962: Chapter 14: 103)

For Hobbes it is axiomatic that, in the state of nature, each individual has an overriding interest in self-preservation. Thus, we may think of a law of nature as a principle of action that can be recommended independently to each individual as a means of furthering his own fundamental interests. When Hobbes formulates the laws of nature, he is making recommendations to each individual separately; and the recommendation to each individual is intended to engage with that individual's interests, as he perceives them. This is a normative analysis that does not take a view from nowhere: it takes the separate viewpoints of individuals. Hobbes's laws of nature apply equally to all individuals, but that is only because of the symmetry of those individuals' positions and interests. They do not reflect an impartial assessment of what is good for everyone, taken as a whole.

For Hobbes's argument, the most important laws of nature are the first, second, and third. The first law is:

> that every man, ought to endeavour peace, as far as he has hope of obtaining it; and when he cannot obtain it, that he may seek, and use, all helps, and advantages of war.   (Hobbes, 1651/1962: Chapter 14: 103–4)

The second is:

> that a man be willing, when others are so too, as far-forth as for peace, and defence of himself he shall think it necessary, to lay down this right to all things; and be contented with so much liberty against other men, as he would allow other men against himself.   (Hobbes, 1651/1962: Chapter 14: 104)

The idea behind these two laws is that everyone's interests are better served by peace than by war, but that peace cannot be achieved by unilateral action: a person who disarms when others do not is merely exposing himself to be someone else's prey. Hobbes's recommendation to each individual is to be ready and willing to enter into a multilateral agreement to achieve peace. Each should be willing to concede as much as everyone else concedes, if this proves necessary to achieve agreement; but no one should make himself prey by conceding more than this. And if everyone acts on these recommendations, it *will* be necessary that each concedes exactly as much as everyone else does.

The interlocking nature of these recommendations suggests a sense in which, even though Hobbes's recommendations are valid for each individual separately, he is addressing everyone together. His stance is analogous with that of a mediator, trying to end a conflict (say, a labour dispute between an employer and a union, or a war between two countries) by guiding the two parties to a mutually advantageous agreement. A mediator who acts in good faith will look for an agreement that she can recommend to both parties as the best that each can hope to achieve, given that the other must agree too. Since it is evidence of good faith that her recommendations to each party can be stated openly to both, one might say that a good mediator is engaged in a kind of public reasoning. But it is a form of reasoning that recognizes the separate interests of the parties; it takes account of what is good for each party, from its own point of view, without needing to consider what is simply good, as viewed from nowhere.

Using this mode of analysis, Hobbes recommends a 'covenant of every man with every man', by which each individual gives up his right of self-government, conditional on everyone else doing the same; all jointly submit themselves to a sovereign ruler or assembly in the expectation that this power will protect each against the others (Chapter 17: 129–133). Since the covenant imposes almost no constraints on the sovereign, Hobbes's analysis can be read as a justification of the absolute monarchies of seventeenth-century Europe. This justification is an example of *social contract theory*: an institution is justified by showing that it could have been created by a contract between rational individuals, each pursuing his or her own interests.

A contract can serve no purpose unless there is some basis for the expectation that its terms will be fulfilled. Hence the third law of nature: 'that men perform their covenants made'. Given what he means by a 'law of nature', Hobbes has to show that performance is in the individual interest of each party to a contract. In one of the most famous passages of *Leviathan*, Hobbes replies to the 'fool [who] hath said in his heart, that there is no such thing as justice', who 'questioneth, whether injustice...may not sometimes stand with that reason, which dictateth to every man his own good'. Hobbes argues that, even in a state of nature, rational self-interest requires an individual to fulfil the terms of any contract he has made, provided he has sufficient assurance that the other party to the contract will perform too. This assurance is present if 'there is a power to make him [the other party] perform', or if (which Hobbes thinks will be unusual in a state of nature) the other party has already performed. The latter case corresponds with the position of the second mover in what would now be called a Trust Game. Hobbes gives the example of a prisoner of war who is released in return for a promise to pay a ransom. This is a mutually beneficial contract between the captor and the captive. The captor performs first, trusting the captive to perform second. Hobbes asks 'whether it be against reason, that is, against the benefit of the other [the second mover] to perform, or not', and concludes that it is not. In essence, Hobbes's argument is that a reputation for fulfilling the terms of the contracts one has made when there is assurance that the other party will do the same is a valuable asset, particularly in a state of nature in which self-preservation depends on alliances (Chapter 14: 110; Chapter 15: 113–15). I will say more about this argument in Section 11.4.

Hobbes gives most attention to the first three laws of nature, which are concerned with explicit contracts. But not all his laws have this property. The fourth law of nature (the law of 'gratitude') is particularly interesting, because of the way it parallels the third. It is:

> that a man which receiveth benefit from another of mere grace [i.e. by a free gift], endeavour that he which giveth it, have no reasonable cause to repent him of his good will. (Hobbes, 1651/1962: Chapter 15: 118)

The characteristically Hobbesian premise for this law is the claim that 'no man giveth, but with intention of good to himself'. (I do not want to endorse this premise, but as a theorist I must confess a certain admiration for Hobbes's brutal clarity of thought.) In other words, a gift is given only on the expectation of some return, just as the first party to fulfil the terms of a contract does so only on the expectation that the other party will do the same. Like the contractual relationship between the captor and the captive, the relationship between the giver and the recipient is mutually advantageous. In the latter case, the giver is the first mover. According to Hobbes, rational self-interest requires the recipient to meet the giver's expectations: otherwise 'there will be no beginning of benevolence, or trust; nor consequently of mutual help; nor of reconciliation of one man to another' (Chapter 15: 118). One might say that the relationship between giver and recipient is an implicit contract.

So Hobbes's first and second laws recommend each individual to try to negotiate a certain kind of mutually advantageous contract with others. His third law recommends each individual to fulfil the terms of explicit contracts, whenever the other party has performed, or there is adequate assurance that he will do so. His fourth law extends this recommendation to at least one form of implicit contract. These recommendations are addressed to all individuals together, but no one is being asked to make any sacrifice, or even to take any unreasonable risk, for the benefit of anyone else. In summary: each individual is being advised how to achieve his own purposes by entering into and maintaining mutually advantageous relationships with others. These are characteristic features of the mode of argument that I will call 'contractarian'.

3.2 Hume's Contractarianism

My second example of contractarian argument—the analysis of convention developed by Hume in his *Treatise of Human Nature* (1739—40/1978)—may seem very different from Hobbes's theory.[1] One very obvious difference is that Hume, writing against the relatively stable political background of lowland Scotland in the middle of the eighteenth century, is much more optimistic about the possibilities of spontaneous social order than is Hobbes, writing in an earlier era of civil war and religious conflict. But I am less concerned with these writers' political conclusions than with the structure of their arguments.

Even so, the claim that Hume is a contractarian may surprise readers who know Hume's essay *Of the Original Contract* (1748) and the passages in the *Treatise* dealing with the origin of government and the obligation of allegiance (1739–40/1978: 534–67). In these texts, Hume takes obvious enjoyment in demolishing the form of social contract theory dear to the Whigs of his time, according to which legitimate government can be founded only on the consent of the governed. But I still want to maintain that Hume's theory of conventions (which underpins his analyses of both justice and political allegiance) follows a contractarian approach.

Hume deviates from traditional social contract theory by analysing social institutions and moral practices as ongoing and self-reproducing conventions that have emerged from evolutionary processes, rather than as the outcomes of some original agreement. In the part of the *Treatise* entitled 'Of Justice and Injustice', Hume begins with an analysis of three principles of justice or 'fundamental laws of nature'. These are the laws of 'stability of possession', 'transference [of possession] by consent', and 'performance of promises' (1739–40/1978: 526). These are laws *of nature* in the sense that they are recognized even in stateless societies. Appealing to evidence from the native societies of North America, Hume conjectures that the earliest human societies were small enough to be able to regulate their internal affairs according to the laws of justice without established governments; government—in the form of military leadership—was needed only to coordinate warfare between societies. He recognizes that, in larger societies, there has to be some public system of enforcement of the rules of justice, but the suggestion seems to be that public enforcement is a backup device: in a well-ordered society, most of the time, these rules are self-enforcing (1739–40/1978: 540–1).

Hume argues that, in contrast to 'natural' virtues such as benevolence, justice is an 'artificial virtue'. In modern language, what Hume means is that the sense of justice is not hard-wired into human psychology in the way that sympathy is. In support of this hypothesis, Hume argues that actions that are naturally perceived as virtuous are ones that *immediately* induce positive affective responses, such as those linked with sympathy. In contrast, actions that are 'artificially' virtuous are perceived as virtuous *indirectly*, by being understood as instances of general rules; it is only by recognizing the value of the relevant rule that we can recognize the value of individual instances of rule-following (1739–40/1978: 477–84). Typically, rules of justice are not consciously designed: a rule of justice 'arises gradually, and acquires force by a slow progression, and by our repeated experience of the inconveniences of transgressing it' (1739–40/1978: 489–90). Although we come to 'annex the idea of virtue to justice', the rules of justice must be prior to the sense of their moral force (1739–40/1978: 498). So the first task for a theory of justice is to explain the origin of these rules without using moral concepts.

Hume begins with the law of 'stability of possession', developing a theory of the origin of property rights in external goods (that is, goods that are capable of being transferred between individuals). The content of this law is

> a convention enter'd into by all the members of the society to bestow stability on the possession of those external goods, and leave everyone in the peaceable enjoyment of what he may acquire by his fortune and industry.
>
> (Hume, 1739–40/1978: 489)

But what does Hume mean by 'convention'?

> This convention is not of the nature of a *promise*: For even promises themselves, as we shall see afterwards, arise from human conventions. It is only a general sense of common interest; which sense all the members of the society express to one another, and which induces them to regulate their conduct by certain rules. I observe, that it will be for my interest to leave another in the possession of his goods, *provided* he will act in the same manner with regard to me. He is sensible of a like interest in the regulation of his conduct. When this common interest is mutually express'd, and is known to both, it produces a suitable resolution and behaviour. And this may properly enough be call'd a convention or agreement betwixt us, tho' without the interposition of a promise; since the actions of each of us have a reference to that of the other, and are perform'd on the supposition, that something is to be perform'd on the other part.   (Hume, 1739–40/1978: 490)

Notice how Hume treats 'convention' and 'agreement' as cognate concepts. When he says that the rule of stability of possession *may properly enough be called* a convention, he seems to be acknowledging that, in its linguistically proper sense, 'convention' implies agreement. In calling the rule a convention he is claiming that, in significant respects, it *is like* an agreement. At the same time, he is stressing that it *is not* an agreement in the usual sense of an exchange of promises. He is formulating a philosophically precise concept that has some of the content of 'agreement' but is more fundamental than that of an exchange of promises: according to Hume's analysis, the institution of promising, and hence also the institution of contract, are themselves conventions.

For Hume, a convention rests on a *general sense of common interest*; each member of society has this sense and is aware that the others have it too. The content of a convention is *reciprocal*: each individual constrains his own actions as part of a general practice in which other people constrain theirs. As Hume puts it:

> A single act of justice is frequently contrary to *public interest*... Nor is every single act of justice, considered apart, more conducive to private interest, than to public; and 'tis easily conceiv'd how a man may impoverish himself by a signal instance of integrity, and have reason to wish, that with regard to that single act, the laws of

> justice were for a moment suspended in the universe.... [But] 'tis certain, that the whole plan or scheme is highly conducive, or indeed absolutely requisite, both to the support of society, and the well-being of every individual. 'Tis impossible to separate the good from the ill.... And even every individual person must find himself a gainer, on ballancing the account; since, without justice, society must immediately dissolve... (Hume, 1739–40/1978: 497)

As this passage makes clear, the idea of mutual advantage is an essential part of Hume's account of a conventional practice: on balancing the account, each individual construes the practice as a whole as beneficial *to him*. Thus, although a convention is not an exchange of promises, it *is* a form of mutually beneficial exchange. In this respect, Hume's analysis is in the same spirit as Hobbes's analysis of the implicit contract between the giver of a gift and the recipient.

However, Hume is concerned with stability of possession not only as a social fact, but also as a rule of justice, to which the idea of virtue has been 'annexed'. Unlike Hobbes, Hume recognizes a distinction between an individual's perception that *it is in her interest* to follow some rule and her perception that *she has a moral obligation* to do so. In Hume's analysis, morality does not belong to some non-naturalistic realm of moral truth or reason; it is a matter of empirical psychology. Moral rules encode social regularities of approval and disapproval, and approval and disapproval are sentiments that are determined by mechanisms of sympathy. Actions that cause harm induce sympathetic negative emotions even in individuals who are not directly affected. If some type of action consistently induces such emotions, it will be the subject of general disapproval—which is to say that it will be perceived as morally wrong.

Hume's explanation of how people come to perceive the rules of justice to be morally obligatory is rather brief and is open to various interpretations, but it seems to depend on the assumption that the rules of justice are mutually advantageous. Hume argues that the earliest societies were sufficiently small that self-interest provided each individual with sufficient motivation to act in accordance with the rules of justice. This is no longer the case; but because justice is understood as a system of general rules which works to everyone's benefit overall, acts of injustice are the object of general disapproval:

> But tho' in our own actions we may frequently lose sight of that interest, which we have in maintaining order, and may follow a lesser and more present interest, we never fail to observe the prejudice we receive, either mediately or immediately, from the injustice of others; as not being in that case either blinded by passion, or byass'd by any contrary temptation. Nay when the injustice is so distant from us, as no way to affect our interest, it still displeases us; because we consider it as prejudicial to human society, and pernicious to every one that approaches the person guilty of it. We partake of their uneasiness by *sympathy*.... *Thus self-interest*

is the original motive to the establishment *of justice: but a* sympathy *with public interest is the source of the* moral approbation, *which attends that virtue.*

(Hume, 1739–40/1978: 499–500; italics in orginal)

The implication is that moral approval and disapproval supplement self-interest and public enforcement in maintaining practices of justice.

It might seem that Hume's concept of 'public interest' could be interpreted in a utilitarian way, as some kind of aggregate of the interests of all individuals. But, given the earlier emphasis on the sense of *common* interest, it is more natural to suppose that Hume is building some notion of common interest into what he calls 'public interest'. And in Hume's account, one of the steps by which people come to sympathize with public interest is their sense of the 'prejudice' that *they* receive from the injustice of others. This would not be possible if the rules of justice were not mutually advantageous.

So for Hume, as for Hobbes, mutual advantage is a central explanatory and normative concept. The two writers offer very different political models—very different descriptions of what social order is and of how it can be maintained—but each presents his model as a configuration of mutually beneficial relationships between individuals. Thus, each writer can recommend his model to every member of society, as a means by which that person can achieve his or her own interests in interaction with others. In this sense, Hobbes and Hume are both contractarians.

Certainly, *explicit* contract plays a smaller part in Hume's argument than in Hobbes's. But Hume's analysis allows us to understand explicit contract as an instance of a more fundamental concept, that of a mutually beneficial interaction grounded on reciprocal expectations. And by showing how such interactions induce generalized sentiments of approval, Hume provides a *moral* understanding of mutually advantageous practices. This allows us to see contracts not only as instruments by which the relevant parties achieve their separate ends, but also as relationships of mutual trust which create moral obligations.

3.3 The Contractarian Perspective

The social theories developed by Hobbes and Hume exemplify the contractarian perspective from which the present book is written.[2]

In the sense in which I will use the term 'contractarian', the most fundamental characteristic of this perspective is that a recommendation is addressed to a set of individuals, showing those individuals how they can coordinate their behaviour to achieve mutual benefit. In making some recommendation *R* to some set of individuals, the contractarian says: 'It is in the interest of each of you separately that all of you together agree to do *R*'.

Notice that this is *not* the same thing as saying: '*R* is in the collective interest of the group of which you are the members'. The latter recommendation treats the addressees as a collective, and allows the possibility that *R* requires some individuals to incur losses for the greater good of others. In contrast, the contractarian recommendation is about the good of *each*, not about the good of the *whole*. But notice too that the contractarian recommendation aims at *mutual* benefit, and it is about the terms on which individuals should *agree*. For these reasons, it is not just a collection of separate recommendations addressed to separate individuals. It is a recommendation (in the singular) addressed to individuals (in the plural). Although those individuals are not addressed as components of a collective entity, they are addressed *together*.

As I said when discussing Hobbes's laws of nature, the stance taken by a contractarian is that of a mediator, helping the parties to a negotiation to find an agreement that they can recognize as mutually beneficial. Pursuing this analogy, the stance of the mediator can be contrasted with that of someone who advises one of the parties to a negotiation on how best to achieve its interests, given the likely behaviour of the others. Such an adviser can look for ways in which the party she is advising can out-think the others. But since the contractarian mediator is advising all the parties together, the idea that one might out-think another can have no place in her reasoning. If there is a range of alternative terms of agreement, all of which ensure positive benefits to all parties but some of which particularly favour one party, some another, a contractarian mediator must appeal to some principle, whether of rationality or fairness or salience, which all parties acknowledge. Hobbes's second law of nature, requiring each man to be contented with as much liberty against other men as he would allow other men against himself, is an example of this kind of contractarian reasoning.

Since a contractarian recommendation is about how to achieve mutual benefit, contractarian reasoning necessarily presupposes some *baseline* of non-agreement from which benefit is measured. And since this reasoning is addressed to individuals together, and is intended to engage with each individual's own interests as he perceives them, this baseline must be acknowledged by each individual. That is, each party to a potential agreement must recognize that, for all the parties severally, agreement must be more beneficial than non-agreement.

Contractarian writers differ on what is involved in this acknowledgement of a baseline. I share the view of Buchanan (1975) that, for contractarian reasoning to be possible, it is sufficient that individuals acknowledge the baseline *as a fact of life*—that, as Buchanan puts it, 'we start from here, and not from some place else' (1975: 78). In Buchanan's theory of 'ordered anarchy', there is a 'natural distribution' of resources that has emerged in a Hobbesian state of nature, as an equilibrium between individuals whose relationships with one another are those of predator and prey. As an example of this kind of baseline, consider the leaders of the two opposing sides in a civil war, trying to negotiate a political settlement after the war has reached a stalemate. Each may believe his own party to be the legitimate government of the country, and entirely deny the moral legitimacy of the other's claims. Still, if each recognizes the reality of the stalemate—that warfare is costly for both sides and that neither has a realistic prospect of outright victory—there may be sufficient basis for negotiation, and hence for contractarian reasoning about mutual benefit.

As a less dramatic example of the same idea, consider two private individuals Joe and Jane in a society with reasonably secure property rights, negotiating over the sale of a car; Joe is the potential seller and Jane the potential buyer. If this is a normal market transaction, their negotiation is structured by their common acknowledgement of the property rights that are to be exchanged—Joe's initial rights in the car and Jane's initial rights in the money. This does not mean that each person has to believe that those rights are legitimated by some comprehensive theory of social justice, but only that issues of social justice are bracketed out of their reasoning about the terms on which they might trade. Thus, whatever the relative wealth of Joe and Jane, and whatever their respective political opinions about how wealth ought to be distributed, neither of them expects to trade on terms that impose a net loss on one party for the benefit of the other.

I have claimed that, for contractarian reasoning to be possible, it is sufficient that the parties acknowledge some non-agreement baseline as a fact of life. Nevertheless, one might think that the parties' perceptions of the moral status of their agreement would be influenced by their perceptions of the moral status of the baseline. This is not quite as obviously true as it appears at first sight. A recurring theme in Hume's work, developed in my own contractarian theorizing (Sugden, 1986), is that ongoing conventions can come to be perceived as having moral status, without reference to any beliefs about the fairness of their actual or hypothetical origins. But if, as some contractarian thinkers do, one wants to provide moral justifications for social rules or institutions construed as mutually beneficial agreements, it is natural to make that justification conditional on the fairness of the baseline. For example, David Gauthier (1986), whose contractarian project is to derive 'morals by agreement', requires that the relevant agreements are made from a baseline in which there is no coercion. Recall that even Hobbes claims that his state of nature, which might seem completely devoid of morality, is a state of approximate equality—equality, that is, in the faculties of body and mind that can be used for self-preservation. I will say more about the problem of specifying a baseline for contractarian reasoning in Chapters 8 and 10.

Hume's account of convention highlights another significant feature of contractarian reasoning—that it typically leads to recommendations in favour of *general rules*. When a particular rule is recommended to individuals, the claim need not be that each individual benefits from *every* application of that rule, considered separately. Instead, it may be that each can expect to benefit *overall* from the general application of the rule—or, as Hume puts it, that each can expect to find himself in credit when he balances his account. As a modern example, consider the rule that requires vehicles entering a traffic roundabout to give way to vehicles that have already entered. It is easy to see that this rule is efficient in ensuring smooth traffic flows. (If the opposite rule is used, as is apparently the case in Uzbekistan, there seems to be no way of unravelling a traffic jam at a roundabout, once it has formed.[3]) Nevertheless, if one considers the application of this rule to a specific interaction between two drivers at a particular moment, it benefits one at the expense of the other. A traffic engineer who takes the viewpoint of a social planner might point out that, on average, the gain in time to the driver who is favoured by the rule is greater than the loss of time to the one who is disfavoured, and so recommend the rule as a means of reducing the *total* time spent by all road users making a given set of journeys. Viewed in the contractarian perspective, this is not an adequate recommendation. A recommendation has to be addressed to each individual separately, and each individual's interest is in her own journey times, not in the total. The contractarian argument for the rule is that, because each individual can expect to be favoured by the rule approximately as often as she is not, everyone can expect to benefit.

In the case of the roundabout rule, the formula 'everyone can expect to benefit' can be read as 'if the rule is applied, everyone *will* benefit in the long run'. But there is another way in which contractarian arguments can use the concept of expectation. Consider the rule (whether legal or moral) that if there has been a serious road accident, the first person to arrive on the scene must provide assistance, at least to the extent of calling the emergency services if the accident victims are incapable of doing so. In each specific case, this rule imposes significant costs on the person who has to provide assistance, but provides much greater benefits to the people who are being assisted. Because serious accidents are rare events, it would not be true to say that, for each individual separately, the *ex post* benefits of the rule exceed the *ex post* costs. But one might reasonably claim that, for each individual *ex ante*—that is, looking ahead and considering the probabilities of his being involved in an accident in the two possible roles—the *prospective* benefits exceed the *prospective* costs. To use an idea developed by Buchanan and Gordon Tullock (1962: 77–81), when an individual considers the future application of a general rule, a *veil of uncertainty* limits his ability to see exactly how that rule will affect him. The veil of uncertainty represents the uncertainty faced by real individuals when thinking about the possible consequences to them of general rules; it is not a device for creating a view from nowhere.[4]

A further characteristic feature of contractarian recommendations is the attention they give to *compensation*. If, in the absence of compensation, a specific policy proposal would impose significant harms on particular individuals, the addition of compensation payments may make the overall proposal mutually beneficial. The principle of analysing policy proposals in conjunction with compensation payments is standard practice in cost–benefit analysis, in the form of the 'compensation test' or 'potential Pareto improvement criterion'. A proposal satisfies this test if it can be combined with a package of compensation payments such that no individuals are no net losers and some are net beneficiaries. Viewed in the contractarian perspective, a cost–benefit analysis that is structured in this way is a first step in identifying opportunities for mutual benefit.

Some readers may object to what they see as the excessive conservatism of a criterion that apparently requires that losers are always compensated. But it is important to recognize the distinction between the contractarian perspective and the view from nowhere. The contractarian is not claiming that the payment of compensation is a necessary means to achieving the overall good of society, viewed impartially. He is not saying that, in an impartial assessment of the social good, one individual's greater gain never outweighs another's lesser loss. He is addressing individuals, advising them about how to achieve their separate interests through mutually beneficial agreements. If a policy imposes a net loss on some individual, the contractarian cannot tell *her* that it is in *her* interest to accept a loss because others are gaining more. The idea that losers are to be compensated is not a moral assumption of contractarian reasoning; it is another expression of the fundamental idea that that reasoning is addressed to individuals.

Ultimately, the concept of a contractarian recommendation is only a model. In this respect, its status is analogous with that of the two approaches to normative economics that I discussed in Chapter 2—the model of the benevolent autocrat, and the model of impartial public reasoning. If we economists are to think clearly about our normative recommendations, we need some way of construing politics that allows those recommendations a point of engagement. In other words, we need a model of politics in which there are actors to whom our recommendations can be addressed. Since our recommendations are structured by the logic of economic theory, the model must be one in which the addressees have some reason or motivation to act on recommendations that are structured in this way. And, obviously, if the model is to be useful, it must capture significant features of real politics. I suggest each of the three models—the benevolent autocrat, impartial public reasoning, and contractarian reasoning—is a viable option.

Each model isolates a different aspect of the complex reality of politics in a way that allows economists' recommendations to gain traction. In real politics, there are decision-makers—presidents, ministers of state, senior pub-lic servants—who sometimes have both discretionary power and the desire to use this power for the social good. The model of the benevolent autocrat provides a stylized representation of this form of *politics as executive action* and of the corresponding role of normative economics. In real politics, too, there are arenas of debate about the public good where the participants—legislators, academics, religious thinkers, journalists, ordinary citizens—strive to deploy impartial and reasoned argument. The model of public reasoning provides a stylized representation of this form of *politics as debate*, allowing a different point of engagement for economists' recommendations. The con-tractarian model represents politics in a yet another manifestation—*politics as negotiation*. In real politics, there are parties and interest groups whose prefer-ences are neither fully aligned nor completely opposed; politics provides a space in which acceptable compromises are negotiated and mutually benefi-cial policy packages are identified. The contractarian model allows normative economic reasoning to be brought to bear on this kind of politics.

To some extent, the choice between these models comes down to horses for courses: which model is most useful depends on the problems with which one is dealing. But I think that there is more to the choice than this. Most readers will probably agree that democratic politics, as actually practised, involves elements of executive action *and* of debate *and* of negotiation. They will probably also agree that each of these elements has some legitimate place in democratic politics. But the relative importance of these elements—the importance that they do have, and the importance that they ought to have—is a matter of political judgement and opinion. I would not be writing this book if I did not believe negotiation to be a major part of what politics is, and of what it should be.

3.4 Why a Contractarian Cannot be a Paternalist

The distinction between the contractarian perspective and the view from nowhere is particularly significant in relation to questions about paternalism.[5] Suppose that, in some domain of economic life, individuals appear to be making choices that are not in their own best interests, perhaps because of deficient information, faulty reasoning, lack of attention, or failures of self-control. Suppose too that these choices are neither beneficial nor harmful to others. How should such choices be viewed in normative economics? Is it the job of the economist to propose ways of aligning individuals' private choices more closely with what she judges to be their interests, and if so, what kinds of proposals should be considered and to whom should they be addressed?

It should go without saying that any proposals should be made with decent humility. We should not assume (as economists too often do) that the axioms of conventional decision and game theory are uncontestable standards of human rationality. But suppose that all due humility has been shown. Suppose that I, as a behavioural economist, am dealing with a case in which, in my judgement, individuals are acting contrary to their own best interests. As far as I can see, those individuals are not pursuing genuine interests that my theoretical framework has failed to represent. Nor are they acting on heuristics which, all things considered, are well-adapted to the decision problems they face. They are simply making mistakes. What then?

On the face of it, the obvious answer is that, if I feel some concern about these mistakes, I should address my concerns *to the individuals themselves*. Take an analogy from epidemiology—a science which, like economics, deals with issues of individual behaviour and public policy. Consider an epidemiologist who discovers a statistically significant causal relationship between consumption of some common food product and the prevalence of some illness. An obvious next step is for her to make her findings public in such a way that (perhaps through the mediation of other health professionals) potential consumers of the product are informed. As the history of smoking from the 1950s illustrates, the dissemination of information about health risks can precipitate major shifts in consumption patterns—shifts that may begin well before significant public policy interventions are seen as politically feasible. Indeed, some degree of risk awareness on the part of private individuals may be a precondition for successful public intervention. So there is nothing obviously absurd in thinking that the role of a professional economist might include telling the general public how to avoid decision-making errors.

Given that economists often characterize their discipline as the science of rational choice, one might expect them to recognize the potential value of helping individuals to make better decisions in their private lives. An example of how normative economics can be oriented in this way can be found in the work of one of the pioneers of neoclassical economics. Philip Wicksteed's *Common Sense of Political Economy* (1910/1933) was one of the first attempts to express the theoretical innovations of neoclassical economics in plain prose rather than the mathematics of calculus. Wicksteed presents economics as a study of the 'general laws of the administration of resources'—that is, the principles of optimization—and insists that these laws apply 'from end to end of life' (1910/1933: 159). Although much of his analysis depends on the assumption that individuals act on consistent preferences, he acknowledges that the art of rational decision-making 'by no means looks after itself' (1910/1933: 93). In a chapter entitled 'Economical administration and its difficulties', he gives the reader practical advice on how to avoid common mistakes in decision-making. These mistakes include a surprising number of phenomena that have since been investigated by behavioural economists, including the sunk cost effect, failures of self-control, part–whole inconsistencies, and bad-deal aversion.[6]

Wicksteed's concern with promoting rationality in private life can still be found in the teaching of economics, where there is an informal tradition of asserting, to the satisfaction of both teacher and student, that people who understand economics are capable of making better decisions than those who do not. (I remember, as an undergraduate student of economics, learning that bygones are bygones and feeling superior to those non-economists who succumbed to the sunk cost fallacy.) But the application of rational choice theory to private decision-making has not been taken very seriously as a branch of normative economics. In its respectable forms, normative economics has almost always been addressed to *public* decision-makers.

This orientation is perhaps understandable when it is taken by economists who model individuals as ideally rational agents. Such economists are used to thinking about individuals—admittedly, imaginary ones—who have no need for advice about how to make better decisions. But it is surely odd that this approach has been carried over to behavioural economics. Of course, an economist who works as a paid consultant has to address herself to whoever pays her, and academic economists are perhaps more likely to be consulted by government agencies than by private individuals. But I am thinking about the huge body of work in normative economics that is not written to meet the demand of any particular client, but is presented at academic conferences and published in academic books and journals. Although the authors of such work may refer to the 'policy implications' of their research, there is usually no actual policy-maker waiting to put these implications into effect. No doubt the authors hope that their findings will eventually filter into the consciousness of some politician or public official, but the idea that normative economics is addressed to a public decision-maker is, as I said in Section 2.2, no more than a literary device. This device seems rather out of place when what are being discussed are (supposed) mistakes in decisions that are made by private individuals and that do not affect anyone else. At any rate, something is clearly wrong if economists think that their response to the discovery of mistakes in individual decision-making *must* take the form of a recommendation about public policy. Advising individuals about how to pursue their own interests in their private lives is a natural counterpart to advising them about how to pursue common interests through agreement.

But what if we are dealing with a mistake which, although made by a private individual, is partly attributable to some feature of that individual's environment that is under the control of some commercial firm or public agency? This is a central issue in the literature of behavioural welfare economics. A common view, first proposed by Cass Sunstein and Richard Thaler, is that the professional role of behavioural economists should include acting as, or as advisers to, choice architects—that is, the designers of the infrastructure associated with decision problems. Thaler and Sunstein (2008: 88) argue that well-designed choice architecture steers or *nudges* the chooser towards the choices that are in her best interests. One of their examples is the design of cash machines. To withdraw cash from a machine, the customer must first insert a bank card. There is a risk that, through lack of attention, she will forget to retrieve her card. The tendency to make this mistake is augmented by the psychological salience of the money relative to the card: it is easy to think that one's interaction with the machine is closed by taking the money. Thus, it is less likely that anything (money or card) will be left in the machine if the card is returned before the cash is delivered, particularly if the removal of the card is a precondition for the delivery of the cash. Most cash machines now have this feature. Sunstein and Thaler assume, reasonably enough, that their readers will approve of cash machines that are designed to minimize the risk that customers will forget to retrieve their cards. They suggest that the paternalistic nudges they propose, such as displays of food items in retail outlets which steer customers towards healthier options, have a similar rationale.

But if one thinks in terms of recommendations and their addressees, the cash machine case is not entirely analogous with a paternalistic nudge. Imagine a time when no one had realized the significance of the order in which cash and card were returned; some cash machines followed one order, some the other. Suppose I am a behavioural scientist researching the loss of bank cards, and I discover that losses are much less frequent with the 'card-first' design than with the 'cash-first' design. I want to recommend the general adoption of the card-first design and, provided the costs are not too great, the retrofitting of existing machines. To whom should I address this recommendation?

If I were to follow the usual practice of economics, I would formulate my conclusion as a 'policy implication'—that is, as a recommendation to an imagined social planner or policy-maker. Taking a view from nowhere, I would argue that the adoption of the card-first design would increase social welfare, and that a policy to this effect should be implemented, perhaps by governmental regulation. But there is a contractarian alternative. I can identify a mutually beneficial transaction between customers and banks (or, more accurately, the shareholders who receive the banks' profits). My recommendation to each bank is: Adopt the card-first design; publicize its advantages to customers as one of your selling points. My recommendation to each customer is: Other things being equal, patronize banks which use the card-first design, even if their charges are marginally higher. Notice that, in the spirit of contractarianism, these recommendations are addressed *to individuals together.* Each individual will benefit by acting on the recommendation I make to him, provided that other individuals act on the recommendations I make to them. There is no paternalism in these recommendations. I am advising each customer to recognize her own propensity to error, and hence her interest in paying a premium for good choice architecture. And I am advising the owners of banks that, if customers are willing to pay such a premium, it is in their interest to cater to that demand.

In saying that these recommendations are not paternalistic, I am using 'paternalism' in the sense used by Julian Le Grand and Bill New (2015: 23), who say (I think rightly) that a government intervention 'is paternalistic towards an individual if it is intended to address a failure of judgement by that individual [and to] further the individual's own good'. This definition makes paternalism a matter of *intention*: its key feature is the substitution of the government's judgement for that of the individual on the grounds that the individual's judgement of her own good is in error. Such an intention should not be conflated with that of an agent who acts on behalf of a principal. Suppose my car breaks down. I employ a mechanic to repair it because I believe that her judgements about car repair are better than mine. But in acting on those judgements she is not correcting an error of reasoning on my part: my reasoning led to an entirely sensible decision, namely to employ her. Advocates of behavioural welfare economics sometimes seem to suggest that all forms of hired expertise are paternalistic (as when Sunstein [2018] claims that a GPS device is paternalistic because 'it purports to know, better than you do, how to get where you want to go'). To define 'paternalism' so broadly is to fail to recognize how paternalism in general could ever be thought objectionable.

Without being paternalistic, a contractarian can recommend an individual to make use of types of choice architecture that nudge her away from mistakes that she knows she is liable to make and that she wishes to avoid. He can make this recommendation in relation to a propensity for error that she was not *previously* aware of. That is, he can say: This is a mistake that you are liable to make; if you want to avoid making it, I recommend this piece of choice architecture. The contractarian might even recommend the individual to make use of a choice architect whom she trusts, just as someone who is building an extension to his house might make use of a real architect. For example, think of how a firm which sells technologically complex products can gain a reputation for good design; a customer might choose to patronize such a firm in the expectation that its products will be easy to use, even though she cannot specify the problems that good designs can overcome. Thus, a citizen who was aware of his liability to make certain kinds of mistakes might be advised to delegate the task of designing and implementing nudges against these mistakes to a regulatory agency that *he* trusts to act in what *he* perceives as his interests.[7]

But what a contractarian economist cannot do is to propose nudging an individual *who chooses not to be nudged*. Compare the cash machine case with the case of Sunstein and Thaler's cafeteria, discussed in Section 2.2. Consider Jane, one of the cafeteria's customers. Suppose that Jane is currently in good health but seriously overweight. Almost all professional dieticians would concur with the judgement that her long-term health prospects would be better if she ate less high-fat, high-sugar food (such as the cafeteria's cream cake) and more fruit and vegetables (such as the cafeteria's fresh fruit option). In fact, however, she usually chooses the cake. Sunstein and Thaler's recommendation (at least if all customers are like Jane) is that the fruit should be displayed more prominently than the cake, so as to nudge Jane towards the healthier choice. As I pointed out in Section 2.2, this recommendation is addressed to the cafeteria director, in the role of benevolent social planner. But if it is to be a contractarian recommendation, it must be addressed *to the individuals whom it will affect*, and that clearly includes Jane. And it must engage with Jane's interests, *as she understands them*.

There is no problem in advising Jane to choose fruit rather than cake, just as one might advise a bank customer to try to remember not to leave his bank card in a cash machine. But unless Jane is a hermit, she will already know that this is what professional dieticians recommend to people like herself. If she acted on this advice, there would be no need for nudging. The problem is that she doesn't. So the recommendation in favour of nudging has to be compatible with whatever reasons Jane finds adequate to explain why, despite knowing what dieticians advise, she usually chooses cake. Within the limits set by those reasons, it must show Jane why she would benefit by being nudged away from cake-eating.

What might those reasons be? Suppose Jane is given a questionnaire which asks which of the following seven statements best represents her reason for eating as she does, contrary to expert advice:

(a) *I get a lot of pleasure from eating sweet and fatty foods, and the thought of living to a great age doesn't appeal to me.*

(b) *When I am a few years older I will adopt a healthier diet, so my current eating habits are not a problem.*

(c) *The expert advice sets unrealistic standards. Most of the people I know eat at least as much sugar and fat as I do.*

(d) *Expert health advice is always changing; in a few years time, experts may be recommending high-fat, high-sugar diets.*

(e) *All my grandparents were thin but died relatively young. It's quite likely that I will die young too, whatever I eat.*

(f) *Whatever I eat, I put on weight, so for me there is no point in trying to eat healthier food.*

(g) *I always go into the cafeteria having resolved not to choose cake, but when I see the cake at the front of the counter, I can't resist the temptation.*

If Jane's answer is (g), she is acknowledging a problem of self-control. A recommendation in favour of nudging then has some chance of engaging with her reasons: she wants to resist the temptation to eat the cake, and the temptation will be less if the cake is displayed less prominently. But behavioural science provides a lot of evidence of psychological mechanisms that might induce other answers. These include lack of empathy for one's older self (a), procrastination (b), matching one's behaviour to that of others (c), cognitive dissonance (d), over-weighting personal experience (e), and self-deception (f). My conjecture, based both on casual social experience and general scientific knowledge about these mechanisms, is that answers like (a), (b), (c), (d), (e), and (f) are much more likely. Their common feature is the denial that any mistake is being made. If Jane sees nothing wrong with the choices she is making, she will see no reason to want to be nudged.

Of course, this is not to say that these answers are *good* reasons for choosing a high-fat, high-sugar diet. As stated, they are not exactly illogical, but they depend on assumptions which, one might think, Jane ought to know are unlikely to be true, or on beliefs that she ought to know are not well-founded.[8] A benevolent social planner might brush them aside and invoke his preferred interpretation of Jane's best interests. But a contractarian cannot appeal against the reasoning of the real Jane by invoking the supposed fact that she *would have chosen* to be nudged, if only she had been better informed, less impulsive, or better able to understand sound reasoning. All of these putative justifications for nudges are paternalistic. They are the kinds of reason that a parent might use to justify her management of a child's behaviour. The parent who tells the child to eat up the vegetables on his dinner plate or to come home before it gets dark will typically say that she is not imposing her own preferences on the child: the behaviour she is demanding is in the child's best interests, and the child would recognize this fact if he were as well-informed and rational as the parent. The paternalism is embedded in the presumption that the parent is entitled to act as the agent of the child's supposed rational self and as the judge of what that self would have chosen.

Why, in the contractarian perspective, is paternalism out of bounds? The answer is *not* that, all things considered, paternalism has undesirable consequences. Nor is it that paternalism violates individuals' rights or compromises their autonomy, and that rights or autonomy have moral value, as viewed from nowhere. It is that, within the contractarian framework, a paternalistic recommendation *lacks a valid addressee*. Contractarian recommendations are not addressed to imagined benevolent autocrats or to self-appointed guard-ians. They are addressed to individuals as the directors of their own lives, advising those individuals about how to pursue their own interests. Paternal-istic proposals are not recommendations of this kind; in a contractarian analysis they are simply out of place. One might say that they are *ultra vires*, not properly on the agenda for contractarian discussion.[9]

When justifying specific proposals for nudging, Sunstein and Thaler some-times claim more than that nudgees (the people being nudged) will be made better off, as judged by themselves. They sometimes make the further claim that the nudgees *want* to be nudged, in a sense that corresponds with the answer (*g*) in my questionnaire. But the evidence offered in support of this claim is typically quite casual. (I will say more about this in Section 4.8.) Sunstein and Thaler might reasonably say that the issue of whether people want to be nudged is peripheral to their main argument. The normative criterion of libertarian paternalism is the satisfaction of individuals' latent preferences. Concerns about liberty and autonomy are taken into account by means of the constraint that individuals' freedom of choice is not restricted. If this constraint is satisfied, it might be argued, it does not really matter whether or not nudgees want to be nudged.

A related thought is made explicit when Sunstein and Thaler consider the objection that autonomy has moral value, and that 'people are entitled to make their own choices even if they err'. Their response is:

> We do not disagree with the view that autonomy has claims of its own, but we believe that it would be fanatical, in the settings we discuss, to treat autonomy, in the form of freedom of choice, as a kind of trump, not to be overridden on consequentialist grounds.... [W]e think that respect for autonomy is adequately accommodated by the libertarian aspect of libertarian paternalism.
>
> (Sunstein and Thaler, 2003a: 1167, note 19)

Notice that the objection to which Sunstein and Thaler are responding is another view from nowhere. They are imagining a critic who maintains that autonomy is a component of individual well-being, and so ought to be included in any assessment of what is good, all things considered. They 'do not disagree' with this general idea, but think that only a fanatical libertarian would appeal to it as an objection to the sort of nudges they are proposing. When an individual's own choices—say, through excessive drinking or over-eating—are so much in error that they seriously impair his health, how can the effects on his autonomy of a mere nudge outweigh the prospective bene-fits in the form of better health?

If one takes the view from nowhere, this argument has some force. But it is not an argument against the contractarian position. The contractarian does not claim that unchosen nudges—that is, nudges that are not chosen by the nudgees whose behaviour they are designed to affect—are bad, all things considered. The claim is only that such nudges cannot be recommended to their nudgees. From long experience of giving talks on this topic, I know that many economists and philosophers *do* think that the contractarian position is fanatical. A typical questioner will describe some case in which (as judged by the questioner) a mild but unchosen nudge would be very beneficial to its nudgees. Perhaps the nudgees are morbidly obese, and the nudge is a government policy that will make unhealthy fast food less readily available. The questioner asks me: What would you do in this case? To which my reply is: What do you mean, what would *I* do? What is the hypothetical scenario in which I am supposed to be capable of doing something about the diets of my morbidly obese fellow-citizens?

If the scenario is one in which Robert Sugden is in a roadside restaurant and a morbidly obese stranger is sitting at another table ordering a huge all-day breakfast as a mid-afternoon snack, the answer is that I would do nothing. I would think it was not my business as a diner in a restaurant to make gratuitous interventions into other diners' decisions about what to eat. But of course, this is not the kind of scenario the questioner has in mind. What is really being asked is what I would do, *were I a benevolent autocrat*. My answer is that I am not a benevolent autocrat, nor the adviser to one. As a contractarian economist, I am not imagining myself in either of those roles. I am advising individuals about how to pursue their common interests, and paternalism has no place in such advice.

3.5 The Four Alls

Some readers may by now have been persuaded of the internal coherence of the contractarian approach, but still be surprised that anyone would *want* to think about normative economic issues in this way. It may be true (they may think) that paternalism is out of bounds to contractarian analysis, but is that not just a symptom of the deficiencies of that approach? I will end this chapter with an attempt to express how, if one looks at the world in a certain way, the contractarian approach can be seen as attractive.

Sunstein and Thaler devote a chapter of *Nudge* to the issue of retirement savings. The content of this chapter is summarized in the final paragraph:

> Saving for retirement is something that Humans [as contrasted with ideally rational agents] find difficult. They have to solve a complicated mathematical problem to know how much to save, and then they have to exert a lot of willpower for a long time to execute this plan. This is an ideal domain for nudging. In an environment in which people have to make only one decision per lifetime, we should surely try harder to help them get it right.   (Thaler and Sunstein, 2008: 117)

Look at the final sentence. Sunstein and Thaler are telling their readers that *we* should try harder to help *them* get their decisions right. But who are the 'we' and who are the 'they' here? What 'we' are supposed to be doing is designing and implementing choice architecture that nudges individuals to save more for retirement; so presumably 'we' refers to government ministers, legislators, regulators, human resource directors, and their respective assistants and advisers; 'they' are the individuals who should be saving. As an expert adviser on the design of occupational pension schemes, Thaler is certainly entitled to categorize himself as one of the 'we'. But where do his readers belong? Very few of them will be in any position to design savings schemes, but just about all of them will face, or will have faced, the problem of saving for retirement. From a reader's point of view, Sunstein and Thaler's conclusion would be much more naturally expressed as: *They* should try harder to help *us* get it right. Sunstein and Thaler are writing from the perspective of insiders to the public decision-making process: they are writing as if they were political or economic decision-makers with discretionary power, or the trusted advisors of such decision-makers. And they are inviting their readers to imagine that they are insiders too—that they are the people in control of the nudging, not the people who are being nudged.

I suggest that the benevolent autocrat model appeals to people who like to imagine themselves as insiders in this sense. By imagining yourself into a suitable insider role, you can forget about all the real obstacles that lie between your having (what you believe to be) a good idea about how other people's welfare might be improved and there being a public decision to implement that idea. If you have been trained as an economist, you can imagine advising a decision-maker who shares your belief in the importance of economics and who has the good sense to consult sound economists such as yourself. You do not have to ask whether real decision-makers would want to take your advice. Nor do you have to ask whether other people's ideas about how *your* welfare might be improved—ideas that *they* believe to be good, but you perhaps don't—might get implemented instead.

The public reasoning model has something of the same appeal to people who like to imagine themselves as insiders in a different sense. That model invites you to imagine a public discussion in which each participant presents reasoned arguments in support of his or her judgements about the overall good, and all try to reach agreement about the validity and force of these arguments. If you have been trained as a philosopher, you have professional expertise in reasoned argument. You can imagine having a prominent role in a public discussion, presenting arguments which carry the day by virtue of their philosophical merits. It is easy to forget that other people's arguments, based on reasons which they believe to be sound but you do not, might prove more persuasive.

In contrast, the contractarian approach appeals to people who take an outsider's view of politics, thinking of public decision-makers as agents and themselves as principals. The sort of person I have in mind does not think that he has been unjustly *excluded* from public decision-making or debate; he is more likely to say that he has (what for him are) more important things to do with his time. He does not claim to have special skills in economics or politics, and is willing to leave the day-to-day details of public decision-making to those who do—just as he is willing to leave the day-to-day maintenance of his central heating system to a trained technician. But when public decision-makers are dealing with his affairs, he expects them to act in his interests, as he perceives them. He does not expect them to set themselves up as his guardians.

This way of thinking about politics is encapsulated in a traditional English inn sign, the sign of the Four Alls. The sign is divided into quarters, on the model of a shield in a coat of arms. The first quarter shows a picture of a king, with the words 'I rule all'. The second shows a soldier: 'I fight for all'. The third shows a parson: 'I pray for all'. The fourth shows a farmer, with the words 'I pay for all'. The sign expresses the farmer's view of public affairs. The farmer, I take it, recognizes the value he derives from the activities of the government, the army, and the church. He does not pretend to possess the skills that those activities require, and has no particular wish to do so: he has his own skills, which are at least as valuable in the overall scheme of things. But he expects the king, the soldier, and the parson to remember that it is his taxes that pays for their work. He does not defer to them: he is their employer.

4

The Inner Rational Agent

In Chapter 1, I explained how the findings of behavioural economics have created problems for welfare economics. I said that a consensus about how to resolve these problems was beginning to emerge, based on the idea that observed 'anomalies' in individual behaviour—deviations from the patterns of behaviour represented in neoclassical models—are the result of errors, and that the satisfaction of individuals' underlying error-free preferences should be used as a normative criterion. In this chapter, I examine the *behavioural welfare economics* that is favoured by this consensus.

4.1 Behavioural Welfare Economics: The New Consensus

Since Cass Sunstein and Richard Thaler have been particularly influential in the development and advocacy of behavioural welfare economics, I begin by looking at their proposals.[1] Their principal original paper (Sunstein and Thaler, 2003a) was addressed to legal scholars; a shorter version was addressed to economists (Sunstein and Thaler, 2003b). These papers set out a manifesto for *libertarian paternalism*. Their later book *Nudge* (Thaler and Sunstein, 2008) extends and popularizes these ideas.[2]

One of Sunstein and Thaler's key claims is that the findings of behavioural economics make paternalism unavoidable: the anti-paternalist position is 'incoherent', a 'nonstarter'. In all three works, this claim is developed in relation to the cafeteria example that I mentioned in Section 2.2. The premise is that customers' choices between alternative food items are influenced by the prominence with which those items are displayed on the cafeteria counter. Knowing that some items are healthier than others, the cafeteria director has to choose the relative prominence with which different items are displayed. Sunstein and Thaler consider two apparently reasonable strategies that the director might adopt: she could 'make the choices that she thinks would make the customers best off, all things considered' or she could 'give consumers what she thinks they would choose on their own'. We are told that the second option is 'what anti-paternalists would favor', but that the anti-paternalist argument for this option is incoherent. By assumption, the customers

> lack well-formed preferences, in the sense of preferences that are firmly held and preexist the director's own choices about how to order the relevant items [along the counter]. If the arrangement of the alternatives has a significant effect on the selections the customers make, then their true 'preferences' do not formally exist.
>
> (Sunstein and Thaler, 2003a: 1164)

Sunstein and Thaler conclude that the first strategy, despite being paternalistic, is the only reasonable option for a well-intentioned director (2003a: 1164–5, 1182; see also 2008: 1–3).

To avoid confusion later, it is important to clarify what Sunstein and Thaler mean by 'true preferences' in the passage I have just quoted. Given the context, it seems clear that 'preference' is being used in the sense that it is used in conventional economic theory—that is, as a binary relation over potential objects of choice that is reliably revealed in an individual's decisions. In this 'formal' sense, the cafeteria customer does not have well-defined ('true') preferences over food items. As I will explain later, Sunstein and Thaler's analysis attributes to the customer what might, in a different sense, be called 'true preferences'.

Notice that, as in the 'loss aversion', 'attention', and 'Allais Paradox' cases described in Section 1.3, the choices of the cafeteria customers are context-dependent in a way that has a psychological explanation (more prominently-displayed items are more likely to engage attention) but which does not seem relevant to customers' interests or goals. Such cases are central to Sunstein and Thaler's argumentative strategy. The key innovation of libertarian paternalism is the idea that individuals' choices from given sets of (objectively defined) options can be influenced by *nudges*—that is, interventions which affect only the (subjectively perceived) framing of the decision problem. Thus, it is possible to achieve paternalistic objectives without restricting individuals' freedom of choice over objective options. But nudges can work only in cases in which choices are context-dependent.

Notice also that the cafeteria problem is presented as a problem *for the cafeteria director*. The director is understood as someone who acts on her own authority and responsibility, but with the objective of benefiting her customers. Sunstein and Thaler describe this role as that of a 'planner' (in their 2003 papers) or 'choice architect' (in their later book). As I explained in Chapter 2, the idea that normative recommendations are addressed to a benevolent planner is a common device in welfare economics. It leads naturally to the further idea that those recommendations should be directed at increasing the well-being of the individuals for whom the planner is planning. In *Nudge*, this idea is given a significantly different twist: Sunstein and Thaler say that their recommendations are designed to 'make choosers better off, *as judged by themselves*' (2008: 5; italics in original). The italicized clause recurs with minor variations throughout *Nudge* (2008: 10, 12, 80). The implication seems to be that although the planner acts on her own responsibility, she tries to respect each individual's subjective judgements about what makes him better off.

Sunstein and Thaler's approach to normative economics requires that the planner can reconstruct each individual's judgements about his own well-being, even though these judgements are not always revealed in his choices. But how, at the conceptual level, are we to understand these judgements? And how is the planner to reconstruct them? The closest that Sunstein and Thaler come to addressing these questions systematically is in their discussion of decision-making errors.

Immediately after presenting the principle of trying to make choosers 'better off, *as judged by themselves*', Sunstein and Thaler undertake to show that

> in many cases, individuals make pretty bad decisions—decisions that they would not have made if they had paid full attention and possessed complete information, unlimited cognitive abilities, and complete self-control.
>
> (Thaler and Sunstein, 2008: 5)

The corresponding passage in one of their earlier papers uses almost the same characterization of decisions that would not have been made if individuals had been fully rational, and refers to these as 'inferior decisions in terms of their [i.e. the individuals'] own welfare' (2003a: 1162). The implication is that, for Sunstein and Thaler, the criterion of individual well-being is given by the preferences that the relevant individual would have revealed, had his decision-making not been affected by limitations of attention, information, cognitive ability, or self-control—limitations which, for short, I will call *reasoning imperfections*. So the task for the planner is to try to reconstruct individuals' underlying or *latent* preferences by simulating what they would have chosen, had they not been subject to reasoning imperfections.[3] Following Daniel Hausman (2012: 102), I will call such a reconstruction exercise *preference purification*.

That this is what Sunstein and Thaler have in mind is confirmed by Thaler (2015: 325–6) in a later book, where he emphasizes 'a point that critics of our book [i.e. *Nudge*] seem incapable of getting'. The point is that Sunstein and Thaler 'have no interest in telling people what to do. We want to help them achieve their *own* goals'. Pointing the reader to the '*as judged by themselves*' clause, Thaler says: 'The italics are in the original but perhaps we should also have used bold and a large font, given the number of times we have been accused of thinking that we know what is best for everyone. . . . We just want to reduce what people would themselves call errors'.

Notice that preference purification cannot provide the welfare criterion that Sunstein and Thaler need unless latent preferences are context-independent. The context-dependence of revealed preferences, with the supposed implication that paternalism is unavoidable, provides the starting point for Sunstein and Thaler's argument for libertarian paternalism. But if the choice architect's decision criterion turned out to be context-dependent too, that argument would be fatally undermined. The assumption that latent preferences are context-independent is implicit in Sunstein and Thaler's arguments, but is never defended.

One of Sunstein and Thaler's favourite rhetorical strategies is to characterize their opponents as maintaining that human beings are not subject to reasoning imperfections. Recall the passage from *Nudge* that I quoted in Section 1.3, in which Sunstein and Thaler tease conventional economists for assuming that human beings can 'think like Albert Einstein, store as much memory as IBM's Big Blue [sic], and exercise the willpower of Mahatma Gandhi' and report that 'the folks we know are not like that' (2008: 6–8). Since this contrast between Humans and Econs follows closely after the cafeteria example, the reader is surely being encouraged to infer that the imperfection of human reasoning is *the reason why* ordinary folks' choices have the apparently irrational patterns that behavioural economists and psychologists have discovered, and that can be turned to those folks' advantage by carefully designed choice architecture. *If that inference were justified*, it would support the conclusion that, in the absence of reasoning imperfections, individuals' choices would reveal context-independent preferences. But *is* it justified?

I will return to this issue later, but to lay a foundation for later arguments I invite the reader to think about the following question. Imagine a being—let us call him SuperReasoner—who has the intelligence of Einstein, the memory of Deep Blue, and the self-control of Gandhi. Imagine in addition (since this is also part of Sunstein and Thaler's characterization of perfect reasoning) that SuperReasoner's capacious memory contains every item of information that can be extracted from any existing publication or database. Otherwise, however, SuperReasoner is just like some ordinary human, whom I will call Joe. If Joe were in Sunstein and Thaler's cafeteria, his choices between food items would be influenced by the prominence of their displays. Now imagine taking SuperReasoner into the cafeteria. The desserts offered by the cafeteria include cream cake and fresh fruit. Would the probability of his choosing cake be independent of the position of cake on the counter?

For the moment, I postpone answering this question and look at the work of other advocates of behavioural welfare economics. Contemporaneously with Sunstein and Thaler's original manifesto for libertarian paternalism, Colin Camerer, Samuel Issacharoff, George Loewenstein, Ted O'Donaghue, and Matthew Rabin (2003) advocated *asymmetric paternalism* as a normative response to the findings of behavioural economics. There are close similarities between the two proposals. Both are made by authorial teams which combine prominent behavioural economists and legal scholars. Both claim that behavioural findings provide justifications for paternalistic policies, and that these justifications are immune to traditional anti-paternalist arguments. (The title of Camerer et al.'s paper is 'Regulation for conservatives'.) The paternalistic policies that Camerer et al. recommend are asymmetric in the sense that they benefit boundedly rational individuals by helping them to avoid 'decision-making errors' that 'lead people not to behave in their own best interests', while imposing minimal costs on individuals who are 'fully rational' (2003: 1211–12). Camerer et al. give even less guidance than Sunstein and Thaler about how individuals' interests are defined or how they can be identified. However, the obvious implication is that an individual's interests are revealed in the choices he would have made in the absence of errors, and hence that Camerer et al.'s normative criterion is equivalent to the satisfaction of latent preferences. This is preference purification again.

Douglas Bernheim and Antonio Rangel (2007, 2009) propose an approach to behavioural welfare economics that is similar to preference purification. This approach is developed further by Bernheim (2016). Presuming it to be self-evident that welfare economics is addressed to 'the planner', Bernheim and Rangel characterize the conventional approach as requiring the planner to respect the choices that individuals would make for themselves. Their objective is to extend this form of welfare economics to cases in which choices are context-dependent. The key concept in their theoretical framework is a *generalised choice situation* (GCS) for a given individual, consisting of a set of 'objects' from which the individual must choose one, and a set of 'ancillary conditions'. Ancillary conditions are properties of the choice environment that may affect behaviour but which the planner treats as normatively irrelevant. (Applying this conceptual scheme to the cafeteria, food items are objects while ways of displaying them are ancillary conditions.) The individual's choice behaviour is represented by a correspondence which, for each GCS, picks out the subset of objects that the individual is willing to choose. Bernheim and Rangel's first line of approach is to propose a criterion that respects the individual's revealed preferences over pairs of objects if those preferences are not affected by changes in ancillary conditions, and instructs the planner 'to live with whatever ambiguity remains' (2009: 53). They then suggest that this rather unhelpful criterion might be given more bite by the deletion of data derived from 'suspect' GCSs. A GCS is deemed to be suspect if its ancillary conditions induce impairments in the individual's ability to attend to or process information, or to implement desired courses of action. In effect, this approach purifies choice data by eliminating any choices that were made when the individual's reasoning was impaired. Considering only the purified data, it then uses the satisfaction of context-independent revealed preferences as the normative criterion. Although Bernheim and Rangel do not assume that context-independent latent preferences always exist, their approach yields welfare rankings only for those pairs of objects for which revealed preferences, after purification, are context-independent.

A different way of using the idea of purification is to begin by assuming the existence of context-independent latent preferences, and to propose some specific model of the psychological processes that intervene between those preferences and actual choices. Given such a model, one can then investigate how far and under what assumptions latent preferences can be reconstructed from observations of choices. Yuval Salant and Ariel Rubinstein (2008) follow this approach within a general theoretical framework similar to Bernheim and Rangel's. They define an *extended choice problem* for an individual as a pair (A, f) where A is a set of mutually exclusive and exhaustive alternative objects of choice, and f is a 'frame'. The individual's choices are determined by the interaction of her frame-independent 'underlying preferences' with decision-making heuristics that are activated by, and conditional on, the frame (2008: 1288). Salant and Rubinstein's 'social planner' uses these underlying preferences as the normative criterion for choosing which frame the individual should face (2008: 1294).

A related approach is followed by Paola Manzini and Marco Mariotti (2012), who discuss the welfare implications of a model of boundedly rational choice. In this 'categorize then choose' model, each individual has context-independent preferences over all relevant objects of choice. However, these preferences are not necessarily revealed in her choices. When facing a large menu of options, the individual first assigns options to categories, then eliminates less desired or less salient categories, and finally chooses the most preferred of the non-eliminated options. Thus, as in Salant and Rubinstein's model, the individual's choices are determined by the interaction of integrated underlying preferences with a context-dependent decision-making heuristic. (In Manzini and Mariotti's model, the relevant contextual feature is the composition of the menu.) A welfare economist who understands this decision-making process may then be able to reconstruct the individual's underlying preferences from observations of her choices. Manzini and Mariotti (2014) argue that this 'model-based' form of preference purification is more soundly-based than Bernheim and Rangel's method of ignoring choices made in 'suspect' decision environments.

The preference purification approach is developed with a more applied emphasis by Han Bleichrodt, Jose-Luis Pinto-Prades, and Peter Wakker (2001). These authors are primarily concerned with cases in which a professional specialist has to make a decision in the best interests of a client. For example, consider a physician who has to choose between alternative medical treatments for an unconscious patient. The physician has access to data from a stated-preference survey in which the patient made various hypothetical choices between alternative probability distributions over health states. However, these responses are not fully consistent with one another, given the background assumption that 'the right normative model for decision under uncertainty' (2001: 1498–9) is expected utility theory—an assumption to which Bleichrodt et al. are committed. According to Bleichrodt et al., such inconsistencies in stated-preference responses 'designate deficiencies in our measurement instruments that, even if the best currently available, do not tap perfectly into the clients' values' (2001: 1500). The problems resulting from inconsistencies in stated preferences can be mitigated if those preferences are elicited in face-to-face interviews in which the client is asked to reconsider inconsistent choices (2001: 1499 and 1510). Notice the implicit assumption that the client has (or can be guided to form) preferences that are consistent with one another and with expected utility theory; the use of interviews is presented as a method of purifying preferences by the elimination of error.

But what if the physician has to make do with the patient's inconsistent survey responses? The real novelty of Bleichrodt et al.'s approach is their proposal of an econometric method for 'correcting biases' (2001: 1499). They use cumulative prospect theory (Tversky and Kahneman, 1992) as the *descriptive* model of choice while retaining expected utility theory as the *normative* model. There are two main differences between these models. First, cumulative prospect theory uses a *probability weighting function* to transform objective probabilities into their subjective counterparts; this transformation can be interpreted as taking account of psychological biases in the processing of probability information. Second, it has a *loss aversion* parameter which can be interpreted as picking up a bias induced by the framing of decision problems. Given these interpretations, an expected utility model of preferences can be constructed from an empirically estimated prospect theory model by replacing the estimated probability weighting and loss aversion parameters with the 'unbiased' values implied by expected utility theory. Bleichrodt et al. propose that the patient's stated preferences should be used to estimate a prospect theory model, and that the 'corrected' expected utility model should be used to make choices on behalf of the patient.

A somewhat similar methodology is proposed by Botond Kőszegi and Rabin (2007, 2008) as a way of making inferences about individuals' preferences from observations of their choices while recognizing that the reasoning that led to these choices may have involved mistakes. Their main examples are of choice under uncertainty. Their approach is to infer an individual's subjective beliefs from the choices he makes between gambles with money outcomes, on the assumption that he prefers more money to less (contingent on any given state) and prefers higher probabilities of preferred outcomes to lower probabilities. If subjective beliefs, elicited in this way, do not coincide with objective relative frequencies, a 'revealed mistake in beliefs' is deemed to have occurred. The individual's preferences are then purified by working out what he would have chosen, had he acted on correct beliefs.

The analyses developed by Kőszegi and Rabin and Bleichrodt et al. illustrate how a modelling strategy that is common in descriptive behavioural economics can be adapted to generate normative conclusions. This strategy is to use conventional rational-choice theory as a template, and to model the individual as maximizing a *behavioural utility* function that retains many of the properties of the utility functions used in neoclassical economics and game theory. Psychological factors that are neglected in conventional theory are modelled by introducing additional parameters to the utility function. Typically, the standard utility function is represented as a special case of the behavioural function, defined by assigning default values to the additional parameters. (For example, cumulative prospect theory uses expected utility theory as a template, but adds parameters which allow loss aversion and non-linear probability weighting. When these parameters take their default values, cumulative prospect theory reduces to expected utility theory.) If one accepts (as many behavioural economists do) that the predictions of conventional economic theories are often good first approximations to the truth, this modelling strategy has obvious practical merits, as Hausman (2012: 114–15) and Rabin (2013) have pointed out. But it has an additional feature that can be put to use in normative analysis. It makes it possible to construct two parallel utility functions for an individual—a behavioural utility function that describes the individual's actual behaviour, and a hypothetical utility function in which the 'behavioural' parameters of the behavioural function are given their default values. If—and this is a big 'if'—one assumes that non-default values of behavioural parameters reflect errors of reasoning, the hypothetical utility function can be interpreted as a representation of the individual's latent preferences. And, by construction, those latent preferences satisfy the coherence properties of conventional rational-choice theory.

Another example of the advocacy of behavioural welfare economics can be found in a paper by John Bershears, James Choi, David Laibson, and Brigitte Madrian (2008). Bershears et al. distinguish between *revealed preferences* and *normative preferences*. Revealed preferences are 'tastes that rationalize an economic agent's observed actions'. Normative preferences 'represent the economic actor's true interests' and are taken to be what is ultimately relevant for 'practical policy analysis'. The findings of behavioural economics are interpreted as showing that people's choices often 'do not reveal a true preference, but rather reflect the combined influence of true preferences and decision-making errors' (2008: 1787). Bershears et al. propose various strategies for identifying normative preferences by filtering out the effects of errors from choice data. (For example, they propose a method of 'structural estimation' that is similar to the methods proposed by Bleichodt et al. (2001) and Kőszegi and Rabin (2007, 2008).)

My final example of behavioural welfare economics comes from a book by Julian Le Grand and Bill New (2015), written from the perspective of social policy analysis. (Le Grand is a theorist of the economics of social policy and a one-time adviser to a British Prime Minister.) Le Grand and New defend a certain kind of 'government paternalism' as a means by which a government 'can help its citizens achieve their own ends, and thereby promote their own well-being and that of the whole society' (2015: 182). The policies they recommend are paternalistic in the sense that the government's intention, in its interaction with each individual citizen, is to address problems of 'reasoning failure' by that individual and thereby to promote his good. However, the paternalism is *means-related*: the government respects each individual's chosen ends, and seeks only to assist him in achieving those ends (2015: 2–3). Le Grand and New's account of the nature of 'reasoning failure' and the evidence of its existence is similar to that presented by Sunstein and Thaler. Like Sunstein and Thaler, Le Grand and New point to many predictable patterns in individuals' revealed preferences that are inconsistent with the neoclassical theory of rational choice and explain the psychological mechanisms that lie behind them, but they have very little to say about how error-free latent preferences are to be reconstructed, or indeed to justify the assumption that such preferences exist at all (2015: 79–110).

The various proposals I have reviewed in this section can all be understood as belonging to a common programme for reconciling normative economics with behavioural findings. This programme takes the objective of normative economics to be the measurement of the effects of economic policies on individual well-being, as assessed from the viewpoint of a social planner or entrusted professional (such as a physician, dietician, or 'choice architect') who wishes to respect individuals' judgements about their own well-being. It treats cases in which an individual's choices depend on 'irrelevant' properties of framing as errors, 'error' being defined relative to the latent preferences that the individual would have revealed if not subject to reasoning imperfections. The satisfaction of latent preferences is taken as the normative criterion.

Implicit in this programme, as I understand it, is the idea that latent preference is a subjective concept. By this I mean that latent preferences are judgements or perceptions that are formed within the minds of individual human beings; they do not correspond directly with objective properties of the external world. Thus, the intention is that each individual's interest or well-being should be assessed in terms of that individual's own judgements about what he wants, or about what matters to him. In this sense, behavioural welfare economics remains in alignment with the liberal tradition of economics, as I described it in Chapter 1. In the transition from neoclassical to behavioural welfare economics, actual preferences (as revealed in choices) are replaced by latent preferences as the criterion of individual well-being. Behavioural welfare economists are right to acknowledge that this is a move in the direction of paternalism. However, by maintaining that latent preference is a subjective concept, they can claim to have avoided the stronger form of paternalism in which a social planner imposes *her own* judgements about the well-being of the people for whom she plans. This, I take it, is the point of Sunstein and Thaler's repeated insistence that their aim is to make people better off *as judged by themselves*, and of Bernheim and Rangel's description of their approach as an attempt to respect the choices that individuals would make for themselves.

If this approach is to work in any particular case, the relevant latent preferences must be integrated (in the sense defined in Section 1.2). That is, they must satisfy conventional principles of rational consistency—in particular, context-independence. The clause 'in any particular case' is significant here: the logic of behavioural welfare economics does not require that each individual has integrated latent preferences over *all conceivable* states of affairs. Behavioural welfare economists are entitled to claim that their approach is intended for use only in cases in which latent preferences with the right properties can in fact be reconstructed from individuals' decisions. But if this qualification is taken seriously, the domain in which behavioural welfare economics can be applied may turn out to be rather small.

If latent preferences are subjective judgements or perceptions, the properties of integration that behavioural welfare economics needs to attribute to them cannot be explained by the hypothesis that latent preferences map some objective concept that already has those properties. So the preference purification approach, as applied to any given individual, must presuppose that the individual has potential access to some mode of *latent reasoning* that generates subjective preferences that satisfy conventional principles of rational consistency. Typically, however, the advocates of behavioural welfare economics do not explain what that mode of reasoning is, or how it generates integrated preferences. All they tell us is that it is free of the 'imperfections' that behavioural economists and cognitive psychologists have identified in actual human reasoning. This is true even of those variants of behavioural welfare economics, such as those proposed by Salant and Rubinstein and by Manzini and Mariotti, that are based on models of the decision-making process. Recall that these models assume the existence of the latent preferences that the welfare economist is to elicit; the decision heuristics represented in the models are able to access and process these preferences, however imperfectly.

Needless to say, this limitation of the preference purification approach is shared by the standard theory of rational choice. That theory is formulated in terms of axioms of consistency among preferences, and between preferences and choices; it does not try to explain the reasoning by which individuals construct their preferences. Implicitly, rational-choice theory assumes the existence of a mode of reasoning that generates preferences that satisfy the consistency axioms, but it treats that reasoning as a black box. But a companions-in-guilt defence would be out of place here. Behavioural economics has grown out of (and, one might say, has traded on) scepticism about the psychological plausibility of rational-choice theory. (Recall Sunstein and Thaler on the difference between Humans and Econs.) Its empirical findings have supported that scepticism. A reconciliation of normative and behavioural economics should not depend on black-box assumptions about latent rationality.

4.2 Autonomy and the Model of the Inner Rational Agent

It would be easy to say that the concept of latent rationality used in behavioural welfare economics is simply a hangover from neoclassical theory. However, it may have deeper roots. Over many years of arguing against the assumption of latent rationality, I have been surprised to discover how reluctant many of my academic colleagues—not only economists, but also philosophers and psychologists—are to give it up. I have come to think that the kind of rational-choice theory that is used in neoclassical economics is just one instance of a much wider class of models that human beings are inclined to use when thinking about their own thinking. Latent rationality, albeit in different guises, is a common feature of this class of models. So giving up the idea of latent rationality is a more drastic step than merely accepting the limitations of neoclassical economics.

To illustrate how ideas of latent rationality are used outside economics, I will look at a paper in which two philosophers express their reservations about Sunstein and Thaler's nudge policies. Beginning their paper with a review of libertarian paternalism, Hausman and Brynn Welch (2010) express agreement with many of Sunstein and Thaler's conclusions *about welfare*, acknowledging that those authors 'catalogue many factors that can lead to mistakes in human judgment and decision-making'. For the purposes of their paper, Hausman and Welch do not need to defend Sunstein and Thaler's specific judgements about which psychologicial factors 'interfere with rational deliberation', but they endorse those judgements as 'generally plausible' (2010: 125–6).

Hausman and Welch's reservations about libertarian paternalism are not about its analysis of welfare, but about the nudging policies that it recommends. These reservations are formulated in terms of *autonomy*, defined as 'the control an individual has over his or her evaluations and choices'. If one is concerned about autonomy, Hausman and Welch say, 'there does seem to be something paternalistic, not merely beneficent, in designing policies so as to take advantage of people's psychological foibles for their own benefit' (2010: 128). Throughout the paper, nudges are contrasted with 'rational persuasion'. For example:

> The reason why nudges such as setting defaults seem ... to be paternalist, is that in addition to or apart from rational persuasion, they may 'push' individuals to make one choice rather than another. . . . [W]hen this 'pushing' does not take the form of rational persuasion, their autonomy—the extent to which they have control over their own evaluations and deliberations—is diminished. Their actions reflect the tactics of the choice architect rather than exclusively their own evaluation of alternatives.   (Hausman and Welch, 2010: 128)

And (having defined 'shaping' as 'the use of flaws in human decision-making to get individuals to choose one alternative rather than another' [2010: 128]):

> [R]ational persuasion respects both individual liberty and the agent's control over her own decision-making, while, in contrast, deception, limiting what choices are available or shaping choices risks circumventing the individual's will.
> (Hausman and Welch, 2010: 130)

But what do Hausman and Welch mean when they refer to 'the individual' or 'the agent' as an entity that may or may not have control over his or her evaluations, deliberations, and choices? Notice that this agent is not a real human being whose thoughts and actions are governed by psychological mechanisms. If the choices of the real human being are influenced by factors that cannot be construed as good reasons, Hausman and Welch are able to claim that this agent's will has been circumvented. But circumvented by whom? The only available answer seems to be: by the real human being. The implication seems to be that 'the agent', whatever it is, is capable of error-free autonomous reasoning that is undistorted by 'problematic' human psychological mechanisms. It is open to rational persuasion, but impervious to attempts to influence it by other means. Given any decision problem, it can identify the option that it wishes to choose, referring 'exclusively' to its own evaluations of alternatives. This seems to imply that the agent's reasoning can generate evaluations with sufficient structure to determine what should be chosen from any set of options, and that the preferences revealed in those choices are free from psychological foibles and thereby stable and context-independent. This agent is beginning to sound very much like the rational individual of neoclassical economics and game theory. I will call this mysterious and disembodied entity the *inner rational agent*.

Notice how ordinary human psychology is being treated as a set of forces that are liable to restrict the inner agent's ability to act according to the implications of its own reasoning. It is as if the inner rational agent is separated from the world in which it wants to act by a *psychological shell*. The human being's behaviour is determined by interactions between the autonomous reasoning of the inner agent and the psychological properties of the outer shell. However, in relation to issues of preference and judgement, the inner agent is the ultimate normative authority.

Something like this model of human agency seems to be implicit in the project of preference purification that is central to behavioural welfare economics. Preference purification can be thought of as an attempt to reconstruct the preferences of the inner rational agent by 'seeing through'—by abstracting from the distorting effects of—the psychological shell. Recall that Sunstein and Thaler's criterion of well-being is given by the preferences that the relevant individual would reveal, were she to pay full attention to decision problems and to possess complete information, unlimited cognitive abilities, and complete self-control. One might think of these preferences as those of an inner rational agent whose reasoning is free of internal errors but which depends on faulty psychological machinery to provide it with information, to carry out complex information-processing operations, and to execute its decisions. Lack of attention can cause faults in the flow of information to the inner agent; limited cognitive ability can cause faults in information processing; lack of self-control can cause faults in decision execution. Preference purification is an attempt to reconstruct the decisions that the inner agent would execute if the faults in the psychological shell were corrected. On this view, supposed faults in the psychological shell are construed as limitations on the autonomy of the inner agent—an idea that is made explicit when Le Grand and New (2015: 119) characterize reasoning failure as 'a limited loss of autonomy'.

Of course, behavioural economists do not maintain that a human being is *really* made up of an entity that is rational in the sense of neoclassical theory, encased in an error-prone psychological shell. But it is both true and illuminating that behavioural welfare economics proceeds *as if* human beings were like that. Behavioural welfare economics invokes a model of rational agency when it assumes that, in the absence of error, an individual's choices would reveal integrated preferences. This rationality is modelled as an 'inner' property of the individual in the sense that, although rationality is not always revealed in actual behaviour, it is a continuing property of the individual—a continuing capacity to form context-independent subjective judgements on the basis of error-free reasoning. The inner rational agent of behavioural welfare economics is no more and no less than that assumed capacity.

As used by behavioural welfare economics, the model of the inner rational agent might be interpreted as a methodologically questionable attempt to conserve the neoclassical theory of rational choice in the face of disconfirming evidence by re-interpreting it as applying, not to real human beings, but to imaginary disembodied agents. This interpretation is the core of Nathan Berg and Gerd Gigerenzer's (2010) critique of 'as-if behavioural economics'. Despite agreeing with the main thrust of that critique, I think Hausman and Welch's argument illustrates how the model of the inner rational agent has resonance beyond neoclassical economics.

Hausman and Welch are led to the model of the inner rational agent through their attempts to reconcile the idea of human autonomy with the facts of human psychology. To view a human being as an autonomous agent is to view her as the conscious author of her own actions. But viewed in the perspective of empirical psychology, her actions are caused by mental processes that are ultimately matters of physics and chemistry. Whether these two viewpoints can be reconciled, and if so how, is one of the classic problems of philosophy—the Mind-Body Problem. There is a long history of attempts to solve this problem by using *dualist* theories in which properties of the mind (or, in some older versions, properties of the soul) are in some sense or other fundamentally different from properties of the body. Thinking in this way leads naturally to a conception of human agency in which the relationship of mind to body is that of an autonomous inner agent to an outer psychological (and biological) shell. But then one faces the question of what the inner agent is actually doing when it deliberates about what to choose.

Analytical philosophers are inclined to represent the workings of the mind as the processing of propositions that express attitudes such as preference, belief, or intention. For example, a person who is choosing between two drinks might maintain the propositions 'I must drink either tea or coffee' and 'All things considered, I prefer drinking tea to drinking coffee'. Processing these propositions in her mind, she might form the intention 'Let me drink tea'. If one accepts this kind of propositional representation of the workings of the mind, it is difficult to make sense of autonomous agency unless the propositions that the person maintains are mutually consistent. So rationality, in the sense of sound reasoning about choice-relevant propositions, may seem to be an essential property of an autonomous inner agent. Conversely, if some person's choices *cannot* be justified by sound reasons, it may seem that the only way to maintain a conception of her as an autonomous agent is to attribute those choices to the effects of alien mechanisms—alien, that is, to the inner agent, even if an integral part of her human psychology. And so philosophers, like economists, can be drawn to the model of the inner rational agent. However, the idea that the mind works by processing propositions is not a self-evident truth. It is an empirical hypothesis about human psychology, and one that may turn out to be false.

4.3 System 1 and System 2

I still find it surprising that so many behavioural economists have wanted to use the model of the inner rational agent. However attractive that model may be to rational-choice theorists and to analytical philosophers, one might have thought that it would have less appeal to the sub-group of economists who pride themselves on taking psychology seriously. One of the first impulses for what is now called behavioural economics was a recognition that the mental processes that people actually use in decision-making do not necessarily generate choices with the rationality properties traditionally assumed in economics. An obvious corollary of this idea, pointed out by Daniel Kahneman (1996), is that rational choice is not self-explanatory: cases in which behaviour is consistent with the conventional theory of rational choice are just as much in need of psychological explanation as are deviations from that theory. The model of the inner rational agent seems to depend on a denial of this corollary. In that model, human psychology is represented as a set of forces that affect behaviour by *interfering with* rational choice, but rational choice itself—represented by the error-free reasoning of the inner agent—is not given any psychological explanation. Kahneman is right to say that this modelling strategy is 'deeply problematic' (1996: 251–2).

It might be objected that the model of the inner rational agent has psychological foundations in dual-process theories of the mind. The idea that the workings of the mind can be separated into two 'systems'—the fast and automatic *System 1* and the slow and reflective *System 2*—has been suggested by a number of psychologists, including Peter Wason and Jonathan Evans (1975) and Kahneman (2003) himself. Indeed, it is the central theme of Kahneman's (2011) overview of his contributions to psychology and behavioural economics. Kahneman even uses notions of autonomy to describe System 2, in a way that parallels Hausman's and Welch's account of the inner rational agent: 'When we think of ourselves, we identify with System 2, the conscious, reasoning self that has beliefs, makes choices, and decides what to think about and what to do' (Kahneman, 2011: 21). Since Sunstein and Thaler (2008: 19–39) use the same idea as an organizing principle when reviewing behavioural findings, it is plausible to conjecture that they are thinking of the inner rational agent as System 2 and the psychological shell as System 1.

But even if one accepts the dual-process theory as a useful way of organizing ideas about human psychology, the model of the inner rational agent remains vulnerable to Kahneman's critique. One is not entitled simply to assume that the mental processes of System 2 can generate preferences and modes of strategic reasoning that are consistent with conventional decision and game theory. Indeed, that assumption does not fit easily with the logic of dual-process theory. One of the fundamental insights of that theory is that the automatic processing mechanisms of System 1 are evolutionarily older than the conscious mechanisms of System 2. Thus, except in so far as its original features have atrophied, we should expect System 1 to be capable of generating reasonably coherent and successful actions without assistance from other processes. But if System 2 processes are later add-ons, there is no obvious reason to expect them to be able to work independently of the processes to which they have been added. Despite his claim that each of us sees his System 2 as his true self, Kahneman sometimes seems to suggest that System 2 may be no more than a collection of disparate decision support routines. For example: 'When System 1 runs into difficulty, it calls on System 2 to support more detailed and specific processing that may solve the problem of the moment' (2011: 24). It is not obvious that System 2 always needs to be capable of making decisions in its own right, as the inner rational agent is supposed to be. To put this another way, it is not obvious that System 2 is capable of generating the kind of latent preferences that behavioural welfare economics needs.

4.4 Does the Concept of Latent Preference Have Empirical Content?

Another way in which the concept of latent preference might be given psychological foundations is by locating latent preferences in a model of the mental process of decision-making.[4] One might look for a model of mental processing that generates latent preferences (rather than merely assuming their existence) and in which the mechanisms that generate those preferences interact with other mechanisms that induce biases or errors.

Some idea of the difficulties involved in this strategy can be had by considering an example I discussed in Section 1.3—people's choices between alternative snacks to be delivered a week after that choice was made. What has been found is that a typical individual's choices between specific food items (say, between Mars bars and apples) are influenced by his *current* degree of hunger, even though the date and time of delivery of the snack (and hence, the presumably predictable degree of hunger *at the time of delivery*) is held constant. Thus, the individual's choices are influenced by a contextual cue which seems to have no relevance for his welfare. A natural psychological explanation starts from the observation that Mars bars and apples are goods with different mixes of attributes: the Mars bar is tastier and more energy-giving, the apple is more refreshing and, considered as an addition to the individual's normal diet, healthier. In deliberating about which of the two snacks to choose, the individual has to bring these various attributes to mind and strike a balance between them. The hungrier he is, the more attention he gives to those attributes on which the Mars bar is superior, and so the more likely it is that his deliberation will end in the choice of that option.

Viewed in this way, what might seem to be irrational context-dependence is evidence about the underlying structure of the decision-making mechanism. If one thinks in terms of the evolutionary origins of human psychology, the role played by attention in decision-making can be understood as an integral part of a general-purpose mechanism for choosing between multi-attribute options—a mechanism that is (as if) efficiently designed to make use of other mental processes that tend to distribute attention towards what is currently important. (For example, the hungrier one is, the more important it is to be alert to possible sources of nutrition.) But how, then, are we to separate the decision-making mechanism into components of 'rationality' and 'error', and to be able to claim that the rational component retains the subjectivity of the real human individual? The only way forward I can see is to try to identify some particular distribution of attention as 'correct'. But how are we to do this? Recall that it is fundamental to the preference purification approach that the individual's latent preferences represent his own subjective judgements. Thus, we cannot define the correct distribution of attention in terms of some *objective* standard of the individual's interest, analogous with fitness in an evolutionary model. In the absence of such a standard, the idea of a 'neutral' distribution of attention between different attributes of choice options is ill-defined. The core of the problem is that the attention-based mechanisms that explain the individual's decisions also explain what, given the relevant choice context, he actually prefers or desires to do: he feels the desires that prompt him to choose as he does. Viewed in the perspective of empirical psychology, the idea that he might have 'true' preferences that are different from his actual ones seems free-floating and redundant.

To provide some support for this sceptical conclusion, I consider an example of how the concept of latent preference has been used by behavioural economists in modelling attention. Pedro Bordalo, Nicola Gennaioli, and Andrei Shleifer (2013) present an analysis of 'salience and consumer choice' that is motivated by experimental findings from psychology, economics, and marketing. The key idea is that, when valuing any good, individuals tend to give most attention to those attributes on which it stands out relative to the goods with which it is being compared. In Bordalo et al.'s leading example, a consumer is choosing between a bottle of French wine and a bottle of Australian wine. The consumer thinks the French wine is 50 per cent better than the

Australian. In one version of the problem, the choice is made in a supermarket, where the wines are priced at \$20 and \$10. Because the ratio of prices is greater than the ratio of qualities (the French wine is 100 per cent more expensive), price is the *salient attribute* and so tends to receive more attention. In a second version of the problem, the choice is made in a restaurant, where the prices are \$50 and \$40 (and so the French wine is only 25 per cent more expensive). Now quality is the salient attribute. Bordalo et al. present a model that can explain why the same consumer might choose Australian at the supermarket prices and French at the restaurant prices. Leaving aside the possibility of perverse income effects, this pattern of choice is inconsistent with standard economic theory, but it has long been recognized as a common feature of human decision-making (see, for example, Savage, 1954: 103).

In Bordalo et al.'s (2013) model, a consumer faces a set of two or more *goods*, one and only one of which is to be chosen. Each good k in this *opportunity set* is characterized by the pair $\langle q_k, p_k \rangle$, where q_k and p_k are non-negative magnitudes, respectively representing the *quality* and *price* of that good. The consumer knows the value of q_k and p_k for each good in the opportunity set. Higher-quality goods are assumed to have higher prices. The model is specified so that, in the absence of 'salience distortions', the consumer values each good k according to the linear utility function $u_k = q_k - p_k$. This gives a family of linear and parallel indifference curves in $\langle$quality, price$\rangle$ space, which Bordalo et al. call 'rational indifference curves' and attribute to 'the rational consumer'. That the marginal rate of substitution between units of price and quality is constant is a substantive modelling assumption; that each unit of quality is worth \$1 to the 'rational consumer' is (I take it) merely a convenient normalization.[5]

Bordalo et al. then specify how 'salience distorts the valuation of a good' (2013: 810). The behaviour of a 'salient thinker' (that is, a non-rational consumer) is modelled by assuming that salience distorts the utility weights that the consumer applies when evaluating goods. For the rational consumer, both attributes have a normalized weight of 1 in the evaluation of every good. In contrast, when valuing any given good, the salient thinker uses a weight greater than 1 for its salient attribute and a weight less than 1 for its non-salient attribute. Bordalo et al. apply this model to a wide range of consumer behaviour problems. In these applications, the behaviour of a non-rational consumer is determined by the interaction of two systems or processes—a context-independent latent preference relation that is deemed to be rational, and a psychological mechanism which distorts latent preferences. The consumer's actual choices are determined by the distorted preferences, but the hypothetical choices of the rational consumer—that is, the consumer who acts on undistorted preferences—provide the normative benchmark. This is a model with an inner rational agent.

But what is the function of this benchmark? The essence of the model is that the relative weights of the two attributes differ according to which attribute is salient. But which attribute is salient for any given good in any given opportunity set depends only on the qualities and prices of the goods in that opportunity set, and these are defined independently of the consumer's latent preferences. Thus, any results that come about because of changes in relative attribute weights are independent of latent preferences. *The concept of latent preference serves no explanatory purpose.*

Does this mean that rational preferences, as defined by Bordalo et al., are unobservable? Not quite. Bordalo et al. go to some lengths to show how, given the specification of their model, these preferences can be revealed in choices. Consider a decision problem in which there is only one good in the everyday sense of the word, but the consumer can choose whether or not to buy it. Bordalo et al. represent this as a choice between $\langle p_1, q_1 \rangle$ and $\langle p_2, q_2 \rangle$, with $\langle p_2, q_2 \rangle = \langle 0, 0 \rangle$ representing 'not buying'. In this special case, the definition of salience implies that the two attributes are equally salient, and so the salient thinker's choices coincide with those of the rational consumer. Thus, rational preferences are revealed in the consumer's willingness to pay for individual goods in situations in which only one good is on offer.

But what makes this the right definition of rationality? Bordalo et al. do not explain. Here is my best guess about what they have in mind. They are presupposing that the consumer has well-defined latent preferences between goods, defined as $\langle$quality, price$\rangle$ pairs, and that the latent utility of any good is independent of which other goods are in the opportunity set. Since the supposedly distorting effects of salience are induced by comparisons between the goods in the consumer's opportunity set, the best way to recover the consumer's latent preferences is to observe his choices in situations in which there is as little scope as possible for cross-good comparisons. Willingness-to-pay tasks meet this requirement, provided they are set up so that the relevant good 'is evaluated in isolation and without price expectations'. Bordalo et al. suggest that such settings can be created in 'lab experiments' (2013: 828).

In the light of decades of attempts to elicit willingness-to-pay valuations in experiments and surveys, this suggestion is extraordinarily optimistic. Responses to willingness-to-pay and willingness-to-accept questions are known to be influenced by many kinds of irrelevant cues which draw attention to particular answers (Parducci, 1965; Slovic and Lichtenstein, 1968; Johnson and Schkade, 1989; Ariely, Loewenstein, and Prelec, 2003). For example, if the elicitation exercise begins with a question of the form 'Would you be willing to pay $x?', final responses are pulled towards $x; if respondents are asked to pick a point on a scale of possible values, responses are pulled towards the middle of the scale. These 'anchoring' and 'range/frequency' effects are particularly strong when (as in stated preference studies which try to elicit valuations for non-marketed goods, such as changes in environmental quality) there is no customary price that the respondent can use as a benchmark. A natural interpretation of this evidence is that people find it very difficult to give a monetary valuation of any good *in isolation* and that, when required to do so, they unconsciously search for comparators and reference points.

But in any case, the proposition that latent preferences are revealed in willingness-to-pay valuations plays no part in Bordalo et al.'s explanations of observed regularities in consumer behaviour. The truth is that, in their empirical model, the concepts of rationality and distortion are redundant. This redundancy is not an accident of some detail of the model; it reflects the fact that latent preferences serve no psychological function.

4.5 SuperReasoner in the Cafeteria

It is time to return to a question that I asked, but did not answer, in Section 4.1—the question about SuperReasoner in the cafeteria.

Recall that SuperReasoner is a re-engineered version of an ordinary human being, Joe. He differs from Joe in not being subject to reasoning imperfections: he has no limitations of information, attention, cognitive ability, or self-control. In all other respects, however, he is the same as Joe. According to Sunstein and Thaler, SuperReasoner's choices reveal Joe's latent preferences. The options available at the cafeteria include cake and fruit. Were Joe to go to the cafeteria, he would choose (and would be willing to pay at least a small premium for) whichever of those two options was displayed more prominently—let us say, whichever was displayed at the front of the counter, the other item being displayed at the back. The cafeteria director has read *Nudge*, and wants to use the display that best satisfies Joe's latent preferences. Thus, she needs to know what SuperReasoner would choose. Hence the question: Would the probability of his choosing cake be independent of the position of cake on the counter? The logic of behavioural welfare economics requires that the answer to this question is 'Yes'.

If we are to answer this question, we need to know more about the mental operations that SuperReasoner uses when he makes decisions. We know that these are the same operations that Joe uses, except for two features: where Joe uses incomplete or false information, SuperReasoner uses information that is complete and correct; and where Joe makes errors of reasoning, SuperReasoner does not. So we need a representation of the mental operations that Joe uses; we need a specification of what counts as complete and correct information; and we need a specification of what counts as erroneous reasoning.

To the extent that Joe's mental operations involve the processing of propositions, an examination of the propositions that support his decisions may reveal incomplete or incorrect information or erroneous reasoning. If this is the case, SuperReasoner's decisions may differ from Joe's. For example, suppose that the energy contents of fruit and cake are labelled in different units; the fruit is labelled as 250kJ and the cake as 200kcal. In fact, 1kcal = 4.184kJ. But suppose Joe does not understand the difference between the two units. He maintains the propositions 'I prefer a low-calorie diet to a high-calorie diet' and 'The cake has fewer calories than the fruit'; on the basis of these propositions, he forms the intention 'Let me eat the cake'. Whether we describe this as resulting from incorrect information or from a reasoning error, the second proposition is clearly false. Since SuperReasoner would know that the fruit had fewer calories than the cake, he might reach a different conclusion.

But the case we are concerned with is rather different. The anomalous feature of Joe's behaviour is not an error in his response to any decision problem, considered in isolation; it is an apparent inconsistency between his responses to two different decision problems. What we know is that Joe's choice between fruit and cake depends on how these items are displayed. We may think that the difference in display is not a good reason for the difference in choice, but does that tell us that Joe's information or reasoning is at fault?

Suppose that the context-dependence of Joe's decisions is explained by the psychology of attention and desire. Whichever way the two items are displayed, the information he has about them is the same. However, his attention fluctuates between them. He tends to give more attention to the item at the front, and so to have a more vivid sense of its desirable attributes and a greater inclination to choose it. As experienced by Joe, this inclination may be simply a *feeling*, not a *proposition* to which he assents. This might be all there is to the decision process: Joe feels the inclination, and he acts on it. If this is the truth about Joe's mental operations, the fact that he chooses cake when cake is displayed at the front of the counter and fruit when fruit is displayed at the front does not reveal any error in his reasoning. And so we are not entitled to infer from this fact that SuperReasoner's decisions would be different from Joe's.

If we are to have any chance of attributing error to Joe, we need to assume that his mental operations have some propositional content. So let us suppose that Joe is aware of how he responds to the cafeteria display. Suppose that he assents to the following proposition: 'If the cake were at the front, I would feel an inclination to choose the cake, and I would act on that inclination; but if the fruit were at the front, I would feel an inclination to choose the fruit, and I would act on that inclination.' But this proposition is simply a true statement about Joe's psychology; it reveals self-knowledge, not an error of reasoning. If Joe has this degree of self-knowledge, SuperReasoner must have it too.

Remember that SuperReasoner's feelings are the same as Joe's. So SuperReasoner can make the same decisions as Joe does, and assent to a proposition that correctly describes how he comes to those decisions.

Let us try another line of argument. So far, I have said nothing about Joe's *preferences*. How the concept of preference should be understood in economics is not a settled matter. On one possible interpretation, a preference for *x* over *y* is simply an inclination to choose *x* rather than *y*. Given this interpretation, Joe and SuperReasoner can both assent to the proposition 'If the cake were at the front, I would prefer the cake to the fruit; but if the fruit were at the front, I would prefer the fruit to the cake'. As before, assent shows self-knowledge, not error. But a case can be made—and has been made by Hausman (2012)—for a different interpretation.

As part of a philosophical attempt to clarify 'current practice' in economics, Hausman proposes the following definition: 'To say that Jill prefers *x* to *y* is to say that when Jill has thought about everything she takes to bear on how much she values *x* and *y*, Jill ranks *x* above *y*' (2012: 34–5). Thus, a preference is *comparative* (*x* is *ranked* above *y*); the comparison is in terms of *value*; the valuation is *subjective* ('how much *she* values . . . '); and it takes account of the *totality* of factors that the individual thinks relevant to the comparison ('*everything* she takes to bear on . . . '). In short, a preference is a total subjective comparative evaluation. Crucially, preferences are 'more like judgements than feelings' (2012: 135). Given this interpretation, and assuming that Joe's psychology and behaviour are as I have previously described them, suppose he assents to the proposition 'If the cake is at the front, the cake is preferable to the fruit; but if the fruit is at the front, the fruit is preferable to the cake'. Now Joe is not reporting his inclinations; he is declaring that the *comparative subjective values* of the cake and the fruit depend on their relative positions on the counter. Hausman argues that such statements are subject to rational scrutiny. Thus, we are entitled to ask whether the positions of the items on the counter are *relevant* in judging their relative value. For the purposes of the argument, let us stipulate that they are *not* relevant. Then the proposition to which Joe has assented is not rationally defensible: in reasoning about the value of the cake and the fruit, Joe has made an error. SuperReasoner will not make this error. In other words, SuperReasoner's *preferences* over cake and fruit will not be context-dependent. But what about his *choices*?

Since SuperReasoner's feelings are the same as Joe's, he too feels an inclination to choose the cake if the cake is at the front, and to choose the fruit if the fruit is at the front. Were his Einstein-like powers of reasoning to lead him to the conclusion that (say) the fruit was more valuable, his Gandhi-like powers of self-control would allow him to overcome any inclination to choose the cake. But what if, given the premises and inference rules that characterize his mode of reasoning, the relative value of cake and fruit is undetermined?

If, as I have argued, latent preference is a subjective concept, we are not entitled to assume that fully-informed error-free reasoning can determine a person's latent preference over every pair of options. It is true that, by virtue of his special powers, SuperReasoner can access all the information that is relevant for the choice between fruit and cake. For example, he knows all the respects in which eating fruit would be good for his health, and all the respects in which eating cake would give him immediate enjoyment. If the uniquely correct choice could be determined by applying some well-defined algorithm to this multi-dimensional information, SuperReasoner would have the computational powers to solve the problem. But what is at issue is whether, for a given person (such as Joe), there exists an algorithm which, for any pair of options x and y, can identify the truth of exactly one of the following three propositions: 'x is preferred to y', 'y is preferred to x', and 'x and y are equally preferred'. Such an algorithm generates a preference ranking that is *complete*. I know of no argument, either in behavioural economics or in the theory of rational choice, that would justify the assumption that such an algorithm exists. Indeed, Hausman (2012: 19) explicitly denies that sound reasoning necessarily generates a complete preference ranking.

So let us maintain the supposition that SuperReasoner cannot determine whether, all things considered, the cake is more valuable than the fruit or vice versa. In Hausman's sense, he has no (strict or weak) preference between these options. Still, he feels an inclination to choose whichever of cake or fruit is more prominently displayed. I cannot see any principle of sound reasoning that he would contravene by acting on this inclination, just as Joe would. It seems that SuperReasoner's choices, like Joe's, can be context-dependent.

4.6 Savage and Allais

A possible line of defence remains for behavioural welfare economics. If we are to insist that SuperReasoner's choices must be context-independent, we seem to need to make completeness of preferences an *axiom* of reasoning, rather than a property that, depending on circumstances, reasoning may show to be true or false. One might perhaps stipulate that, if an agent is to be truly rational, his choices must always be justified by preferences. One might then claim that rationality requires the agent to ensure that the set of preference propositions he holds to be true is sufficient to pick a nonempty set of justified choices from any nonempty set of options. My own view is that this requirement would be unwarranted; but let us set any reservations aside and press on.[6] If SuperReasoner wanted to comply with the requirement, he would have to fill in the gaps in his otherwise incomplete preference ordering by constructing additional preferences whose content was *not* justified by reasoning.

But this conclusion is of no help to behavioural welfare economics. The problem that needs to be solved is that of discovering Joe's latent preference between fruit and cake. The line of argument we are exploring leads to the conclusion that, were Joe truly rational, he would have *some* context-independent preference between the two options. But that means only that the imaginary SuperReasoner would have responded to the demands of rationality by constructing such a preference, arbitrarily if necessary. We may have no way of discovering what that imaginary preference would be. In any case, if we can discover this at all, it will not be by investigating the psychology, preferences, or beliefs of the real Joe; it will be by postulating additional properties of the imaginary SuperReasoner. There is no real sense in which this imaginary preference is latent *in Joe*.

Leonard Savage's (1954: 101–3) discussion of the Allais Paradox nicely illustrates the issues involved here. Recall from Section 1.3 that respondents are asked to imagine two different situations, in each of which there is a choice between two gambles. In Situation 1, the choice is between Gamble 1, which gives $500,000 with probability 1, and Gamble 2, which gives $2,500,000 with probability 10/100, $500,000 with probability 89/100, and nothing with probability 1/100. In Situation 2, the choice is between Gamble 3, which gives $500,000 with probability 11/100 and nothing with probability 89/100, and Gamble 4, which gives $2,500,000 with probability 10/100 and nothing with probability 90/100. Savage reports that, when he was first presented with Allais' two choice problems, he expressed a preference for Gamble 1 in Situation 1 and for Gamble 4 in Situation 2—the response that constitutes the Paradox and that is inconsistent with Savage's own expected-utility axioms (one of which is an axiom of completeness). He confesses that he 'still feel[s] an intuitive attraction to those preferences'. However, since his analysis of expected utility is intended as a normative theory, it would be an 'intolerable discrepancy' for him to maintain two preferences that together were inconsistent with the axioms of the theory:

> In general, a person who has tentatively accepted a normative theory must conscientiously study situations in which the theory seems to lead him astray; he must decide for each by reflection—deduction will typically be of little relevance—whether to retain his initial impression of the situation or to accept the implications of the theory for it. (Savage, 1954: 102)

Savage reassures himself of the validity of his axioms by re-framing the four gambles so that their outcomes all depend on the same draw from a set of lottery tickets numbered 1–100. Prizes are assigned to tickets so that the prizes for Gambles 1, 2, 3, and 4 respectively, in units of $100,000, are (5, 0, 5, 0) for ticket 1, (5, 25, 5, 25) for tickets 2–11, and (5, 5, 0, 0) for tickets 12–100.[7] Since, in each situation, the two gambles on offer differ only in the event that one of tickets 1–11 is drawn, Savage concludes that the other tickets are irrelevant to the decisions that have to be made. Conditional on this event, Gambles 1 and 3 are identical, as are Gambles 2 and 4. Thus, Savage's original preferences are unacceptably context-dependent. Both of them cannot be right. But which of them is wrong? Savage tells himself that, in both situations, the choice problem reduces to 'whether I would sell an outright gift of $500,000 for a 10-to-1 chance to win $2,500,000'. Consulting his 'purely personal taste', he finds that he prefers the former. He then accepts the implication that he prefers Gamble 3 to Gamble 4, saying: 'It seems to me that in reversing my preferences between Gambles 3 and 4 I have corrected an error'.

Notice that Savage has invoked a third situation (let us call it 'Situation 3') in which he has to choose *either* $500,000 with probability 1 ('Gamble 5') *or* $2,500,000 with probability 10/11 and nothing with probability 1/11 ('Gamble 6'). According to his axioms, his ranking of Gamble 3 relative to Gamble 4 (and, equivalently, his ranking of Gamble 1 relative to Gamble 2), should be the same as his ranking of Gamble 5 relative to Gamble 6. He finds an inclination to prefer Gamble 5 to Gamble 6. So far, this is not a resolution of the original problem; it is merely an expansion of the set of inconsistent preferences. However, it seems that Savage feels more confident about his inclinations in Situation 3 than in the other two situations, and so decides to use those inclinations as his arbiter. There is nothing wrong with that: as Savage says, this is a matter of reflection, not deduction. But there seems no reason to suppose that this particular sequence of reflections leads to the uniquely correct resolution of the original inconsistency (if inconsistency it is). At most, this story tells us that if someone genuinely accepted the expected-utility axioms as requirements of rationality and was not cognitively constrained, he would be able to settle on *some* preferences, consistent with those axioms, which he was willing to live with (but which might still be contrary to his actual inclinations). That is not particularly helpful if we are trying to identify the actual latent preferences of an ordinary Joe whose choices and inclinations have the Allais Paradox pattern.

4.7 Purifying Allais Paradox Preferences

The preferences that constitute the Allais Paradox can be used as a test case for the preference purification method proposed by Bleichrodt et al. (2001), described in Section 4.1.

Recall that Bleichrodt et al. use cumulative prospect theory as the descriptive model of choice. Viewed in the perspective of that theory, Allais' four gambles can be differentiated in terms of two characteristics—the probability of winning at least $500,000, and the probability of winning $2,500,000.

In terms of the second characteristic, Situations 1 and 2 are equivalent to one another. (In each situation, the probability of winning $2,500,000 is either zero or 0.10, depending on whether the first or the second gamble is chosen.) So an explanation of the Allais Paradox must work through the first characteristic. The probability of winning at least $500,000 is 1.00 in Gamble 1, 0.99 in Gamble 2, 0.11 in Gamble 3, and 0.10 in Gamble 4. The difference between the two relevant probabilities (1.00 and 0.99 in Situation 1, 0.11 and 0.10 in Situation 2) is the same in both situations, which is another way of explaining why the Paradox contravenes expected utility theory. However, cumulative prospect theory transforms each objective probability p into a subjective decision weight $w(p)$. The Allais Paradox is possible if $w(1.00)-w(0.99)$ is sufficiently greater than $w(0.11)-w(0.10)$. That inequality is consistent with intuition: the difference between the certainty of a very large prize and a 99 per cent chance of it *feels* more significant than the difference between an 11 per cent chance and a 10 per cent chance. So it is plausible to suppose that cumulative prospect theory is picking up a psychological mechanism that contributes *in some way* to the Allais Paradox. Bleichrodt et al.'s purification methodology treats the non-linearity of the probability weighting function as a reasoning error that needs to be corrected if we are to identify latent preferences. But where is the error?

Of course, there would have been an error *if* the decision-maker had known the utility to him of the three possible outcomes, *and if*, believing expected utility theory to be the right normative model, he had tried to calculate the expected utility of each of the four gambles, *and if* in doing so he had used decision weights in the mistaken belief that they were objective probabilities. But that is not a remotely plausible account of the reasoning that leads real people to choose Gambles 1 and 4. To point to just one problem with this account, remember that when people respond to Allais' problems, they are *told* all the relevant objective probabilities. If you were to ask a respondent what he believed to be the percentage probability of an outcome that he had just been told had a probability of 1 per cent, what answer would you expect to get?

I do not want to suggest that Bleichrodt et al. are assuming that the decision-maker is reasoning in this way. No doubt what they are assuming is not that he *believes that* the decision weights of the relevant events are objective probabilities, but rather that his feelings about those events have properties that are captured by the model of decision weights. But then we are back with the problem of showing how those feelings constitute or give rise to an error of reasoning. For example, one might argue that the psychological mechanism that generates non-linear decision weights is one of differential attention, and that the Allais Paradox reveals an error of giving too much attention to low-probability events. But this claim would raise the problem that I have already discussed in the context of Bordalo et al.'s (2013) model of salience in consumer choice: How is the correct distribution of attention to be defined? It would be circular to define it as whatever distribution of attention generates choices that are consistent with expected utility theory.

What Bleichrodt et al.'s purification methodology reveals is that, *relative to the benchmark of expected utility theory*, a person who makes the Allais Paradox choices has behaved *as if* he held false beliefs about the probabilities of the relevant events. If expected utility theory could be interpreted as a first approximation to a true description of how people actually reason, it might be plausible to move from that as-if proposition to the conjecture that the person's actual reasoning followed the general logic of expected-utility reasoning but with some error in the processing of beliefs. But the truth is surely that expected utility theory provides a first approximation to *the choices that people actually make*, not to the reasoning by which they arrive at those choices.

It is not surprising that expected utility theory has this approximation property, at least when applied to lotteries with monetary outcomes and explicit objective probabilities. Whatever mental processes people use in decision-making about such lotteries, one would expect larger money prizes to be perceived more favourably than smaller ones, other things being equal. Similarly, for any given money amount x, one would expect larger probabilities of winning at least x to be perceived more favourably than smaller probabilities, other things being equal. By generalizing these two intuitions and by organizing them in a simple and tractable functional form, expected utility theory picks up some of the main patterns in the decisions that are generated by actual human reasoning. In the case of the Allais Paradox, however, cumulative prospect theory provides a more accurate description of actual decisions. In the absence of a theory of how people reason, that is just about all that can be said. One is certainly not entitled to infer that Allais Paradox choices reveal errors of reasoning that are not committed by people whose choices are consistent with expected utility theory.

4.8 Akrasia

In behavioural welfare economics, as I have characterized it, latent preference is a hypothetical construct: a person's latent preferences are the preferences that would be revealed in her choices, were her reasoning not distorted by error. I have argued that the kind of normative economics that I have discussed in this chapter is best understood as using the satisfaction of such latent preferences as the normative criterion. I stand by that argument. However, behavioural welfare economists sometimes appeal to a different concept of latent preference. On this alternative view, a person's latent preferences are the preferences that she *actually* endorses in some independently definable circumstances, and which in some sense she acknowledges as her true preferences even when she is acting contrary to them. Thus, to discover a person's latent preferences, an outside observer does not need to use the methodology of purification illustrated by my story of SuperReasoner. Instead, the observer has to discover what *the person herself*—the real human being, not her supposed inner rational agent—judges to be her true preferences. The underlying model of human agency is one of *akrasia*—of lack of self-control, acting contrary to one's own better judgement.

I return again to Sunstein and Thaler's mantra of making choosers better off, *as judged by themselves*. The 'as judged by themselves' clause would certainly have more argumentative force if it could be read as an appeal to individuals' actual judgements, rather than to the hypothetical judgements of their inner rational agents. I maintain that that alternative reading is not consistent with Sunstein and Thaler's argument as a whole, or with the practice of behavioural welfare economics. Recall that among the causes of the 'pretty bad decisions' that Sunstein and Thaler want to help people avoid are limitations of information and cognitive ability, neither of which can be understood as a lack of self-control. A typical example of the role of such limitations in Sunstein and Thaler's arguments comes in their discussion of the circumstances in which nudges are most useful. They say: 'Someone can eat a high-fat diet for years without having any warning signs of a heart attack. When feedback does not work, we may benefit from a nudge' (2008: 75). The point of this example is that people are liable to make errors because of lack of opportunities to learn the effects of alternative choices. But in such cases, one cannot claim that the person who makes the error is conscious at the time of acting contrary to his better judgement: the person eating the high-fat diet does *not* think that this is bad for his heart.

Nevertheless, Sunstein and Thaler often claim that the people they are proposing to nudge *want* to be nudged. This claim is usually made in vague terms and with little supporting evidence. For example, Sunstein and Thaler sometimes appeal to the 'New Year's resolution test'. Thus, in support of proposals to nudge individuals towards healthier lifestyles, they ask: '[H]ow many people vow to smoke more cigarettes, drink more martinis, or have more chocolate donuts in the morning next year?' (2008: 73). Notice that the evidence we are being asked to consider here shows only that individuals' preferences are context-dependent: preferences about alcohol consumption are different when elicited through the formation of New Year's resolutions than when revealed in choices in a restaurant. But just as the restaurant gives cues that point in the direction of drinking, so the traditions of New Year give cues that point in the direction of resolutions for future temperance. If an argument based on akrasia is to work, we need to be shown that *in the restaurant*, the individual acknowledges that her true preferences are the ones that led to her New Year's resolution and not the ones she is now acting on. In many cases that fit the story of the resolution and the restaurant, the individual in the restaurant will be thinking that resolutions should not be followed too slavishly, that there is a place in life for spontaneity, and that having an extra glass of wine would be an appropriately spontaneous response to the circumstances. A person who thinks like this as she breaks a previous resolution is not acting contrary to what, at the moment of choice, she acknowledges as her true preferences.

I do not want to claim that individuals are *never* conscious of akrasia. Certainly, there can be cases in which an individual feels an apparently irresistible urge to pour another glass of wine, while still genuinely endorsing the resolution that forbids this action. Later in this book, I will consider self-control problems in more detail (Section 7.3). However, it is worth asking now why behavioural welfare economists so often choose to model cases of context-dependent preferences as self-control problems.

A large part of the answer, I suggest, is that behavioural welfare economists are seeing the world through the lens of the model of the inner rational agent. Suppose that I (as a behavioural economist) start from the premise that, in the absence of reasoning errors, an individual would act on context-independent preferences. Then any observation of context-dependent choice calls for an explanation in terms of error. Take the case of the resolution and the restaurant. I observe an individual (say Jane) whose preferences about drinking are context-dependent. I must infer that *either* Jane's New Year's resolution *or* her decision in the restaurant reveals an error of reasoning. Suppose I think that reasoning errors about alcohol consumption are less likely when people are thinking about New Year's resolutions than when they are thinking about pouring drinks in restaurants. That naturally suggests the hypothesis that Jane's decision in the restaurant was a mistake. I now have to explain what the mistake was and why it occurred. That explanation has to be consistent with the fact that, in the context of making resolutions, Jane avoided the mistake. Why didn't she use the same reasoning in the restaurant as she did when making the resolution? One obvious way forward is to conjecture that, in the restaurant, Jane was capable of that reasoning, but that some psychological mechanism prevented her from acting on its conclusions. In other words, Jane has a self-control problem.

But notice how this line of thought is activated by the model of the inner rational agent. If one has no prior commitment to the idea of latent preferences, there is no reason to suppose that Jane has made any mistake at all. The question of how much she should drink may have no uniquely rational answer. Both when she was making New Year's resolutions and when she was in the restaurant, she had to a strike a balance between considerations that pointed in favour of alcohol and considerations that pointed against it. The simplest explanation of her behaviour is that she struck one balance in the first case and a different balance in the second. This is not a self-control problem; it is a change of mind.

4.9 Summing up

In arguing for libertarian paternalism, Sunstein and Thaler (2008: 6) criticize conventional economists for assuming that ordinary human beings are 'Econs'—an imaginary species which 'thinks and chooses unfailingly well'. They claim that their approach to behavioural welfare economics—an approach that is becoming part of the mainstream of behavioural economics—breaks away from this mistaken assumption, and models human psychology as it really is. But it would be closer to the truth to say that behavioural welfare economics models human beings as faulty Econs. Its implicit model of human decision-making is that of a neoclassically rational inner agent, trapped inside and constrained by an outer psychological shell. Normative analysis is understood as an attempt to reconstruct and respect the preferences of the imagined inner Econ.

If behavioural and normative economics are to be satisfactorily reconciled, the first essential is that economists learn to live with the facts of human psychology. We need a normative economics that does not presuppose a kind of rational human agency for which there is no known psychological foundation.

5

Opportunity

To follow the contractarian approach is to use a particular model of the role of the normative economist. In this model, the individual members of a society are considered as potential parties to voluntary agreements. The economist addresses these individuals together, recommending terms on which they might agree. The content of a recommendation is that a certain agreement is in the interests of each individual, as he or she perceives those interests. So a first essential is to have a criterion for determining whether or not a proposal is in a person's interests. What this criterion should be is the topic of this chapter.

It is fundamental to the contractarian approach that the ultimate authority for judging what is in a person's interests is that person himself. The economist's job is to design proposals that individuals will want to accept. But part of that job is to explain the nature of the proposals and *why* it is in each individual's interests to accept them. This requires that the economist has some representation of individuals' interests that is independent of those individuals' prior attitudes to any specific proposal. She needs to be able to say: 'Having represented your interests in this way, I can show you that it is in your interest to agree to this proposal'. To fill in 'this way', we need a criterion of individual interest.

5.1 The Individual Opportunity Criterion

In thinking about what this criterion should be, we must keep in mind the uses to which it will be put. We are looking for a criterion that can be used by economists when they make recommendations about economic policies and institutions. To be useful for this purpose, it must satisfy certain design constraints.

One such constraint is that the criterion should be *general with respect to individuals*. That is, whatever formula it uses to represent an individual's interests should apply to individuals in general. It is simply impractical to have a separate criterion for every individual, tailored to his particular requirements. For similar reasons, the criterion should be *general with respect to applications*—that is, capable of being applied to a wide range of economic problems. Since the criterion is to be used in economics, often in conjunction with predictions derived with the help of theory, it needs to *engage with economic theory*. Thus, it should be framed in terms of concepts that, while being intelligible to the individuals on whose behalf it is to be used, can be processed in economic analysis. (To say this is not to be imperialist on behalf of economics. Normative economics is not the only kind of normative analysis there can be; it is just the kind that economists do.) And the criterion needs to be *operational*. By this, I mean that there must be some reasonably well-defined method for satisfying its informational requirements. Here we must remember that a contractarian economist has to be able to *show* individuals that her recommendations are in their interests, as they perceive them. It is not enough for her to assert this and to appeal to their trust in her superior judgement or expertise. So the method by which the informational requirements are satisfied must be *transparent*—that is, capable of being stated openly and laid open to public scrutiny. And, as far as possible, that method should be *objective*: it should not depend on subjective or contestable judgements.

Of course, the most fundamental requirement for a contractarian criterion is that it can be endorsed by the individuals to whom the economist's recommendations are to be addressed. Each of those individuals must be able to recognize it as a representation of his interests, as he perceives them. Or, more precisely, he must be able to recognize it as a representation of what he wants to achieve from agreements with others, in the kinds of cases that economists make recommendations about: the word 'interest' is only a shorthand for that. Remember that a contractarian economist does not have to endorse the criterion as a representation of what *she* judges to be the individual's best interests, or of what in *her* judgement the individual ought to want to achieve from agreements. She is his agent, not his guardian.

The idea that an individual endorses a particular criterion must be understood in relation to the design constraints that any criterion has to satisfy. In endorsing a criterion, the individual need not affirm that it gives a perfect representation of his interests in each and every possible case to which it might be applied. Rather, he accepts it as a satisfactory representation of his interests, given the design constraints.

The criterion I propose to use is that of *opportunity*. In its simplest terms, the idea is that it is in each individual's interest to have more opportunity rather than less. An individual's opportunities can be thought of as the set of options from which he can choose, options being described in such a way that they are mutually exclusive and jointly exhaustive. Such a set is an *opportunity set*.

(It is also known to economists as a 'choice set', 'feasible set', or 'menu'.) For example, consider an air traveller who is offered a choice of onboard complimentary drinks. His opportunity set might be the set O = {water, orange juice, coffee, nothing}. A different airline might offer the set O' = {water, orange juice, coffee, beer, nothing}. If 'water', 'orange juice', and 'coffee' mean the same in the two cases, O' offers strictly more opportunity than O in the simple sense that O' contains all the options that O does, and something in addition that the individual might conceivably want to choose. According to my criterion, it is in the traveller's interest that the set of complementary drinks is O' rather than O. I will make no attempt to compare opportunity sets that are not nested in this way.[1]

In the rest of this chapter I explain this *Individual Opportunity Criterion* in more detail, and defend the claim that each member of society can endorse it as representing his interests, as he perceives them.

5.2 Preference-satisfaction

As a first step in explaining and defending the Individual Opportunity Criterion, it is useful to consider how it relates to the criterion that has traditionally been used in normative economics—preference-satisfaction. Economists who have used the preference-satisfaction criterion have usually assumed that individuals have integrated preferences over all outcomes that are relevant to the problem at hand, and that individuals' choices are consistent with those preferences. As I pointed out in Chapter 1, how far these assumptions correspond with reality is open to serious question. But for the purposes of this and Section 5.3, I will bracket out those doubts and suppose that the assumptions *are* satisfied. Given this supposition, one way of justifying the use of the Individual Opportunity Criterion is to say that the more opportunity a person has, the more effectively his preferences will be satisfied. I will present and defend this justification and then consider whether it can be extended to cases in which individuals do not act on integrated preferences.

Let me introduce an imaginary character: Norman the Neoclassical Agent. With respect to all decision problems that he could meet in his private life, Norman has preferences that satisfy all the postulates of the conventional theory of rational choice. That is, he has consistent preferences over all relevant consequences, and those preferences can be represented by a well-behaved utility function. He has consistent beliefs about all relevant states of the world, and those beliefs can be represented by subjective probabilities. In every decision problem, he chooses an action that maximizes the expected value of utility. Whatever opportunity set he faces, the act of choosing from it is costless to him. His preferences are stable over time and are independent of irrelevant features of context or framing. His beliefs are stable too, except in so far as they are updated in the light of new information, as Bayesian probability theory requires. In line with an assumption that is implicit in most rational-choice theory, Norman's preferences are consequentialist. That is, they are defined over objects that can be interpreted as the final outcomes of decisions, and not as properties of the procedures by which decisions are made.

Clearly, any expansion in Norman's opportunity set maintains or increases the degree to which his preferences are satisfied. Take the case of the complimentary drinks. If Norman faces the opportunity set O = {water, orange juice, coffee, nothing}, he will choose an option in O that he weakly prefers to all the others. Suppose this is coffee. Now consider the effect of expanding his opportunity set to O' = {water, orange juice, coffee, beer, nothing}. Now he will choose an option in O' that he weakly prefers to all the others. If this is coffee too, there has been no change in preference-satisfaction. If it is another option that was also in O, say water, the only explanation consistent with Norman's being a neoclassical agent is that he is indifferent between coffee and water. So again, there has been no change in preference-satisfaction. The remaining possibility is that Norman chooses beer from O'. Since he has chosen beer when coffee was available, either he is indifferent between beer and coffee, in which case preference-satisfaction is unchanged, or he strictly prefers beer to coffee, in which case preference-satisfaction has increased. Thus, if Norman endorses the preference-satisfaction criterion as a representation of his interests, he has no reason to object to any recommendation that satisfies the Individual Opportunity Criterion. (Sometimes that criterion will positively support proposals that Norman is merely indifferent about, but it never supports proposals than are contrary to his preferences.) So one way of justifying the Individual Opportunity Criterion to a neoclassical agent like Norman is to convince him of the merits of the preference-satisfaction criterion.

Assessed against my list of desirable properties, and given that we are dealing with a neoclassical agent, the preference-satisfaction criterion scores rather well. Since, by assumption, Norman has consistent preferences over all consequences that are relevant to the problems an economist might address, that criterion is extremely general. Preference is a readily intelligible concept, and it is central to economic theory. Since Norman's preferences are revealed in his private choices, the informational requirements of the criterion can be met by observing those choices. By assumption, there are no inconsistencies between the preferences he reveals at different times, in different decision problems or in different contexts. So, if the criterion is accepted, identifying Norman's interests—that is, identifying what he wants to achieve from agreements with others—is a technical problem in economics, in much the same way that discovering the height of a mountain is a technical problem in surveying.

The most important question, of course, has still to be asked: Can the preference-satisfaction criterion be endorsed by Norman himself? In posing this question, let us take it as given that the domain of collective decision-making in which the contractarian economist makes recommendations is distinct from the domain of private life in which Norman's choices have been assumed to reveal his preferences. Thus, the assumption that Norman acts on his preferences when making private decisions does not, as a matter of logical necessity, entail that he prefers it to be the case that the satisfaction of his preferences is used as the criterion of his interests for collective decision-making. Nevertheless, the latter proposition is very plausible.

It surely *is* a tautology that what a person chooses voluntarily is what, at the moment of choice and in the light of whatever deliberation he has engaged in, he most wants to choose. By assumption, Norman's private choices reveal an integrated system of preferences. To use the satisfaction of those preferences as the criterion of Norman's interests is to identify his interests with what, in all his private decisions, he most wants to choose. On the face of it, one might expect Norman to endorse this representation of his interests, at least for the purposes of arriving at and justifying economic recommendations.

Why might he *not* endorse it? If Norman is to reject the preference-satisfaction criterion, it seems that he must assert that what he consistently wants when he makes private choices is not what he wants to achieve from collective agreements. I can see two different ways of making sense of that assertion.

The first is to draw a distinction between private and collective decision-making. Norman might believe that some considerations that are relevant in one of these domains are not relevant in the other. For example, he might believe that the political community to which he belongs has a collective responsibility to promote particular forms of human excellence or to conserve distinctive features of its culture, and yet not attach any value to those matters in his private decision-making. This way of thinking about collective decision-making is not incoherent, but it is contrary to the spirit of the contractarian approach. As I explained in Chapter 3, this approach rests on a model of politics *as negotiation*. Politics is represented as a search for mutually beneficial agreements between individuals with given interests, not as public reasoning about what is socially valuable. I have already said what I can to persuade the reader of the virtues of the contractarian approach; I have nothing more to add here.

The second way in which one might understand how Norman might reject the preference-satisfaction criterion depends on a distinction, sometimes made by economists, between two personae or 'selves' of a given individual—the *acting self* and the *reflective self*. The acting self oversees acts of choice; the reflective self oversees the overall assessments that the person makes about his life. By assumption, Norman has an entirely consistent acting self, whose choices reveal a well-articulated system of preferences. But it is still just about conceivable that the reflective Norman believes that those preferences, despite their internal consistency, do not reflect his interests. When he is thinking about his life as a whole, he might be convinced that his private choices are systematically distorted by errors of reasoning or failures of self-control, and as a result do not serve what (in his reflective moments) he regards as his true interests. And, despite recognizing this fact, he might believe that his future choices will be similarly flawed. (For example, the acting Norman might have consistent preferences with respect to smoking, revealed in his behaviour when he buys his daily supply of cigarettes, but the reflective Norman might consistently think that smoking was contrary to his true interests.) The reflective Norman might then have reservations about endorsing the preference-satisfaction criterion.

Even so, that is not to say that, all things considered, there is any better option. A criterion designed to implement individuals' reflective judgements about their own interests would require some operational and transparent procedure for discovering those judgements, at least to some degree of approximation. A reflective Norman who thought carefully about the difficulties and risks of licensing any decision-making authority to act as the interpreter of his judgements about his interests might well decide that those interests were more reliably represented by the preferences of his acting self. I do not want to claim that there are *no* circumstances in which people, thinking reflectively about their best interests, are so conscious of (what they then see as) their error-proneness or weakness of will as choosers that they are willing to empower certain kinds of decision-makers to act as their guardians. But I submit that these cases are exceptional. I shall say more about them in Section 7.3, when I look at some of the implications of using opportunity as a normative criterion.

Any practicable form of normative economics depends on modelling simplifications. It would be unrealistic to expect to find a general, operational, and transparent criterion of individual interest that would be endorsed by *every* person in *all* circumstances. But were we able to assume that individuals act on integrated preferences, there would surely be a strong case for using preference-satisfaction as the criterion of individual interest. And that case would provide equally strong support for the Individual Opportunity Criterion.

5.3 'Mere' Preferences?

Although most normative economists have used preference-satisfaction as the criterion of each individual's interests, moral philosophers have often objected to this practice. They have argued that preference-satisfaction in itself does not have normative significance. If the satisfaction of preferences has value (it is claimed), that must be because preferences are indicators of something else, something that *does* have value in itself. And then we can look for principles for screening out those preferences that are *not* indicators of value.

Typically, the principles that moral philosophers propose can be construed as conceptions of individual *well-being*, broadly conceived. The idea is that what really matters is each person's well-being, and that preference-satisfaction matters just to the extent that it contributes to well-being. The philosophical literature provides a range of subtly-nuanced alternative conceptions of well-being, with corresponding screening principles. Some proposals appeal to *informed desires*, understood counterfactually as what a person would prefer for herself after ideally rational and informed deliberation (Arneson, 1989). Recall that Thaler and Sunstein (2008) use a similar criterion to determine when paternalistic interventions make choosers better off (see Section 4.1 above). Some proposals appeal to *considered preferences*, understood as preferences that are internally consistent and that are stable under experience and reflection (Gauthier, 1986). Some appeal to *objective lists* of the supposed components of human well-being, allowing that each individual may, within reasonable limits, weight these components in different ways (Griffin, 1986; Nussbaum, 2000). Some appeal to a *reasoned consensus*, reached through public discussion, about what human beings have reason to desire (Sen, 1999). And so on.

In denying that preference-satisfaction has normative value in itself, many philosophers argue that 'mere' preferences do not provide reasons for action. If a person is to reach a reasoned decision about what to do (it is said), she cannot treat her own preferences as data.

To understand this argument and how it relates to economics, one needs some knowledge of how choice is represented in the philosophy of mind. Philosophers make a distinction that is absent from conventional economics, between 'desire' and 'intention'. To *desire* something is to have an inclination to choose it. That inclination is understood as a mental state that is in some sense external to the cognitive part of the mind that engages in reasoning. The cognitive mind is aware of the inclination and may treat its existence as a premise in its reasoning but, except in pathological cases, is not constrained by it. The cognitive mind's reasoning leads to the formation of *intentions*. These are mental states that record decisions reached by the cognitive mind. Intentions can act as direct instructions to the acting parts of the body, or they may be stored to be used as premises by the cognitive mind in making more fine-grained decisions. For example, suppose I am in a pub, having just finished my first glass of beer. I am conscious of an urge to have to a second. That is a desire. Having thought about that urge and about other factors that bear on my decision problem, I decide to have a second beer. That is the formation of an intention. I then set about acting on that intention (walking to the bar, engaging the bartender's attention, . . .), making finer-grained decisions in doing so. After carrying out the intention, I experience the pleasurable sensations of drinking the second beer. Those sensations are conceptually distinct from the desires that prompted the decision that caused them.[2]

It is far from obvious how (or indeed if) the economic concept of preference fits into this framework. On one reading, favoured by some philosophical critics of the preference-satisfaction criterion, 'preference' is the comparative form of 'desire': to prefer x to y is to have a stronger desire for x than for y. This makes preference an input to the individual's reasoning about what to choose. On another reading, 'preference' is the comparative form of 'intention': to prefer x to y is to have a settled intention to choose x rather than y. This makes preference an output of reasoning. On a third reading, favoured by Daniel Hausman (2012) and discussed in Section 4.5, a preference between two options is an all-things-considered comparative evaluation of them. For the moment, I will leave open the question of how the economic and philosophical frameworks map on to one another, and focus on what philosophers have actually said.

Consider the following passage from a philosophical critique of preference-satisfaction as a normative criterion. The author is Philip Pettit:

> in deliberating our way to action we have to take our start, not from the fact that we desire certain goals, but from the fact that, as we see things, those goals are desirable or good or valuable or whatever. This line fits with our ordinary practice and with the long tradition of thinking that the major premise in a practical syllogism should not mention that some state of affairs is desired but rather the fact that is worthy of being desired. . . . Deliberation tries to track the true and the valuable, not the believed and the desired.   (Pettit, 2006: 144)

According to Pettit, a substantive theory of rational or reasonable choice must provide an account of the value-making properties that make some goals desirable and others not: hence the need for theories of well-being. Thus Pettit is able to conclude that 'preference-satisfaction should not normally figure as a deliberative concern', either when 'individuals deliberate about what they ought individually to do' or when 'authorities or commentators deliberate about what good government ought to try to do for its people' (2006: 131).

Pettit's idea, as I understand it, can be illustrated by the following example. Suppose I am ordering a meal in a restaurant. There are two dishes on the menu, steak and salmon. Consider the following schema of practical reasoning (that is, reasoning about what to do), in which P1 and P2 are premises and C is the conclusion to be drawn from those premises:

Schema 1
(P1)   I must choose steak or salmon.
(P2)   I desire salmon more than I desire steak.
So (C)   Let me choose salmon.

Here 'Let me...' represents an intention to perform a particular action.

In this schema, a proposition about desire is being used as a premise in deliberating about what to do. Pettit would object to this as an unsatisfactory form of practical reasoning. It might be more accurate to say that, for Pettit, it is not *reasoning* at all. The schema describes a form of mental activity in which the cognitive mind moves straight from the recognition of a desire to the formation of an intention to act on that desire. According to Pettit, an individual whose behaviour is governed in this way is *not an agent*: 'The fundamental tenet of our common sense psychology of human agents is that agency involves acting to realize various goals in a way that is sensible in light of the apparent facts' (2006: 138). Pettit seems to be hinting that the abdication of agency, as exemplified by Schema 1, is unfitting for a human being.

Pettit presumably thinks that my reasoning in the restaurant ought to be more like this:

Schema 2
(P1)   I must choose steak or salmon.
(P2)   I would enjoy the salmon more than I would enjoy the steak.
(P3)   Enjoyment is worthy of being desired.
So (C)   Let me choose salmon.

In Schema 2, unlike Schema 1, none of the premises refers to my prior inclinations towards the actions I am deliberating about. P2 makes predictions about the mental states to which these actions will lead; P3 attaches value to those mental states. As Pettit would say, my deliberation about what to do is trying to track the true (how much I would in fact enjoy the two dishes) and the valuable (what truly is worthy of being desired).

Hausman (2012: 88) makes a similar argument, claiming that 'satisfying preferences does not by itself contribute to welfare. Preference satisfaction theories of welfare are untenable'. Hausman is explicit that his argument does not depend on challenges to the conventional assumption that individuals have integrated preferences: it applies 'even when preferences are informed, rational, and generally spruced up' (2012: 77). Like Pettit, Hausman begins by looking at choice from the first-person perspective of the chooser. He claims that when a person thinks about what she should choose, she looks for *reasons* for doing one thing rather than another. Desires are not reasons in this sense:

From the first-person perspective of someone thinking about what to do, *reasons* are paramount. The question agents ask themselves is not 'Given my beliefs and desires, what do I predict that I will do?' but 'What should I do' or 'What do I have most reason to do?' ... To decide what to do, I try to be guided by what the facts are and by what is valuable. ... That I happen to believe *P* and desire *X* is not decisive, because I can step back and question my beliefs and my desires. My awareness of a desire to do X does not automatically incline me to do X intentionally unless I can see some *reason* to do X.   (Hausman, 2012: 5)

From the proposition that first-person reasoning about what to do should refer to reasons and not desires, it is a short step to an apparently similar proposition expressed in the third-person perspective of normative economics: that a criterion of what is in an individual's interests should refer to what that individual *has reason to* choose, rather than to what he in fact desires or prefers. Thus, having asserted that 'preference-satisfaction theories of well-being are mistaken', Hausman immediately goes on to say:

> Another way to support this conclusion is to ask what moral 'pull' satisfying someone's preferences should have on others. In my view, ... none at all. If something is valuable to people *only* because they want it, then their getting it has *no* direct moral importance for others. I have reason to help others to get what they want only if I can see how what they want is worth wanting, or why their lives will be in some way better if they get what they want.   (Hausman, 2012: 86)

Notice how, in a discussion about how to practise normative economics, Hausman has taken the standpoint of a disinterested philanthropist who gratuitously 'helps others'. A similar standpoint is implicit in Pettit's critique of the use of the preference-satisfaction criterion in deliberation 'about what good government ought to try to do for its people'. If one imagines a wealthy and philanthropic private individual, leafing through unsolicited requests for money and deciding which of these she will accede to, requests that simply take the form 'I want...' do indeed seem out of place. The philanthropist is entitled to expect the writer of a begging letter to provide reasons why his wants are worthy of being met, rather than merely reporting his preferences. But is the relationship between a philanthropist and the objects of her charity the right model of the relationship between government and citizen?

Consider a different model. Suppose I have a friend who is confined to her house by illness. I offer to do her shopping for her, spending her money. She tells me what she wants to have bought, and I do my best to buy it. When I act on her behalf at the supermarket, her preferences surely *are* reasons for me. Suppose she has told me that she prefers whole milk to skimmed. Then, when I am at the supermarket, I choose whole milk because that is what she prefers. I don't ask myself whether skimmed milk would be better for her, all things considered. That is a question that she might (or might not) want to ask herself when deliberating about her diet. But if I know what her preferences are, and if there is no ambiguity about what they imply with respect to what is on sale at the supermarket, it is not part of my role as her shopper to enquire into the reasoning that lies behind them.

I take this example to show that, when two people are in a principal–agent relationship, the preferences of the principal can be reasons for the actions of the agent. And, more relevantly for the contractarian approach, *the principal can want it to be the case* that, when the agent is acting on her behalf, he treats her preferences as reasons. In other words, the principal can want the agent to use preference-satisfaction as the criterion of her interests. Pettit's and Hausman's arguments provide no objection to that proposition.

Here is a related example, which touches on questions about paternalism.[3] Suppose I am the parent of a six-year-old child. It is early December and I am buying Christmas presents. I know that my child has a very intense desire for a certain toy. It is rather expensive, but can be bought within the budget that I have set aside for her presents. I see it as harmless but rather tacky, and predict that it will provide only brief excitement before she loses interest in it. There are alternative presents that I think would give her more pleasure over the coming year. Is her preference *in itself* a reason for me as parent, choosing what presents to give her? My own view (as author, and as one-time parent of young children) is that this *is* a significant reason, even though it is not necessarily decisive. The child's preference has a moral pull on the parent that an unsolicited 'I want . . . ' letter from a stranger does not. Why? The child is too young to control a budget sufficient to buy major items for herself, but she is still a full member of the family with preferences of her own, not a passive object of the parent's benevolent concern. In buying toys for the child from the family budget, the parent's relationship to the child has some of the characteristics of that of the shopper to the housebound friend. Even parents of young children should not be too paternalistic.

Now consider another way in which preferences might be thought of as reasons. Suppose that, instead of ordering a meal in a restaurant, I have decided that I want to buy a pre-prepared meal to eat at home. The next step is to choose which of two nearby shops, A and B, to go to in order to buy the meal. Both shops are operated by the same retail chain. The main difference between them is the number of products they stock. A is a convenience store, with a limited product range. B is a large supermarket which stocks everything that can be bought at A and much more besides. In keeping with the assumption I have maintained up to now in this chapter, suppose that my preferences over meals are stable and coherent. I know what my preferences are, but I do not know exactly which products the two shops stock. Still, I know that the opportunity set I will face if I go to B is a strict superset of the one I will face if I go to A. Is that a reason to go to B? It seems entirely reasonable to say that it is.

The most obvious way of reasoning to the conclusion that I should go to B is to use the criterion of preference-satisfaction. If my preferences are stable and coherent, and if I will act on those preferences whichever shop I go to, it is clear that the meal I end up buying will satisfy my preferences at least as well, and possibly better, if I go to B rather than A. (Compare the case of Norman and the complimentary drinks, discussed in Section 5.2.) My reasoning can be represented as:

Schema 3

(P1)   I must choose shop *A* or shop *B*.

(P2)   Shop *B* will satisfy my preferences at least as well as, and possibly better than, shop *A*.

So (C)   Let me choose shop *B*.

There is no circularity and no abdication of agency here. This schema treats the preferences I will act on in the shop I go to (whichever shop that turns out to be) as reasons for choosing between shops. But the reasoning is not circular: P2, the premise that refers to preferences, concerns preferences *between meals*, while the conclusion is an intention to choose *between shops*. There is nothing in Schema 3 that excludes the possibility that, when I get to the shop, my choices will be influenced by reasons, as Pettit and Hausman think they should be. But when I am choosing which shop to visit, I do not need to anticipate those reasons.

A critic might object that Schema 3 needs an additional premise, analogous with P3 in Schema 2, to the effect that preference-satisfaction is worthy of being desired. I disagree. I am using the concept of preference-satisfaction as it is normally used in economics. To say that, at the moment of choice in the shop, I prefer some product *x* to some other product *y* is to say that, at that moment, I want to choose *x* rather than *y*. If it then matters to me that what I choose is worthy of being desired, considerations of desire-worthiness will influence what I then want to choose, and so will be reflected in my preferences. If not, not. I am not abdicating agency; I am merely deferring the exercise of it. If there is an unstated premise in Schema 3, it has nothing to do with what is desire-worthy; it is something like 'Let me be able to have what I want'.

In each of the three cases I have discussed—shopping for the housebound friend, choosing the child's present, choosing between the two shops— preferences act as reasons for decisions; but the context in which preferences are revealed is distanced in some way from the problem for which they are treated as reasons. When I shop for my housebound friend, or when I choose a present for my child, another person's preferences are reasons for a decision that I make. When I choose which shop to visit, my future preferences between products are reasons for my current choice between shops. In using preference-satisfaction as a decision criterion, I do not need to deny the possibility of asking whether preferences are based on good reasons. But that question is not relevant for the problem at hand. Thinking about reasons for the preferences that are to be satisfied can be left to another person (the friend, the child) or to another time (when I get to the shop).

There is a similar distancing when preference-satisfaction is used as a criterion of individual interest in contractarian economics. The individual licenses the economist, when making her recommendations about collective actions, to use that criterion as a representation of what he (the individual) wants to achieve from those actions. Whether there are good reasons for those preferences is a matter for the individual himself; the economist can quite properly bracket out that question. Indeed, the individual might reasonably say that it is not the economist's business to enquire into his reasons for wanting what he wants.

I must say, however, that I do not share Pettit's and Hausman's belief that, from the first-person perspective of the chooser, reasons *must* be paramount. I think Hausman is wrong when he says: 'My awareness of a desire to do X does not automatically incline me to do X intentionally unless I can see some *reason* to do X.' Nor do I agree with his suggestion that the question 'What should I do?' is equivalent to 'What do I have most reason to do?' As a matter of psychology, a desire for something surely *is* an inclination to choose it. I cannot see why one needs to look for reasons for doing what one desires to do, although of course one needs to keep a lookout for reasons for *not* doing so. And, in my experience, deliberation about what to do often calls for insight into one's own feelings rather than the appraisal of reasons. (Suppose I am buying a new car and have narrowed down the choice to two models. One is more reliable and more economical, the other has cuter looks and is more fun to drive. I have desires pulling in both directions. It seems that I have to ask myself 'What do I have more *desire* to do?')

The relationship between reason and desire in choice is a deep topic in the philosophy of mind. Some philosophers, like Pettit and Hausman, give reason the primary role. Others, following David Hume (1739–40/1978), argue that when applied to decision problems, reason is inert unless it has desires to engage with, and that what a person desires is ultimately a matter of feeling. As an amateur philosopher, I side with Hume.[4] For the purposes of this book, however, I do not need to take any particular position on these issues. The criterion of preference-satisfaction can be endorsed from either point of view.

Consider two more imaginary characters, Rachel the Reason-following Agent and Desirée the Desire-following Agent. For the moment, I assume that both of them have integrated preferences. Rachel thinks of her preferences as grounded on good reasons. Her preferences follow her desires only when she believes that what she desires is worthy of being desired. Desirée thinks of her preferences as grounded on her desires. Notice that nothing that I have said implies that Desirée's preferences are less prudent or less moral than Rachel's. To the extent that Rachel's preferences are prudent or moral, she can attribute this to her recognition of reasons for not acting myopically or selfishly. To the extent that Desirée's preferences have the same properties, she can attribute this to whatever genetic, psychological, and social influences have made her desires what they are.

When Rachel endorses preference-satisfaction as a criterion of her interests, she is endorsing a criterion that identifies those interests with what, in her judgement, she has most reason to choose. When Desirée endorses preference-satisfaction as a criterion of her interests, she is endorsing a criterion that identifies her interests with what she in fact most desires to choose. Each can endorse the criterion, as applied to her, from her own philosophical standpoint. For a contractarian analysis, that is enough. It is not necessary that Rachel thinks that the satisfaction of Desirée's preferences is a good criterion of Desirée's interests, or vice versa. Rachel may think that Desirée is misguided in believing that the preference-satisfaction criterion represents her interests, when it 'merely' implements her desires. She may even think that Desirée's attitude to choice shows that she is not an agent in the sense that *she* (Rachel) thinks fitting for a human being. But that is not how it looks to Desirée herself. Desirée (as I wish to represent her) does not think of her desires as alien forces that have somehow subverted the reasoning of her true self and led her to make unintended choices. She sees herself as an autonomous agent who does not need reasons in support of her desires. In so far as she can make any sense of the idea of a true self, she thinks that her desires are just as much part of that self as her ability to reason. If one takes the contractarian approach, there is no need to adjudicate between Rachel and Desirée. Neither has any standing to question the other's judgement of her own interests.

5.4 Opportunity when Preferences are Liable to Change

So far, I have argued that a person with stable and well-articulated preferences can endorse the Individual Opportunity Criterion as a means of satisfying those preferences. I shall now argue that one of the advantages of using opportunity rather than preference-satisfaction as the criterion of individual interest is that it can deal more easily with *changes* of preference.

Here I am not referring to the kind of preference change that occurs as a rational response to new information, and which Bayesian decision theory can represent as an updating of beliefs. The cases I am concerned with are ones in which a person simply changes her mind about what she wants, given her beliefs about how the world is. Changes of mind may not fit easily into the framework of rational-choice theory, but they are surely one of the constants of human life.

Consider again the case in which I have to choose between two shops at which to buy a pre-prepared meal. I know that shop B stocks every product that is stocked by shop *A*, and more besides. In the original version of the example, my preferences over products were stable, but I did not know exactly which products were stocked by each shop. The criterion of preference-satisfaction recommended me to go to *B*. But suppose instead that my preferences are *not* stable. Suppose I know that, between setting out for the shop and taking a chosen product to the check-out, I am liable to change my mind about what I want to eat. These changes of mind are not responses to new information. But that does not mean that (as viewed by me) they are the result of forces that compromise my autonomy as an agent. Perhaps, like Rachel, I always try to choose what I have most reason to choose, and my judgements about the relative weights of different reasons are liable to change. Or perhaps, like Desirée, I always act on my desires, and my desires are liable to change. Either way, I cannot choose to go to *B* as the best means of satisfying my *given* preferences: when I am choosing between shops, my preferences are not given. But it is still true that, *whatever my preferences turn out to be*, I will be better able to satisfy them at *B* than at *A*. And that still provides a strong reason in favour of going to *B*. Expressing this idea more generally, I do not need to have stable preferences in order to endorse the principle that my interests are served by my having a larger opportunity set. It is sufficient to say that I want to be able to satisfy my preferences, whatever they turn out to be, as fully as possible.

It might seem that this argument does not apply if, at the time that a person is choosing between alternative opportunity sets, he knows that his preferences over the options *in* those sets are liable to be affected by factors that will be determined by his choice *between* the sets. Continuing with the story of the two shops, suppose that both shops stock a particular kind of paella and a particular kind of pizza. *A* displays the paella in a way that, for me, is particularly effective in arousing a desire to eat it; *B* displays the pizza in a correspondingly attractive way. Were I to go to *A*, I would choose the paella; were I to go to *B*, I would choose the pizza. Given all this, is the fact that *B* offers more choice overall than *A* a reason for me to go to *B*?

It might be argued that if my preferences depend on how products are displayed in a shop, I cannot be acting as an autonomous chooser; I must be acting under the causal power of forces that are in some sense external to me. And if I know that this is the case, I cannot at the same time treat the non-chosen elements of my opportunity sets as genuine options for me. Thus, once I have decided which shop to go to, I have effectively decided to subject myself to forces that will result in my choosing paella (if I have gone to *A*) or pizza (if I have gone to *B*). So when I am choosing between the shops, it is as if that choice is between the opportunity sets {*paella*} and {*pizza*}, and the Individual Opportunity Criterion is silent on which of these better serves my interests.

But remember that what is at issue is whether each individual can endorse the principle that it is in *her own* interests that *she* has more opportunity rather than less. So, in discussing autonomy, what matters is each individual's understanding of her own preferences and choices, and not how these are viewed by anyone else. When an individual acts on context-dependent preferences, does she think of herself as the author of her own actions, or as the prisoner of a body that is responding to alien causal forces? Suppose I have gone to the shop that has the particularly attractive display of the pizza. As I take the pizza to the checkout, can I think of this as *my* choice, even though I realize that some of my desire to buy it has been triggered by the display?

I suggest that this question is ultimately about my sense of identity. If I define myself as an inner rational agent with an integrated set of neoclassical preferences, I might be troubled by the realization that my physical body seems to be behaving in ways that I cannot rationalize. But my guess is that most people do not think of themselves like this. If instead I think of my psychology as part of who I am, I can recognize that my choices are influenced by psychological mechanisms and still see them as mine. Why should I think of myself as lacking in autonomy because my choices are governed by mechanisms that operate through ordinary human psychology? Indeed, one might ask: What else could govern them? Once one thinks of identity in this way, it is no longer puzzling that a person might recognize that her preferences are context-dependent and still think it in her interests to have more opportunity rather than less.

The idea that opportunity has value for a person whose preferences are liable to change has implications for an influential critique of the preference-satisfaction criterion presented by Amartya Sen (1999: 58–63). This critique follows on from Sen's discussion of alternative 'informational bases' for normative economics—the discussion that I commented on in Section 2.3. One of the informational bases considered by Sen is 'utility', interpreted as a representation of preferences. The core of Sen's critique of the preference-satisfaction criterion is summed up in the following claim: 'The mental metric of pleasure or desire is just too malleable to be a firm guide to deprivation and disadvantage'. Sen is particularly concerned with the mechanisms by which a person's desires and capacities for pleasure adapt to unfavourable circumstances. Among his examples of people who can be affected in this way are 'perennially oppressed minorities in intolerant communities, traditionally precarious sharecroppers living in a world of uncertainty, routinely overworked sweatshop employees in exploitative economic conditions, hopelessly subdued housewives in severely sexist cultures'. As a survival strategy, such persistently deprived people may 'adjust their desires and expectations to what they unambitiously see as feasible' (1999: 62–3).

Sen wants to say that the utility-based approach can support unjust restrictions on the opportunities of people whose preferences have adapted to deprivation. Take the case of the hopelessly subdued woman in the sexist culture. The rules of her society debar her from activities that are seen as normal for men, such as taking paid work outside the home. Viewed in the perspective of the conventional preference-satisfaction criterion, whether that is a deprivation depends on her preferences. If she prefers her current activities in the home to paid employment, expanding her opportunity set to include paid employment would not increase her preference-satisfaction (but, of course, would not worsen it either). Sen's response is that if that preference came about as her adaptation to the infeasibility of any other way of life, she is the victim of an injustice—whether or not she has any desire to change her situation. He proposes an approach to normative analysis in which '[t]he basic concern . . . is with our capability to lead the kind of lives we have reason to value' (1999: 285). The subdued woman is the victim of injustice because she has reason to value a life that includes paid work, even if she does not recognize that value.

Because the Individual Opportunity Criterion does not take preferences as given, it is not vulnerable to Sen's critique. According to that criterion, any expansion of a person's opportunity set promotes her interests, irrespective of her actual preferences and independently of any argument about what, among the options that might be available to her, she has reason to prefer. The essential idea is that it is in each individual's interest to have opportunities to satisfy not just those preferences that she currently has, but any preferences she might come to have.

This idea is central to John Stuart Mill's *The Subjection of Women* (1869/ 1988), which I discussed briefly in Section 1.1. Mill is at least as conscious of adaptive desires as Sen is. He argues that the status of women in mid-Victorian Britain is a survival from the 'primitive state of slavery' that was once common for both sexes (1869/1988: 5–6, 31–5). In making this claim, Mill has to confront the fact that most mid-Victorian women do not perceive themselves as unfree. How can this be? Mill's answer is that, because all but the most brutal men want their wives to be willing 'favourites' rather than forced slaves, women have been trained to develop those self-abnegating dispositions that are most attractive to, and most useful for, men. But, despite his belief that women's desires are an adaptation to a form of slavery, Mill does not argue for the emancipation of women on the grounds that they have reason to desire a different form of life. Instead, he appeals to the principles of liberty and free trade. For example, responding to opponents who argue that it is essential for society that women marry and have children, and that this is proof that the natural vocation of a woman is that of wife and mother, Mill points out that goods and services that really are valued can always be supplied in the market, so long as those who demand them are willing to pay the costs of supply. If men have a sufficiently strong desire for women to be housewives and mothers, the terms of freely-negotiated marriage partnerships will be such that women find it worthwhile to agree to them, given the opportunities available to them in a free labour market. In a free society, men will have to pay the price of the services they want, or go without (1869/1988: 28–30).

Notice that Mill does not need to address the question of how many women in fact desire a mode of life other than that of wives and mothers, or of whether women in general have reason to desire such a life. It is sufficient for his proposal that women and men should have the same opportunities with respect to marriage partnerships and labour contracts. Those opportunities are valuable to anyone who might ever want to use them, whatever their current preferences. The difference between Mill's and Sen's understandings of opportunity can be expressed in terms of the familiar problem of the 'contented slave' (which, according to Mill, is exactly the status of a happily married mid-Victorian woman). The problem is this: If slaves are contented, on what grounds can we condemn slavery? If our criterion is the satisfaction of actual desires, there seems to be nothing to criticize. Sen's approach is to ask whether the contented slave has reason to desire a different way of life, from which she is debarred by her slavery. In contrast, Mill's approach is to ask what would happen if the slave ceased to be contented: if she came to desire a different way of life, could she walk away from her existing one? Sen's approach leads to a critique of slavery that can be opposed by those who claim that slaves have no reason to value a life outside slavery. In contrast, Mill's argument retains its force against opponents who claim exactly this. If the slaves are so contented, why do they need to be prevented from walking away? And if the slaves really *are* contented, they can still recognize that their preferences might change.

5.5 The Continuing Person

So far, I have presented the Individual Opportunity Criterion as applying to decision problems that are faced at a single point in time.[5] For example, in discussing the case of the two shops A and B, I used that criterion to compare the opportunity sets that the individual would face, *having arrived at the respective shops*. Let us call these sets O_A and O_B. However, in interpreting that comparison, I discussed the decision problem that the individual would face *if choosing which of the two shops to go to*. If, as I have assumed, the relevant features of the two shops can be described by the sets of options available at them, the choice between the shops can be represented as the opportunity set $\{O_A, O_B\}$, each of whose elements is itself an opportunity set. We might want to ask whether the individual's interests are better served by his having this choice than, say, by having no choice but to go to A, a possibility that can be represented as the singleton set $\{O_A\}$. In this section, I consider how the Individual Opportunity Criterion might be generalized so that it applies to *nested* opportunity sets such as $\{O_A, O_B\}$ and $\{O_A\}$. This problem highlights some important issues about how the identity and agency of an individual should be understood if his preferences are not consistent over time. I will first present a generalization of the Individual Opportunity Criterion in abstract terms, and then explore its implications for a specific multi-stage decision problem.

As a starting point, consider two alternative options, v and w, which, if chosen by a given individual, would be experienced in some period t. (I will use the concept of 'periods' to refer to stages in a decision problem.) I leave open whether these options are opportunity sets in their own right. I introduce a formal concept of *weak dominance* among options; the proposition 'option v weakly dominates option w in period t' is written as $v \geqslant_t w$. The intuitive idea is that if v weakly dominates w, the opportunity provided by v is unambiguously at least as great as that provided by w. Here, 'unambiguous' is to be understood without reference to the actual preferences of the individual we are considering: to say that v weakly dominates w is to say that *whatever* the individual's preferences (perhaps within some minimal bounds of reasonableness or plausibility), those preferences can be satisfied at least as well by v as by w. If v weakly dominates w but w does not weakly dominate v, I will say that v *strictly dominates* w, written as $v >_t w$. If each of v and w weakly dominates the other, I will say that they are *dominance-equivalent*, written as $v \sim_t w$; the interpretation is that the individual's preferences, whatever they may be, can be satisfied equally well by v or w. I stipulate that weak dominance is reflexive—that is, $v \geqslant_t v$ (and hence $v \sim_t v$) for all options v that can be faced in period t. However, I do not require that this relation is complete. If neither of v and w weakly dominates the other, I will say that they are *not dominance-comparable*, written as $v \#_t w$.

Given a weak dominance relation among options that might be experienced in period t, we might look for an analogous relation among the opportunity sets of which they can be elements. I propose the following *dominance extension* principle. Let V and W be alternative opportunity sets of this kind, and let $t-1$ denote the period in which those opportunity sets would be faced (and in which an option would be chosen from them). V weakly dominates W if, for every option w' in W, there is some option v' in V such v' weakly dominates w' in period t. I will write this as $V \geqslant_{t-1} W$. The intuitive idea is that there can be no loss of opportunity in facing V rather than W if, for each option w' that can be chosen in W there is an option v' in V which unambiguously provides at least as much opportunity. The relations of strict dominance, dominance equivalence, and dominance non-comparability are defined from weak dominance in the same way as before. These definitions imply that reflexivity is preserved—that is, that for all opportunity sets V that can be faced in period $t-1$, $V \sim_{t-1} V$. Thus, given a weak dominance relation among options than can be experienced in any period t, the dominance extension principle induces a dominance relation among the opportunity sets themselves. This principle can be applied repeatedly to induce dominance relations at successively higher levels of nesting (or, equivalently, in successively earlier periods).

This set of definitions can be interpreted as a generalization of the Individual Opportunity Criterion, as that was presented in Section 5.1. Take the case of the air traveller for whom opportunity sets are sets of alternative complimentary drinks. The period in which a drink might be consumed is t; the period in which an opportunity set is faced is $t-1$. Compare the sets $O = \{water, orange\ juice, coffee, nothing\}$ and $O' = \{water, orange\ juice, coffee, beer, nothing\}$. If we take it that any one of the five options (that is, the four drinks and 'nothing') might plausibly be preferred to all of the others, every pair of distinct options is dominance non-comparable. Thus, for every option x in O there is an option (the same x) in O' which weakly dominates it, but the converse is not true; and so O' strictly dominates O (i.e. $O' \succ_{t-1} O$). If we read 'strictly dominates' as equivalent to 'provides strictly more opportunity than', we have reproduced the implication of the Individual Opportunity Criterion.

A model of a specific multi-stage decision problem may help to explain the intuitions behind this rather abstract analysis. The story behind the model is that the agent, Jane, is offered a rare opportunity to buy a ticket to attend some important sporting event. Going to the event would satisfy a long-felt desire and would give her intense but brief enjoyment. However, the ticket is expensive; buying it would require painful economies in other areas of her life. I begin with the version of the model in which Jane has the greatest freedom of action. There are four periods. Jane enters period 1 with an endowment m of money. In this period she has two options, *buy* and *don't buy*. If she chooses *don't buy*, she keeps her endowment and has no decision to make in period 2. If instead she chooses *buy*, she pays a price p_1 (less than m) and receives the ticket. Then in period 2 she has two more options, *hold* and *return*. If she chooses *hold*, she keeps the ticket and what is left of her money. If she chooses *return*, she returns the ticket and receives an amount of money p_2 that is slightly less than she originally paid. In period 3, there are no further opportunities to buy or sell tickets. If she has chosen *don't buy*, her opportunity set in period 3 contains the various ways she could spend her original endowment m. Let this set be X. If she has chosen *buy* and *hold*, her opportunity set in period 3 is such that she can choose whether or not to go to the event and also how to spend $m-p_1$, the relatively small amount of money she still holds. Let this set be Y. If she has chosen *buy* and *return*, her opportunity set in period 3 contains the various ways in which she could spend $m - p_1 + p_2$. Let this set be Z. Since the only difference between X and Z is the amount of money that Jane is able to spend on things other than going to the event, I assume that Z is a strict subset of X.[6] In period 4, she experiences whichever option she chose in period 3. All of this is known to Jane at the start of period 1.

Jane's entire decision problem is described by the nested set $S = \{\{X\}, \{Y, Z\}\}$. The outer pair of curly brackets defines the choice facing Jane in period 1. This is a choice between the elements of the set that is specified by that pair of brackets—that is, the elements $\{X\}$, corresponding with *don't buy*, and $\{Y, Z\}$, corresponding with *buy*. Each of these elements is a (possibly degenerate) choice problem that will be confronted in period 2 if the relevant action is chosen in period 1. The singleton $\{X\}$ represents the fact that, if *don't buy* is chosen in period 1, there is no choice to be made in period 2, and the options that will be available in period 3 are the elements of X. The set $\{Y, Z\}$ represents the fact that, if *buy* is chosen in period 1, there will be a further choice to be made in period 2, between one action (*hold*) which leads to the period 3 opportunity set Y, and another action (*return*) which leads to Z. In this notation, each matched pair of curly brackets is associated with a specific period; the succession of periods is represented by successively deeper nesting of sets.[7]

Notice that if Jane acts on a single set of integrated preferences throughout the four periods (and knows that this is how she acts), she has no reason to choose *buy* followed by *return*. Whatever those preferences are, she can satisfy them at least as well (and typically better) by choosing *don't buy*. This raises the question of whether the opportunity to choose *buy* followed by *return* is of any value to her. This question can be posed more precisely by considering a variant of the model in which the option of returning the ticket is not available: there are choices to be made only in periods 1 and 3. In this variant model, Jane's entire decision problem is described by the nested set $S' = \{\{X\}, \{Y\}\}$. How should the opportunities offered by S and S' be ranked?

As a first step in answering this question, consider the three alternative opportunity sets, X, Y, and Z, that Jane might face in period 3. If these sets are considered independently of any preceding choices, they are the kind of objects to which the Individual Opportunity Criterion, as defined in Section 5.1, can apply. Since Z is a strict subset of X, we have $X \succ_3 Z$. Since neither of X and Y is a weak subset of the other, we have $X \#_3 Y$. Similarly, since neither of Y and Z is a weak subset of the other, we have $Y \#_3 Z$. Now consider the opportunity sets $\{X\}$, $\{Y\}$, and $\{Y, Z\}$ that Jane might face in period 2. Applying the dominance extension principle, we have $\{X\} \#_2 \{Y\}$, $\{X\} \#_2 \{Y, Z\}$, and $\{Y, Z\} \succ_2 \{Y\}$. Finally, consider the alternative decision problems that Jane might face in period 1. Applying the dominance extension principle again, we have $\{\{X\}, \{Y, Z\}\} \succ_1 \{\{X\}, \{Y\}\}$. So the answer to the original question is that S gives more opportunity than S': being able to choose *buy* followed by *return* counts as an addition to Jane's opportunities, even though the combined effect of the two actions is an unambiguous loss.

Why does this count as an additional opportunity? Think about how, facing the decision problem S, Jane might choose *buy* in period 1 and *return* in period 2. Suppose that, as I suggest is entirely plausible, there is no uniquely correct answer to the question of how much Jane should be willing to pay for the ticket. She can predict both the pleasures she will enjoy if she goes to the event and the sacrifices she will have to make in order to pay for the ticket, but she knows of no objective way of making these effects commensurable. In some states of mind, she finds herself giving particular attention to the pleasures of the event, and the price p_1 seems worth paying; in other states of mind, when she attends more to the sacrifices, the ticket does not seem to be worth as much as p_2. In period 1, she has to choose between $\{X\}$ and $\{Y, Z\}$. Both options are eligible choices for her. Suppose she is then in the first state of mind, and doesn't expect this to change. She buys the ticket. In period 2, she has to choose between $\{Y\}$ and $\{Z\}$. Both of these options are eligible too: the fact that Z is inferior to an option she previously rejected does not make Z a bad choice *now*. Suppose that in period 2, she is the second state of mind, and returns the ticket. In neither period has she made an irrational decision; she has simply changed her mind. The added value of S relative to S' is that it gives Jane the opportunity to act on this change of mind. My claim is that it is Jane's interest to have this additional opportunity.

Some readers may want to object that, since Jane does not have a consistent set of preferences, it is a mistake to treat her as a single agent with definable interests. When representing individuals whose preferences change over time, decision theorists often use *multiple-self* models in which a person's agency is broken down into that of two or more *selves*, each with its own integrated preferences; at different times or in different situations, different selves are in control of the individual's actions. These selves are then treated as if they were distinct agents. In some models, the different selves of a single person interact strategically with one another, in the same way that players interact with one another in game theory. Sometimes, normative analysis privileges the preferences of one self, treating these as the 'true' preferences of the whole person. Sometimes, the preferences of the different selves are given equal moral status, and the whole person is treated as if she were a society with the individual selves as members. Sometimes, the person is assumed to have a coherent higher-level *metapreference* ranking of the various lower-level preference orderings which govern her day-to-day behaviour; normative authority is then located in each person's supposed higher moral self.[8]

Applying this approach to the case of Jane, we might distinguish between an 'experience-seeking' self (Jane$_1$, the self whose preferences are acted on in period 1) which is willing to pay a high price to go to the event, and a 'prudent' self (Jane$_2$, the self whose preferences are acted on in period 2) which is willing to pay only a low price. We might conclude that Jane$_1$'s preferences would be better satisfied if the decision problem were S', while Jane$_2$'s preferences would be better satisfied if it were S. And then we (as impartial spectators or social planners) might try to decide which of these selves is truly Jane.

This modelling strategy, like that of the inner rational agent (to which it is closely related), often looks suspiciously like an attempt to continue to use rational-choice theory while describing the behaviour of people whose actual choices are inconsistent with that theory. One of its least attractive features is that it cannot recognize the continuing identity and agency of ordinary human beings who happen to choose in ways that disconfirm received theory. A failure of the theory is being re-cast as a failure of the individuals whose behaviour the theory is supposed to explain. As I explained in Chapters 3 and 4, this strategy opens the way to kinds of paternalism that are out of bounds to a contractarian.

I think we need a radically different conception of the continuing person. We should think of the continuing Jane—let us call her Jane*—as the *composition* of the selves which perform the various parts of whatever sequence of actions is in fact performed. For theorists who insist on modelling identity in terms of some kind of preference relation, this idea may seem strange. But, viewed from outside the framework of decision theory, it is a very natural way of thinking of identity. The continuing Jane* is just whatever Jane the human being is over time. What the continuing Jane* does is just whatever Jane does over time; what the continuing Jane* values is just whatever Jane values over time. In this perspective, it becomes clear how the continuing person can value the absence of constraints on her present and future actions.

Think again about Jane, facing the decision problem S. In period 1, Jane$_1$ wants to choose, and does choose, *buy*. Since Jane* *is* Jane$_1$ at this moment, it is also true that Jane* wants to choose, and does choose, *buy*. In period 2, Jane$_2$ wants to choose, and does choose, *return*. Since Jane* *is* Jane$_2$ at this moment, it is also true that Jane* wants to choose, and does choose, *return*. So Jane* wants and chooses to *buy* in period 1, and wants and chooses to *return* in period 2. In allowing this sequence of actions, S gives Jane* an opportunity to do something that she wants to do. If Jane* values opportunities to do as she wants, this feature of S has value for her.

Consider how, at the end of period 3, Jane (the human being) might reflect on the actions she has taken. A conventional decision theorist might point out to her that she has acted on preferences that are inconsistent over time, and that in consequence she has incurred an unambiguous loss—she has bought dear and sold cheap. Jane can concede this, yet still see both buying and selling as *her* autonomously chosen actions: she wanted to buy, and she bought; she wanted to sell, and she sold. She does not have to disown either of those actions as the work of an alien self, or as the result of weakness of will.

She can say that she has done what she wanted to do, when she wanted to do it. And she can say that it was in her interests that she was able to do this.

5.6 Responsibility

My proposal is that the continuing agency of a person across time and across contexts should be understood as the continuing existence of a self-acknowledged *locus of responsibility*. The intuitive idea is that a person is a continuing locus of responsibility—for short, a *responsible agent*—to the extent that, at each moment, she identifies with her own actions, past, present, and future. A responsible agent treats her past actions as her own, whether or not they were what she now desires them to have been. She treats her future actions as her own, even if she does not yet know what they will be, and whether or not she expects them to be what she now desires them to be.[9]

This conception of responsibility provides philosophical underpinning for the claim that opportunity has value. Consider the set of opportunities that are open to some individual across time. Is it a good thing that this set is larger rather than smaller? In conventional welfare economics, more opportunity is better than less only to the extent that it allows the individual to achieve a more preferred outcome; if the individual lacks integrated preferences, there seems to be no way of answering the question. In a model of multiple selves, the question has to be posed separately in relation to each self, and increases in lifetime opportunity may be judged to be good from the viewpoint of one self and bad from that of another. If appeal is made to metarankings, increases in the opportunities of selves which act on 'inferior' preferences may be judged to have negative value. But if an individual is understood as a continuing locus of responsibility, any increase in that individual's opportunity is good for her in an unambiguous sense. The more opportunities she has, the more she—construed as responsible agent with a continuing existence through time—is free to do. This is true whether or not her actions across time are consistent with any one set of coherent preferences.

Benjamin Disraeli is supposed to have said, apropos of the attacks that any leading British politician faces in Parliament, 'Never complain and never explain'.[10] This aristocratic sentiment captures something of what it is to be a responsible agent. In relation to matters that affect only himself, the responsible agent asks of government only that it ensures him as wide a range of opportunities as possible. How he uses those opportunities is up to him, and he accepts sole responsibility for the consequences. He has no need to explain the decisions he has made, because they were no one else's business. And because they were *his* decisions, he can have no complaint against anyone else about how they turn out.

6

The Invisible Hand

Adam Smith's metaphor of the invisible hand captures an idea that is at the heart of the liberal tradition of economics—the idea that the market can generate socially beneficial consequences that no human agency has consciously planned, or even *could* consciously plan. As I pointed out in Chapter 1, modern economics has represented this idea in terms of the two fundamental theorems of welfare economics. These theorems assume that each individual's economic behaviour is rational with respect to integrated preferences, and define social benefit in terms of the satisfaction of those preferences. If real individual behaviour is not rational in this sense, and if real preferences are not integrated (or do not exist at all), the theorems lose their relevance. But that is not to say that the underlying idea of the invisible hand is mistaken. It is not self-evident that this idea depends on the rational-choice theory that economists thought up a hundred or so years after Smith wrote *The Wealth of Nations*. In this chapter, I will argue that it does *not* depend on the validity of that theory.

A traditional device in economic writing is to invite the reader to think about just how much order there is in economic life, how much we all depend on this, and how little of it is the result of deliberate planning. This device allows the writer to express his or her sense of the significance and depth of economics as an area of enquiry. Economic life, the economist wants to say, has an astonishing degree of order and complexity which, just like the subject matter of the natural sciences, calls for explanation. If this order tends to work to everyone's benefit, and if it depends on human institutions that can be sustained by some kinds of political action and obstructed or damaged by others, it is important to understand what those institutions are and how they work. The idea behind the metaphor of the invisible hand is that the competitive market is one of those institutions. As a first step in reconstructing this idea without assuming rational choice, it is useful to look at how Smith first expresses his sense of wonder at the spontaneous order of the market.

Smith (1776/1976: 22–3) asks his readers to observe 'the accommodation of the most common artificer or day-labourer in a civilized and thriving country' and to recognize that 'the number of people of whose industry a part, though but a small part, has been employed in procuring him this accommodation, exceeds all computation'. The day-labourer's woollen coat may seem coarse and rough to a well-off eighteenth-century reader, but the process by which it was produced required the specialized labour of the shepherd, the wool-sorter, the wool-comber, the dyer, the scribbler, the spinner, the weaver, the fuller, and the dresser; carrying material between these workmen required ship-builders, sailors, and rope-makers; each of these workmen used tools whose production processes were at least as complicated as that of the woollen coat itself; and so on. Part of Smith's intention is to show that the economy of a thriving country is an enormously complicated and unplanned scheme of cooperation, most of whose properties are unknown to the people who participate in it. It is also his intention to show that this scheme provides even the poor day-labourer with a standard of living that would be unattainable in an 'uncivilized' country. Thus, Smith (conscious of the climate of his native Scotland) gives special mention to the glass window of the day-labourer's cottage, reminding the reader how much specialized labour has gone into that, and how much the 'beautiful and happy invention' of glass contributes to human comfort in northern parts of the world.

Having been shown the astounding properties of this self-organizing cooperative scheme, Smith's reader is expected to want to understand the principles on which it operates. Smith's answer is that it works through the division of labour, which in turn results from the human propensity to 'truck, barter and exchange'. Since the division of labour requires exchange, it is limited by the extent of the market. Thus, the market is central to the cooperative scheme by which the inhabitants of civilized countries satisfy their wants.

Perhaps reflecting the state of economic development at the time at which he was writing, Smith's account of exchange does not give much emphasis to the finer details of individuals' preferences. Nevertheless, it is essential to his analysis that the market benefits individuals by allowing them to give up what they prefer less in return for what they prefer more. The suggestion is that the economic goods that the day-labourer most wants are such things as bread to eat, beer to drink, a coat to wear, a room to live in, and fuel to heat it. The market allows him to get these valuable things by selling his labour. The day-labourer experiences the market in terms of the wage at which he can sell his labour and the prices at which he can buy these various goods. However, if one looks at his transactions with the eye of an economist, one can see that he is engaging in mutually beneficial exchange with a vast number of other individuals. Ultimately, the day-labourer is exchanging his own labour for tiny quantities of the labour of the shepherd, the wool-sorter, the wool-comber, the dyer, and many, many others.

An invisible-hand argument for the market needs to reconcile these two viewpoints. In order to understand *what* the market achieves, one has to see it as making possible complex multilateral transactions between people who do not and cannot know one another, let alone negotiate directly with one another. But in order to understand *how* this is achieved, one has to see the market as presenting each individual with a much simpler set of options. The ordinary worker or consumer is presented with opportunities to acquire goods and services that he might want to consume, or money that can be used to buy such goods and services, in return for giving up goods, services or money that he already owns. In terms of the analysis developed in Chapter 5, the individual is presented with an opportunity set. In a competitive market, this opportunity set can be defined in terms of the individual's endowment of each tradable commodity and the price at which each commodity can be bought and sold.

The ability of the market to induce a spontaneous order of mutual benefit stems from the way in which, under suitable conditions, each individual's opportunity set encapsulates the terms on which other people are willing to transact with him. All that the day-labourer needs to know about the coat is how much he has to pay to get it, but that price is the sum of the amounts of money that the shepherd, the wool-sorter, the wool-comber, and so on are willing to accept in return for the amounts of their labour that are embodied in the coat. Conversely, the terms on which the day-labourer is willing to exchange his labour for money make up one component of the prices at which other people are able to buy the goods that embody that labour. In other words, the properties of each individual's opportunity set are determined by the choices that other people make from *their* opportunity sets.

Because of this mutual dependence between opportunity sets and choices, what each person can expect to gain from participating in the market cannot be described by any particular set of opportunities for that person, specified independently of how other people choose to use *their* opportunities. Roughly speaking, what each person can expect from the market is a rich array of opportunities to transact with others on terms that those others are willing to accept. But if that statement is to capture the reciprocal nature of opportunity, we must interpret the clause about the terms that other people are willing to accept as referring to other people's *opportunities* to choose what they will and will not accept, rather than to their preferences, taken as given. It is less ambiguous to say that people *collectively* can expect the market to provide them with a rich array of opportunities to transact with one another on terms that they might find *mutually* acceptable. The latter formulation makes clear that the opportunities offered by the market are opportunities for voluntary transactions between individuals. It is crucial to the concept of opportunity, as I understand it, that an individual's opportunities are defined independently of her actual preferences: in assessing a person's opportunities, we consider what she *might* conceivably want to choose, not what, given her preferences, she *does* want to choose (see Section 5.4). Similarly, in assessing opportunities for voluntary transactions, we consider what individuals might find mutually acceptable.

My aim in this chapter is to identify more precisely the sense in which the market provides opportunity, and to explain how this property of markets can be seen as beneficial, even by people who do not act on integrated preferences.

6.1 The Basic Idea

This chapter engages with general equilibrium theory, one of the more mathematical areas of economics. Unavoidably, it will involve analysis that is more abstract and formal than that in previous chapters. However, its central idea can be expressed fairly simply. In this section, I present an initial sketch of that idea, using as little mathematics as possible. In subsequent sections I develop the idea more fully and more formally.

A normative appraisal of the market has to start from a specification of the economic problem to which the market is a possible solution. If such an appraisal is to be at all tractable, it is unavoidable that that specification will be highly stylized: it will be a simple *model* of the problem, not a realistic *description* of it. There is a long tradition in economics of using models of one-period 'exchange economies' as a first step in understanding how markets work and what they can and cannot achieve. I will do the same.

In the simplest version of the model I will develop in this chapter, trade takes place among a set of individual 'consumers'. There is a set of (infinitely divisible) commodities. There is a fixed stock of each commodity. Prior to trade, these stocks are distributed among consumers in some given way: each consumer's initial holding of a commodity is her 'endowment' of that commodity. One of the commodities, 'money', serves as the unit of value and as the medium of exchange. Economic activity consists in the exchange of commodities between consumers. After all such exchange has taken place, each individual consumes the commodities she then holds. I make no assumptions about individuals' preferences except that money is always seen as desirable.

In an equilibrium state of a competitive economy, each non-money commodity has a single market price in terms of money. Each consumer is free to buy and sell non-money commodities in any quantities at these prices, subject to the constraint that her holdings of a commodity cannot be negative. It is convenient to describe an individual's opportunities in terms of her 'acquisition' of commodities—that is, in terms of changes (positive or negative) in her holdings of commodities, defined relative to her endowments. Any combination of acquisitions has a market value—that is, the net increase in the total money value of the individual's holdings (including holdings of money itself), measured at market prices. Since all trade takes place at market prices, the market value of every consumer's acquisitions must be zero. Thus, a consumer's opportunity set contains every combination of acquisitions that has a market value of zero (and that satisfies the constraint that holdings cannot be negative). Each consumer chooses one such combination of acquisitions from her opportunity set. In a competitive equilibrium, prices and choices are such that all markets clear. That is, for each commodity separately, chosen acquisitions by all consumers together sum to zero.

Such a configuration of opportunity sets has a normatively significant property, which I now describe. I define a 'transaction' among a group of individuals as a list of combinations of acquisitions, one combination for each member of that group. It is 'feasible' if and only if, for each commodity considered separately, acquisitions of that commodity by all members of the group sum to zero. (In other words: a feasible transaction for a group consists of some redistribution of that group's total endowment of commodities.) In relation to a given specification of individuals' opportunity sets, a transaction among a group of individuals is 'allowable' if and only if each group member's component of that transaction is an element of her opportunity set. The central claim of this chapter is that, in every competitive equilibrium, individuals' opportunity sets satisfy a condition that I will later define more formally as the 'Strong Interactive Opportunity Criterion' (see Section 6.4). This condition requires that every group of individuals has the collective opportunity to make any feasible transaction among themselves which, given the assumed desirability of money, they might find mutually acceptable.

Here is a sketch of how that claim can be proved. Consider any competitive equilibrium and any group S of individuals. Consider any potential transaction T among this group that is feasible but *not* allowable. Since T is feasible, acquisitions by group members must sum to zero for each commodity separately. Thus, the market value of the acquisitions of all group members together must sum to zero. But if *every* individual's acquisitions had zero market value, T would be allowable. Since T is not allowable, and since the total market value of acquisitions by group members is zero, there must be some group member, say i, for whom the market value of acquisitions is strictly negative. But i's opportunity set allows him to choose any combination of acquisitions that has zero market value. Since, by assumption, money is always desirable, T gives i a combination of acquisitions that is clearly inferior to some combination that he could achieve by trading at market prices. So i has no reason to want to take part in T. The implication is that T is not a transaction that the members of S might find mutually acceptable.

In the opening section of this chapter, I claimed that what people can expect from the market is a rich array of opportunities to transact with one another on terms that they might find mutually acceptable. The Strong Inter-active Opportunity Criterion formalizes that concept of richness, and the demonstration that this criterion is satisfied in every competitive equilibrium formalizes that claim.

6.2 Exchange Economies

I begin my formal analysis by defining an exchange economy.[1] In my model of an exchange economy, there is a set of *consumers*. This set will be written as $I = \{1, \ldots, n\}$, with $n \geq 1$; typical consumers will be referred to as i and j. There is a set of *commodities*. This set will be written as $G = \{1, \ldots, m\}$, with $m \geq 2$; a typical commodity will be referred to as g. Commodities are infinitely divisible. Each consumer i enters the economy with an *endowment* of some quantity $e_{i,g}$ of *claims* on each commodity g. At the level of the individual consumer, endowments may be positive or zero, but not negative. For each commodity, the sum of all consumers' endowments is strictly positive. For each consumer i, the *endowment vector*, written as $\mathbf{e}_i$, is the array $(e_{i,1}, \ldots, e_{i,m})$ of i's endowments of the m commodities. The *endowment profile*, written as $\mathbf{e}$, is the array $(\mathbf{e}_1, \ldots, \mathbf{e}_n)$ of endowment vectors for the n consumers. (I will use bold letters to refer to arrays of objects. Arrays that include one object for each consumer will be called 'profiles'. I will reserve the word 'vector' for any array that includes one quantity or one price for each commodity.) An *exchange economy* is defined by the quadruple $\langle I, G, \mathbf{e}, \mathbf{f}(.) \rangle$, where $\mathbf{f}(.)$ is a function, to be defined later, that specifies the choices that consumers make in this economy, given whatever opportunities are available to them. In my analysis, 'the' economy is taken as fixed; but the results of this analysis will apply to any exchange economy.

Economic activity consists in consumers' taking on further claims to add to their endowments, or disposing of claims from their endowments. This activity will be called *acquisition*, which can be either positive (taking on additional claims) or negative (disposing of endowments). Acquisition takes place in a single period, during which the total stock of claims on each commodity g remains constant: claims are merely transferred between consumers. At the end of this process, each consumer i holds $x_{i,g}$ claims on each commodity g, which he then *consumes*. Summing over all consumers, total consumption of each commodity g is equal to total endowments.

A claim on a unit of commodity g confers on its holder both an entitlement and an obligation to consume one unit of that commodity at the end of the period. In my model there is no option of 'free disposal' of unwanted commodities—hence the obligation to consume. In general, consumption need not be interpreted as something that consumers value positively; it represents whatever opportunities and obligations a consumer incurs by virtue of holding a claim at the end of the period. For example, a commodity might be an obsolete type of electronic equipment, for which 'consumption' takes the form of unwanted storage or costly disposal. Commodities will be interpreted as *private* goods (or bads, if consumption is valued negatively). That is, each consumer is concerned only about how much of each commodity *he* consumes, and not about how much other individuals consume. This property of the model has to be treated as a matter of interpretation, because the model has no formal concept of preference. Commodity 1 (which I will call *money*) will be interpreted as having the special property that holdings of it are always valued positively. This too has to be a matter of interpretation, because of the absence of a concept of preference. However, it provides the motivation for a concept of 'dominance' that is built into the normative criteria that I will use to assess consumers' opportunities. When I model processes of exchange, I will treat money as the medium through which exchange takes place. Thus, in effect, I am assuming that generalized purchasing power is always valued positively.

One might say that the economic problem posed by an exchange economy is that of reallocating the fixed stocks of claims between consumers so as to satisfy some normative criterion. However, it is more useful to say that the fundamental problem is to design a *trading institution* which can bring about such reallocations, and to specify the rules by which it operates. This institution might be thought of as a 'social planner' in the sense of modern welfare economics, or as an 'auctioneer' in the sense of the general equilibrium theory first developed by Léon Walras (1874/1954), or (as in the model I present in Sugden [2004a]) as a population of competing profit-seeking arbitrageurs who come to the economy from outside and make offers to buy commodities from, and to sell commodities to, consumers in the economy.

I shall describe trading institutions in terms of the opportunities for net acquisition that they make available to consumers. Consider any consumer i and any commodity g. Let $q_{i,g}$ denote consumer i's (net) *acquisition* of claims on commodity g; thus, i's consumption of commodity g is given by $x_{i,g} = e_{i,g} + q_{i,g}$. I stipulate that a consumer's holdings of claims on a commodity can never be negative; thus, $q_{i,g} \geq -e_{i,g}$. Let $\mathbf{q}_i = (q_{i,1}, \ldots, q_{i,m})$ be the array of i's acquisitions of commodities; I will call this an *acquisition vector*. An *opportunity set* for i, denoted O_i, is a non-empty set of alternative acquisition vectors (satisfying the non-negativity condition for holdings), from which i must choose one. An *opportunity profile* $\mathbf{O} = (O_1, \ldots, O_n)$ is an array of opportunity sets, one for each of the n consumers. I will say that an acquisition vector $\mathbf{q}_i$ for consumer i is *allowable* in $\mathbf{O}$ if it is an element of O_i. A profile $\mathbf{q} = (\mathbf{q}_1, \ldots, \mathbf{q}_n)$ of acquisition vectors will be called an *acquisition profile*; such a profile will be called allowable in $\mathbf{O}$ if each $\mathbf{q}_i$ is allowable in $\mathbf{O}$. I will say that an acquisition profile is *jointly feasible* in a given exchange economy if, for each commodity separately, the sum of acquisitions by all consumers is zero. Notice that I do not require that each O_i contains the acquisition vector $(0, \ldots, 0)$. In other words, I do not require that each individual has the option of consuming exactly as much of each commodity as he is endowed with. Thus, I am allowing the possibility that the trading institution simply takes claims from one consumer and gives them to another.

I want to allow the possibility that consumers do not act on integrated preferences. Thus, I do not want to assume that, for any given specification of the set of consumers I, the set of commodities G, the endowment vector $\mathbf{e}$ and the opportunity profile $\mathbf{O}$, the behaviour of each consumer is fully determined. Instead, I want to allow consumers' behaviour to be context-dependent. One way of doing this would be to introduce a variable to represent 'contextual features' that might influence consumers' choices and then to include this variable both in the definition of an economy and as an argument in consumers' choice functions.[2] However, the effects of these features can be captured in the specification of choice functions, as I now explain.

For each consumer i, there is a *choice function* $f_i(.)$ which assigns a unique acquisition vector $f_i(\mathbf{O})$ to every opportunity profile $\mathbf{O}$. The *jointly chosen* acquisition profile $[f_1(\mathbf{O}), \ldots, f_n(\mathbf{O})]$ will be written as $\mathbf{f}(\mathbf{O})$; $\mathbf{f}(.)$ is the *joint choice function*. Recall that an 'exchange economy' is defined by the quadruple $\langle I, G, \mathbf{e}, \mathbf{f}(.) \rangle$. Thus, two economies may share the same I, G, and $\mathbf{e}$ while having different joint choice functions, say $\mathbf{f}'(.)$ and $\mathbf{f}''(.)$. The interpretation is that these economies differ in their contextual features; in one economy, those features induce the choices represented by $\mathbf{f}'(.)$; in the other, they induce those represented by $\mathbf{f}''(.)$. My analysis will be concerned with properties of a *given* economy, that is, an economy for which I, G, $\mathbf{e}$, and $\mathbf{f}(.)$ are all fixed.

Apart from the implicit assumption that money is always valued positively, the only assumption that I make about the behaviour of consumers is that, from the viewpoint of the modeller, a consumer's choice from any given opportunity set is predictable, given the contextual features of the economy.[3] Consumers' decisions may be rational or irrational, context-independent or context-dependent. For example, a consumer's revealed preference between two given acquisition vectors may vary according to the opportunity set in which they appear, as in theories of salience (Bordalo, Gennaioli, and Shleifer, 2013) and bad-deal aversion (Isoni, 2011; Weaver and Frederick, 2012). Because consumers' endowments are treated as properties of the fixed economy, and because choice functions are specific to that economy, the model imposes no restrictions on how choices respond to changes in endowments. Thus, an individual's revealed preferences over given bundles of consumption might vary according to his endowments, as in theories of reference-dependent preferences (Tversky and Kahneman, 1991; Munro and Sugden, 2003).

A crucial question to ask of any opportunity profile **O** in relation to a given exchange economy is whether **f(O)** is jointly feasible. If **f(O)** is jointly feasible, I will say that **O** is *market-clearing*. Notice that this question is being asked in relation to the acquisition vectors that consumers *actually choose* from the opportunity sets they face, and not in relation to all the combinations of such vectors that they *might have chosen*. Unless all opportunity sets are singletons (that is, unless the trading institution does not allow consumers to make any choices at all), it is inevitable that some—typically, most—combinations of allowable choices will not be jointly feasible. Joint feasibility of actual choices is an equilibrium condition which one might expect to be satisfied by at most only a tiny fraction of the opportunity profiles that are possible for a given exchange economy. A useful institution needs to have some mechanism that constructs opportunity profiles in such a way that, given the choices that consumers can be predicted to make, joint feasibility is achieved. For the moment, I bracket out the question of how this might be achieved and focus on the normative appraisal of institutions which *do* achieve it.

6.3 The Interactive Opportunity Criterion

From the viewpoint of neoclassical welfare economics, the economic problem posed by an exchange economy is that of reallocating commodities between individuals so that their preferences are satisfied as effectively as possible. Opportunity sets are not treated as having any normative significance in their own right; all that matters is the bundle that each individual finally consumes, and where this stands in his preference ordering. My approach will be the opposite. It will attach normative significance to opportunity sets without explicit reference to individuals' preferences.

In this section, I formulate a normative criterion that can be used to assess opportunity profiles in an exchange economy. As a preliminary step, I define a relation of dominance between acquisition vectors. For any consumer i, for any acquisition vectors q_i and q'_i, I will say that q'_i *dominates* q_i if the two vectors differ only in terms of acquisition of money, and acquisition of money is strictly greater in q'_i. Given the interpretation of money as a commodity that is always valued positively, a dominating acquisition vector can be interpreted as unambiguously more choiceworthy than the vector it dominates. To put this another way, if q'_i dominates q_i and if i's opportunity set contains q'_i, then q_i is not an option that i could plausibly want to choose.

I now present the criterion itself. For any given exchange economy, consider any market-clearing opportunity profile **O**. The idea behind my criterion is to assess any such **O** by asking whether it allows the set of all consumers to implement every feasible transaction that all of them could plausibly want to participate in. Consider what this means. Since the only economic activity is acquisition, a feasible transaction must be described by some acquisition profile which is jointly feasible. So the criterion sets a two-part test which is applied to every jointly feasible acquisition profile q. The first part of the test is to ask whether q is allowable in O. If the answer is 'Yes', the set of all consumers *is* allowed to implement the relevant transaction, and so the test is passed. If not, an additional question has to be asked: Is there any consumer j such that q_j is dominated by some element of O_j? If the answer to this question is 'Yes', q is not a transaction that every consumer could plausibly want to participate in, and so, for a different reason, q passes the test. Every jointly feasible acquisition profile is required to pass this two-part test. More formally, the criterion is:

Interactive Opportunity Criterion.[4] For a given exchange economy, an opportunity profile O satisfies the Interactive Opportunity Criterion *if* (i) it is market-clearing *and* (ii) for every jointly feasible acquisition profile q, *either* q is allowable in O *or* there is some consumer j such that q_j is dominated by some element of O_j.

To say that an opportunity profile satisfies the Interactive Opportunity Criterion is to say, of every transaction that is feasible for all consumers collectively and is non-dominated for each consumer separately, that each consumer's component of that transaction is an element of her opportunity set. It is important to understand the significance of the clause 'is an element of her opportunity set'. What is being said is not that consumers are free to negotiate jointly feasible transactions among themselves. It is that, for every jointly feasible transaction that all consumers could plausibly want to participate in, the trading institution makes each consumer's component of that composite transaction available to him as an option that he can choose *as an individual agent*. (Compare the difference between saying that Smith's day-labourer is free to negotiate with the thousands of workers whose labour is embodied in the woollen coat and saying that the terms of a contract with those workers are embodied in the price of the coat.)

I have deliberately formulated the Interactive Opportunity Criterion in a way that avoids any mention of preferences. However, to understand how this criterion relates to conventional welfare economics, it is useful to consider what it would imply under the additional assumption that individuals act on preferences that satisfy standard conditions of coherence. To investigate this issue, I introduce the concept of a *neoclassical consumer*. A neoclassical consumer has a (context-independent) preference ordering over all vectors of quantities of commodities consumed. In relation to a given endowment profile, an equivalent statement of this property is that a neoclassical consumer *i* has a preference ordering over all acquisition vectors q_i. I also stipulate that a neoclassical consumer always prefers more money to less, and always chooses an option in his opportunity set that is at least as preferred as every other option in that set.

If all consumers are neoclassical, it is possible to apply the familiar normative criterion of Pareto-optimality. Consider any opportunity profile **O**. To say that **O** induces a Pareto-optimal outcome is to say that, given consumers' actual preferences, no feasible reallocation of commodities away from the jointly chosen acquisition profile **f(o)** is Pareto-improving (that is, makes at least one consumer better off in terms of her preferences, and makes none worse off). To say that **O** satisfies the Interactive Opportunity Criterion is to say, without any reference to consumers' actual preferences, that every feasible reallocation of commodities away from **f(o)** that consumers jointly could conceivably want is in fact allowable to them. The latter statement is stronger. In other words, if all consumers are neoclassical, any opportunity profile that satisfies the Interactive Opportunity Criterion induces a Pareto-optimal outcome. However, the converse proposition does not necessarily hold. For example, one might imagine an omniscient social planner who identifies a Pareto-optimal acquisition profile **q*** and then allows each consumer *i* only the singleton opportunity set $\{q_i^*\}$. In such an economy there would be many jointly feasible, non-dominated transactions that were not allowable: the opportunity profile would be catering to consumers' *actual* preferences but not to the whole range of preferences that they might plausibly have held. In this sense, the Interactive Opportunity Criterion is more demanding than Pareto-optimality.

6.4 The Strong Interactive Opportunity Criterion

The Interactive Opportunity Criterion assesses an opportunity profile by asking whether it allows *the set of all individuals* to implement every feasible transaction that all of them could plausibly want to participate in. But it does not ask about the presence or absence of opportunities for feasible combinations of choices by sets of individuals that do not contain everyone.

This can be seen most clearly by considering any one consumer *i* in an economy in which $n > 1$. Consumer *i* comes to the economy with some vector of endowments e_i. Given these endowments, it is feasible *for him* that his acquisition of every commodity is zero, with the implication that his consumption of each commodity is equal to his endowment of it. But nothing in the Interactive Opportunity Criterion requires that this option is an element of (or is dominated in) *i*'s opportunity set. To put this another way, the Interactive Opportunity Criterion takes no notice of the fact that the *n*-person economy contains a smaller economy, in which the only consumer is i and the only endowments are i's endowments.

Similarly, consider any two consumers i and j in an exchange economy in which $n > 2$. The n-person economy contains a smaller economy, in which the only consumers are i and j and the only endowments are i's and j's endowments. The Interactive Opportunity Criterion does not ask whether i and j collectively are allowed to implement every transaction that involves only *their* acquisitions, is feasible for *them* in terms of *their* endowments, and that each of *them* might plausibly want to participate in.

This line of thought suggests a natural way of strengthening the Interactive Opportunity Criterion. Consider any exchange economy, and any market-clearing opportunity profile **O**. The Interactive Opportunity Criterion tests whether **O** allows I (the set of all consumers) to implement every jointly feasible transaction that all of them could plausibly want to participate in. The intuitive idea is to strengthen the criterion so that it tests whether **O** allows every non-empty set $S \subseteq I$ to implement every transaction that is jointly feasible for the members of S and that all those members could plausibly want to participate in.

More formally, let $S \subseteq I$ be any non-empty set of consumers. For any opportunity profile **O**, the *opportunity profile for S*, denoted by $\mathbf{O}_S$, is an array of opportunity sets O_i, one for each consumer i in S. An *acquisition profile for S*, denoted $\mathbf{q}_S$, is an array of acquisition vectors $\mathbf{q}_i$, one for each consumer i in S. Such a profile is *allowable in* $\mathbf{O}_S$ if each of its component vectors $\mathbf{q}_i$ is allowable in O_i. It is *jointly feasible for S* if, for each good g, the sum of acquisitions of g by all members of S is zero. The strengthened criterion is:

> *Strong Interactive Opportunity Criterion.* For a given exchange economy, an opportunity profile **O** satisfies the Strong Interactive Opportunity Criterion *if* (i) **O** is market-clearing *and* (ii) for every non-empty set of consumers $S \subseteq I$, for every jointly feasible acquisition profile $\mathbf{q}_S$ for S, *either* $\mathbf{q}_S$ is allowable in $\mathbf{O}_S$ *or* there is some consumer j in S such that q_j is dominated by some element of O_j.

Notice that, by virtue of the fact that the set of all consumers is one of the sets S in the statement of the Strong Interactive Opportunity Criterion, any opportunity profile that satisfies that criterion necessarily satisfies the Interactive Opportunity Criterion too.

One might ask what the Strong Interactive Opportunity Criterion would imply under the assumption that all consumers are neoclassical. Given this assumption, to say that an opportunity profile satisfies the Strong Interactive Opportunity Criterion is to say that the chosen acquisition profile is Pareto-optimal, not only in the whole n-person economy, but also in every 'sub-economy' that is populated by a subset of the set of all consumers, each member of that population having the same endowment vector as in the original economy. In conventional welfare economics, an acquisition profile that has this property is said to be in the *core* of the economy.

6.5 Competitive Equilibrium

In Sections 6.3 and 6.4, I proposed normative criteria for assessing opportunity profiles in an exchange economy. But my ultimate objective is to assess the opportunities provided by a particular institution—the competitive market. This requires some representation of the properties of the opportunity profiles that competitive markets can be expected to create.

Neoclassical economic theorists have investigated the concept of *competitive equilibrium* as a representation of a general tendency of competitive markets. The underlying idea is that, in a competitive market, each commodity has a single *market price* (expressed in units of some specific benchmark or *numéraire* commodity) at which each consumer can buy and sell it in whatever quantities he chooses, subject only to the budget constraint that, summing over all commodities, the total value of his gross purchases must be equal to the total value of his gross sales. Thus, each consumer's opportunity set is fully determined by his endowments and the list of market prices: it is the set of acquisition vectors for which the net total market value of acquisitions is zero. A competitive equilibrium is a list of prices such that, when opportunity sets are specified in this way, consumers' choices are jointly feasible (or, in other words, such that all markets clear). It is a common practice in economics to use competitive equilibrium as a general-purpose model of the normal state of competitive markets.

When economists use this model, they usually also assume that consumers' choices in the market reveal integrated preferences that satisfy standard neoclassical conditions. But that is not to say that the concept of competitive equilibrium *requires* that individuals behave in this way. I will argue that it does not.

Consider any exchange economy. Treating money as the *numéraire*, I define a *price vector* as an array $\mathbf{p} = (p_1, \ldots, p_m)$, where $p_1 \equiv 1$ as a matter of definition and $p_2, \ldots, p_m$ are finite prices of the non-money commodities. The latter prices may be positive, zero, or negative. For any consumer i, any acquisition vector $\mathbf{q}_i$ and any price vector $\mathbf{p}$, I define the *net value* of $\mathbf{q}_i$ in terms of $\mathbf{p}$ as the increase in the total money value of i's holdings as a result of the acquisitions described by $\mathbf{q}_i$, valued at the prices $\mathbf{p}$. In other words, the net value of $\mathbf{q}_i$ in terms of $\mathbf{p}$ is $q_{i,1} + p_2 q_{i,2} + \ldots + p_m q_{i,m}$. Then the concept of competitive equilibrium can be defined as follows:

Competitive equilibrium in an exchange economy. For a given exchange economy, an opportunity profile $\mathbf{O}$ is a competitive equilibrium *if* (i) $\mathbf{O}$ is market-clearing *and* (ii) there is a price vector **p** such that, for each consumer i, O_i is the set of acquisition vectors for i whose net value in terms of **p** is zero.

Suppose that commodities change hands only through trade, and that each non-money commodity is traded separately against money. That is, for any consumer, an acquisition vector describes the combined effect of a set of transactions, in each of which he buys or sells some quantity of one non-money commodity in exchange for some amount of money. Each of these transactions must take place at some (explicit or implicit) rate of exchange between the relevant commodity and money. Then the definition of competitive equilibrium requires that, for each non-money commodity, all transactions between that commodity and money take place at *the same* rate of exchange. This property of transactions has been known to generations of economists as the *Law of One Price*. The definition also requires that, at these prices, all markets clear: for each commodity, supply (that is, the total quantity that consumers attempt to sell) is equal to demand (the total quantity that consumers attempt to buy). This used to be known as the *Law of Supply and Demand*.

The usual explanation for the Law of One Price is that, in any case in which it does not hold, there is an opportunity for profitable arbitrage. This idea can be presented most clearly by using a model in which all transactions between the 'consumers' in the economy—the people who come to the economy with endowments and who leave it with holdings which they consume—are mediated by a distinct class of *traders*. Traders are agents who buy and sell commodities with the sole aim of making monetary profits. They have no interest in holding commodities other than money; they aim to sell exactly as much of each non-money commodity as they buy, and to make profits by buying cheap and selling dear. There is free entry into the activity of trading, and many potential entrants. There is also free exit. The only assumption I make about the behaviour of consumers is that they are *price-sensitive*—that is, whenever a consumer engages in trade, he buys at the lowest prices that are available to him and sells at the highest.

Representing this scenario in a formal model involves some theoretical complexity.[5] However, the intuitive idea that the Law of One Price and the Law of Supply and Demand are equilibrium conditions for such a model is quite straightforward. Here, I use the concept of 'equilibrium' in the generic sense of a situation with no tendency for change. Given the assumption that profit-seeking traders have free entry to the market, equilibrium requires that, given the behaviour of traders who are currently in the market, no potential entrant could earn positive profits. Given the assumption of free exit, equilibrium also requires that no trader is making a loss. Finally, given the assumption that each trader aims to sell exactly as much of each non-money commodity as she buys, equilibrium requires that each trader succeeds in this aim.

Consider any non-money commodity g for which at least one consumer is a net buyer and at least one consumer is a net seller. Let p_g^H be the highest price that is paid by any consumer who buys the commodity, and let p_g^L be the lowest price that is received by any consumer who sells it. Now suppose that $p_g^H > p_g^L$. If this were the case, a trader could enter the market offering to buy at a price slightly higher than p_g^L and to sell at a price slightly lower than p_g^H, while still allowing a positive profit margin. Consumers who are currently buying or selling the commodity would be able to make unambiguous gains by transferring their custom to the new entrant. Since (by assumption) consumers are price-sensitive, they would transfer their custom in this way, and the new entrant would make a profit.[6] Thus, for the market to be in equilibrium, it is necessary that for every commodity g, $p_g^H \leq p_g^L$. That is, for each commodity g, the highest price at which *any* trader sells it to *any* consumer is no greater than the lowest price at which *any* trader buys it from *any* consumer. But it is also an equilibrium condition that no trader makes an overall loss from his dealings. The implication is that, in equilibrium, all trade in any given commodity takes place at the same price. This is the Law of One Price. Since equilibrium requires that each trader sells exactly as much of each non-money commodity as she buys, the Law of Supply and Demand must also be a property of equilibrium.

Notice that this argument does not require that consumers' behaviour reveals integrated preferences. Of course, price-sensitivity is a strong assumption, but the kind of rationality it describes is quite different from the (supposed) rationality of neoclassical assumptions about preferences. The idea that, at any given time, people would rather buy given items at lower prices than at higher ones, and that they would rather sell given items at higher prices than at lower ones, does not seem particularly controversial. This is not to say that, as a matter of economic fact, ordinary consumers are always able to identify the most favourable prices in a complex market. Thus, there can be a role for the regulation of markets in ways that make price comparisons easier for consumers; I will say more about this in Section 7.4. Nevertheless, it is significant that one does not need to postulate that consumers are neoclassical in order to explain the Law of One Price and the Law of Supply and Demand.

It might be objected that, although my argument has not required much rationality on the part of consumers, it has attributed a high degree of rationality to traders. Notice, however, that traders have been assumed to be rational only in the pursuit of monetary profit. Further, there is no need to assume that *all* potential traders are motivated in this way; for the arbitrage argument to work, it is sufficient that *some* are. No assumptions have been made about traders' preferences about consumption, since their choices among alternative consumption plans are irrelevant to their role as arbitrageurs.

The most problematic rationality assumption may be hidden in the concept of equilibrium. My argument shows that *equilibrium requires* that the Law of

One Price and the Law of Supply and Demand hold. But should we expect a market to be in a state of equilibrium?

In its essentials, the concept of equilibrium I am using is that of Nash equilibrium in a game played between profit-seeking traders. The alternative strategies between which a trader chooses specify the terms on which she will transact with consumers. The profit she earns depends on the combination of strategies chosen by all traders, given whatever principles (whether rational or not) govern the behaviour of consumers. In Nash equilibrium, each trader is maximizing her profit, given the strategies chosen by other traders. I certainly do not want to claim it to be a general property of games that players' chosen strategies make up a Nash equilibrium. Indeed, I share the view of Michael Bacharach (1987) that, even given the assumption that the players of a one-shot game are fully rational and that this rationality is common knowledge between them, it cannot be proved that for all such games, players' strategy choices will be in Nash equilibrium with one another. Like most economists, however, I take Nash equilibrium to be a reasonable general-purpose assumption for modelling agents with well-defined objectives, playing games that are repeated sufficiently often for those agents to be able to make reliable predictions about the consequences for themselves of choosing alternative strategies. In the present context, what has to be assumed is that, when considering a pricing strategy that appears to have some chance of being profitable, a professional trader is able to predict the quantities in which consumers in the aggregate would choose to trade with her. That does not seem an extravagant assumption, at least for markets in everyday consumption goods.[7]

6.6 The Strong Market Opportunity Theorem

It is now time to state the central theoretical proposition of this chapter:

Strong Market Opportunity Theorem. For every exchange economy $\langle I, G, \mathbf{e}, \mathbf{f}(.)\rangle$ and for every opportunity profile $\mathbf{O}$ for that economy, if $\mathbf{O}$ is a competitive equilibrium, then it satisfies the Strong Interactive Opportunity Criterion.

The proof of this result is surprisingly simple. Consider any exchange economy and any opportunity profile $\mathbf{O}$ for that economy. To initiate a proof by contradiction, suppose that $\mathbf{O}$ is a competitive equilibrium but does not satisfy the Strong Interactive Opportunity Criterion. By the definition of a competitive equilibrium, there exists a price vector $\mathbf{p}$ such that, for each consumer i, O_i is the set of acquisition vectors whose net value in terms of $\mathbf{p}$ is zero. (For the rest of the proof, I will omit 'in terms of $\mathbf{p}$' when using the concept of 'net value'.) By the same definition, the jointly chosen acquisition profile $\mathbf{f}(O)$ is jointly feasible. Since O does not satisfy the Strong Interactive Opportunity Criterion, there must be some non-empty set $S \subseteq I$ of consumers, and some acquisition profile $\mathbf{q}_S$ for S, such that (i) $\mathbf{q}_S$ is jointly feasible for S, (ii) $\mathbf{q}_S$ is not allowable in O_S, *and* (iii) there is no consumer j in S such that q_j is dominated by some element of O_j. But (i) implies that, for each commodity g, the sum of acquisitions $q_{i,g}$ by all members of S is zero. Thus, summing over all consumers i in S, the total net value of their acquisition vectors $\mathbf{q}_i$ is zero. Since acquisition vectors with zero value are always allowable, (ii) implies that there is some consumer i in S for whom the net value of $\mathbf{q}_i$ is *not* zero. And (iii) implies that there is no consumer j in S for whom the net value of $\mathbf{q}_j$ is negative. Since these three implications are mutually inconsistent, the original supposition is false. Thus, the Strong Market Opportunity Theorem is true.[8]

I showed in Section 6.3 that if consumers are neoclassical, every opportunity profile that satisfies the Interactive Opportunity Criterion is also Pareto-optimal. Thus, viewed in the perspective of neoclassical economics, the Strong Market Opportunity Theorem can be interpreted as a stage in the proof of the First Fundamental Theorem of welfare economics—that is, the theorem that every competitive equilibrium of an exchange economy is Pareto-optimal. Under the same neoclassical assumption, every opportunity profile that satisfies the Strong Interactive Opportunity Criterion is also in the core of the economy. In fact, the strategy I have followed in proving the Strong Market Opportunity Theorem is used in many proofs of the First Fundamental Theorem. The close relationship between the two theorems may prompt the suspicion that assumptions equivalent to neoclassical rationality have somehow been smuggled into the Strong Market Opportunity Theorem. I plead Not Guilty.

The truth is that the proof of the First Fundamental Theorem does not depend on any strong assumptions about the rationality of individuals' preferences. In order to define a competitive equilibrium, we have to specify each consumer's opportunity set and the option that he chooses from it in such a way that, taken together, consumers' chosen options are jointly feasible. That need not involve any rationality assumptions. For the purposes of the proof, one has to assume that, for each consumer, the chosen option is at least as preferred as every non-chosen option. But that assumption has content only to the extent that restrictions are imposed on preferences, and all that is necessary for the proof is that preferences satisfy some property of non-satiation (such as that more money is preferred to less).

Of course, when the neoclassical theory of consumer behaviour is considered in its entirety, rationality assumptions *do* have significant implications. But those implications come about because of the crucial assumption that, for any given individual, choices made *in different decision problems* reveal the same preference ordering. That assumption imposes various restrictions on relationships between choices from different opportunity sets.[9] It also implies that if the opportunity set is held constant, an individual's choice from that set does not vary according to the context of the decision problem. As I explained in Chapter 1, the fact that individuals' choices often *are* context-dependent poses fundamental problems for neoclassical welfare economics. But these problems do not impinge on the proof of the First Fundamental Theorem. Rather, they impinge on the normative significance of that theorem. If an individual has stable, context-independent preference orderings over economic outcomes, it may seem reasonable to use the extent to which her preferences are satisfied as a criterion of her well-being. But if individuals' preferences are unstable and context-dependent, it is difficult to interpret the First Fundamental Theorem as saying anything useful about the implications of competitive markets *for well-being*. Nevertheless, it turns out that the analysis that underlies that theorem can be adapted to say something useful about the implications of competitive markets *for opportunity*. In particular, it can be adapted to show the truth of the Strong Market Opportunity Theorem.

6.7 Production

The Strong Market Opportunity Theorem is a theorem about exchange economies. As I said in Section 6.1, models of exchange economies are often used in economics as a first step in understanding markets. To anyone who is not familiar with economics—and, more specifically, with neoclassical economics—this may seem surprising. In an exchange economy, nothing is actually *produced*. There are no firms in the sense of organizations that produce goods or services. The only possible form of entrepreneurship, and hence the only possible source of profit, is arbitrage. How (one might ask) can an investigation of exchange economies help us to understand the workings of real market economies in which most goods come into existence only through a process of production, and production is organized by profit-seeking firms?

Neoclassical economics has a surprisingly simple method for extending the basic model of competitive equilibrium in an exchange economy to include production and firms. This is certainly not the only way in which the basic model can be adapted to take account of production; it is merely the simplest. But variants of it are used in some of the classic proofs of the existence of competitive equilibrium, including that of Kenneth Arrow and Gérard Debreu (1954).[10] This method represents production by means of 'production functions'. A *production function* for a given 'output' commodity specifies the terms on which that commodity can be produced by combining 'input' commodities. A typical production function can be written as $y_g = \varphi_g(x_1, \ldots, x_m)$ where $x_1, \ldots, x_m$ are quantities of the input commodities $1, \ldots, m$, and y_g is the quantity of the output commodity g that can be produced by combining those inputs. A *firm* can then be represented as an economic agent that has access to a production function, can buy inputs at their market prices, transform these into output, and sell that output at its market price. In a model of this kind, the role of firms is very similar to that of arbitrageurs in an exchange economy. Just as arbitrageurs seek to buy cheap and sell dear, firms seek to maximize profit—that is, to maximize the excess of revenue from the sale of output over expenditure on inputs. Adapting a distinction I introduced in Section 6.2, one can think of the activities of firms as part of the workings of a 'trading institution' which intermediates transactions between 'consumers'. At the start of the trading period, commodities (such as labour, raw materials, land, and physical capital) that can be used as inputs to production are owned by consumers. Firms buy their inputs from, and sell their outputs to, consumers.

Competitive equilibrium in an exchange economy is defined by the Law of One Price and the Law of Supply and Demand. That definition extends straightforwardly to the kind of model I have just described. However, it is not so easy to extend the argument that explains *why* profit-seeking by arbitrageurs induces competitive equilibrium. As I explained in Section 6.5, competitive equilibrium in an exchange economy can be interpreted as a state of Nash equilibrium among profit-seeking arbitrageurs. The difficulty is that that interpretation depends on the assumption that each arbitrageur can trade in commodities *on any scale*. Thus, if any consumer is buying any quantity of any commodity at a price higher than the price at which some other consumer is selling any quantity of it, there is an arbitrage opportunity to be exploited. If we are to extend this argument to an economy with production, we have to interpret 'arbitrage' as including activities than involve production. That raises the question of whether productive activities can be replicated on different scales.

From a modelling point of view, the simplest way of dealing with this problem (or, at least, of shunting it to one side) is to assume that production functions have constant returns to scale. To say that a production function $\phi_g(x_1, \ldots, x_m)$ has constant returns to scale is to say that, for any positive number a, $\phi_g(ax_1, \ldots, ax_m) = a\phi_g(x_1, \ldots, x_m)$. In words: if all inputs are multiplied by some constant, output is multiplied by the same constant. Under this assumption, any firm can replicate the activities of any other firm on any scale. Thus, there can be equilibrium in an economy with many profit-maximizing firms only if every firm makes zero profit, and so competitive equilibrium can sensibly be defined in terms of the Law of One Price and the Law of Supply and Demand. It is well known that, if consumers have neoclassical preferences and if production functions have constant returns to scale, the First Fundamental Theorem holds for economies with production: every competitive equilibrium in such an economy is Pareto-optimal.

It should be no surprise that an analogue of the Strong Market Opportunity Theorem holds too: provided that production functions have constant returns to scale, the Strong Interactive Opportunity Criterion is satisfied in every competitive equilibrium, whether or not consumers act on integrated preferences. As the proof of this result follows the same logic as that of the Strong Market Opportunity Theorem, I do not present it here. In Section 7.5 I will consider the implications of relaxing the assumption of constant returns to scale.

6.8 Storage Economies

Despite what I said in Section 6.6 in support of my plea of Not Guilty, there is something slightly unsatisfactory about using the model of a one-period economy when discussing how to reconcile normative and behavioural economics.[11] To prove the Strong Market Opportunity Theorem, we need to examine only a single (but typical) competitive equilibrium state of an exchange economy. But, looking only at such a state, we can never see any evidence of non-integrated preferences. All we see of the behaviour of any individual is that he chooses one option from an opportunity set which does not contain any dominated options. For all we know, the individual may be a neoclassical consumer choosing the option that ranks highest in a consistent preference ordering. For the reasons I explained in Section 6.6, that does not detract from the significance of the Strong Market Opportunity Theorem. But it detaches the theorem from any discussion of how competitive markets cater to non-integrated preferences.

It is therefore illuminating to consider the properties of competitive markets in economies in which non-integrated preferences, if they exist, have more visible consequences. For this purpose, it is useful to work with models of *storage economies* (a concept developed by McQuillin and Sugden, 2012). Roughly speaking, a storage economy is a multi-period exchange economy. As in a one-period exchange economy, the total stock of each commodity is fixed and each unit of this stock is ultimately consumed by someone. There are no storage costs. In a storage economy, however, individuals may have opportunities to choose how this consumption is distributed over periods, and transfers of claims from individual to individual may take place in more than one period. A model of a storage economy can represent the possibility that an individual changes his mind between one period and another, making a choice in one period which he later reverses. In this section, I generalize the analysis presented in Sections 6.2 to 6.6 so that it applies to storage economies. I explain how competitive equilibrium can be defined for such economies, and show that every competitive equilibrium of a storage economy satisfies a generalized form of the Strong Interactive Opportunity Criterion.

Let me concede straight away that it would be a huge leap of faith to maintain that, with respect to transactions across time periods, there is a general tendency for market economies to gravitate to states of competitive equilibrium. As I argued in Section 6.5, competitive equilibrium can be interpreted as a Nash equilibrium among profit-seeking arbitrageurs, and Nash equilibrium is best understood as a way of modelling general tendencies of behaviour in games that are repeated sufficiently often for players to make reliable predictions about the effects of alternative strategy choices. If one is considering time scales over which there may be changes in knowledge, technology, or tastes, or unpredictable shocks such as wars and revolutions, it would be hard to justify the assumption that market participants can predict future prices. (Indeed, the long-run unpredictability of markets will be important for an argument I develop in Chapter 8.) I will use storage economy models only to investigate how markets respond to consumers who act on *predictably* non-integrated preferences. In order to represent the possibility that a consumer may change his mind about the trades he wants to make, I need a model in which trade can take place in more than one period. If the changes of mind that are being modelled are the product of reliable psychological mechanisms, it seems reasonable to assume that profit-seeking traders can predict how these changes of mind will affect the terms on which consumers are willing to trade with them.

The concept of a storage economy has been deliberately constructed to maintain as close an analogy as possible with an exchange economy, while allowing economic decisions to have a temporal dimension. The theoretical principles underlying the analysis that follows are essentially the same as those developed in previous sections. However, because of the need to refer to a sequence of periods rather than just one, the notation becomes rather cumbersome. Readers who prefer to avoid mathematical formalism might want to go straight to Section 6.9, which uses a very simple storage economy to illustrate how competitive markets provide opportunity when individuals act on preferences that are not consistent over time.

Formally, a model of a storage economy has non-empty sets $I = \{1, \ldots, n\}$ of *consumers*, $G = \{1, \ldots, m\}$ of infinitely divisible *commodities*, and $T = \{1, \ldots, z\}$ of *periods*. Typical consumers will be referred to as i and j, a typical commodity as g, and a typical period as t. Each consumer i enters the economy in period 1 with an *endowment* of some quantity $e_{i,g}$ of *claims* on each commodity g.[12] Individual endowments may be positive or zero, but not negative; for each commodity, the sum of all consumers' endowments is strictly positive. Endowment vectors e_i and the endowment profile e are defined as in Section 6.2. For each commodity g, the sum of all consumers' endowments constitutes the stock of that commodity in the economy. A storage economy is described by the quintuple $\langle I, G, T, \mathbf{e}, \mathbf{f}(.) \rangle$, where $\mathbf{f}(.)$ (to be defined later), specifies the choices that consumers make in every period, given whatever sequences of opportunities are available to them. An exchange economy can be understood as the special case of a storage economy in which $T = \{1\}$.

Each consumer i enters each period t with an *inheritance* $r^t_{i,g}$ of claims on each good g; the inheritance vector $(r^t_{i,1}, \ldots, r^t_{i,m})$ is written as $\mathbf{r}^t_i$. In period 1, inheritances are equal to endowments (that is, for each consumer i, $\mathbf{r}^1_i = \mathbf{e}_i$). As I will explain in a moment, inheritances in each period $t = 2, \ldots z$ depend on what has happened in previous periods. In each period t, each individual i faces a *t-period opportunity set* O^t_i. The elements of this set are alternative *t-period behaviours*. A *t-period behaviour* for consumer i is an array $\mathbf{b}^t_i = (\mathbf{q}^t_i, \mathbf{x}^t_i)$, where $\mathbf{q}^t_i = (q^t_{i,1}, \ldots, q^t_{i,m})$ is a vector of *acquisitions* of commodities by i in period t and $\mathbf{x}^t_i = (x^t_{i,1}, \ldots, x^t_{i,m})$ is a vector of *consumption* of commodities by i in period t. In order for an array $(\mathbf{q}^t_i, \mathbf{x}^t_i)$ to count as a 't-period behaviour', it must satisfy the following conditions. First, as in my analysis of an exchange economy, I require that consumers' holdings of claims can never be negative. Thus, for all i, g, and t, $q^t_{i,g} \geq -r^t_{i,g}$. Second, consumption cannot be negative. Thus, for all i, g, and t, $x^t_{i,g} \geq 0$. Third, I interpret consumption of commodity g by consumer i in period t as something that i's opportunity set might allow him to do *with his current holdings* of that commodity. I therefore require that consumption never exceeds current holdings. Thus, for all i, g, and t, $x^t_{i,g} \leq r^t_{i,g} + q^t_{i,g}$. Finally, I require that in the final period z, all remaining holdings are consumed. Thus, for all i and g, $x^z_{i,g} = r^z_{i,g} + q^z_{i,g}$.

I now explain how inheritances are determined. My previous definitions imply that, in each period $t = 1, \ldots, z - 1$, a consumer may consume less than (but no more than) his current holdings of claims on a commodity g. I will say that claims that are converted into consumption in period t are *retired* in that period. Claims that are held by consumer i in period t but *not* retired in that period make up i's inheritance in the following period. Thus, for all $t = 1, \ldots, z - 1$ and for all i and g, $r^{t+1}_{i,g} = r^t_{i,g} + q^t_{i,g} - x^t_{i,g}$.

As in my analysis of exchange economies, I will say that opportunities are provided to consumers by some 'trading institution'. In an environment in which individuals can make consumption decisions over time, a useful analysis needs to allow the trading institution to condition an individual's opportunity set in one period on his decisions in previous periods. (Otherwise, individuals could not be given opportunities to choose between current and deferred consumption.) I therefore define the concept of a *t-period opportunity function*. For a given consumer i and a given period t, a *t-period opportunity function*, denoted by O^t_i, assigns a *t-period opportunity set to every possible t-period inheritance vector $\mathbf{r}^t_i$. The opportunities that are made available to any consumer i are fully determined by the *opportunity function sequence* $O_i = (O^1_i, \ldots, O^z_i)$. (Arrays that include one object for each period will be called 'sequences'.) In period 1 consumer i faces the opportunity set $O^1_i(\mathbf{r}^1_i)$, where

$\mathbf{r}^1_i$ is the endowment vector $\mathbf{e}_i$. He chooses a period-1 behaviour from this set. This behaviour determines his holdings of non-retired claims at the end of period 1, and hence his period-2 inheritance vector $\mathbf{r}^2_i$. So in period 2, consumer i faces the opportunity set $O^2_i(\mathbf{r}^2)$. And so on.

For a given storage economy, the opportunities made available to all consumers in all periods can be described by a profile $\mathbf{O} = (\mathbf{O}_1, \dots, \mathbf{O}_n)$ of opportunity function sequences. Any such profile is a *regime*. I now consider how the normative criteria presented in Sections 6.3 and 6.4 might be generalized to apply to regimes in a storage economy.

For any consumer i, I define a *behaviour sequence* for that consumer as a sequence $\mathbf{b}_i = (\mathbf{b}^1_i, \dots, \mathbf{b}^z_i)$, where each $\mathbf{b}^t_i$ is a t-period behaviour. With respect to a given regime $\mathbf{O}$, a behaviour sequence $\mathbf{b}_i$ is *allowable* in $\mathbf{O}_i$ if it is the outcome of a sequence of choices that are consistent with the opportunities offered by $\mathbf{O}_i$. (That is, $\mathbf{b}^1_i$ is an element of the period-1 opportunity set $O^1_i(\mathbf{e}_i)$; $\mathbf{b}^2_i$ is an element of the period-2 opportunity set $O^2_i(\mathbf{r}^2_i)$, where $\mathbf{r}^2_i$ is the inheritance vector that results from i's period-1 choice of $\mathbf{b}^1_i$; and so on.) For a given regime, the set of behaviour sequences for i that are allowable in that regime is i's *overall opportunity set*. I will say that a behaviour profile $\mathbf{b} = (\mathbf{b}_1, \dots, \mathbf{b}_n)$ is allowable in $\mathbf{O}$ if each $\mathbf{b}_i$ is allowable in $\mathbf{O}_i$.

Generalizing an assumption that I made about exchange economies, I assume that, for any given storage economy, for any given regime $\mathbf{O}$, and for any given consumer i, the chosen behaviour sequence is uniquely determined. I will write this behaviour sequence as $\mathbf{f}_i(\mathbf{O})$. The chosen behaviour profile $[\mathbf{f}_1(\mathbf{O}), \dots, \mathbf{f}_n(\mathbf{O})]$ will be written as $\mathbf{f}(\mathbf{O})$. This is the function $\mathbf{f}(.)$ that appears in the definition of a storage economy.

The concept of 'joint feasibility' can be generalized so that it applies to behaviour profiles. I will say that a behaviour profile is *jointly feasible* in a given storage economy if, for each commodity separately, total consumption (summed over all periods) is equal to the total of consumers' endowments. This definition has an implication which will be significant for my normative analysis of markets. To say that total consumption of some commodity is equal to total endowments is necessarily to say that acquisitions of that commodity, by all consumers *in all periods taken together*, sum to zero. (That follows from the fact that, for each consumer separately but summing over all periods, consumption of any commodity is equal to endowments plus acquisitions.) However, this does *not* imply that acquisitions of the commodity by all consumers *in each period considered separately* sum to zero. Thus, when consumers implement a jointly feasible behaviour profile, there can be periods in which they hold claims on specific commodities that are not fully backed by currently-existing stocks of those commodities. Joint feasibility requires only that the trading institution is able to honour claims *when the holders of those claims choose to convert them into consumption*.

One way of dramatizing this idea is to imagine that the economy's stocks of commodities are held in *repositories* operated by the trading institution. A claim on a commodity is an entry in the accounts of some repository, in much the same way that bank balances are entries in the accounts of a bank. When a consumer 'acquires' or 'disposes of' a claim, all that happens is that a positive or negative entry is made in some account of his. However, if and when he converts a claim into consumption, the trading institution does not merely debit his account; the corresponding physical quantity is taken from a respository and delivered to him. (Compare a cash withdrawal from a bank.) To say that a behaviour profile is jointly feasible is to say that, if consumers implement that profile, the trading institution is always able to deliver when called on to do so. If the trading institution is interpreted as the combined activities of a population of profit-seeking traders, different traders should be understood as operating different repositories and using different sets of accounts: any claim on a commodity is a claim against a specific trader.

Next, I need to generalize the concept of 'dominance'. As in my analysis of exchange economies, I treat commodity 1 (*money*) as the medium of exchange, and interpret it as having positive value for all consumers in all periods. Consider any consumer i and any two behaviour sequences $\mathbf{b}_i$ and $\mathbf{b}'_i$. I will say that $\mathbf{b}'_i$ *dominates* $\mathbf{b}_i$ if (i) the two sequences differ only in terms of acquisition and consumption of money, (ii) in every period, the net change in i's holding of money (i.e. acquisition minus consumption) is the same in both sequences, (iii) in all periods, consumption of money is at least as great in $\mathbf{b}'_i$ as in $\mathbf{b}_i$, and (iv) there is at least one period in which consumption of money is strictly greater in $\mathbf{b}'_i$ than in $\mathbf{b}_i$. Notice that, for this dominance relationship to hold, $\mathbf{b}'_i$ must be unambiguously more desirable than $\mathbf{b}_i$ in *every* period in which the two sequences differ. Thus, to say that individuals want to avoid choosing dominated behaviour sequences is to say only that, in each period *considered in isolation*, they attach positive value to money. It is not to say that they want to avoid sequences of choices which, *in combination*, result in losses of money. For example, recall the case of Jane in Section 5.5. In changing her mind between one period and the next, she makes a sequence of choices which results in an unambiguous loss of money relative to the outcome of an alternative sequence that was available to her. But, although she buys dear in one period and sells cheap in another, she does not pay an unnecessarily high price *when she buys* or accept an unnecessarily low price *when she sells*. Thus, her chosen behaviour sequence is not dominated in the sense that I have defined.

I can now generalize the Interactive Opportunity Criterion:

Generalized Interactive Opportunity Criterion. For a given storage economy, a regime $\mathbf{O}$ satisfies the Generalized Interactive Opportunity Criterion *if*

(i) the jointly chosen behaviour profile $f(O)$ is jointly feasible *and* (ii) for every jointly feasible behaviour profile b, *either* b is allowable in O *or* there is some consumer j such that b_j is dominated by some behaviour sequence that is allowable in the opportunity function sequence O_j.

To say that a regime satisfies the Generalized Interactive Opportunity Criterion is to say, of every transaction that is feasible for all consumers collectively and is non-dominated for each consumer separately, that each consumer's component of that transaction is an element of his overall opportunity set. In this context, a 'transaction' is any combination of the acquisitions, disbursements, and retirements of claims made by all consumers in all periods.

The Strong Interactive Opportunity Criterion can be generalized in a similar way. Recall that the distinctive feature of the Strong form of the Interactive Opportunity Criterion is that it considers 'sub-economies' that are populated by subsets of the set of all consumers, each member of that population having the same endowment vector as in the original economy. It is straightforward to apply this idea to storage economies. Consider any storage economy $\langle I, G, T, \mathbf{e}, \mathbf{f}(.)\rangle$. Let $S \subseteq I$ be any non-empty set of consumers. For any regime O, the implications of that regime for S are described by the array O_S of opportunity function sequences, one such sequence for each member of S. A *behaviour profile for S*, denoted b_S, is an array of behaviour sequences b_i, one for each consumer i in S. Such a profile is *allowable in O_S* if each of its component sequences b_i is allowable in O_i. The generalized criterion is:

Generalized Strong Interactive Opportunity Criterion. For a given storage economy, a regime O satisfies the Strong Interactive Opportunity Criterion *if* (i) the chosen behaviour profile $f(O)$ is jointly feasible *and* (ii) for every non-empty set of consumers $S \subseteq I$, for every jointly feasible behaviour profile b_S for S, *either* b_S is allowable in O_S *or* there is some consumer j in S such that b_j is dominated by some behaviour sequence that is allowable in O_j.

The next step is to generalize the definition of competitive equilibrium. For any consumer i, any behaviour sequence b_i and any price vector $\mathbf{p}$, I define the *net value* of b_i in terms of $\mathbf{p}$ as the total money value of the acquisitions described by b_i, summed over all periods and valued at the prices $\mathbf{p}$. Notice that $\mathbf{p}$ is not dated: it is one vector of prices that applies to all periods. Then competitive equilibrium for a storage economy can be defined as follows:

Competitive equilibrium in a storage economy. For a given storage economy, a regime O is a competitive equilibrium *if* (i) there is a *price vector* $\mathbf{p}$ such that, for each consumer i, i's overall opportunity set is the set of behaviour sequences for i whose net value in terms of $\mathbf{p}$ is zero *and* (ii) the chosen behaviour profile $f(O)$ is jointly feasible.

This definition requires that, for each non-money commodity, all transactions between that commodity and money *in all periods* take place at the same rate of exchange. In Section 6.5 I argued that if all transactions are mediated by profit-seeking traders, if there is free entry to and free exit from this activity and if consumers are price-sensitive, then equilibrium requires the Law of One Price to hold in a one-period economy. The same argument implies that, in equilibrium, this Law holds *in any given period* of a storage economy. But why must the price of a given commodity be the same in *different* periods? The answer is that if there are no storage costs and if the rate of exchange between some commodity and money is different in different periods, there is an opportunity for profitable arbitrage: a trader can buy claims on the commodity at the lower price and sell them at the higher price.

Here I am making a crucial assumption, that traders are able to sell short. In terms of the story of repositories, imagine that, at the start of period 1, consumers' endowments are held in traders' repositories. Consumers merely hold claims on the commodities with which they are endowed. A claim is a promissory note written by a trader: the trader promises to deliver the commodity if and when the holder of the claim chooses to convert it into consumption. A trader sells short by selling promises that are not backed by physical quantities in her repository. Indeed, a trader can sell such promises without having a repository at all. (That is how there can be free entry into the activity of trading.) For example, suppose that claims on some non-money commodity g are traded in both period 1 and period 2. Suppose that the price of these claims were higher in period 1 than in period 2. A trader could make a pure profit by selling claims in period 1 to consumers who chose not to convert them into consumption in that period, and then buying back the same quantity of claims at a lower price in period 2.

Notice that when a trader sells short, the liabilities she incurs (the value of the commodities she is promising to deliver) are backed by the additional money that she holds as a result of the sale. If there is a single price vector $\mathbf{p}$ that applies in all periods, and if in every period it is possible to buy and sell freely at those prices, the value of the liabilities of short-selling traders are always exactly covered by the value of their assets. That is another way of saying that, in competitive equilibrium, traders can always honour their promissory notes. Out of equilibrium, however, short-selling can generate profits and losses from arbitrage; under the assumptions of my model, traders who make losses will not be able to honour all their promises.[13]

I can now generalize the Strong Market Opportunity Theorem:

Generalized Strong Market Opportunity Theorem. For every storage economy $\langle I, G, T, \mathbf{e}, \mathbf{f}(.)\rangle$ and for every regime $\mathbf{O}$ for that economy, if $\mathbf{O}$ is a competitive equilibrium, then it satisfies the Generalized Strong Interactive Opportunity Criterion.

This result can be proved by a simple adaptation of the proof of the Strong Market Opportunity Theorem, given in Section 6.6. The original proof works by summing net acquisitions of given commodities across consumers and by summing given consumers' net acquisitions of different commodities, valued at equilibrium prices. In the generalized proof, the corresponding summations are made across all periods. From now on, unless there a specific reason to distinguish the original Strong Market Opportunity Theorem from the generalized version, I will refer to the two theorems collectively as the 'Market Opportunity Theorems'.

6.9 The Wine Economy and the Responsible Agent

One of my reasons for presenting the model of a storage economy was to show how competitive equilibrium can involve short-selling. The essential feature of short-selling is that an agent sells a promise to perform an action whose feasibility depends on future market conditions that are outside that agent's control. In varying degrees, this feature is present in most kinds of real-world borrowing. For example, a person who takes out a mortgage to buy a house promises to repay the amount borrowed, with interest. Typically, that promise is secured by the borrower's expected future employment income and by the value of the house in the event of a default, but there is no guarantee that future wage levels and property prices will allow the promise to be kept. Short-selling in this generic sense is an essential part of the mechanism by which competitive markets provide opportunities to individuals whose preferences are non-integrated. I will illustrate this claim by using a model of a very simple storage economy—the *wine economy* analysed by McQuillin and Sugden (2012).

This storage economy has two or more identical consumers, two periods, and two commodities—*money* (commodity 1) and *wine* (commodity 2). Each consumer is endowed with one unit of each commodity. Thus, the economy is defined by $\langle I, G, T, \mathbf{e}, \mathbf{f}(.) \rangle$ where $I = \{1, \ldots, n\}$ with $n \geq 2$, $G = \{1, 2\}$, $T = \{1, 2\}$ and, for each consumer i, $\mathbf{e}_i = (1, 1)$. The assumptions about consumer behaviour that are encoded in $\mathbf{f}(.)$ will be explained in the following paragraph. In competitive equilibrium there is a single money price p_2 at which wine can be bought and sold in both periods.

Consumers are not rational in the neoclassical sense. Instead, they have preferences that are dynamically inconsistent. Specifically, their willingness to pay money for wine is greater in period 2 than in period 1. In period 1, they act myopically, choosing their end-of-period holdings of the two commodities as if these holdings would constitute their period-2 consumption (naïvely ignoring the opportunities for further trade that they will face in period 2). In choosing these holdings, they act on their period-1 preferences, rather than on the preferences on which they will in fact wish to act in period 2. I leave open the question of whether this represents a forecasting error (they do not realize that their preferences will change) or an attempt to commit their period-2 selves to act on their period-1 preferences.

I represent this scenario in the following numerical model. In period 1, each consumer i has preferences over alternative consumption sequences $x_i = (x^1_i, \ x^2_i)$ where $x^1_i = (x^1_{i,1}, \ x^1_{i,2})$ and $x^2_i = (x^2_{i,1}, \ x^2_{i,2})$ are consumption vectors for periods 1 and 2. I assume that these preferences are represented by the utility function

$$u^1_i = 0.5[0.75 \ \ln(x^1_{i,1}) + 0.25 \ \ln(x^1_{i,2})] \tag{1}$$
$$+ 0.5[0.75 \ \ln(x^2_{i,1}) + 0.25 \ \ln(x^2_{i,2})].$$

This equation has a very simple interpretation. Given that the price of wine in both periods is p_2, the consumer's endowment has a market value of $1 + p_2$. This constitutes a 'budget' which he can allocate on consumption in the two periods. If he plans to maximize the value of this utility function, then (irrespective of the value of p_2) he will divide his budget equally between consumption in the two periods. Within each period, three-quarters of the total value of his planned consumption will be consumption of money and one-quarter will be consumption of wine. Thus, planned consumption of money is given by $x^1_{i,1} = x^2_{i,1} = (1 + p_2)/8$ and planned consumption of wine is given by $x^1_{i,2} = x^2_{i,2} = 3(1 + p_2)/8p_2$.

In period 2, each consumer i has preferences over alternative period-2 consumption vectors x^2_i. These preferences are represented by the utility function

$$u^2_i = 0.25 \ \ln(x^2_{i,1}) + 0.75 \ \ln(x^2_{i,2}) \tag{2}$$

Notice that, relative to the period-1 utility function, 0.75 and 0.25 have been transposed, indicating an increase in willingness to pay for wine. Given the consumer's decisions in period 1, as described in the previous paragraph, his period-2 inheritance has a total value of $(1 + p_2)/2$. If he then maximizes the value of the utility function (2), one-quarter of the value of his period-2 consumption will be consumption of money and three-quarter will be consumption of wine. Thus, actual consumption of money and wine in period 2 is given by $x^2_{i,1} = (1 + p_2)/8$ and $x^2_{i,2} = 3(1 + p_2)/8p_2$.

The equilibrium value of p_2 is defined by the condition that the chosen behaviour profile is jointly feasible. Since all consumers are identical, this is equivalent to the condition that each individual's chosen consumption of wine, summed over the two periods, is equal to his endowment—that is,

$(1 + p_2)/2p_2 = 1$, which implies $p_2 = 1$. Thus, each individual's *actual* consumption sequence is given by $x^1_{i,1} = 3/4$, $x^1_{i,2} = 1/4$, $x^2_{i,1} = 1/4$, $x^2_{i,2} = 3/4$. In period 1, however, each individual's *planned* consumption sequence is $x^1_{i,1} = 3/4$, $x^1_{i,2} = 1/4$, $x^2_{i,1} = 3/4$, $x^2_{i,2} = 1/4$. Since each consumer's holdings of each commodity at the end of period 1 are equal to his planned consumption in period 2, each consumer must sell 1/2 unit of claims on wine in period 1, receiving in return 1/2 unit of claims on money. This trade must then be reversed in period 2. This reversal is the visible evidence of consumers' dynamic inconsistency.

This pattern of trade implies that, at the start of period 2, consumers' holdings of claims on commodities are not exactly backed by remaining stocks. Since each of the n individuals consumed 1/4 unit of wine in period 1, the remaining stock of wine is $3n/4$, but consumers hold claims on only $n/4$ units. Conversely, the remaining stock of money is only $n/4$, but consumers hold claims on $3n/4$ units. This imbalance is possible only if the trading institution has made promises to deliver money that it would be unable to honour, were it called on to do so. In other words, it has taken a position that is short on money and long on wine. It has done this in the expectation that, in period 2, consumers will use some of their claims on money to pay for consumption of wine. If this expectation is correct (as, in the model, it is), the institution will be able to honour all those demands that are in fact made on it.

The significance of this story emerges when one recalls that a competitive equilibrium of a storage economy satisfies the Generalized Strong Interactive Opportunity Criterion. The implication is that, if a trading institution is to make available to individuals all opportunities for jointly feasible transactions, there are situations in which some form of short-selling is required. The fundamental reason for this is easy to explain. The concept of a transaction, as I have defined it, implicitly includes transactions between an individual in one period and *the same individual* in a different period. In the wine economy, for example, a representative consumer wants to sell 1/2 unit of claims on wine in period 1 at a price of 1 and to buy the same quantity at the same price in period 2. This is a jointly feasible transaction in the sub-economy that contains only that consumer. In competitive equilibrium, the regime allows the consumer to carry out both components of this one-person transaction. What is more, it allows him to carry out the period-1 component without requiring him to make any commitment to carry out the period-2 component. This is possible only because the trading institution offers to take the other side of each of these components. Since the consumer makes no commitment to complete the transaction, this offer amounts to a kind of short-selling.

Can an individual value this kind of opportunity? I maintain that the answer is 'Yes', for the reasons I gave in Chapter 5. But I must remind the reader that my argument rests on a particular normative understanding of the relationship between an individual's actions in different periods, encapsulated in the idea of the 'continuing person'. The wine economy illustrates some of the differences between this approach and more conventional models of 'multiple selves'.

A conventional multiple-selves approach would treat the utility functions (1) and (2) as representing the preferences of two different 'selves' of the representative consumer—the period-1 self and the period-2 self. Each of these selves would be treated as having its own preferences about consumption in period 2, and each set of preferences would be treated as potentially relevant for an assessment of the welfare that the consumer derives from that consumption. Since the preferences of the two selves are different, that assessment would require some kind of adjudication between them. In such an analysis, the competitive equilibrium regime (as I have defined it) would not necessarily be judged optimal. For example, compare the *precommitment* regime in which trade takes place only in period 1, and all such trade takes place at a single market-clearing price p'_2. Since (by assumption) consumers are myopic, the preferences of the period-2 self have no effect on trade in this regime. It is easy to work out that $p'_2 = 1/3$, and that each individual's consumption sequence is given by $x^1_{i,1} = x^1_{i,2} = x^2_{i,1} = x^2_{i,2} = 1/2$. If we confine attention to feasible solutions which treat all consumers alike, this is the solution that maximizes period-1 utility. Thus, if the preferences of the period-1 self were deemed to be the consumer's latent preferences, each consumer could be said to have a latent preference for the outcome of the precommitment regime rather than that of competitive equilibrium.

Nevertheless, the precommitment regime fails to make available to consumers a behaviour profile (namely, the profile that is chosen in competitive equilibrium) that is jointly feasible and non-dominated. What it fails to make available is not the profile of *consumption* that is chosen in competitive equilibrium. (Each consumer can arrive at his component of that profile without engaging in trade at all.) It fails to make available a profile of *net acquisitions* in which consumers sell claims on wine in period 1 and reverse that trade in period 2. As I argued in Section 5.5 in relation to the example of Jane, if individual agency is interpreted as a continuing locus of responsibility, an opportunity to act on a change of mind is a genuine opportunity. In the competitive equilibrium of the wine economy, each consumer wants to sell claims on wine in period 1 and wants to buy claims on wine in period 2. In allowing these trades, competitive equilibrium allows continuing persons to do what they want to do, when they want to do it.

6.10 How the Invisible Hand Works

The invisible hand of Adam Smith's *Wealth of Nations* (1776/1976: 456) works through the behaviour of 'merchants'. We are told that a typical merchant 'intends only his own gain', but that '[b]y pursuing his own interest he frequently promotes that of the society more effectually than when he really intends to promote it'. Some modern commentators are sceptical about the ways in which Smith's invisible hand argument is used in economics: they see the argument (at least in the form in which it is now used) as an implausible and ideologically motivated claim about the socially beneficial effects of economic selfishness. A characteristic example of this response can be found in Richard Layard's (2005) advocacy of making happiness the goal of public policy. Bemoaning the growth of 'the non-philosophy of rampant individualism', Layard associates this way of thinking with what he claims are now 'the two dominant ideas in the West'—Charles Darwin's concept of natural selection and Smith's invisible hand:

> From Darwin's theory of evolution many people now conclude that to survive you have to be selfish. . . . From Adam Smith they also learn, conveniently, that even if everyone is completely selfish, things will actually turn out for the best: free contracts between independent agents will produce the greatest possible happiness. (Layard, 2005: 91–2)

Layard is inviting us to think that the mechanism by which the selfishness of merchants is supposed to promote the interest of society is unexplained and mysterious. In this chapter I have presented a model in which the actions of profit-seeking traders promote consumers' collective interest in the existence of opportunity. But, I maintain, there is nothing mysterious about this invisible-hand mechanism.

In my model of a storage economy, the socially valuable but unintended consequence of traders' actions is the provision of opportunities that satisfy the Generalized Strong Interactive Opportunity Criterion. That criterion requires that, for every set of consumers, for every combination of acquisitions, disposals, and retirements of claims that is jointly feasible for those consumers collectively and that all of them could plausibly want to participate in, each consumer's component of that combination is made available to him as a potential object of choice. Putting this in different words, let us say that a person is willing to pay for a commodity if he is willing to give up what would induce others (or, as in the case of the wine economy, himself at another point in time) to supply it. Then to say that the Generalized Strong Interactive Opportunity Criterion is satisfied is to say that each consumer is able to get whatever he wants and is willing to pay for, when he wants it and is willing to pay for it. The idea that profit-seeking traders might provide this kind of opportunity is hardly mysterious.

Consider what is implied by the proposition that, for some storage economy and some regime, the Generalized Strong Interactive Opportunity Criterion does *not* hold. If that is so, we can identify some feasible potential transaction involving some set of consumers, each of whom might plausibly want to participate in it; and we also know that, even if all of them wanted to participate in it, they would not be able to do so. But if all of them *did* want to participate in the transaction and were willing to pay to do so, that would be just the kind of arbitrage opportunity that profit-seeking traders look for.

The concept of an arbitrage opportunity can be viewed in two different ways. From the viewpoint of an alert trader who intends only her own gain, it is an opportunity for pure profit—an economic location at which a 'money pump' might be set up to extract value from potential trading partners. Alternatively, leaving the trader out of the picture, one might take the viewpoint of the parties to the potential transaction. From their viewpoint, an arbitrage opportunity is an opportunity for mutual benefit. It is in the interest of society, one might say (and a contractarian *would* say) that such opportunities are realized. But these are just different ways of describing the same phenomenon.

In simple terms, an arbitrage opportunity arises when some consumers are willing to sell something at a lower price than other consumers (or the same consumers at another time) are willing to pay to buy it. The excess of willingness to pay over willingness to accept constitutes a surplus that can be realized through a transaction between buyers and sellers. To say that this surplus is strictly positive is to say that there is an opportunity for a mutually beneficial transaction. At the same time, the surplus is a source of value that a trader can try to appropriate by acting as an intermediary between the buyers and the sellers. Thus, a trader who takes advantage of an arbitrage opportunity makes a pure profit *and* brokers a mutually beneficial transaction. In competitive equilibrium, however, there are no pure profits to be earned from arbitrage: pure profit is competed away in the process by which traders undercut one another in an attempt to appropriate surplus. Thus, if traders act on the intention of making profits from arbitrage, the unintended consequence of their actions is the facilitation of mutually beneficial transactions between consumers on terms which do not include any appropriation of surplus by intermediaries.

In saying that this invisible-hand mechanism is not mysterious, I am referring only to what happens in the world of my model. As I made clear at the outset, this chapter has been concerned with a highly stylized model of a market economy, rather than with any kind of realistic description of one. In Chapter 7, I will consider some of the many ways in which real market economies differ from this model, how far these differences affect the conclusions that can be drawn about the beneficial consequences of markets, and whether the workings of the invisible hand need to be supplemented by governmental regulation. Nevertheless, generations of economists have seen the analysis of simple models of exchange economies as a useful first step in understanding how real markets work. They have seen the First Fundamental Theorem of welfare economics, and the extension to that theorem that shows that every competitive equilibrium of an exchange economy is in the core, as telling us something, however sketchily, about normatively significant properties of real competitive markets. Given this tradition of economic analysis, it is surely useful to know that analogues of these results can be proved without assuming that individuals act on integrated preferences.

It is often said that theoretical models in economics can be valuable by providing new and insightful ways of 'seeing' the world. Having understood the role that some mechanism plays in an abstract model, one starts to notice real-world phenomena that are similar to those in the model, and to entertain the possibility that something like the mechanism in the model is at work in the real world. Even if no claims to realistic description have been made on behalf of the model, it may help us to discover genuine empirical regularities or (as a methodological realist would say) to discover real causal mechanisms. I believe that this is the case for the invisible-hand mechanism of my model. It allows us to see the fundamental truth in the idea that markets are, at the same time, both money pumps and networks of mutually beneficial transactions. And it allows us to see how, by virtue of the duality between these two properties, profit-seeking by competing arbitrageurs generates opportunities for individuals to get whatever they want and are willing to pay for—whether or not those individuals are rational according to the standards of neoclassical theory.

7

Regulation

I began this book with a discussion of John Stuart Mill's conception of the market as a 'community of advantage'. This idea, I said, encapsulates three core components of a liberal tradition of economic thought: that, in a well-ordered society, cooperation for mutual benefit is a governing principle of social life; that a competitive market is a network of mutually advantageous transactions; and that, in cooperative relationships, it is for each individual to judge what counts as his or her benefit. In Chapter 6, I developed simple models of exchange and storage economies to illustrate how, under idealized conditions but irrespective of whether or not individuals act on integrated preferences, the market promotes transactions that are mutually advantageous in Mill's sense. In this chapter, I will relax some of these idealizations. I will consider what role governmental regulation can play in helping to provide individuals with opportunities for mutually beneficial cooperation.

In keeping with the objectives of this book, my concern will be with the implications of taking a contractarian viewpoint rather than that of a social planner, and of using opportunity rather than preference satisfaction as a normative criterion. Many important aspects of market regulation are orthogonal to these concerns. I will refer to some of these aspects in Section 7.1, but I will not say much about them. This is not because they are not important, but because I have no need to add to what is already well known in economics. In Sections 7.2 to 7.4, I will consider arguments for regulation that respond to problems that result from individuals having non-integrated preferences. In Sections 7.5 to 7.7, I will consider forms of regulation that are usually thought to require measures of consumers' welfare or surplus, and so might seem to depend on assumptions about integrated preferences.

7.1 Neoclassical Arguments for Regulation

Neoclassical welfare economics recognizes a wide range of arguments for the regulation of markets. Many of these arguments carry over immediately to the contractarian, opportunity-based normative economics that I am proposing. In this section, I explain why.

The Market Opportunity Theorems that I presented in Chapter 6 state that the following is true for every equilibrium state of a competitive market in an exchange or storage economy: For every set of consumers, for every combination of transactions that is jointly feasible for those consumers and that all of them could plausibly want to participate in, each consumer's component of that combination is made available to him as a potential object of choice. I have interpreted this result as showing that competitive markets have properties that can be seen as valuable in a contractarian perspective. As I also showed in that chapter, it is straightforward to extend this result to show that if all consumers act on integrated 'neoclassical' preferences, every competitive equilibrium is Pareto-optimal and (a stronger condition) is in the core of the economy. The latter conclusions are well known and are generally interpreted as showing that competitive markets have properties that can be seen as valuable in the perspective of neoclassical welfare economics. Although the contractarian and neoclassical conclusions appeal to different normative criteria and make different assumptions about preferences, they are based on a common understanding of how markets work, namely that markets intermediate mutually beneficial transactions between consumers.

Once we move away from the idealized model of competition, we find various properties of real markets that can obstruct this process of intermediation. Forms of regulation that are directed at removing such obstacles can be recommended on both contractarian and neoclassical grounds, and for essentially the same reasons. For example, collusion among firms to raise prices typically requires that firms do not intermediate certain transactions which, considered in isolation, would be profitable. (Each firm agrees to a profit-reducing restriction on its own output or sales in return for corresponding restrictions by other firms.) Almost all economists recognize that, if competitive markets are to be maintained, regulation is required to deter firms from colluding and to prevent the accumulation of monopoly power. Similarly, there is general recognition that regulation is needed to prevent firms from taking excessive risks in situations in which, because of limited liability provisions, their owners do not have to bear the full costs of bad outcomes. Here the problem that calls for regulation is that firms are able to make profits by intermediating transactions that are *not* mutually beneficial. One of the major research programmes of economics is to identify obstacles to the intermediation of mutually beneficial transactions and to design regulatory responses. This programme is just as relevant for contractarian normative economics as it is for neoclassical.

A further justification for market regulation, recognized by neoclassical economists since the work of Arthur Pigou (1920), is to correct externalities. To keep things concrete, take the case of carbon emissions. One of the most important contributions of environmental economics has been the design of market-based regulatory regimes. Consider a *cap-and-trade* regime for regulating carbon emissions. Within some jurisdiction, an upper limit for emissions per period is set. Permits matching these limits are issued, and emissions are allowed only to agents who possess the requisite permits. Initial ownership rights in permits may be vested in governments and auctioned to the highest bidders. Alternatively, permits may be allocated free of charge (as 'grandfather' rights) to existing emitters. A market in permits is then allowed to operate. Neoclassical economic analysis shows that, for any given emissions ceiling, a cap-and-trade regime induces an economically efficient pattern of emissions. An alternative way of achieving essentially the same result as would follow from vesting permits in governments is to impose a single rate of tax on carbon emissions with the commitment that the tax rate will be adjusted over time to ensure that the emission ceiling is not exceeded.[1]

Over recent years there has been slow but real progress in setting up market-based regulatory regimes and in persuading policy-makers and opinion-formers of their virtues. But more dirigiste methods of regulation continue to be widely used and advocated. Governments persist in imposing ad hoc regulations on specific uses of carbon (for example, regulations about the fuel efficiency of home insulation, vehicles, and lighting), ad hoc 'green' taxes (for example, on fuel used by private cars), and ad hoc 'green' subsidies (for example, for wind- and wave-powered electricity generation). The consensus view among economists has been that this kind of regulation is economically inefficient: it restricts the scope for economic agents to make mutually beneficial exchanges which would have no net effect on total emissions.

If a nation commits itself to a specific emissions ceiling to be enforced by some kind of regulation, an economic good of 'emission rights' (that is, being permitted to make emissions) necessarily comes into existence. By virtue of the ceiling, this good is in fixed supply. Since units of the good are simply permissions, there is no technical obstacle to their being transferred between economic agents. Thus, the economic problem of allocating emission rights between agents has many of the characteristics of an exchange economy. In a suitably simplified model, neoclassical analysis shows that a competitive market in emission rights induces an allocation that is Pareto-optimal subject to the constraint set by the ceiling. It is straightforward to develop a corresponding contractarian analysis which shows that a competitive market in emission rights makes available opportunities for all transactions that agents might plausibly want to participate in and that are feasible, given the ceiling.

7.2 Choice Overload

The normative criterion for my analysis of markets has been opportunity.[2] According to that criterion, a person's interests are better served by her being able to choose from a larger rather than a smaller opportunity set. In offering a contractarian justification for this criterion, I have argued that most people, in most situations, will recognize that they benefit from the addition of options to their opportunity sets (see Chapter 5). However, there is a substantial body of literature in psychology and behavioural economics dealing with a phenomenon that may seem to cast doubt on that claim, and to suggest a role for regulation that neoclassical economics has not recognized. This phenomenon is *choice overload*.

Choice overload is said to occur when consumers face so many options that the quality of their decisions declines, or they feel dissatisfaction with their final choices, or their motivation is so undermined that they avoid choosing altogether. An extreme version of the claim that choice overload is a serious problem in developed economies has been popularized by Barry Schwartz (2004) in a book whose premise is that when the number of options becomes too large, 'choice no longer liberates, but debilitates. It may even be said to tyrannize' (2004: 2). Researchers who investigate choice overload sometimes suggest that their findings reveal a fundamental failure of the market system—that it provides *too much* choice. In some versions of this argument, consumers *want* more choice, but only because they do not understand that more choice does not benefit them. For example, Nicola Bown, Daniel Read, and Barbara Summers (2003: 307) interpret an experiment on choice overload as supporting the view that 'The needs of most consumers . . . could be met by offering much less choice than there is. Yet the inherent attractiveness of choice, even when it is disconnected from any ultimate benefits, leads retailers to offer it and consumers to be lured to it'. In their advocacy of libertarian paternalism, Cass Sunstein and Richard Thaler sometimes suggest that people might be better off with less choice rather than more. When they first propose this approach, they say that libertarian paternalists 'want to promote freedom of choice, but they need not seek to provide bad options, and among the set of reasonable ones, they need not argue that more is necessarily better' (Sunstein and Thaler, 2003a: 1196). In their later book *Nudge*, there is a hint of the same thought when they discuss dining out: '[I]t can be smart to let someone else choose for you. Two of the best restaurants in Chicago . . . give their diners the fewest choices. . . . The benefit of having so little choice is that the chef is authorized to cook you things you would never have thought to order' (Thaler and Sunstein, 2008: 76).

The most often cited evidence of choice overload is a field experiment reported by Sheena Iyengar and Mark Lepper (2000). The experimenters set up a 'tasting booth' in an up-market American grocery store. Visitors to the booth were invited to sample from a range of high-quality jams and were given coupons giving a $1 discount against purchases from that range of jams at the store. The number of jams that could be sampled was sometimes six and sometimes twenty-four. The rate of visits to the booth was slightly higher when it had more jams, but the proportion of coupons redeemed was much higher when there were only six jams. Iyengar and Lepper interpret this and similar results as illustrating Schwartz's idea of the 'tyranny of choice' and as showing that the provision of a wide range of choice 'though initially appealing to choice-makers, may nonetheless undermine choosers' subsequent satisfaction and motivation' (2000: 1003).

It is difficult to reconcile this interpretation with one of the most obvious trends in retail markets—the success of those retail business models that offer the widest ranges of choice. Think of the success of Wal-Mart and Amazon, compared with the decline of neighbourhood groceries and high-street book-shops. Admittedly, there has been a recent trend for large grocery chains to open small supermarkets close to where people live or work. But these stores cater to the growing demand for 'quick-stop' shopping, as contrasted with driving to an out-of-town hypermarket to stock up with a week's supply of groceries. This, I think, is one aspect of a general trend towards business models that minimize the delay between a consumer's desire for something and the gratification of that desire—of giving people what they want and are willing to pay for, *when they want it*. (A crucial ingredient in the success of internet shopping has been the development of courier services which allow internet retailers to offer very short delivery times.) This is the temporal dimension of the demand for choice.

In any event, the range of choice offered by a modern supermarket, let alone an internet shopping site, is vastly greater than that of the twenty-four jams of Iyengar and Lepper's tasting booth. If the demotivating effects of a wide range of choice reduce the propensity of customers to buy, how do retailers make profits by offering it? It should not be surprising that Iyengar and Lepper's result has not proved robust to other experimenters' attempts to replicate it.[3]

There is stronger evidence of choice overload in some situations that are interestingly different from the supermarket case.[4] In the US, the most commonly available form of saving for retirement is the '401(k)' plan. (Employees and employers contribute jointly to a savings plan that has tax relief. The employee chooses how those savings should be distributed among a defined set of fund options, typically including money market funds, bonds, and equities.) After other factors have been controlled for, increases in the number of fund options are associated with lower participation in 401(k) plans, and with more risk-averse portfolio choices by participants. Similar effects have been found in medical decision-making. From 2006, Medicare (the US health insurance plan for people over the age of 65) offered subsidised insurance to cover expenditure on prescription drugs; as with 401(k) plans, individuals choose from a defined set of (typically 40 or more) privately-supplied plans. Survey evidence suggests that slow enrolment in these plans was partly attributable to the large number of choices on offer. There is also evidence that patients' preferences for making their own decisions between alternative medical treatments are negatively correlated with the severity of their illness, and are overestimated by people who are in good health.

Why are these decisions different from those made in supermarkets? One difference is the extent to which choosers know their own preferences. It is generally recognized in the choice overload literature (even if sometimes overlooked in rhetorical flourishes about the tyranny of choice) that overload does not occur when choice takes the form of 'preference matching'—that is, scanning through a set of options to find the one that is best according to a pre-existing preference ranking. Thus, a supermarket shopper who has already decided that he wants to buy a particular breakfast cereal is not de-motivated by seeing other products on the shelves. One might expect this effect to extend to families of related products. For a shopper who knows the general features of breakfast cereals and who knows his tastes with respect to those features, it is not such a daunting task to choose one breakfast cereal in a supermarket, even if some of the brands on display are unfamiliar to him. People are much less likely to know their own preferences over saving and insurance plans, or over alternative medical treatments.

Another factor, also recognized in the literature, is that choice overload is less likely to occur if the set of options is organized into categories that the chooser perceives as relevant. For reasons of experimental control, investigations of choice overload often strip out navigational aids which could help choosers to impose structure on the opportunity set. When (as in the examples from US social insurance) publicly-financed programmes allow individuals to choose between privately-supplied products, the presentation of choice options has to satisfy standards of impartiality. As a result, the choice environment tends to be more like that of a controlled experiment than a supermarket.

In an early internet discussion of libertarian paternalism, one participant quoted the American politician Newt Gingrich as having said:

> If you were to walk into a Wal-Mart and say to people, 'Don't you feel really depressed by having 258,000 options; shouldn't it be their obligation to reduce the choice you must endure?', they would think you were nuts.[5]

Gingrich is surely right: most supermarket customers *would* be astonished at the suggestion that the range of choice presented to them was too large. But why are they *not* intimidated by the vast number of options they are being offered?

Imagine a store which stocks the 258,000 Wal-Mart options, but in which these goods are arranged on the shelves in a random order, changed every 24 hours. Further, imagine that all products are packaged in plain white containers; on each package, the nature of its contents is described in black print in a standard typeface. If consumers had no choice but to shop at such a store, they would find shopping an extremely onerous task, and would probably welcome a reduction in the number of options. The point of this thought experiment is that our ability to navigate supermarkets is highly dependent on the existence of conventions about how options are displayed. One such set of conventions governs retailers' decisions about which products are placed close to which. For example, in just about all supermarkets, the different coffee products are placed close together, and relatively close to the different tea products. A customer who is looking for tea knows she is in roughly the right part of the store when she sees coffees; when she locates the tea section, she can readily compare the different teas. Another set of conventions governs producers' decisions about the packaging of their products. For example, there are family resemblances among the package designs used by different tea producers. Because of these features, the customer can quickly locate tea products against a background of other groceries. Clearly, there are mechanisms at work in retail markets which favour the emergence and persistence of conventions that reduce the complexity of consumers' choice problems.

The driving force behind these mechanisms is the interest that sellers have in attracting buyers. In intermediating between wholesale producers and consumers, retailers sell shopping environments—locations where consumers can inspect what producers are offering, compare alternative products and prices, and carry out desired transactions. Retailers compete to provide environments that consumers want to visit and in which they will want to buy products that can be sold to them at a profit. If consumers prefer shopping environments that are easy to navigate, retailers who do not cater to this preference will lose business. Similarly, if consumers find tea products in supermarkets by looking for packages with certain conventional features, it is in the interest of each tea producer to use packages which follow these conventions.

Of course, retailers sometimes find it profitable to create shopping environments that are less easily navigable than they might be. For example, supermarkets sometimes place their special offers away from the shelves used to display similar but normally-priced goods. The relative positioning of different brands of a product on supermarket shelves is sometimes determined by differential fees charged by supermarkets to producers, eye-level displays commanding premium prices. Some common pricing strategies work by introducing artificial complexity into consumers' decision problems. In Section 7.4, I will consider a role for regulation in ensuring transparent pricing and in making it easier for consumers to compare alternative products and tariffs. But, I submit, the available evidence about choice overload does not suggest that individuals would generally be better off, according to their own understanding of their interests, if their opportunity sets were smaller than those that competitive markets can offer.

Nevertheless, the idea that markets offer too much choice seems to have some resonance in public debate, as evidenced by the success of Schwartz's book and by the fame of Iyengar and Lepper's experiment with jams. My sense is that it appeals to culturally conservative or snobbish attitudes of condescension towards some of the preferences to which markets cater. This may seem harmless fogeyism, as when Schwarz (2004: 1–2) begins his account of the tyranny of choice by complaining that Gap allows him to choose between too many different types of pairs of jeans ('The jeans I chose turned out just fine, but it occurred to me that buying a pair of pants should not be a daylong project'). But it often reflects a misunderstanding of the facts of economic life, and a concealed interest in restricting other people's opportunities to engage in mutually beneficial transactions.

Imagine you are asked to describe your ideal shopping environment. For many people, and I suspect for Schwartz, the description would be something like this. Your Perfect Shop is a small business, conveniently located in your own neighbourhood (perhaps just far enough away that you are not inconvenienced by other customers who might want to park their cars in front of your house). It stocks a small product range, tailored to your particular tastes and interests, but at prices that are similar to those charged by large supermarkets. There are some categories of goods (such as jeans if you are Schwartz) which you sometimes need to buy but whose detailed features do not much interest you. The Perfect Shop stocks a small but serviceable range of such items. There are other categories of goods (breakfast cereal might be an example) for which you have a strong preference for a specific brand and feel no need to try anything different; the Perfect Shop sells a limited range of this type of good, but your favourite brand is always on sale. However, there are a few categories of goods in which you are something of a connoisseur and like to experiment with different varieties. Here, the Perfect Shop offers a wide range of options, imaginatively selected to appeal to people who want to experiment in just the kinds of ways that you do. No shelf space is wasted on categories of goods which you have no desire to buy.

Compared with such an ideal, real shopping may well seem to offer too much choice, not to mention clutter and vulgarity. But, of course, in a world in which there are economies of scale in retailing and people have different tastes and interests, the idea that each of us can have a Perfect Shop is an economic fantasy. A less fantastic possibility is that there are Perfect Shops for some people, but everyone is constrained to use them. Because these shops are well-used, prices can be kept low. But then the viability of what are some people's Perfect Shops depends on the absence of opportunities for other people to buy what *they* want. Restricting other people's opportunities to buy goods that have no appeal to you can be a way of conserving your preferred shopping environment without your having to pay for it. Describing these restrictions as defences against the tyranny of choice can be a convenient camouflage for a form of protectionism.

Sunstein and Thaler's remark about Chicago restaurants draws attention to a third possibility—businesses that are like Perfect Shops in all respects except their prices. Such an Almost Perfect Shop caters to a niche clientele whose members share similar tastes and who are willing to pay premium prices to avoid confronting options that they do not wish to choose. If enough people were willing to pay enough to cover the costs of this kind of retailing, Almost Perfect Shops would tend to emerge in a market economy.[6] Conversely, the dominance of large retail outlets in real market economies suggests that most people are *not* willing to pay these costs. The restaurants recommended by Sunstein and Thaler seem to be extreme examples of the business model of the Almost Perfect Shop. (Since these restaurants are supposed to be among the best in Chicago, we can assume that they are not cheap.) The suggestion is that diners can benefit by deferring to the expertise of a chef, rather than by making their own choices from a larger menu. But the customers at these restaurants are not subjecting themselves to expertise in the abstract; they are buying the expertise of a particular chef whom they themselves have chosen in a market offering a vast range of alternative dining experiences. This is not a serious counter-example to the principle that it is in each person's interest to have more opportunity rather than less.

7.3 Self-constraint

Many economists and philosophers have been interested in analysing cases in which people can choose to constrain their future opportunities so as to prevent themselves from doing what, when the future arrives, they will actually want to do. Indeed, as the story of Odysseus and the Sirens attests, people have been fascinated by this kind of problem for thousands of years. Thomas Schelling (1980: 96) has written eloquently (and from personal experience) about how smokers who are trying to quit can alternate between trying to impose constraints on themselves and, having imposed those constraints, trying to evade them:

How should we conceptualize this rational consumer whom all of us know and some of us are, who in self-disgust grinds his cigarettes down the disposal swearing that this time he means never again to risk orphaning his children with lung cancer and is on the street three hours later looking for a store that's still open to buy cigarettes...?

Clearly, there *are* cases in which people choose strategies of self-constraint, or would choose such strategies if they were available. For the moment, I leave aside the question of how common these cases are, and focus on whether, when they occur, they give rise to a contractarian case for some form of regulation of markets.

Viewed in a contractarian perspective, the issue is not whether individuals would be better off, as judged by some planner or social commentator, if they were subject to external constraints. It is whether they themselves want to be subject to them. This prompts the question of whether markets tend to provide individuals with opportunities to constrain their later choices, if and when they want to do so. A rough and ready answer is that, in a competitive market, self-constraint technologies tend to be made available to those people who are willing to pay for them, but so too are the counter-technologies that allow people to escape from constraints they no longer wish to be bound by. Thus, the market satisfies Schelling's smoker's demand for the sink disposal unit that he uses to prevent himself from smoking the cigarettes he has previously bought, but it also provides him with the convenience stores at which he can replace them. Similarly, profit-seeking banks can offer long-term savings contracts with severe penalties for early cancellation, and these contracts may be attractive to people who want to commit themselves to long-term savings plans. But if, having taken out such a contract, a saver feels the desire to consume more than her original plan allows, she may be able to cancel out the effects of the contract by borrowing from another bank, perhaps even using the assets in her savings account as security.

An American internet company, StickK, has found a way of selling self-constraint to individuals. It runs a social networking site at which individual clients post personal commitments to achieve self-defined goals, and then self-report success or failure in achieving them. A client can choose to appoint 'referees' to verify her self-reports, and 'supporters' who will be kept informed about her progress. She can also choose to make a 'financial commitment' by staking a chosen amount of money which will be refunded only if the goal is achieved. As part of this commitment, the client chooses whether, in the event of failure, the stake will be transferred to a specific other person, to a pool of charities selected by StickK, or to an 'anti-charity' chosen from a menu designed to allow clients to choose organizations they dislike. (Catering to American tastes, the range of options includes the National Rifle Association and the Educational Fund to Stop Gun Violence; British clients are offered the fan clubs of Arsenal and Manchester United.) If you read the small print of the 'Terms and Conditions', you find that 19.5 per cent of transfers to charities and 50 per cent of transfers to anti-charities are deducted as fees. StickK also takes the interest on the stakes it holds.[7] Later, I will consider the volume of business that StickK conducts. For my present purposes, StickK is interesting as an example of how some forms of self-constraint can be bought and sold on markets.

Nevertheless, I think we must conclude that competitive markets do not always satisfy preferences for self-constraint. Does this matter? A first, formal answer is that the Market Opportunity Theorems, as formulated in Sections 6.6 and 6.8, are not invalidated by preferences for self-constraint. The reason is that the normative criteria that I have used treat self-constraint opportunities as having zero value. This can be seen most easily in relation to the Individual Opportunity Criterion, as formulated in Sections 5.1 and 5.5. Consider a person Jane for whom there are two possible consumption options, *fruit* and *cake*; *fruit* is healthier, but *cake* has more visceral appeal. These options will be available, if at all, in period 2. In period 1, Jane believes that, were both options available in period 2, she would choose *cake*, but she would now like to constrain herself to choose *fruit*. Using the notation developed in Section 5.5, if there are no opportunities for self-constraint, Jane's choice problem (viewed from period 1) is described by the nested opportunity set $O = \{\{fruit, cake\}\}$. (The inner pair of curly brackets encloses the options that will be available in period 2; the outer pair encloses the single option available in period 1, namely that the choice problem in period 2 will be $\{fruit, cake\}$.) If instead Jane has a self-constraint option in period 1 which allows her to make y unavailable in period 2, her choice problem is $O' = \{\{fruit, cake\}, \{fruit\}\}$. We now need to ask how O and O' are ranked by the Individual Opportunity Criterion. Since each of *fruit* and *cake* might plausibly be strictly preferred to the other (indeed, Jane herself prefers *fruit* in some states of mind and *cake* in others), neither option dominates the other. Thus, applying the dominance extension principle, $\{fruit, cake\} \succ_2 \{fruit\}$: Jane has strictly more opportunity in period 2 if she can choose between *fruit* and *cake* than if she is constrained to take *fruit*. But that implies that, for each option that one of the sets O and O' makes available in period 1, that option is at least weakly dominated by an option that the other set makes available in the same period. Thus, $O \sim\succ_1 O'$: Jane has just as much opportunity if she faces O as if she faces O'.

Of course, one might reply that this merely reveals the limitations of the Individual Opportunity Criterion as a representation of an individual's interests. If a person knows that she sometimes wants to constrain her future choices, she might reasonably think it in her interest to have certain opportunities for self-constraint.[8] Or, just as reasonably, she might think the opposite. Knowing that, if there are opportunities for self-constraint, she will sometimes find that she is unable to do what she wants because of a constraint that she had previously imposed on herself but now wishes she hadn't, she might think it in her interest that such opportunities are *not* made available. Which view she takes seems to depend on whether, at the time she is making the judgement about her interests, she identifies with the self that imposes the constraint or with the self that is constrained. How far a regime of voluntary transactions should be regulated so as to support individuals in imposing constraints on themselves is a deep problem that generations of economists have struggled with. I can only say that my analysis, as I have so far developed it, abstracts from this problem.

Let me say in my defence that the same problem has to be faced by any approach to normative economics that uses preference-satisfaction as its criterion. As I pointed out in Chapter 4, behavioural welfare economists sometimes claim to be able to solve this problem by distinguishing between latent preferences and mistakes. If an individual's inner rational agent chooses self-constraint and if attempts to evade these constraints are mistakes, social planners (it is said) should respect preferences for self-constraint. Conversely, if it is the desire for self-constraint that is the mistake, that desire does not qualify for respect. But unless there is a method for identifying latent preferences, that conclusion does not help at all.

But how common are genuine preferences for self-constraint? (By a 'genuine preference for self-constraint', I mean a willingness to choose to be subjected to a constraint which, once imposed, will be enforced by some mechanism external to one's own will. Self-constraint is not to be confused with the formation of aspirations or resolutions, which are intended to influence subsequent choices without actually constraining them.) Alongside Schelling's all-too-real account of struggling to escape addiction, the literature of behavioural economics contains many models based on assumptions about preferences for self-constraint that seem psychologically implausible or are not supported by the evidence. As I suggested in Section 4.8, behavioural economists' propensity to interpret context-dependent preferences as evidence of self-control problems may be a side effect of their commitment to the model of the inner rational agent.

A characteristic example is the model used by Drew Fudenberg and David Levine (2006) to explain the high levels of risk aversion observed in laboratory experiments in which student subjects make choices between lotteries with small monetary prizes. Fudenberg and Levine hypothesize that a representative subject has two selves—a 'long-run self' with a preference for a relatively high rate of saving and a 'short-run self' with a preference for immediate consumption. Recognizing the conflict between these preferences, the long-run self restricts the short-run self's access to cash (for example, by deliberately making only small cash withdrawals from a bank account). In the experimental lab, the short-run self is in command, and views the small money prizes available as opportunities to evade the constraints the long-run self has imposed. Given that there is no shortage of simple and psychologically well-grounded explanations of risk aversion with respect to small gains and losses (to say nothing of the ease of finding a cash machine on a typical university campus), Fudenberg and Levine's dual-self model strikes me as lacking in both plausibility and parsimony.

A more serious example, often cited in discussions of self-constraint, is gym membership. Many gyms offer two alternative types of tariffs. A *pay-as-you-go* tariff charges a fee per visit. A *membership* tariff has a fixed fee (say, per month or per year) which allows unlimited visits at no additional cost. Choices between pay-as-you-go and membership tariffs (or season tickets) are common in many sectors of the economy: think of public transport or spectator sport. The standard economic explanation is that this is a form of price discrimination: by allowing customers to select between alternative tariffs, a firm can charge different prices to customers with different demand functions and thereby gain more revenue. In the case of gyms, however, it is sometimes suggested that membership tariffs are a response to a demand for self-constraint. The idea is that a typical individual has a long-run self with a strong preference for regular exercise and a short-run self which, on any particular day, is liable to prefer not exercising. When the long-run self is active, the individual chooses a membership tariff and pays the fixed fee with the aim of making subsequent gym visits more appealing to the short-run self: gym visits will still involve the pain of exercising, but at least the pain of paying will be removed.

Stefano DellaVigna and Ulrike Malmendier (2004, 2006) discuss this hypothesis as a possible explanation of evidence that they have collected from the records of three commercial health clubs in New England. From this evidence, they derive two main findings, encapsulated in the title of their 2006 paper, 'Paying not to go to the gym'. The first is that, on average, people who choose monthly membership tariffs pay around 70 per cent more than the total pay-as-you-go prices of the visits they actually make. The second finding is that people who choose monthly membership are more likely to stay enrolled for over a year than those who choose annual membership. Annual membership is cheaper per month, but is not rolled over automatically at the end of a year; monthly membership is rolled over automatically unless the customer chooses to cancel.

In principle, the observation that customers on membership tariffs pay more than the pay-as-you-go prices of their visits is consistent with the hypothesis of deliberately chosen self-constraint. Conceivably, the long-run selves of these customers might have predicted that they would have visited the gym even less frequently if they had used the pay-as-you-go tariff, and might have thought the 70 per cent excess payment a price worth paying to induce their short-run selves to make more visits. But the size of the excess payment suggests that if monthly membership really is being chosen as a self-commitment device, it is a device that does not work particularly well. It is as if customers have the economic sophistication to predict that their future will-ingness to go to the gym will be much greater if the marginal price is zero, but lack the psychological self-awareness to realize that this prediction is in fact false.

DellaVigna and Malmendier conclude that the most plausible and parsimo-nious explanation of their two findings is *not* that customers choose self-constraint; it is that customers make the errors of 'overestimation of future self-control or of future efficiency' (2006: 716). In this context, 'efficiency' means cancelling monthly memberships that are not being used, while 'over-estimation of future self-control' means overestimation *of future gym visits*. The interpretation of gym visits as acts of self-control plays no part in the explan-ation of the choice of membership tariffs. As DellaVigna and Malmendier point out, their results 'are at least as much about naiveté as they are about self-control' (2004: 394).

An alternative and simpler explanation is that when people are choosing between tariffs, they tend to attribute their current attitudes to their future selves. Thinking about an extended series of gym visits, they focus on the long-term health benefits and overestimate their day-to-day willingness actu-ally to go to the gym. Thinking about a choice between tariffs, they imagine that the issues that are now at the front of their minds will be equally salient at other times, and so overestimate the likelihood of reconsidering their decision in the light of new information. The underlying psychological mechanism here is closely related to the *focusing illusion* summed up in Daniel Kahneman's (2011: 402) maxim: 'Nothing in life is as important as you think it is when you are thinking about it'. Notice that this mechanism works *against* self-constraint: if (whether correctly or not) you attribute your current preferences to yourself in the future, you will see no need to con-strain your future choices.

This is not to deny that the New England gym users are choosing options that are unambiguously dominated (in the sense that these people are paying more than they need to pay, and getting nothing extra in return). This might be a case in which consumers' interests would be served by regulations which made pricing more transparent; I will say more about such regulations in Section 7.4. But it does not support the interpretation of gym membership as self-constraint.

To find evidence about the prevalence of preferences for self-constraint, we need to look for cases in which consumers are offered options that are explicitly presented as self-constraint and consider how frequently these offers are taken up. Such options are not very common, but (partly as a result of diffusion of ideas from behavioural economics) regulators sometimes require firms to offer them. An interesting example featured in a recent news item, when the chief executive of William Hill (one of the largest betting firms in the UK) claimed that a rule introduced by the Gambling Commission (the industry regulator) was adversely affecting its profits:

> A 'panic button' making it easier for problem gamblers to take a break from online betting by locking their accounts has damaged the profits of William Hill, the firm has announced. As part of a new feature introduced to the website last year, punters can choose to lock themselves out of their accounts for 24 hours, a week, a month or up to six weeks with just the click of a button. The option was introduced by the UK Gambling Commission last November as part of a raft of measures designed to improve the industry's social responsibility. William Hill's chief executive James Henderson said the number opting to take a break had risen by 50 per cent since the turn of the year, with about 3,000 accounts now being locked every week. . . . William Hill's online business, with 2.7 million users, made £126.5m last year.[9]

The panic button certainly provides a useful service to internet gamblers who recognize that they suffer from self-control problems. The Gambling Commission is entitled to justify its regulation as a response to a demand for self-constraint. But notice the rate of take-up: at any given time, approximately one in every thousand internet gamblers is choosing to be constrained. Given that gambling is a particularly addictive form of consumption, this evidence does not suggest that, across the economy as a whole, there is a large and unsatisfied latent demand for self-constraint.

What about StickK? In the period from its start-up in 2008 to the time at which I am writing (October 2017), it claims to have handled 374,000 commitment contracts and $32.6 million in stakes.[10] Clearly, StickK has found a successful business model for a niche market. But, like the take-up rate for the panic button, this volume of traffic on a social networking site is hardly evidence that preferences for self-constraint are a major feature of economic life.

As a final example of a case in which behavioural welfare economists assume preferences for self-constraint, recall Thaler and Sunstein's (2008: 103–31) argument for nudging people to save more for retirement, on which I commented in Section 3.5. Sunstein and Thaler point out that, for many Americans, retirement savings are very low in relation to what most experts would judge necessary to ensure a reasonable standard of living in old age. They also cite survey evidence that two-thirds of employees describe their savings rate as 'too low' while only 1 per cent describe it as 'too high'. As explanations of low savings rates, Sunstein and Thaler refer to the mathematical complexity of rational financial planning and the willpower needed to execute a long-term savings plan. They recommend various nudges that have been found to increase enrolment in employment saving plans (particularly the use of opt-in rather than opt-out defaults), and present these nudges as helping individuals to overcome self-control problems that those individuals themselves recognize.

On this view, executing a long-term savings plan is analogous with keeping to a diet, maintaining a resolution to give up smoking, or enrolling in an old-fashioned Christmas club. But it is interesting to compare the emotional intensity of retirement saving decisions with that of dieting, trying to give up smoking, or planning for Christmas. Although retirement saving decisions have extremely important consequences, both for the savers' current disposable incomes and for their future standards of living, the evidence suggests that people find it hard to maintain interest and attention when dealing with them.[11] People are content to accept arbitrary default options or to use crude rules of thumb; if there are more than a handful of alternative saving options, they are liable to respond by choosing none of them. If people really would choose to be nudged towards a saving plan chosen by supposed experts, that might be explained more plausibly as a way of avoiding having to deal with a difficult, unengaging, and worrying problem than as a sophisticated attempt to resist a temptation to spend.

However, it is worth asking whether part of the explanation for low rates of household saving is that people are conscious of the huge economic, political, and personal uncertainties involved in planning for a retirement that may be several decades away. Experts' estimates of the future returns to saving typically depend on assumptions about the stability of existing institutional structures and the continuation of existing regularities and trends. (For example, Thaler and Sunstein [2008: 121] are unnervingly confident in asserting, on the strength of the evidence that equities have out-performed bonds in every twenty-year period up to the unfortunate date at which they are writing, that savers who do not hold most of their assets in equities are making a mistake: 'Over a twenty-year period, stocks are almost certain to go up'.) In contrast, ordinary savers (and non-savers) may have some inchoate awareness of the possibility of such unexpected shocks as stock market crashes, bank collapses, hyperinflations, and governments reneging on pension commitments. It may also cross their minds that if most people do not save for retirement, when non-savers reach retirement age they may be able to use their collective voting power to secure transfers from the working population.

I suggest that much of the political driving force for policies to increase household savings does not come from a desire to help individuals solve self-control problems. Rather, it comes from a recognition that low savers undermine the credibility of policy regimes in which private savings play an important part in financing retirement and social care. Policy-makers are trying to solve a collective action problem, in which the aim is to create sustainable institutions and to induce consistent and realizable expectations. In a democratic society that guarantees a minimum living standard for all and in which the imprudent have votes, a contractarian solution to this problem may require some form of compulsory saving.

7.4 Obfuscation

Industrial economists are becoming increasingly interested in a phenomenon variously known as 'spurious complexity', 'shrouding', and 'obfuscation'. Firms engage in obfuscation when they deliberately price their products, or present information about prices, in unnecessarily complex ways. Obfuscation is seen as a practice that can obstruct competition and exploit unwary consumers, and therefore an appropriate target for regulation. Since ideally rational consumers would presumably be able to deal with complex price information, this argument for regulation has become more prominent with the accumulation of evidence about how far individuals' economic behaviour deviates from the predictions of traditional rational-choice models.

Recent academic interest in obfuscation also reflects the increasing salience of the topic in public debate as people come to terms with the effects of the information revolution and the explosion of internet commerce. These innovations have made it much easier for firms to use complex pricing schemes. In many cases, this has led to greater economic efficiency in pricing. For example, it is now possible for airlines to vary the prices of seats on individual flights minute by minute so as to match demand to supply, reducing the waste of empty seats. Products that were previously sold as single-price packages can now be more easily broken down into separately-priced components, allowing purchases to be tailored to consumers' individual requirements. As the example of airline prices also illustrates, price discrimination has been made easier. Minute-by-minute price flexibility allows higher prices to be charged to passengers who do not want to commit their travel plans far in advance and who are not willing to substitute a cheap destination for an expensive one. But this too can be seen as efficiency-enhancing, since price discrimination helps to ensure that goods are supplied whenever the total benefits to consumers exceed the cost of production (see Section 7.5 below). However, there is a downside. The same changes in technology give sellers more control over the information that consumers receive about what is on offer. For example, the designer of a website has much more control than the manager of a department store over the process by which consumers access price information.

This gives sellers more opportunities to misrepresent prices and to frustrate price comparisons.

It is well known that search costs—the costs that consumers have to incur to gain information about the offers made by individual suppliers—tend to reduce the effectiveness of price competition and so lead to higher prices.[12] Many forms of price complexity can be viewed as anti-competitive strategies designed to increase consumers' search costs.[13] *Drip pricing* is the practice of advertising a low headline price to attract consumers to a firm's store or website. As the consumer invests time in gaining more information about the firm's offer or in initiating the process of placing an order, additional and unexpected price components (such as taxes, fees for the use of payment cards, or delivery charges) are added. The more firms in a market that use this strategy, the higher is the cost in time and effort of finding the lowest final prices. So, despite the unpleasant surprises of the later information, the consumer may do better (or may think she will do better) by accepting the offer than by looking elsewhere. *Baiting* works in a similar way: a low headline price is later revealed to be available only 'while stocks last' or subject to conditions that are almost impossible to meet. Other strategies use unnecessary price complexity to make it harder for mathematically-challenged or time-constrained consumers to compare different firms' final prices. Such strategies include *price partitioning*, that is, quoting separate prices for component parts of an indivisible offer (for example, by quoting tax or delivery charges separately) and *complex offers* (such as 'three for the price of two'). A more direct way of obstructing price comparisons is the use of *exploding offers* or *buy-now discounts*—offers that will be withdrawn unless accepted immediately, and so do not allow buyers time to investigate alternative offers.

Another family of strategies exploits consumers' inaccurate forecasts of their own demands, or their mistaken beliefs about the likelihood of particular contingencies.[14] Firms that offer service contracts (for example, for current account banking, credit cards, or mobile phone use) may load their charges disproportionately onto contingencies that consumers under-predict (such as unarranged overdrafts) or even do not think about at all. Multi-part tariffs can be designed to offer low total charges for consumers who forecast their demand correctly, but impose large penalties on those who under- or over-predict how much they will use a service. As in the case of the gyms (Section 7.3), firms may exploit consumers' over-estimation of their future attention to price information by offering service contracts that are automatically rolled over unless positive action is taken to cancel them. By offering a low 'teaser' price for the first period of a contract and progressively increasing this at each rollover, a firm can hide its long-term price at the initial sign-on stage—the stage at which potential buyers are giving most attention to contract terms.

However, it should also be recognized that markets have some self-regulating mechanisms which work against obfuscation. The most obvious of these is reputation. If consumers are aware (as they can hardly fail to be) of the search costs they incur when dealing with complex pricing, they may choose to patronize firms that are known to offer less confusing tariffs and more easily navigable websites. This gives incentives for firms to build reputations for transparent pricing. Information-sharing websites for consumers, such as tripadvisor.com, can make even one-off transactions subject to the effects of reputation. When physical and online supermarkets act as platforms for the sale of other firms' products, they are effectively selling search opportunities to consumers, and their reputations depend on consumers' perceptions of how easily they are able to find what they want. Thus, it may be in the interests of the owner of a platform to require the firms that sell on it to use transparent pricing practices.[15] Because firms' offers are easier to compare when they are expressed in terms of common standards (for example, standard package sizes, standard units of measurement, or common conventions about what is included in the headline price), consumers who are drawing up shortlists before making final choices may be more likely to include offers that are expressed in common standards. Thus, once common standards are established, firms that deviate from them may be penalized by losing market share.[16]

It seems that in real-world markets we are observing an interplay between forces which tend to induce obfuscation and forces which work in favour of transparency. Nevertheless, there is a strong contractarian case for regulation which shifts the balance towards greater transparency.

The central argument of Chapter 6 was that competitive markets are highly effective in providing people with opportunities for mutually beneficial transactions. Recall that the essential mechanism by which these opportunities are generated is competition between would-be arbitrageurs, each trying to make profit by intermediating transactions between willing sellers and willing buyers. One arbitrageur competes with another by offering to sell at a lower price than the competitor, or to buy at a higher price. It is because of this mechanism that, at least in an equilibrium state of an idealized model, a competitive market satisfies the Law of One Price and the Law of Supply and Demand. These two properties of competitive equilibrium are at the core of the proofs of the Market Opportunity Theorems. By obstructing the workings of this mechanism, obfuscation undermines the capacity of a market to intermediate mutually beneficial transactions.

The implication, I suggest, is that regulators should try to ensure that pricing is as transparent as possible, while not restricting firms from making offers that consumers might plausibly be supposed to want to accept. Thus, regulators might require price information to be presented in standardized ways (for example, by requiring prices to be quoted inclusive of unavoidable taxes and 'booking charges', and by requiring the most commonly bought add-ons to be included in headline prices). Sellers might be required to provide information about the total cost of defined packages of complementary goods, representative of the purchases of typical consumers, in the same way that car manufacturers already have to provide standardized information about fuel consumption. (For example, sellers of printers which use dedicated ink cart-ridges might be required to report the annual operating cost for a typical user.) Rollover contracts might be constrained by requiring an opt-out rather than opt-in default at specified intervals, or in the event of price changes. Some of the anti-competitive effects of exploding offers might be countered by requir-ing contracts to be subject to cooling-off periods, during which consumers can cancel them without penalty.

However, it is important that transparency is not achieved by restricting significant opportunities for mutually beneficial transactions. For example, if suppliers were allowed to sell only full-service packages, price comparisons would be made easier, but the emergence of valuable new business models, such as budget hotels and low-cost airlines, might be obstructed. If airlines, hotels, theatres, and spectator sports were not allowed to vary their advance ticket prices over short periods of time, the efficient matching of demand to capacity would be frustrated. If all add-ons were required to be priced on a cost-plus basis, legitimate forms of price discrimination would be prevented. (Think of the price premiums for higher-specification models of mass-market cars. These clearly exceed any cost-plus standard, but the practice is transpar-ent and buyers know what they are paying for.)

There is a similar case for regulations which enforce transparency in other kinds of information that sellers provide to potential buyers. If the opportun-ities that markets offer are to be genuine, people need to know what those opportunities are; if there is to be price competition, buyers need to be able to compare like with like. Thus, there is a place for regulations which require that certain kinds of product information—for example, the nutritional content of food items, the alcohol content of drinks, the working life of lighting products—are provided in standardized formats that are easy for buyers to understand. But again, a contractarian regulator would not want to restrict firms from offering consumers what they might in fact want to buy. Thus, a regulation requiring restaurants to declare the calorie counts of their menu items should not be deemed to have failed just because diners continue to choose high-calorie dishes, or because, in providing their customers with what they want and are willing to pay for, restaurants tend to stack their menus with those dishes.

7.5 Fixed Costs and Price Discrimination

The Market Opportunity Theorems, as formally stated in Sections 6.6 and 6.8, apply to exchange and storage economies. As I explained in Section 6.7, it is not difficult to extend these theorems to economies in which production takes place under constant returns to scale. But things are not so straightforward if there are increasing returns to scale, or if production on any scale requires certain minimum quantities of inputs. It is well known that, under these conditions, neoclassical results about the Pareto-optimality of competitive equilibrium tend to break down. This problem—sometimes called the problem of *natural monopoly*—has usually been seen as identifying a potentially useful role for market regulation. Not surprisingly, the Market Opportunity Theorems break down under the same conditions. In this section, I consider what regulatory responses to this problem are appropriate if consumers lack integrated preferences.

I will discuss this question using a famous example, introduced to economics by Jules Dupuit (1844/1952). I have an ulterior motive for stepping so far back in time. At the beginning of this book, I pointed out that the liberal tradition of economics is much older than the rationality-based style of theorizing that took off with the 'marginal revolution' of the 1870s. I declared that my strategy for reconciling that tradition with behavioural economics would be to avoid making the theoretical moves that characterized the marginal revolution. Dupuit (like his now more famous contemporary, Antoine Augustin Cournot) was a pioneer of mathematically rigorous microeconomics, writing several decades before the neoclassical era. The work of these two French writers is a fertile source of ideas about how microeconomics might be developed without the use of rationality assumptions.[17] Dupuit was a civil engineer, interested in trying to assess the 'utility' of public works such as roads, railways, canals, and water supply systems, which typically involve high fixed costs. He proposes general principles for deciding which public works should be carried out, and how the services provided by those works should be priced. He addresses his analysis to 'legislators' who are concerned with such decisions, either because public works are carried out by government, or because they are subject to governmental regulation. His central example is what I will call the case of *Dupuit's bridge*.

Suppose an entrepreneur is considering building a bridge over a river and charging tolls for crossing it. He would incur costs in building and maintaining the bridge, but these costs are independent of the volume of traffic it would carry. Even if no tolls were charged, the bridge would have more than enough capacity to meet the demand for it. If the entrepreneur can design a tariff that will generate revenue in excess of costs, he will build the bridge; if not, not. If the bridge is built and is profitable, one might say that the entrepreneur has intermediated a mutually beneficial transaction between the bridge's users and those people who supply the inputs necessary for building and maintaining it. In this sense, his role is analogous with that of an arbitrageur in my model of an exchange economy. However, there are significant differences between the two cases, stemming from the fact that bridge-building is an activity with fixed costs.

The most fundamental difference concerns the sense in which, even under ideal conditions, opportunities for jointly feasible and non-dominated transactions can be made available to individuals. In a competitive equilibrium of an exchange economy, every such potential transaction corresponds with an option in the opportunity set of each consumer who would be a party to that transaction. In other words, opportunities for jointly feasible transactions that individuals *might* want to take part in are made available as potential objects of individual choice, even if *in fact* those individuals do not choose them. In contrast, suppose that the potential users of an as-yet unbuilt bridge would *not* be willing to pay enough to cover the costs of building and maintaining it. If this is known to entrepreneurs, the bridge will not be built, and so options that involve paying to cross it will not appear in individuals' opportunity sets. Nevertheless, if entrepreneurs are sufficiently alert to profit opportunities, it might still be true to say that, *were it the case that* potential users were willing to pay enough to cover the costs, the bridge would be built, and that there would then be bridge-crossing options in individuals' opportunity sets.

Generalizing from this idea, it is possible to adapt the Strong Interactive Opportunity Criterion so that it takes account of opportunities that exist only in this counterfactual sense. As I originally stated it, that criterion requires that, for every group of consumers, and for every transaction among the members of that group that is feasible for all those members collectively and non-dominated for each of them separately, each member's component of that transaction is an element of her opportunity set (Section 6.4). Consider a counterfactual version of the criterion that requires that, for any such feasible and non-dominated transaction, *were it the case that* all members of the relevant group wanted to participate in it, each member's component *would be* an element of her opportunity set. This formulation continues to capture one of the main normative intuitions underlying the Strong Interactive Opportunity Criterion—that it is in each individual's interest that he is able to get whatever he wants and is willing to pay for.

Applying this counterfactual criterion to the problem of Dupuit's bridge, the crucial question is whether the total amount that potential users are willing to pay to cross the bridge is greater than the costs of building and maintaining it. If consumers have neoclassical preferences, that is a well-defined question. In neoclassical economics, a person's willingness to pay for something—or more formally, his *compensating variation*—is defined in terms of his (assumedly) given preference ordering. To say that a person's willingness to pay to use the bridge is some specific amount is to say that he is indifferent between (on the one hand) paying that amount and using the bridge and (on the other) not paying and not using it. But I need a measure of willingness to pay that does not presuppose that bridge users are neoclassical consumers.

I suggest that the most useful way to proceed is to think of willingness to pay as the maximum revenue that can be appropriated by price discrimination. Consider the problem of setting a tariff for Dupuit's bridge. A given tariff may set different prices for different individuals, for different numbers of journeys made by each individual, for different types of journey, for different times of day, and so on. For the purpose of defining a measure of willingness to pay, I assume that every tariff is *enforceable* (and that enforcement is costless). By this I mean that, if a tariff is implemented, its terms will in fact be binding on buyers. I also stipulate that, in order to be relevant for the measurement of willingness to pay, a tariff must be *pre-announced* and *transparent*. To say that a tariff is pre-announced is to say that potential buyers are informed about all its relevant features before they make any commitment to buy anything. Transparency is a looser concept, but the intuitive idea is that the tariff is presented in a way that potential buyers can understand and can compare with other offers that are being made to them. These conditions express the distinction between price discrimination and obfuscation. For example, an airline which openly charges a premium price for the privilege of boarding its aircraft first and sitting in the same cabin area as other payers of that price is engaging in what I take to be legitimate price discrimination, even if the additional price is far higher than the additional cost of supplying those privileges. But if an airline imposes a penalty charge, similarly in excess of corresponding costs, for the re-issue of a mislaid boarding pass, and if that charge is pre-announced only in the smallest print of the booking conditions, one is entitled to suspect deliberate obfuscation.

If the behaviour of consumers is predictable, and irrespective of whether individual consumers act on integrated preferences, each of these alternative tariffs will generate a predictable pattern of journeys by each individual and hence a predictable amount of revenue. Thus, ranging across all possible pre-announced and transparent tariffs, it is meaningful to define the maximum revenue that can be generated by 'legitimate' price discrimination. This can be interpreted as a measure of the total willingness to pay of potential users for the services that Dupuit's bridge can provide.

If total willingness to pay is greater than the cost of the bridge, it is in principle possible to identify a jointly feasible and mutually beneficial transaction between bridge users and the suppliers of the inputs necessary to build and maintain the bridge. Indeed, it will typically be possible to identify a range of alternative transactions of this kind, each with a different allocation of fixed costs between users. In practice, however, there is no guarantee that unregulated entrepreneurship will intermediate any of these transactions. One problem is that total willingness to pay has been defined in relation to a discriminatory tariff that may not be practically feasible. Even if the aggregate behaviour of consumers is predictable, it may be that no entrepreneur knows *which* identifiable individuals are willing to pay which prices. A second problem is that, because of fixed costs, arbitrage profits will not necessarily be competed away as they would be in a competitive equilibrium. If a bridge *can* be built and operated at a profit, the first entrepreneur to seize this opportunity may be able permanently to appropriate some of the surplus generated by the transaction he is intermediating, since a competitor would have to incur the fixed costs of building a second bridge.

Nevertheless, the analysis I have presented identifies idealized conditions under which, despite the existence of fixed costs, a regulated market economy would satisfy the counterfactual version of the Strong Interactive Opportunity Criterion. Applied to the problem of Dupuit's bridge, there are three such conditions. First, the bridge will be built if and only if it can be financed by revenue from prices that users choose to pay. Second, if it is built, it will in fact be financed in this way, total revenue exactly covering total costs. Third, the prices charged will not deter any users who are willing to pay the marginal costs (zero in Dupuit's example) that they impose. These conditions describe an ideal to which a contractarian regulator might try to approximate. Within the slack allowed by these conditions, the regulator might also try to satisfy principles of distributional fairness in allocating fixed costs between users.

The conditions I have just stated are essentially the same as those that Dupuit seems to have in mind when he declares his intention to show how tariffs for the services provided by public works can be fixed 'according to rational principles, in order to produce the greatest possible utility and at the same time a revenue sufficient to cover the cost of upkeep and interest on capital' (1844/1952: 271). Significantly, Dupuit proposes these principles without making any assumptions about the rationality of consumers. To the contrary, he explicitly denies that the methods of economics can be used to explain or predict consumer choice. He says that (what would now be called) a demand function 'is not known for any commodity, and it can even be said that it will never be known since it depends on the volatile will of human beings; it is today no longer what it was yesterday' (1844/1952: 277). Explaining the principles of price discrimination, he says that '[t]he variable, yea mobile, nature of the value of utility is indeed well known to business men and has long been exploited by them' (1844/1952: 260). To a modern reader, his account of that exploitation seems much more behavioural than neoclassical. Price discrimination works work by setting 'traps for the buyer's vanity and his credulity':

> The same commodity in various guises is often sold in different shops at quite different prices to the rich, the moderately well-off, and the poor. The fine, the very fine, the superfine, and the extra fine, although drawn from the same barrel and although alike in all real respects other than the superlative on the label, sell at widely different prices.   (Dupuit, 1844/1952: 261)

Dupuit is clearly assuming that choices over consumption goods are typically governed by preferences that are labile and context-dependent. Nevertheless, he sees the business practices that take advantage of this context-dependence as good examples to be followed in setting tariffs for public works.

If utility is so mobile, what does it mean to design a regulatory regime to produce 'the greatest possible utility'? Dupuit's answer is so radical that generations of economists have thought that it must have been the result of confusion.[18] It is encapsulated in a simple slogan: 'Hence the saying which we shall often repeat because it is often forgotten: the only real utility is that which people are willing to pay for' (1844/1952: 262). For Dupuit, to say that an object has utility for a person is the same thing as to say that the person is willing to pay for it; the amount he is willing to pay for it *just is* the measure of its utility. Thus, Dupuit is able to use a concept of willingness to pay in his theory of regulation without making any assumptions about individual rationality.

7.6 Public Goods

Now consider another kind of public work. Imagine a town that is subject to flooding from a river. This risk affects many of the town's residents. It could be reduced by an engineering project that would create areas of wetland upstream to slow down the rate at which flood surges pass down the river. Given the engineering specifications of the project (which determine its effects on river flows downstream), its costs are independent of the number of people who enjoy its benefits, just as the costs of Dupuit's bridge are independent of how many people cross it. However, there is a crucial difference between the two cases: the benefits of the bridge are *excludable*, but the benefits of flood protection are not. By this I mean that it is possible to allow individuals separately to choose whether or not to take the benefits of the bridge, and to restrict those benefits to people who pay some price, but there can be no equivalent individual choice about whether or not to take the benefits of the flood protection project. Thus the flood protection project, unlike the bridge, cannot be directly financed through pricing. In this sense, flood protection is a *public good*.

Nevertheless, this project creates benefits for which individuals are willing to pay. Suppose that some public agency carries out the project and finances it by compulsory charges to be paid by those individuals that it deems to be beneficiaries. The combination of project and charges is a multilateral transaction between the beneficiaries and the suppliers of the inputs that the project requires. For the beneficiaries as individuals, participation in this transaction is not voluntary. But one can still ask whether the transaction is mutually beneficial—that is, whether each beneficiary's willingness to pay for the benefits she receives is greater than the charge she is required to pay. In a natural extension of Dupuit's 'rational principles' for the financing of public works (Section 7.5), one might propose as a regulatory ideal that public goods should be supplied if and only if the total willingness to pay of beneficiaries exceeds the total cost, and that costs should be apportioned between beneficiaries in such a way that, for each individual separately, willingness to pay exceeds actual payment. This is perhaps the ideal to which Dupuit (1844/1952) aspired in his work as the founding father of cost–benefit analysis. The same ideal can be found in the *voluntary exchange* theory of public goods, as developed by Knut Wicksell (1896/1958), Erik Lindahl (1919/1958), and James Buchanan (1968).

In its modern neoclassical form, cost–benefit analysis attempts to implement the first part of this ideal by assessing whether, in total, the beneficiaries of a project are willing to pay more for those benefits than would be necessary to compensate those who incur the costs. Willingness to pay and compensation are defined in terms of individuals' assumedly neoclassical preferences. Formally, cost–benefit analysis applies the *Potential Pareto Improvement Criterion*: it asks whether it is in principle possible to combine the relevant project with income transfers in such a way that some individuals strictly prefer the package of project and transfers to the do-nothing alternative, and no one has the opposite preference. This method of making decisions about the provision of public goods is critically dependent on the assumption that individuals have integrated preferences over alternative combinations of public good and private consumption. However, an accumulation of evidence from experiments and stated preference surveys shows that individuals are particularly likely to reveal context-dependent preferences when they are making choices (whether hypothetical or real) between money and goods that are not normally traded on markets.[19] This should not be surprising. If an individual has no experience of buying or selling something, she is unlikely to have formed settled preferences between it and amounts of money. In addition, it is well known that when people are unsure about their preferences, their responses to valuation tasks are often influenced by

165

irrelevant but salient cues which act as 'anchors'. If the market price of a good is known, that price can serve as a cue for valuations even in situations in which it has no objective relevance.[20] In the absence of a known market price, people look for other cues, with the result that their behaviour appears more context-dependent.

Although behavioural welfare economists sometimes suggest that their approach can be implemented through some unspecified form of cost–benefit analysis (e.g. Camerer et al., 2003: 1222; Sunstein and Thaler, 2003a: 1190–1), the problem of how to do cost–benefit analysis when individuals lack integrated preferences has yet to be solved. Of course, that problem would dissolve if individuals were as represented in the model of the inner rational agent, with neoclassical latent preferences waiting to be discovered by cost–benefit analysts. But, as I argued in Chapter 4, no method of identifying latent preferences has yet been found, and there are strong reasons for doubt about whether such preferences exist at all. The best that cost–benefit analysis can do, it seems to me, is to recognize that individuals' preferences are imprecise and that measures of cost and benefit that are directly based on preferences will therefore be imprecise too.

Is it possible to bypass this problem by taking an opportunity-based approach to normative economics? That approach is able to avoid some of the difficulties caused by non-integrated preferences because it does not probe into the reasons, motivations, or intentions that lie behind individuals' choices. In using this approach to assess competitive markets, I have considered only individuals' *opportunities* for choice, and those opportunities can be defined without reference to preferences. In dealing with cases of natural monopoly, I have needed a concept of an individual's *willingness* to pay for a good, but I have been able to define willingness to pay in terms of the individual's actual or hypothetical choices without assuming that those choices reveal integrated preferences. If (as in the case of Dupuit's bridge) the costs of a project are fully covered by prices paid by its users, the claim that the project implements a mutually beneficial transaction does not need to be supported by further evidence about the users' preferences. But when a good is public, willingness to pay and actual payment cannot be linked so directly.

If an opportunity-based approach is to make any headway in dealing with public goods, we need to find some setting in which people can make genuine *individual* choices about whether or not to take and pay for the benefits of public goods. That is the strategy of the voluntary exchange theory of Wicksell, Lindahl, and Buchanan, and it will be my strategy too. I cannot claim to have found a universally applicable and operational criterion for decisions about the provision and financing of public goods, but in this and the following section I will suggest two possible ways in which progress might be made.

Flood protection provides a good example of the first of these lines of approach. Many of the benefits of flood protection accrue, at least in the first instance, to individuals as occupiers of property. If a river overflows, the occupiers of flooded houses may suffer damage to their possessions, the cost and inconvenience of having to move to temporary accommodation, and the distress and unpleasantness of returning to a damp and dirty house. Similarly, the occupiers of business premises may suffer damage to stock and loss of revenue. For any given property on any given day on which it is flooded, there is an occupier who *on that day* has no option of paying to avoid these harmful effects. But if there is a competitive property market, and if some properties are known to be subject to flood risk and others are known not to be, there will be a corresponding difference in their rental values (holding other factors constant). A prospective occupier who is choosing between alternative properties to rent *is* able to make choices about whether to pay a price premium to occupy a property with reduced flood risk. This difference in rental values will be reflected in capital values. So a prospective owner who is choosing between alternative properties to buy is able to make choices about whether to pay a price premium to own a property with reduced flood risk (and with correspondingly higher returns if rented out). The upshot of this is that many of the benefits of flood protection ultimately show up as increases in property values. These effects are unambiguous monetary gains to identifiable property owners. To determine the size of these gains for a specific flood protection project, we need to be able to identify the statistical relationship between flood risk and property value; but if that relationship is known, we do not need to enquire any further into the preferences that lie behind it.

Now suppose that, for some proposed flood protection project, the total increase in the value of the protected property is greater than the cost of the project. (For simplicity, I will assume that the project is sufficiently small that the underlying relationship between flood risk and property value is unaffected.) Thus, it would in principle be possible to finance the project by imposing charges on the owners of protected property, and to set those charges so that each owner remained a net gainer. Since the calculation of net gain is simply the subtraction of one amount of money from another, there is no ambiguity in saying that a positive net gain for any individual implies an expansion in that individual's opportunity set. This package of project and charges can be thought of as a mutually beneficial transaction between property owners and the suppliers of project inputs.

Despite being mutually beneficial, such a transaction would probably need to be intermediated by some agency with the authority to impose compulsory charges. If instead individuals were left to negotiate an agreement among themselves, the achievement of mutual benefit would be vulnerable to the *free-rider problem*—the incentive for individual beneficiaries to refuse to contribute to the costs of the project, in the hope that others will pay for it. Even if all the beneficiaries were willing to contribute and negotiated in good faith, there would still be the problem of agreeing on a division of the costs, and different individuals might try to hold out for different divisions—the *hold-out problem*. When public goods have many beneficiaries, one cannot normally expect them to be supplied through transactions that are entirely voluntary. But it is sometimes possible for a public agency to supply such goods by intermediating mutually beneficial but non-voluntary transactions.

As another example of the same mechanism, consider the provision of public goods that are enjoyed by tourists, such as litter-free beaches, attractive landscapes, public art works, and wildlife habitats. In any given tourist area, such public goods are complementary with a wide range of locally supplied private goods and services, such as hotel accommodation, restaurant meals, coach travel, and car parking. Improvements in the supply of touristic public goods induce increases in total willingness to pay for the private goods supplied by the tourist industry. Thus, combinations of public good provision and sales taxes on tourist services may be mutually beneficial.

The general principle behind these examples is the exploitation of complementarities between public and private goods. Whenever a public good is complementary with a private good, some part of the benefit of the public good can be appropriated by taxing the private good. This provides a mechanism by which a public agency with taxing powers can intermediate mutually beneficial transactions involving public goods. In advocating this mechanism, I am not saying that flood protection is valuable *because* it increases property values, or that litter-free beaches are valuable *because* they increase hotel revenue. It is the other way round. It is because people want to avoid the distress of seeing their homes ruined by flood water that there is a price premium for properties with flood protection. It is because people find the sight of litter offensive that they are willing to pay more to stay in seaside hotels if beaches are kept clean. Through the workings of markets, the subjective attitudes of disparate individuals are combined and transmuted into objective monetary measures. My claim is that these measures can be meaningful for normative analysis even if they encapsulate the effects of non-integrated preferences.

7.7 Otto per Mille

Philosophical commentators on economics are often critical of the use of willingness-to-pay measures of value in cost–benefit analysis. Their objection is that this practice implicitly assumes that individuals think of public goods in instrumental terms, and that in some important cases this assumption is illegitimate. It might seem that the contractarian analysis I have been presenting is vulnerable to this criticism. I will argue that it is not.

One version of this criticism is put forward by Elizabeth Anderson (1993) and Michael Sandel (2012). Anderson argues that economics treats goods as having only instrumental value, as *commodities* to be *used*: 'To merely use something is to subordinate it to one's own ends, without regard for its intrinsic value' (1993: 144). She maintains that certain goods, environmental quality being an example, 'are not properly regarded as mere commodities. By regarding them only as commodity values, cost–benefit analysis fails to consider the proper roles they play in public life'. Cost–benefit analysis makes this error by unquestioningly 'taking individuals' private market choices as normative for public policy'. It is fundamental to Anderson's argument that individuals' market choices express instrumental motivations—and, she thinks, properly so, provided that the goods that are being traded really are mere commodities (1993: 190–1). Agreeing with Anderson, Sandel says that 'when we decide that certain goods can be bought and sold, we decide, at least implicitly, that it is appropriate to treat them as commodities, as instruments of profit and use. But not all goods are properly valued in this way' (2012: 9). Adding an extra dimension to this argument, he claims that by using a privatized conception of value, 'market reasoning...empties public life of moral argument' and 'drain[s] public discourse of moral and civic energy' (2012: 14).

Daniel Hausman (2012: 93–100) presents a related criticism of what he sees as a common misuse of cost–benefit analysis. Hausman takes as given that cost–benefit analysis is 'a method of evaluating policies in terms of welfare, where welfare is measured by the extent to which preferences are satisfied' (2012: 93). He argues that the validity of conclusions derived from cost–benefit analysis depends on the validity of the assumption that preference-satisfaction is an adequate measure of individual welfare. That assumption, he suggests, is probably reasonable if the preferences that are being used in the analysis are based on accurate information and are self-interested. Crucially, however, he claims that preferences that are *not* self-interested are not relevant for cost–benefit analysis. Hausman illustrates this claim by discussing preferences for environmental protection. Consider a person who is willing to pay to secure the continued existence of some endangered species, even though she has no expectation of personal benefit from that outcome. Hausman claims (contrary to a common practice in environmental economics) that a measure of this willingness to pay is not relevant for cost–benefit analysis. What he is saying is not that the reasons that lie behind this willingness to pay are irrelevant for public policy, or that the conservation of endangered species is not a legitimate concern of government, but rather that those reasons and concerns should be put forward and assessed in public debate, not entered as monetary values in cost–benefit analysis. Thus:

> The objective of increasing welfare gives [legislators] no reason to institute policies that satisfy preferences that are not self-interested. The legislator must instead ask whether there are good reasons supporting non-self-interested preferences, and if he or she thinks there are not, then the legislator should attempt to change the minds of his or her constituents.   (Hausman, 2012: 97)

Viewed in a contractarian perspective, these criticisms of cost–benefit analysis seem misplaced. To explain why, it is useful to begin with a case of a non-instrumental, non-self-interested preference for a *private* good. Consider a person who sees a pilgrimage to some distant place (perhaps Jerusalem or Mecca or Varanasi) as an important religious observance or as a fitting expression of her religious identity. Since she lives in a market economy, this pilgrimage is possible only if she buys an airline ticket. Buying the ticket is a private market choice in Anderson's terms. But the person's willingness to pay the ticket price does not make the journey a mere instrument of profit and use: it is still a religious pilgrimage. The preference that the pilgrim reveals in buying the ticket is not self-interested in Hausman's terms. But should it even cross the mind of a legislator to ask whether her preference is less entitled to be satisfied than an otherwise equivalent self-interested one? The pilgrim is spending her own money to buy something that, for reasons that are important to her, she wants to have. That there is a price to be paid registers the fact that her journey can be made possible only through other people's supply of labour and capital; in paying the price, she ensures that these other people's contributions are made voluntarily. Having ensured this, she is entitled to say that her reasons for engaging in the transaction are no one else's business.

Now consider the case of a group of people who share a non-instrumental, non-self-interested preference that some particular state of affairs should obtain. Using Hausman's example, suppose that this state of affairs is the conservation of some endangered species. The people with this preference— let us call them the *environmentalists*—do not think of themselves as benefiting from the existence of this species. They believe that human beings in general have a responsibility to act as stewards of the natural world, and that maintaining biodiversity is one of those responsibilities. Suppose that a group of environmentalists form an organization, financed by their own voluntary contributions, which funds conservation projects. The environmentalists are a minority in their political community. If the majority think that the idea of environmental stewardship is nonsense, does that entitle them to prevent the others from acting on their non-self-interested preferences? Just as in the case of the individual pilgrim, a contractarian would say: No. The environmentalists, taken together, are willing to pay the costs of their joint activity, and they do pay them. Their reasons for valuing this activity are no one else's business.

Now look at the issue from the other side. The environmentalists believe that *everyone* has a duty of stewardship. Are they entitled to demand that the majority contribute too? Notice that the majority are not free-riding. They are not acting like people who try to avoid paying their share of the costs of a flood protection project that will increase the value of their property. They simply do not value the activity that the environmentalists are willing to pay for. The contractarian answer has to be that the environmentalists are *not* entitled to make this demand. The majority's reasons for not valuing this activity are no one else's business either. This is not to deny that there can be public discourse about what people ought or ought not to value, and that such a discourse might lead people to change their ideas about value. But the purpose of a contractarian analysis is to find transactions that are mutually advantageous, as viewed by those individuals who are party to them.

It is important to keep in mind what is involved in taking a contractarian viewpoint. Of course, if you imagine yourself as a benevolent or moral autocrat, or as a contributor to a process of public reasoning in which your ideas will ultimately carry the day, the contractarian approach of looking for mutually advantageous transactions may seem an unnecessary and even ignoble compromise. If you really had sole responsibility for determining which economic outcomes should come about in your society, or if you could expect a majority of your fellow-citizens to be persuaded by your arguments about what should be done, you might think it right to be guided by your own sense of morality. If you believed in a universal moral duty of environmental stewardship, you might decide (as the benevolent autocrat) or propose (as the influential contributor to public debate) that all individuals should pay to conserve endangered species, whether they wanted to do so or not. Conversely, if you thought the idea of stewardship was nonsense, you might decide or propose to promote the true welfare of the environmentalists by prohibiting them from wasting their money on conservation. But contractarian arguments are addressed to people who are trying to negotiate mutually acceptable agreements without necessarily resolving all their moral and political differences.

This leaves the problem of how to ensure that, when people have non-instrumental preferences for public goods, mutually agreeable transactions (and only such transactions) are intermediated. The Italian tax system has an interesting mechanism which, by going a small way towards achieving this objective, illustrates the logic of a contractarian approach to the provision of public goods. I do not want to claim that this mechanism is a universal solution to the general problem I have described, but I believe that it could usefully be adapted to many cases in which there is divergence in people's beliefs about which kinds of public goods are valuable and which are not.[21]

The Italian mechanism is the *otto per mille* (eight per thousand) law, designed to provide funding to religious organizations. The essential idea is that 0.8 per cent of each individual's income tax liability is assigned either to one of a list of recognized religious organizations or to a general fund, originally intended to be used for humanitarian purposes, administered by the Italian government. Religious organizations are required to spend the money they receive on a defined set of recognized activities, such as support for their clergy and charitable work. From a contractarian viewpoint, what is most interesting about this law is that each taxpayer can choose which fund on the list will receive her 0.8 per cent. (If a taxpayer does not make a choice, her 0.8 per cent is divided between the eligible funds in the same proportions as the total payments of those who do choose.)

One might think of the activities of each religious organization as supplying a public good that is valued by some subset of the Italian population. For those who consider themselves Catholic, the Catholic Church provides a public good; for those who consider themselves Jewish, the Union of Italian Jewish Communities provides a public good; and so on. The *otto per mille* procedure provides a rough and ready response to the free-rider and hold-out problems. If (say) you consider yourself a Catholic and if you cannot avoid paying 0.8 per cent of your tax liability to provide *some* religious or humanitarian public good, why not support your own church rather than someone else's? It might be objected that the concept of free-riding does not apply to someone who values a religious or humanitarian activity for non-self-interested reasons. Such a person, it might be argued, does not benefit from the activity, and so there is no sense in which she can take a free ride on other people's contributions to it. But even if this objection is right (and I am not sure it is), the requirement that everyone must pay the 0.8 per cent tax still serves an important purpose. If contributions are voluntary, someone who contributes to the Catholic Church out of a sense of religious duty can claim that people who choose not to contribute are putting self-interest before morality. But a taxpayer cannot be accused of bad faith or improper self-interest for making her own choice between activities from which she receives no private benefit.

The *otto per mille* procedure is also a rough and ready way of ensuring that people contribute to the costs of only those public goods that they actually value. There may be some Catholics who believe that everyone has a moral obligation to pay for the activities of the Catholic Church, and that the Seventh-Day Adventist Church is a propagator of religious error. And there may be Seventh-Day Adventists who have the opposite beliefs. In taking no account of such beliefs, the *otto per mille* procedure is contractarian in spirit. A contractarian would say that how Seventh-Day Adventists choose to spend their own money is no business of Catholics, and vice versa. In saying this, the contractarian is saying that each taxpayer's 0.8 per cent is that person's own money, and not the property of the Italian state. The Italian government is not subsidising religious organizations according to *its* judgements about their relative merits; it is simply intermediating transactions in which individuals pay for activities that *they* value.

In the spirit of Sandel's critique of 'market reasoning', one might object that the tendency of the *otto per mille* procedure is to empty public life of moral argument and to drain public discourse of moral and civic energy. That is probably true. Political argument would be more intense and energetic if a collective decision had to be made about which (if any) religion was, by virtue of the truth of its doctrines, worthy of state support. But in the light of centuries of experience of wars of religion, one might conclude that energy was a mixed blessing.

8

Psychological Stability

In developing his theory of justice, John Rawls (1971: 16, 177, 453–62) defines a concept of *psychological stability*. On Rawls's view, the purpose of a theory of justice is to provide a set of principles for structuring a 'well-ordered society'. Rawls insists that a well-ordered society must be regulated by a *public* conception of justice. That is, the governing principles of the society must be understood by and accepted by its members. But if a conception of justice is to be public, the hypothesis that individuals accept its principles must be consistent with the facts of human psychology. When an ongoing society is regulated by those principles, it must reproduce both a general belief that the principles are fair and a general willingness to abide by them. Principles that are self-reproducing in this sense are psychologically stable.[1] In this chapter, I consider what properties a market economy needs to have in order for its governing principles to be psychologically stable when viewed in a contractarian perspective.

When I first introduced this perspective in Chapter 3, I said that contractarian reasoning about mutual benefit was possible only if the parties to a potential agreement jointly acknowledged some baseline of non-agreement and understood the idea of 'benefit' relative to that baseline. I claimed that, for contractarian reasoning to be possible, it was not essential that the baseline was acknowledged as fair. In this chapter, I will explain and defend that claim. In doing so, I deviate from the main paths of the contractarian literature, but in a direction previously taken by James Buchanan (1975). One might naturally think that the best way to construct a contractarian recommendation for the market would be to imagine a baseline in which the distribution of initial endowments was fair and then to show that it would be in every individual's interests to set up a market economy. However, I will argue that there is a fundamental tension between the idea of a fair baseline and the principles by which market economies work. Psychological stability has to rest on continuing expectations of mutual benefit, defined relative to a baseline that evolves over time and that cannot be justified in terms of abstract principles of fairness.

8.1 Equality of Opportunity

In philosophical discussions of economic fairness, a traditional thought experiment is to imagine a group of individuals who are forming an entirely new society and who have to agree on the principles by which it will operate.[2] It is sometimes argued that, in such a situation, it would be rational for individuals to agree to set up a market economy that satisfied some principle of equality of opportunity. Different authors argue for different versions of that principle as suitable for the society of the thought experiment. In the first two sections of this chapter, I will follow this approach and see where it leads.

The thought experiment of the newly-formed society has a long history. When John Stuart Mill (1871/1909: 202) discusses the ideal form of private property, he imagines a group of colonists settling in a previously uninhabited country, bringing with them only objects that they own in common. He suggests that if the colonists chose to institute a regime of private property, that regime would be (or ought to be) founded on principles of equality of opportunity:

> Every full grown man or woman, we must suppose, would be secured in the unfettered use of and disposal of his or her bodily and mental faculties; and the instruments of production, the land and tools, would be divided fairly among them, so that all might start, in respect to outward appliances, on equal terms. It is possible to conceive also that in this original apportionment, compensation might be made for the injuries of nature, and the balance redressed by assigning to the less robust members of the community advantages in the distribution, sufficient to put them on a par with the rest. But the division, once made, would not again be interfered with; individuals would be left to their own exertions and to the ordinary chances, for making an advantageous use of them. (Mill 1871/1909: 202)

A thought experiment very similar to Mill's is used by Ronald Dworkin (1981), who imagines a group of shipwreck survivors washed ashore on an uninhabited island, with no prospect of rescue. In Dworkin's story, the islanders begin their economic life together by holding an auction to allocate the available stock of external (that is, non-human) resources. Each islander is given the same initial endowment of a unit of account ('clamshells') for use in the auction. The idea is that, since everyone has the same endowment of clamshells and faces the same prices, everyone has the same opportunities to acquire external resources—even if, in the event, different islanders buy different bundles. However, this procedure is not enough to satisfy Dworkin's conception of 'equality of resources'.

Dworkin makes a fundamental distinction between two kinds of luck that a person may enjoy. *Option luck* 'is a matter of how deliberate and calculated gambles turn out—whether someone gains or loses through accepting an isolated risk he or she should have anticipated and might have declined'; *brute luck* 'is a matter of how risks fall out that are not in that sense deliberate gambles' (1981: 293). According to Dworkin, inequalities that result from option luck do not imply any entitlement to compensation. But in Dworkin's ideal society, external resources would be distributed in such a way that inequality could not arise through brute luck. Thus, when he considers differences in income that arise because different people have different occupations, he distinguishes between the effects of 'ambition' and 'talent' (1981: 314). An ambition is a chosen way of living one's life; a talent is a native ability. Dworkin's ideal is that individuals should be free to choose how to live their lives, provided they 'pay the price of the life they have decided to lead, measured in what others give up in order that they do so' (1981: 294). But, he insists, the role of talent must be 'neutralized': there should no differences that are 'traceable to genetic luck, to talents that make some people prosperous but are denied to others who would exploit them to the full if they had them' (1981: 312, 314).

In the case of the shipwreck story, Dworkin implements this ideal by stipulating that, when they set up their society, the islanders are unable to predict their future health states or the future market value of their natural talents. However, they are free to negotiate insurance contracts to protect themselves against these uncertainties. Since everyone starts with the same clamshell endowment and (it is assumed) with the same knowledge of the probability distributions of future health states and future wage rates, any later inequalities in external resources can be attributed to decisions taken in a situation of equality. Thus, these inequalities are analogous with differences in wealth between lucky and unlucky gamblers: they are the result of option luck.

Exactly how this auction is supposed to work is unclear. When Dworkin tries to fill in the details, he (rather incongruously) imagines that the islanders have access to a computer to which someone has already inputted 'information about the tastes, ambitions, talents, and attitudes to risk of each of the immigrants, as well as information about the raw materials and technology available'. This computer then somehow predicts the outcomes of the auction, how each individual will use his or her resources, and the distribution of income that will result from this. It then designs actuarially sound insurance policies which offer individuals 'insurance . . . against failing to have an opportunity to earn whatever level of income . . . the policy holder names'. With a touching faith in economics, Dworkin says that what the computer is expected to do is amenable to standard (but unspecified) forms of economic analysis, and so there should be no problem of principle in writing the required program (1981: 316–17).

Notice that Dworkin's insurance policies are written in terms of individuals' *opportunities to earn* stated levels of income, and that these opportunities are already known to the computer. Thus, the effects of Dworkin's scheme are just as if it worked in the following way. Before the auction begins, the computer generates a set of insurance policies. As part of the auction process, individuals choose which insurance policies to buy. Immediately after the auction, the computer reports its calculations of the future value of each individual's talents, and determines how much each individual is entitled to claim from the insurance policies he has bought, net of the premiums he has agreed to pay. These transfers need not be made immediately; they might instead take the form of future-dated promises to pay. Still, everything pertaining to insurance can be settled on the day of the auction. Then, as in Mill's story, individuals are left to their own exertions and to the ordinary chances of life. And (in a triumph for the predictive power of economics) each individual in fact chooses to use those opportunities exactly as the computer had predicted on the day of the auction.[3]

One might think that this model offers a peculiar picture of economic life. For the moment, however, I simply leave it as an example of an attempt to theorize the concept of equality of opportunity, and look at another such attempt.

Dworkin's distinction between brute luck and option luck has often been seen as a way of reconciling egalitarianism with principles of freedom and responsibility: on grounds of justice or fairness, it is said, each person can legitimately demand the same amount of opportunity as other people enjoy, but what he does with those opportunities is up to him. It is sometimes hinted that this reconciliation allows egalitarians to steal the clothes of their opponents. Gerald Cohen (1989: 933) expresses this thought particularly openly when, crediting Ronald Dworkin with sparking off a new wave of interest in equality of opportunity, he says that Dworkin 'has performed for egalitarianism the considerable service of incorporating within it the most powerful idea in the arsenal of the anti-egalitarian right: the idea of choice and responsibility'. Building on this idea (but moving away from Dworkin's emphasis on equality of resources), Cohen argues that in determining whether inequalities require compensation 'the right cut is between responsibility and bad luck'. Why is this cut the right one? Because, according to Cohen, 'no one should suffer because of brute bad luck'; 'we should compensate for disadvantage beyond a person's control' (1989: 922).

John Roemer (1998) proposes a theory of equality of opportunity based on Cohen's cut. Roemer starts from the principle that people should not have more or less opportunity because of differences in their *circumstances*, defined as 'characteristics of the environment (broadly defined) which influence behaviour yet are beyond the person's control' (1998: 19). Although Roemer does not present it in quite this way, his theory can be understood as resting on two distinct principles.

The first principle, which I shall call *starting-line equality*, is about *ex ante* equality of opportunity. According to this principle, a fair society would be rather like a fair handicap race: at the starting line, no one is disadvantaged relative to anyone else. Here is one of Roemer's statements of the principle: 'there is, in the notion of equality of opportunity, a "before" and an "after": before the competition starts, opportunities must be equalized, by social intervention if need be, but after it begins, individuals are on their own' (1998: 2). Here is another. Roemer says that an opportunity is 'an access to advantage'. Then: 'What society owes its members, under an equal-opportunities policy, is equal access; but the individual is responsible for turning that access into actual advantage by the application of effort' (1998: 24).

The second principle, which I shall call *equal reward for equal effort*, is about the relationship between effort and *ex post* reward. The ideal is to ensure that, across all individuals, equal efforts (assessed relative to the circumstances of the individuals concerned) yield equal rewards. Here again, Roemer seems to be thinking of a fair society as a handicap race. But now the suggestion is that, if the handicaps are fair, the race will be won by whoever tries hardest to achieve what the rules of the race deem to be victory. Thus, Roemer says, 'individuals who try equally hard should end up with equal outcomes' (1998: 15).

Roemer does not distinguish between these two principles; he presents them as aspects of a single conception of equality of opportunity. They correspond with different readings of Cohen's maxim that we should compensate individuals for disadvantages that are beyond their control. Starting-line equality is a principle of *ex ante* compensation for such disadvantages. Equal reward for equal effort requires that these disadvantages should not translate into deficiencies of *ex post* reward. In Roemer's model of an ideal handicap race, the system of handicaps constitutes *ex ante* compensation while also ensuring that *ex post* rewards are determined only by effort.

Roemer argues that this ideal can be implemented, at least to a reasonable approximation, in a social market economy. He presents the following proposal. Individuals are classified into *types*, such that all the members of any given type can be treated as having equal circumstances. (For example, in a comparison of levels of effort at school between teenage students, students from different social classes might be treated as belonging to different types.) Effort is modelled as a one-dimensional entity. Each person's *degree of effort* is measured by the ranking of her level of effort in the distribution of effort by people of her type. Roemer proposes to structure the relationship between circumstances, effort, and reward so that, as nearly as possible, reward as a function of degree of effort is the same for all types. He assigns the task of designing such a reward structure to an economic planning agency. Roemer suggests that the planners in this agency can collect the information they need to solve this design problem by means of 'experiments' on 'sample populations'. Having used these randomized controlled trials to discover how the effort level of each type responds to different allocation rules, the planning agency determines and announces the 'optimal policy' (1998: 29).

Notice the similarities between Roemer's and Dworkin's representations of equality of opportunity. Both writers are trying to reconcile the kind of freedom of choice that is characteristic of a market economy with a conception of equality of opportunity that requires the effects of brute luck to be neutralized. Both present their proposals by using models in which this neutralization can be carried out before anyone crosses the relevant starting line—in Dworkin's model, on the day of the auction, in Roemer's, before anyone chooses how much effort to make. This is possible because, for every potential configuration of the neutralization device (Dworkin's insurance policies or Roemer's reward structures), individuals' responses to that configuration are already known by some social planner (human or electronic). Of course, these are only models, and the world of a model is necessarily much simpler than the real-world phenomena that it represents. But in analysing economies in which everything is known to a social planner before any economic activity takes place, Dworkin and Roemer are assuming away a crucial feature of real economic life—the *division of knowledge*.

In this respect, Dworkin's and Roemer's proposals are in the same spirit as the *market socialism* that was popular in the period from the 1920s to the 1940s, as a result of the work of such writers as Oskar Lange and Fred Taylor (1938). The essential idea of market socialism was to incorporate markets into a system of central planning. The use of markets would allow decision-making to be decentralized, ensure economic efficiency, and leave individuals free to choose their own consumption patterns. Firms would be publicly owned; they would respond to price signals according to specified rules and not (as under capitalism) in the pursuit of profit for their owners. By means of taxes and transfers, the central planners would ensure an egalitarian distribution of income.

A fundamental flaw in market socialism was identified by Friedrich von Hayek (1948). Market socialism, Hayek argued, owed its credibility among economists to the idea that a market economy can be represented by a general equilibrium model after the style of Léon Walras (1874/1954). By focusing on equilibrium states and by neglecting to consider the dynamic processes by which equilibrium is reached, we are able to create model worlds in which nothing of economic relevance remains to be discovered by the actors. Then, by assuming that we—picturing ourselves as the government, the social planners, the designers of economic institutions—already know everything that will be uncovered in the process of reaching equilibrium, we can design compensation schemes to neutralize any market outcomes we dislike. But this is to overlook what Hayek calls 'the really central problem of economics as a social science'—that of explaining how, in any functioning economic system, 'the spontaneous interaction of a number of people, each possessing only bits of knowledge, brings about a state of affairs...which could be brought about by deliberate direction only by somebody who possessed the combined knowledge of all those individuals' (Hayek, 1948: 50–1). The market is a mechanism that integrates dispersed knowledge. The error of market socialism is to suppose that we can access the knowledge that is generated by market processes without actually going through those processes.

8.2 The Division of Knowledge

As an opening illustration of the difficulty of achieving equality of opportunity in the face of the division of knowledge, I offer a different model of a society of shipwreck survivors. My survivors, like Dworkin's, are washed ashore on an uninhabited island. I will call it Hayek Island. In the sense that Mill uses the term in his story of the colonists, the survivors are equally 'robust'. They arrive with no external resources from their previous lives. The island itself has no external resources except land, which is so abundant as to be a free good. There are only two goods, neither of which can be stored. One good, corn, is produced through cultivation; there is only one technology of corn production, known to everyone, which has constant returns to scale. Since land is a free good, the only economic input to the production process is labour: the more labour is applied, the more corn is produced. There is no uncertainty in this process: the amount of corn produced from any labour input is known. All the islanders are capable of supplying the same undifferentiated labour; thus, in relation to corn production, all have equal natural talent.

The other good is a nutritious fruit which can be found in the island's vast and dense forests. At the time they arrive, all that the islanders positively know about this fruit is the following. The trees on which the fruit grow are sparsely distributed in the forest, at as yet unknown locations. At any given time, only a tiny fraction of the trees are in fruit. There is no known fruiting season, or known interval between fruiting periods for a given tree, but it is known that the fruiting period for any tree is very short and the intervals between these periods are very long. However, if a tree is found at just the right moment, large quantities of the fruit can be collected by the expenditure of relatively little labour. In respect of the labour required to gather and transport fruit, everyone has equal natural talent.

Although this is all that is *known*, there are many, often conflicting, beliefs about the fruit among the islanders; and these beliefs are not public knowledge. Some have heard travellers' tales which suggest that fruiting trees are particularly likely to be found at certain times and in certain kinds of locations—some say in June on mountain sides, some say at full moon beside rivers, and so on. Others have heard tales of how trees in fruit can be found by observing certain movements of birds or insects. Some people believe that fruit-gathering expeditions are most likely to be successful if they are preceded by certain elaborate rituals. Others believe a scientific approach will be most effective: one should invest time in collecting and analysing information about the biology of the trees, trying to construct a theory which will predict where and when fruiting trees are to be found. Still others think the most effective method of finding fruit is to treat the location of fruiting trees as entirely random: one simply has to spend as much time as possible searching.

As well as holding different beliefs, the islanders have different preferences over the two goods, and over the different ways in which time can be spent (leisure, cultivating corn, searching for fruit, engaging in rituals, scientific enquiry, and so on). They also have different time preferences and different attitudes to risk. Each person has only a hazy idea about what other people's current and future preferences are or will be. Each person is also uncertain about his own future preferences. Whether there ought to be—or even can be—compensation for these differences is the point of the story.

The islanders organize their economy in accordance with the teaching of John Locke (1690/1960). Each person is allowed to use as much land as he wants for cultivating corn; any corn produced on this land is his property. All other land is common. Fruit is unowned as long as it is on a tree, but if gathered it becomes the property of the person who gathers it. Everyone is free to search for fruit in whatever way he chooses, provided he does not impede others who are similarly engaged. A person who owns a good may consume it or use it in trade. People are also free to negotiate partnerships. Partnerships provide a way of spreading the risks of fruit-gathering.

In principle, it is open to the islanders to negotiate partnerships which would completely spread all those risks. For example, all of them might form a single partnership, agree on what work each person is to do, and share equally all the corn and fruit produced by everyone's labour. But there are two reasons to expect that freely chosen partnerships would not spread risks so completely.

First, there is the fact that different individuals have different beliefs. Relative to the benchmark of complete risk-spreading, there is scope for trades that are mutually beneficial *ex ante*. The effect of such trades is to increase each person's stake in those activities which he thinks more likely to be successful and to reduce his stake in the others. Second, there is the problem of moral hazard or opportunism. Many of the technologies for fruit-gathering involve forms of labour that are not easy to monitor. (The most effective way for a number of people to search for fruit might be for each person to search a different area of forest; but then how does anyone check whether her partners are searching or not?) In markets, this problem is usually solved by ensuring that anyone who might have an incentive to be opportunistic continues to bear a significant share of the relevant risk. Thus, in a partnership of n people, each of whom searches for fruit alone, it might be agreed that each partner takes more than a $1/n$ share of the fruit she gathers, and a correspondingly smaller share of what anyone else gathers.

So, even after partnerships have been negotiated, different individuals will bear different risks. Those people who believe they know particularly effective fruit-gathering strategies will bet on their beliefs, either by using those strategies themselves, or by going into partnership with people who do. Others will adopt the safer strategy of growing corn. But if the corn-growers are expecting to trade some of the corn they grow for fruit, they are subject to risk too: the terms on which they will be able to trade will depend on the overall success of the fruit-gatherers. *Ex post*, there will be inequality of rewards. Other things being equal, those people whose beliefs are closest to the truth will receive the greatest rewards.

Suppose the story continues like this. A wide range of different fruit-gathering methods are used by different individuals and partnerships. It turns out that the biology of the trees is much more complicated than the would-be scientists imagined. Because of this, those people who invested in scientific investigation learn little that is of use to them; on average they do badly. The travellers' tale about insect behaviour is true. The few people who had heard and believed that particular tale do very well. But the rest of the travellers' tales are valueless; the people who believed them do no better than those who search at random. The idea that rituals increase the success of expeditions is merely a superstition; the people who believed in that superstition, like the would-be scientists, incur unnecessary additional costs. Viewed in relation to Cohen's cut, these inequalities are primarily the result of good and bad luck. But is this option luck or brute luck?

Remember that on Hayek Island there is no technology, known to everyone *ex ante*, by which true information can be discovered by the application of some kind of effort. Different individuals have simply stumbled on different pieces of (what appeared to be) information by good or bad luck. With the benefit of hindsight we can say that those people who heard the true travellers' tale had good luck: through no effort of their own, they had access to a valuable resource—knowledge—that was denied to the others. Conversely, those people who heard the false tales had bad luck. This seems to be a clear case of brute luck, of advantage and disadvantage beyond the control of the person concerned. One might argue that some part of the differences in individuals' initial beliefs was not due to differences in information, but rather to differences in subjective beliefs. This is how I would interpret the islanders' attitudes to ritual and to science. But if we follow Roemer, a person should not be held accountable for beliefs that were embedded in him by his environment before he could reasonably be said to have had control over the process. Let us suppose that the islanders' beliefs about ritual and science are the result of different childhood upbringing: some people were brought up to believe in the power of ritual, others to believe in the power of scientific enquiry. As it turned out, both groups were unlucky in the beliefs they were brought up to hold. This, too, is brute luck.

The implication, then, is that the economic institutions of Hayek Island fail to satisfy Roemer's principle of equality of opportunity. There is starting-line equality in the sense of Mill's conception of equality of opportunity (Section 8.1): everyone has the same opportunities to engage in any of the economic activities that are possible on the island. But the principle of equal reward for equal effort is violated: individuals who expend similar degrees of effort receive different rewards, as a result of circumstances beyond their control.

How, if at all, might this supposed defect be corrected? Recall that in Dworkin's and Roemer's model economies, compensation for disadvantage is *ex ante*: those people who are disadvantaged by their circumstances are compensated *before* they make any binding choices in the market. That is how starting-line equality and fair reward for effort are made compatible with a market economy. But on Hayek Island, *ex ante* compensation is not possible. The disadvantage for which compensation is required is that of holding false beliefs. One obstacle in the way of compensation is that each person's beliefs are his own private knowledge: no inventory of beliefs exists in the public domain, prior to trade. But even if everyone's beliefs were publicly known, it would still not be public knowledge, *ex ante*, which beliefs were true and which false. That is discovered only in the process of people's acting on their own beliefs. Cohen's cut cannot be achieved through *ex ante* compensation for disadvantage.

So what would be the implications of keeping Cohen's cut and giving compensation for disadvantage *ex post*? As a starting point, consider a system of full social insurance. Each person chooses whatever mix of corn-growing and fruit-gathering activities he wishes to pursue, and puts as much or as little effort into these activities as he chooses. The total product of everyone's labour is then divided equally amongst individuals. Each day there is a spot market in which current corn and current fruit are traded against one another, so that each person can choose his preferred consumption bundle of the two goods. Since everyone faces the same set of opportunities (even though, *ex ante*, no one knows for certain what reward he will receive for his efforts), there is starting-line equality. And since rewards are the same for everyone and are independent of effort, the principle of equal reward for equal effort is satisfied, albeit trivially. However, everyone's opportunities are impoverished. Each person is free to choose what efforts to make, and to choose between different consumption bundles of equal market value, but no one is free to choose between alternative combinations of effort and reward. If effort—or even effort beyond some fairly low threshold—is generally regarded as painful, full social insurance will impoverish opportunities in another way: the total product of the economy, and hence the set of consumption bundles from which each individual can choose, will be small. For Roemer, as for most egalitarians, the objective is not just to achieve equality of opportunity for advantage at *some* level; it is to achieve equality at the *highest* possible level (e.g. Roemer, 1998: 34). Given this objective, full social insurance is surely a non-starter.

It might seem that these weaknesses of full social insurance could be overcome if the total product was divided between individuals according to the efforts they have made. Suppose the islanders agree at the outset that the relationship between effort and reward should take the form of some particular increasing function—say, that reward should be directly proportional to effort. They agree on some index of effort, such that effort is measured on a ratio scale. This index is intended to measure the pain or difficulty of different kinds of effort, without reference to the value of the results to be expected from those efforts. Suppose—a strong assumption—that effort, as defined by the index, can be measured in a publicly verifiable way. *Ex post*, the total quantities of corn and fruit produced by everyone's labour are shared between everyone; each person's share is proportional to the amount of effort he has expended. As before, there is a daily spot market for trading fruit against corn.

This way of organizing the island economy satisfies both Roemer's principles. As under full social insurance, everyone faces the same set of opportunities, and so there is starting-line equality. Since rewards are proportional to effort, the principle of equal reward for equal effort is satisfied. But there is still a flaw in the design: there is no mechanism to direct people's efforts to those activities which—according to their own or to other people's beliefs—are most likely to be effective in producing goods that people want to consume. In order for a person to earn a reward, it is necessary and sufficient that he engages in some activity, whether useful or not, which requires painful or difficult effort. Thus, in choosing what productive activities to engage in, each individual is guided primarily by his own preferences between those activities as forms of labour, relative to their ratings on the effort index. If the number of people in the economy is large enough to make the individual's share in his own product negligible, he has no reason to take account of the likely success of his activities, or of other people's preferences over the different goods he might produce. One of the essential coordinating devices of a market economy has been disabled. I take it that this flaw is fatal.

Given the conditions of Hayek Island, there cannot be a functioning market economy unless some people are disadvantaged as a result of their acting on false beliefs; and some of those false beliefs result from circumstances beyond the control of the individuals concerned. Of course, Hayek Island is only a thought experiment, a counterpoint to Dworkin's story of the auction. But the features of economic life that make Cohen's cut impossible on Hayek Island are features of real-world economies too. Remember that both Dworkin and Roemer are trying to equalize the resources or opportunities that individuals are able to use over their entire adult lives.[4] In any market economy, individuals' decisions between alternative educational and employment opportunities involve fundamental uncertainties that expose them to brute luck.

It is a commonplace to say that an individual's success in his career often depends on whether he happens to be in the right place at the right time. In most industries and in most firms, a significant element of risk is borne by workers, who are locked in by industry-specific and firm-specific training, by seniority rules and by pension entitlements, and by the costs of moving between different geographical areas. Thus, in choosing between job offers, an individual commits himself to a bet on the success of an industry, a firm, and perhaps even a specific factory, shop, or office. These bets are not lotteries whose probabilities are known to everyone in advance; they are much more like the decisions made by the fruit-gatherers in my island economy.

Young adults often have to decide whether to make irrevocable bets on their own judgements about their talents. Think of a school-leaver who has shown great aptitude for some form of work—say professional tennis or opera singing or academic research—that requires a great deal of training, and in which there are well-paid jobs only for those who prove to have exceptional ability. If she decides to train for a career using her special talent, she takes a risk with lifetime consequences. Whether she really has sufficient talent to succeed is not known for sure in advance; this will be discovered only in the course of her training, if she chooses to pursue it. Again, this is not a lottery with known probabilities; it is a hunch that the school-leaver chooses whether or not to back. If individuals are to be free to take this kind of risk, economic rewards must involve some element of brute luck.

8.3 The Other Invisible Hand

In Chapter 6, I discussed the invisible hand which, in Adam Smith's *Wealth of Nations*, guides merchants towards actions which promote the interests of society (Smth, 1776/1976: 456). This is the most famous appearance of the invisible hand in Smith's economic writing, but it is not the only one. In fact there are two.[5] Smith represents the less well-known invisible hand as a redistributive mechanism that operates in a market economy. This mechanism will play an important role in the argument I develop in the rest of this chapter.

In his *Theory of Moral Sentiments*, Smith (1759/1976) touches on a concept that was prominent in European discourse in the second half of the eighteenth century—the concept of 'luxury'. Critical comment about luxury expressed a deeper unease about the rapid growth of commerce in this period. There was a perception that old notions of rank and distinction, based on family lineage, honour, and obligation, were being supplanted by new norms of conspicuous consumption and display. One theme in Smith's work was to try to explain how the pursuit of wealth and luxury, even if not admirable in itself, can produce real benefit as an unintended by-product.

At the time Smith was writing, direct engagement in 'trade'—that is, commerce or manufacturing—was unthinkable for people with pretensions to gentility, but earning income by renting out one's land to tenant farmers was eminently respectable. It was common and even fashionable for gentlemen to take an interest in agricultural 'improvements', such as land drainage and crop rotations, which increased the productivity and rental value of their land. Smith paints a highly-coloured picture of a supposedly typical landowner, motivated to increase his existing (and, Smith suggests, already excessive) consumption of luxury goods:

It is to no purpose, that the proud and unfeeling landlord views his extensive fields, and without a thought for the wants of his brethren, in imagination consumes himself the whole harvest that grows upon them. The homely and vulgar proverb, that the eye is larger than the belly, never was more fully verified than with regard to him. The capacity of his stomach bears no proportion to the immensity of his desires, and will receive no more than that of the meanest peasant. The rest he is obliged to distribute among those, who prepare, in the nicest manner, that little which he himself makes use of, among those who fit up the palace in which this little is to be consumed, among those who provide and keep in order all the different baubles and trinkets, which are employed in the oeconomy of greatness; all of whom thus derive from his luxury and caprice, that share of the necessaries of life, which they would in vain have expected from his humanity or his justice.   (Smith, 1759/1976: 184)

Smith then makes what, on first reading, is an astonishing claim. The confidence with which he makes this claim suggests that it is based on economic reasoning, but the reasoning is not explained:

The produce of the soil maintains at all times nearly that number of inhabitants which it is capable of maintaining. The rich only select from the heap what is most precious and agreeable. They consume little more [of necessities] than the poor, and in spite of their natural selfishness and rapacity, though they mean only their own conveniency, though the sole end which they propose from the labours of all the thousands whom they employ, be the gratification of their own vain and insatiable desires, they divide with the poor the produce of all their improvements. They are led by an invisible hand to make nearly the same distribution of the necessaries of life, which would have been made, had the earth been divided into equal portions among all its inhabitants, and thus without intending it, without knowing it, advance the interest of the society, and afford means to the multiplication of the species. (Smith, 1759/1976: 184–5)

Perhaps what Smith has in mind is a model of a closed market economy in which the prime necessities of life (let us say 'grain') are products of agriculture, and the main use of agricultural land is the production of grain. The labouring poor spend almost all their income on grain; rich landowners spend almost all theirs on other goods ('luxury') which require the employment of non-agricultural labour. In an equilibrium state of such a model, there will be relatively little inequality *in the distribution of grain* between rich and poor. One might think that this is not such a great achievement to credit to the invisible hand. After all, the landowners' consumption of luxuries requires the diversion of labour from the production of grain, and this presumably reduces the quantity of grain available for the poor to consume.

What is more interesting is that Smith seems to be claiming that, in an eighteenth-century economy, *the benefits of agricultural improvements* accrue mainly to the poor. This claim is not implausible. Each landowner clearly benefits from *his* improvements, considered in isolation (and before deducting the costs of carrying them out); but the combined effect of improvements by all landowners is to raise the real wage rate and so to increase the price of luxuries. It is entirely possible that improvements have no net effect on the distribution of labour between the production of grain and the production of luxuries. In this case, landowners' attempts to increase their consumption of luxuries are completely self-defeating.[6]

It is important to understand how this invisible-hand mechanism works. Consider an eighteenth-century landowner who takes up the fashion for improvements. To keep things simple, suppose he makes his improvements on the home farm of his estate, managed by a paid employee rather than rented to a tenant farmer. And suppose these improvements do not involve any outlay of labour or capital: the landowner simply takes up scientific farming as a way of using his ample leisure time (although with an eye to the profits it will generate). He instructs his farm manager to use the latest crop rotations. These increase the productivity of his land and thereby his profits. He finds that, with the new rotations, he can increase profits still further by taking on more farm workers. He uses these additional profits to employ more domestic servants and so enjoy a more luxurious life. So *his* improvements have clearly benefited him.

However, the landowner's increased demand for labour tends to raise the price of labour. If the labour he buys is only a small part of the amount that is traded in the market, this change will be small as a proportion of the original price, and will have a correspondingly small proportionate effect on *his* profits. But this price change affects many other participants in the labour market. All sellers of labour gain from the increase and all buyers lose. In absolute terms, the value of this transfer of income from employers to workers is of the same order of magnitude as our landowner's additional outlay on labour.[7] Thus, in improving his own land, each landowner brings about a transfer of income from landowners in general to labourers in general. If all landowners make improvements, the net benefits of their efforts might, as Smith suggests, accrue entirely to labourers.

In the language of cost–benefit analysis, these unintended transfers are *pecuniary externalities* of market transactions. They are not involuntary transfers of goods or services. They do not affect what anyone owns, nor do they affect the opportunities for the members of any group of individuals to make feasible transactions among themselves.[8] What they affect are the terms on which people *are willing to* trade, and hence the opportunity sets from which individuals are able to choose. Intuitively, an individual incurs a negative pecuniary externality when the terms on which other people are willing to trade with him change to his disadvantage; he enjoys a positive pecuniary externality when those terms change to his advantage. Pecuniary externalities occur because, in competitive markets, prices continually adjust in response to changes in individuals' trading plans. These adjustments are unavoidable if the market is to continue to provide opportunities for feasible voluntary transactions. Each person's opportunity set must adjust to reflect changes in the terms on which other people are willing to trade with him.

Pecuniary externalities are one of the most significant ways in which market rewards reflect brute luck. For example, suppose that, as conjectured by Smith, the effect of agricultural improvements is to raise the price of labour by just such an amount that the distribution of labour between agriculture and the production of luxuries is unchanged. Consider someone who is employed by an improving landowner as a domestic servant. Suppose there has been no change in the technology of domestic service. Because of the tendency for workers to move between alternative employments in pursuit of higher wages, the wage rate for domestic servants increases in line with that for agricultural labour. The servant continues to do exactly the same work as she did before, but she is paid more for doing it. Even though she has had no direct involvement in the process of agricultural improvement, and even if she has no personal inclination or talent for agricultural work, she has benefited from that process. This is brute luck. Still, what has happened is not arbitrary. In a market, the rewards that each person receives depend on her trading partners' valuations of what she does for them. The services that the servant performs have not changed, but her employer (being richer) is willing to pay more for them—and has to pay more if he is to continue to enjoy them.

In Smith's example, pecuniary externalities mitigate prevailing inequalities: the market gives incentives for individual landowners to create increases in wealth which ultimately flow to the labouring poor. But it is easy to think of cases in which pecuniary externalities have the opposite effect. In the nineteenth century, for example, some British landowners amassed great fortunes from the good luck of owning large tracts of land that could be mined for coal. In this case, the engineers who developed the technology of steam power created increases in wealth which, through changes in the value of mineral rights, ultimately accrued to a leisure class of landowners.

Nevertheless, pecuniary externalities do tend to show certain general patterns, illustrated by the case of Smith's landowner. The landowner recognizes that, given the current price of labour, agricultural improvement is a profit opportunity. But as an unintended by-product of taking advantage of this opportunity, he transfers to new beneficiaries some of the profits that would otherwise have been earned by those landowners who made improvements before he did. To put this in more general terms, when everyone in some class of market agents has access to the same profit opportunity, each agent's attempt to appropriate the available surplus diverts some of that surplus to people outside that class. There is a simple reason why pecuniary externalities tend to work in this way. If the exploitation of a profit opportunity requires some good to be bought, each agent's demand for the good pushes up its price for the others; if it requires some good to be sold, each agent's supply pushes down the price for the others. The underlying mechanism is essentially the same as that of the various forms of arbitrage considered in Chapters 6 and 7.

In Section 6.10, I described the invisible hand of the *Wealth of Nations* as a mechanism by which opportunities for mutually beneficial transactions are realized. I propose to interpret the invisible hand of the *Theory of Moral Sentiments* as a complementary mechanism. As opportunities for mutually beneficial transactions are being realized, some of the surplus created by those transactions is transferred to individuals whose economic role is effectively that of passive bystanders. Sometimes, as in Smith's example, this mechanism works as if implementing some principle of fairness or equality; but sometimes it does not.

8.4 Why Markets Cannot Be Fair

A recurring metaphor in discussions about equality of opportunity is that of a fair race. As I pointed out in Section 8.1, Roemer seems to have some such metaphor in mind when he describes equality of opportunity as a competition in which everyone starts out on equal terms, but 'after it begins, individuals are on their own'.[9] The same metaphor appears in some of the great works of the liberal tradition of economics. When Mill (1871/1909) compares 'Communism at its best' with the 'principle of private property', he says that this principle has never had a fair trial:

> The laws of property have never yet conformed to the principles on which the justification of private property rests....They have not held the balance fairly between human beings, but have heaped impediments upon some, to give advantage to others; they have purposely fostered inequalities, and prevented all from starting fair in the race.   (Mill, 1871/1909: 208–9)

Mill immediately goes on to concede that no practicable system of private property can ensure that 'all...start on perfectly equal terms', but the clear suggestion is that an ideal system of private property would resemble a fair race. The metaphor of the race can also be found in Smith's *Theory of Moral Sentiments*. Discussing how far a person can retain other people's sympathy while showing more interest in his own happiness than in theirs, Smith (1759/1976) says that each person's natural preference for his own interests will normally be indulged by others, provided that it is expressed in fair competition:

> In the race for wealth, and honours, and preferments [i.e. appointments or promotions], he may run as hard as he can, and strain every nerve and every muscle, in order to outstrip all his competitors. But if he should justle, or throw down any of them, the indulgence of the spectators is entirely at an end.   (Smith, 1759/1976: 83)

Again we have the suggestion that economic life is a race that ought to be run fairly.

A similar thought is expressed by Michael Sandel (2009: 3–10) in a discussion of the justice or injustice of markets. In the aftermath of Hurricane Charley in Florida in 2004, some firms charged scarcity prices for such goods as motel rooms, emergency repairs, and bottled water. At the time, there were economists brave enough to argue that market-clearing prices promote efficiency in the use of resources, and that this truth is not invalidated by hurricanes. In contrast, Sandel presents the 'price gouging' of these firms as an example of going beyond the moral limits of markets (and economists' acceptance of this as an example of going beyond the moral limits of economics). For Sandel, justice is about 'giving people what they deserve'.

That requires judgements about 'what virtues are worthy of honor and reward, and what way of life a good society should promote'. He invites his readers to conclude that effort and talent are worthy of reward in the world of business (2009: 12–21), but that principles of justice are violated if the market rewards individuals for the luck of owning motels close to the tracks of hurricanes and for the 'greed' that allows them to take advantage of this luck. In treating effort and talent as the proper grounds for business reward, Sandel seems to be supposing that that justice requires the distribution of earnings in business to be like the distribution of prizes in a fair athletic contest.

But should we think of the market as a race in which individuals compete against one another for prizes? The essence of a race is that it is a zero-sum game: one person can win only because others lose. That is certainly true when people compete for specific appointments or honours (think of the position of President of the United States, or of Oscars or Nobel Prizes), but is it true of market interactions? The market, I have argued, is an institution that facilitates the realization of mutual benefit. If someone wants to gain wealth through market transactions, she has to find ways of transacting with others which benefit them as well as benefiting her. This is not competition in the sense that a race is competitive; it is *cooperation*.

Take the case of the hurricane. Suppose that Sue is a homeowner whose house has been damaged by Hurricane Charley. As soon as the storm moves on, jobbing builders converge on the areas it has passed through, offering repair services. The prices they quote are well above those that prevail in normal times, but still below the maximum that Sue would be willing to pay for their services. She accepts one of these offers. Viewed in a contractarian perspective, this is just another example of the general tendency of the market to facilitate mutually beneficial transactions. The hurricane has created an unexpected opportunity for mutually beneficial transactions between home-owners and builders. It is because these transactions are temporarily so profitable for builders that builders arrive so quickly to offer their services. Sue benefits from this property of the market. So does Bob, the builder whose work she pays for. The fact that Bob is paid much more than the normal rate for the work he does is not a reward for any special effort or talent; it is just his good luck that the value of his work to other people is unexpectedly and temporarily high. Nevertheless, Bob's luck and Sue's opportunity to get the quick repairs that she wants and is willing to pay for are two sides of the same coin.

It is unfortunate that the word 'competitive' is used to describe both zero-sum games and well-functioning market economies. Paradoxically, a competitive market need not involve race-like competition at all. Suppose I set myself up as a self-employed plumber in a town large enough to support many plumbers. I advertise my availability and invite potential customers to phone me. When they phone, I quote prices for the work they want doing, and they choose whether or not to hire me. If I find that I am getting more work than I want to do, I raise my prices. If I am getting too little work, I lower them. If I have to lower my prices too much in order to get business, I will try a different occupation. If all plumbers behave like me, the town will have a competitive market in plumbing—even if I never think about the other plumbers who, in the sense of economics, are my competitors. My objective as a plumber, I might think, is not to race with anyone: it is to provide myself with a living by benefiting my customers in ways that they are willing to pay for.

Of course, success in business often requires alertness, not only to what potential customers are willing to buy, but also to what potential competitors are willing to sell and at what prices. Think of a manufacturing firm that is considering whether to invest in a new product line to respond to what it perceives as a shift in consumers' tastes. In judging whether this would be a profitable investment, the firm needs to take account of how quickly other firms will recognize this shift and respond to it. In a case like this, one might say that competing firms are racing with one another to exploit an opportunity for profit. But that profit is not a prize to be awarded to the most meritorious competitor. It is the value derived from participating with consumers in mutually beneficial transactions.

Because of the division of knowledge and because of pecuniary externalities, a market economy cannot provide the kind of equality of opportunity that is found in a fair handicap race. Even if it were possible to engineer starting-line equality at some fixed point in time (as in the stories of colonists and shipwrecks) or at some fixed point in each individual's life at which adulthood could be deemed to have been reached (as in Roemer's account of equality of opportunity), mutually beneficial market transactions beyond the starting line would inevitably generate inequalities in rewards that could not be attributed to differences in effort or talent. As Robert Nozick (1974: 160–4) famously declared, liberty upsets patterns.

In a market, each person's opportunities are opportunities to transact with willing others. Each individual is free to choose from his own opportunity set, but the contents of that set are largely determined by the choices that other individuals make from theirs. In a developed market economy, most people's most valuable opportunities consist of the terms on which other people are willing to transact with them. It is an unavoidable consequence of this fact that everyone can have a wide range of opportunities only if everyone's opportunity set is liable to expand or contract as a result of other people's decisions about how to use *their* opportunities. In this sense, unfairness is intrinsic to markets.

8.5 Looking Forward

I began this chapter by asking what properties a market economy needs to have in order for its governing principles to be psychologically stable—that is, for the workings of the economy to induce a general sense of the fairness of those principles and a general willingness to abide by them. That stability cannot be provided by a guarantee of immunity from the effects of brute luck: no such guarantee is possible.

It might be more compatible with economic reality to imagine a market economy with some form of starting-line equality, analogous with the starting point of the Lockean economy of Hayek Island. But would that be sufficient to generate psychological stability? Suppose an economy could be organized so that every individual, on reaching the age of eighteen, was endowed with the same total value of claims on human and non-human resources, 'value' being measured at the market prices prevailing on the relevant person's eighteenth birthday. And suppose this could be done in such a way that, within each cohort of eighteen-year-olds, everyone accepted that no one was starting his or her adult life with any predictable advantage relative to anyone else. Each member of the cohort would be able to recognize that they would all be exposed to brute luck over the course of their lives and that, as a result, some would end up enjoying more opportunity than others; but no one would be able to predict which of them would have the good luck and which the bad. That might be sufficient to ensure a general sense among eighteen-year-olds that their relative economic positions *at the age of eighteen* were fair. But, as a matter of human psychology, it seems unrealistic to expect that the memory of this original equality could sustain a sense of fairness that persisted over the whole course of each person's life, whatever advantages or disadvantages that person experienced as a result of the unpredictable workings of a market economy.

One might well think that this would be an unrealistic expectation even in an economy in which there was only option luck. Imagine Dworkin's ideal economy, in which quantified risks of ill-health and injury are known to everyone. Suppose it is well known that insurance against personal accident risks can be bought on actuarially fair terms. Consider the case of Bill, who is twenty-five years old and is earning a good income from self-employment. He chooses not to insure, thinking that the cost of the premium could be better spent on a challenging hiking holiday. On the holiday, he makes a careless mistake and falls down a mountainside. He is permanently disabled; as a result, he lives in poverty for the rest of his life. This is option luck. Someone who had no particular connection with Bill might easily say, following Dworkin, that this is a fair outcome of a principle of equality of resources: Bill is paying the price of the life he decided to lead. Perhaps Bill *ought* to accept responsibility for his decision, and not complain about unfairness or seek compensation. Perhaps he ought to continue to accept this responsibility throughout the rest of his life. But the question I am asking here is whether *in fact* Bill's experience of the economic system will tend to induce in him a sense that the system is fair and a willingness to abide by its rules. Given human psychology as we know it, I suggest that the answer is probably 'No'.

The problem is that human psychology treats memories of the past very differently from anticipations of the future. If (as Dworkin does) we try to measure the total resources available to a person over his whole life, resources that conferred advantages in the past but are now used up count equally with resources that still exist and provide opportunities for future advantages. But evolution has designed us to give more attention to future opportunities than to past ones: in terms of the currency of survival and reproduction, future opportunities matter in a way that past opportunities do not. As Drazen Prelec and George Loewenstein (1998) have shown, people find it particularly painful to have to pay for pleasures that have already been enjoyed. In one of their experiments, for example, most of their subjects said that they would prefer pre-payment to post-payment for a Caribbean vacation, but would prefer post-payment for the delivery of a washer and drier. Prelec and Loewenstein argue that the crucial difference between the two cases of post-payment is that when the payments have to be made, the pleasures of the vacation are in the past, but the usefulness of the washer and drier is still in the present. As they put it, people have mental accounts that they like to keep in the black.

Rawls uses a related argument in relation to what he calls the 'strains of commitment'. In his theory, the principles of justice are 'the principles that free and rational persons concerned to further their own interests would accept in an initial position of equality as defining the fundamental terms of their association' (1971: 11). However, he stipulates that, as rational agents, those persons will not enter into agreements they know they cannot keep. When we enter an agreement, he says, 'we must be able to honor it even should the worst possibilities prove to be the case. Otherwise we have not acted in good faith' (1971: 176). The strains of commitment are important for Rawls's theory because what is being agreed in the initial position is not a contract that will be enforced by some external agency; it is a set of political principles that each of the contracting parties agrees to uphold. Rawls argues that the contracting parties cannot in good faith agree to uphold utilitarian principles, because those principles might require some of them to forgo significant advantages for the greater good of the whole: 'In fact, when society is conceived as a system of cooperation designed to advance the good of its members, it seems quite incredible that some citizens should be expected, on the basis of political principles, to accept lower prospects of life for the sake of others' (1971: 178).

What Dworkin's principle of equality of resources requires of Bill is not quite as bad as that. Bill is not required to think of his disadvantages merely as negative components of a *social* total. But Bill at age twenty-five is required to think of disadvantages that he will experience for the whole of the rest of his life merely as negative components of (the expected value of) a *lifetime* total. Political principles that expect people to think like this are still putting a lot of strain on ordinary human psychology.

The contractarian approach, as I have presented it, is concerned with recommendations that can be made to individuals together, as potential parties to mutually beneficial agreements. Its guiding idea is well expressed by Rawls's conception of society as a system of cooperation designed to advance the good of its members, or (as he puts it in another passage), as a 'cooperative venture for mutual advantage' (1971: 84). I have argued that contractarian recommendations must engage with each individual's interests as she perceives them (Chapter 3). If contractarian principles are to be psychologically stable, that must mean each individual's interests as she *currently* perceives them—not as she perceived them at some initial position in the past.

The implication, I suggest, is that a contractarian recommendation in favour of a market economy needs to show each participant, *looking ahead from where she is now*, that she can expect the institutions of the market to work to her benefit. It needs to be able to do this, not just at some specially tailored starting line, but whenever 'now' happens to be. And the recommendation must acknowledge the unpredictability of markets and the brute luck that is an unavoidable component of the rewards they give.

Hayek (1976) claims to offer just such a recommendation of the market when he writes of a 'Great Society in which the individuals are to be free to use their own knowledge for their own purposes':

> What makes agreement and peace possible in such a society is that the individuals are not required to agree on ends but only on means which are capable of serving a great variety of interests and which each hopes will assist him in the pursuit of his own purposes. (Hayek, 1976: 2–3)

And:

> When we reflect that most of the benefits we currently owe to the market are the results of continuous adaptations which are unknown to us, and because of which only some but not all of the consequences of our deliberate decisions can be foreseen, it should be obvious that we will achieve the best results if we abide by a rule which, if consistently applied, is likely to increase everyone's chances. Though the share of each will be unpredictable, because it will depend only in part on his skill and opportunities to learn facts, and in part on accident, this is the condition which alone will make it in the interest of all so to conduct themselves as to make

as large as possible the aggregate product of which they will get an unpredictable share. (Hayek, 1976: 122)

For the moment, let me bracket out Hayek's empirical claims about the benefits that markets can be expected to deliver. My point is that Hayek's argument has the right structure for a contractarian recommendation of the market.

Notice that Hayek is arguing that individuals can *agree* to follow the rules of the market, and that their reason for agreeing to this is that those rules are *likely to increase everyone's chances*. But agree in what context? And increase relative to what? Hayek is certainly not imagining a social contract agreed in some original position of equality. He explicitly rejects traditional forms of social contract theory as expressing the rationalistic conceit that reason allows us to 'make the world anew' (1960: 57). I think we must read him as imagining individuals in an ongoing society, engaging in what he calls 'immanent criticism' of the rules of that society (1976: 26). It is as if (these are my words, not Hayek's) individuals ask themselves: 'Given where we are now, can we agree to continue to live by these existing rules; or if not, can we agree to any changes?' According to Hayek, if everyone agrees that their future interactions will be governed by the rules of the market, each of them is likely to gain relative to where he is now—wherever that may be. In an ongoing market society, where we are now is the result of a history of previous interactions, governed by rules which, viewed from each point in that history, ensured that everyone was likely to gain. The suggestion is that if these properties of the market are generally understood, its rules will have psychological stability.[10]

A somewhat similar argument is developed by David Hume (1739–40: 502–3) when he discusses 'the rules, which determine property'. Hume begins with a story that anticipates Mill's account of the colonists and Dworkin's of the shipwreck survivors. He imagines a case in which 'several persons, being by different accidents separated from the societies, to which they formerly belong'd, may be oblig'd to form a new society among themselves'. He argues that these individuals would recognize that it would be mutually advantageous for them to establish a 'convention for the stability of property'. This requires an agreement about the initial distribution of property rights. According to Hume, 'it must immediately occur, as the most natural expedient, that every one continue to enjoy what he is at present master of, and that property or constant possession be conjoin'd to the immediate possession'. Significantly, however, Hume distances himself from his own story, presenting it only as a dramatization of the emergence and reproduction of conventions over an extended period of time: 'I am sensible, that this method of proceeding is not altogether natural; [but in this story] I here only suppose those reflexions to be form'd at once, which in fact arise insensibly and by degrees'.

I take Hume to be saying that, in real societies, everyone can recognize the advantages that they all gain from the stability of property rights. In order to enjoy these advantages, they need to acknowledge a common baseline from which agreements about the transfer of rights can be negotiated. In an ongoing society in which particular property conventions already exist, and in which everyone has already benefited from everyone's adherence to those conventions, the most natural expedient is to continue to accept them as the baseline for future agreements.

Throughout this chapter, I have spoken about how a contractarian might *recommend* the market, and not about how she might *justify* it. This choice of words was deliberate. Writing as a contractarian, I am not trying to show that a market economy based on the existing distribution of property rights is morally just. I am not telling each person that he has a moral obligation to respect other people's property rights. I am recommending terms on which individual citizens, each considering his own interests as he understands them, might agree to conduct their economic affairs in the expectation that those terms will have continuing psychological stability. The salience of the status quo as the baseline for negotiation is not an implication of any abstract theory of justice. Ultimately, it is a matter of psychology.[11]

Even so, the argument that I have attributed to Hayek and Hume can be part of a contractarian recommendation of the market only if, relative to the baseline at any given time, everyone has a realistic expectation of benefiting from the workings of the market. We must ask whether that is the case. Or, more usefully: How must a market economy be structured if everyone is to have a realistic expectation of benefit?

8.6 Can Everyone Expect to Benefit from the Market?

The central argument of Chapter 6 was that, in an equilibrium state of a competitive market economy, each consumer is able to get whatever he wants and is willing to pay for, when he wants it and is willing to pay for it. I interpreted this property of markets as a fleshing-out of the invisible hand of Smith's *Wealth of Nations*. To the extent that real markets have this property, each individual has some reason to expect to benefit from the future workings of a market economy. This reason is not conclusive, but it is useful to start by repeating its importance.

The essence of this invisible-hand mechanism is that, in a market economy, traders are rewarded for intermediating mutually beneficial transactions. Thus, each individual has reason to expect traders to seek out potential transactions that can benefit him together with others, and to make those transactions available to the would-be beneficiaries. If any future change in the economic environment—say, a change in his own or other people's preferences, a change in the availability of resources, or a change in technology—makes possible some new, mutually beneficial transaction involving him and others, he can expect to be offered the opportunity to share in this benefit.

This property of markets is hugely advantageous, but it comes with a downside risk. At any given time, the opportunities that the market offers to an individual reflect the willingness of other people to transact with him. If everyone is to be free to take advantage of new opportunities for mutually beneficial exchanges, adapting to new knowledge and to changing tastes, everyone cannot also have the right to demand the repetition of transactions that he still finds beneficial, but that his former trading partners no longer wish to make. Thus, there can be no guarantee that individuals do not incur losses as a result of changes in how other people use their opportunities to transact with one another.

Nevertheless, a contractarian recommendation of the market has to give each individual good reasons for expecting a favourable balance of benefits and costs. One strategy for doing this is to try to show that there is a general tendency for individuals to benefit from one another's prosperity, and hence for each individual to share in the gains from other peoples' market transactions. Arguments of this kind have often been used by economists in the liberal tradition. For example, here is Smith arguing against mercantilism:

> The wealth of a neighbouring nation, however, though dangerous in war and politicks, is certainly advantageous in trade. . . . As a rich man is likely to be a better customer to the industrious people in his neighbourhood, than a poor, so is likewise a rich nation. A rich man, indeed, who is himself a manufacturer, is a very dangerous neighbour to all those who deal in the same way. All the rest of the neighbourhood, however, by far the greatest number, profit by the good market which his expence affords them. They even profit by his under-selling the poorer workmen who deal in the same way with him. (Smith, 1776/1976: 494)

Mill (1871/1909, Book 2, Chapter 17, §5) uses a similar argument against mercantilism in the passage I quoted in Section 1.1, in which he says that commerce has taught nations to see one another's prosperity with good will.

Smith's argument is that other people's wealth is good for you if they demand what you can supply, or if they can supply what you demand. (In Smith's story, the rich consumer demands products that his industrious neighbours can supply; the rich manufacturer supplies goods that his neighbours demand. As a current example of the benign effect of other people's wealth, consider how economic growth in East Asia has reduced the price of manufactured goods in Europe.) However, as Smith acknowledges in the remark about how a rich manufacturer can be a dangerous neighbour, other people's wealth can be bad for you if they supply what you supply, or demand what you demand. (Think of why Denmark imposes restrictions on the purchase of seaside holiday homes by non-nationals.)

I argued in Section 8.3 that there is a general tendency for pecuniary externalities to redistribute surplus, taking it from those people who first take advantage of new opportunities and transferring it to economic bystanders. Although this other invisible hand works in a rather indiscriminate way, it might go some way towards ensuring that everyone benefits overall from other people's realization of mutual benefit. However, some classes of economic agents are better placed than others to benefit from pecuniary externalities. As Henry George (1879) argued in the late nineteenth century, there is a systematic tendency for the ultimate beneficiaries of pecuniary externalities to be the owners of goods that are in fixed supply and who can thereby gain from increases in rent.

Price discrimination provides another mechanism by which, in a market economy, people can benefit from one another's prosperity. Price discrimination allows producers to recover fixed costs by tailoring prices to what different classes of consumers are willing to pay. As Jules Dupuit (1844/1952: 261) recognized in the first analysis of the topic, price discrimination may work by exploiting consumers' vanity and credulity, but its effects are often 'more equitable and fairer than one might expect at first sight'. If willingness to pay for a good increases with income, revenue-maximizing discriminatory prices will tend be higher for the rich than for the poor. Recall Dupuit's example of the different prices charged for the fine, the very fine, the superfine, and the extra fine that are all drawn from the same barrel (Section 7.5). By insisting on the extra fine, the rich defray some of the cost of supplying the merely fine to the poor. A related mechanism works through the supply of public goods, if (as I advocated in Section 7.6) the costs of supplying public goods are divided among beneficiaries according to their willingness to pay. If the same public goods are valued by all income groups, increases in other people's wealth tend to increase the supply of public goods from which you benefit, and to reduce the share of the costs that are levied on you.

However, recent trends in the distribution of income raise serious questions about the robustness of the market mechanisms by which people benefit from one another's prosperity. From about 1980, a large share of the benefits of economic growth in many developed countries, and particularly in the United States and the United Kingdom, has accrued to the very richest people. For example, between 1976 and 2007, real pre-tax family incomes in the United States grew by 1.2 per cent per year. The incomes of the richest 1 per cent (corresponding with incomes above $399,000 per year in 2009) grew by 4.4 per cent per year, those of everyone else by only 0.6 per cent per year. As a result, 58 per cent of all income growth over those thirty years accrued to the richest 1 per cent of the population (Atkinson, Piketty, and Saez, 2011: 9). Since these are statistics about pre-tax income, they do not take account of the redistributive effects of taxation and public spending, but they are still sobering for anyone who expects all boats to be lifted by a rising economic tide.

It is also enlightening to look at changes in the world distribution of income between individuals. According to data compiled by Branko Milanovic (2013) for the period from 1988 to 2008, the greatest increases of real income (around 3 per cent per year) accrued to individuals in two distinct income bands. One of these bands was the top 1 per cent of the world income distribution. The other was the middle third of the distribution, characterized by Milanovic as the middle classes of emerging market economies such as China and India. In contrast, the rate of increase for individuals between the 80th and 95th percentiles was between zero and 1 per cent per year. This income band 'include[s] many from former communist countries and Latin America, as well as those citizens of rich countries whose incomes stagnated'. It seems that in a period of globalization and rapid world economic growth, inhabitants of rich countries who are not individually rich have enjoyed only a small share of the benefits.

This latter effect may be the result of reductions in trade barriers and changes in technology which have brought workers in developed economies into more intense competition with those in emerging economies. These processes, transmitted through markets, have created benefits for hundreds of millions of people who, in terms of income levels in developed economies, are relatively poor. The effects of these processes on working-class and lower-middle-class people in Europe and North America are perhaps analogous with the catastrophic effects of the Industrial Revolution on particular groups of workers—the handloom weavers of the north of England are a case in point—whose skills were rendered obsolete by technological advances.

But what about the astonishing increase in the share of income going to the very rich? One line of explanation focuses on income from (non-human) capital. Since owning capital is a precondition for receiving capital income, and because richer people can save more and so are better able to accumulate more capital, unconstrained markets may have inbuilt tendencies towards highly unequal distributions of capital income. Viewed in this perspective, the period from the 1940s to the 1970s may have been abnormal. The Second World War resulted in massive depletion of capital in the industrialized world, both through physical destruction and through the diversion of savings into military production. In the first three post-war decades, tax rates on the highest incomes remained very high, hindering the rebuilding of private fortunes. What has happened to capital incomes since 1980 might mark a return to the kind of capitalism that preceded the First World War (Piketty and Saez, 2003; Piketty, 2014).

However, one of the most striking trends in income distribution in recent decades has been an increase in the share of wages in the total income of individuals in the top percentiles of the income distribution (Atkinson et al., 2011: 6–8). Some economists interpret the emergence of a class of extremely rich wage-earners as the result of advances in the technology of information and communications, combined with the globalization of markets. These changes, it is argued, are creating 'winner-take-all' labour markets in which the value of the marginal product of the most talented individuals is very high (Frank and Cook, 1995). This mechanism is clearly at work in the worlds of sport and entertainment. In European football, for example, the growth of pay-per-view and subscription television and the liberalization of the labour market for players have created huge wage differentials between the very best players and the many more who, despite having great talent, are not quite good enough to play in the top leagues. But how widely this mechanism operates is a matter of dispute. Many commentators have argued that weaknesses of corporate governance have given senior managers considerable power to set the terms of their own pay packages, and thus to pay themselves more than the marginal value of their work (Core, Holthausen, and Larcker, 1999; Bebchuk and Fried, 2003). If this view is right, the fundamental problem is a failure of market competition: senior managers are extracting continuing rents from the transactions that their firms are intermediating.

Pursuing these questions about income inequality would require a different kind of book from the one I am writing. For my purposes, the important point is that neither theoretical reasoning nor empirical observation allows us to be confident that, in the absence of any extraneous redistributive mechanisms, markets can be expected to work to the benefit of everyone who participates in them. Nevertheless, I stand by what I said in Section 8.5 about Hayek's recommendation of the market: it has the right structure for a contractarian argument. What Hayek claims to show is true of the market system is what a contractarian *needs* to show is true of whatever economic system she recommends.

8.7 Underwriting Expectations of Mutual Benefit

A contractarian recommendation is addressed jointly to the members of some group of individuals, considered as potential parties to an agreement. The content of the recommendation is that it is in the separate interest of each member of the group to agree to some specified scheme of cooperation. If the recommendation is about how an economy should be organized, it is natural to take the addressees to be the citizens of some political entity that is capable of taking collective decisions about economic institutions. That entity might be a nation state, or a union of nation states such as the European Union. For the purposes of exposition, I will assume such a set of addressees. Readers who prefer to imagine a scenario in which the whole planet is a single political entity are free to translate what follows into recommendations to citizens of the world.

I have argued that a contractarian recommendation of a market system needs to show each citizen, looking forward from each point in time, that that system is likely to work to her benefit. But, given the uncertainties inherent in market processes, it is hard to see how such a recommendation could be given for a market-based economic system that did not include some non-market mechanism of redistribution. Because the market offers rewards for the intermediation of mutually beneficial transactions, it is an extremely effective institution for satisfying wants *in general*—for creating what Hayek calls 'aggregate product' and Smith calls 'wealth'. But, on its own, the market does not guarantee that each individual has the opportunity to share in the increases in wealth that it makes possible. If a market-based economic system is to be recommended, there must be some way of under-writing such a guarantee.

If the argument of this chapter is correct, we (as citizens trying to agree about how to organize our economy) cannot have the wealth-creating features of the market while completely neutralizing the effects of brute luck. In this sense, any market-based economy must be unfair. But, if we are willing to accept some weakening of these wealth-creating features, we can make it more likely that each of us will be able to share in any increases in wealth that are created.

As an illustration of this idea, consider again the story of Hayek Island. In my discussion of that example, I argued that *full* social insurance was incompatible with the working principles of a market economy. But the islanders might be able to supplement the Lockean rules of their economy with a workable scheme of *partial* social insurance. Recall that there is a spot market in which the economy's two consumption goods (corn and fruit) are traded against one another. Thus, on any day, the price in this market can be used to measure each individual's total income in equivalent units of corn. Suppose that, when the islanders are setting up the rules of their economy, they agree that at the end of every month, each individual's income for that month will be assessed, and that all income above some fixed threshold will be taxed at some fixed proportionate rate. The proceeds of this tax will then be distributed among the islanders according to some formula. This formula might divide the proceeds equally among everyone, or it might give more to individuals with lower incomes. For individuals capable of work, receipt of a share of the proceeds might be conditional on some minimum level of publicly verifiable productive effort (perhaps in the more easily monitored activity of corn-growing). In effect, such a tax regime appropriates and redistributes a proportion of any surplus generated by transactions involving individuals who earn more than the threshold level of income. In doing so, it imposes certain restrictions on individuals' opportunities for mutually beneficial transactions. But, provided the tax rate is not too high, it allows more individuals to share in the benefits created by the workings of the market. This is the familiar trade-off between economic efficiency and equality, expressed in contractarian terms.

The tax regime I have described is a risk-sharing partnership that everyone is required to join. As I have presented it, it is part of the institutional structure of the economy, along with the other economic rules of engagement. In supposing that the islanders might agree to this regime when first setting up their economy, I am treating it as if it were part of an economic constitution. But in the original version of the Hayek Island story, individuals were free to form risk-sharing partnerships by mutual agreement. Why, it might be asked, is there any need for political agreement on a compulsory risk-sharing arrangement? Why not treat risk-sharing like other economic activities, as a matter for voluntary agreement?

The answer is that psychological stability is a collective concept. Going beyond the metaphor of Hayek Island, the problem we are dealing with is to design (or discover) economic institutions based on principles which, when put into operation, will command continuing general support. Part of the solution to this problem, I have argued, is to underwrite everyone's continuing expectations of benefit from those institutions. Partial social insurance is a means by which those expectations can be underwritten. In participating in a scheme of social insurance, an individual is not simply exercising a private choice to reduce his own exposure to risk. He is participating in a collective activity, the objective of which is to sustain support for institutions from which he, together with everyone else, can expect to benefit. To the extent that it is in his interests that other people continue to support those institutions, it is to his benefit that other people participate in the social insurance scheme. Reciprocally, it is to other people's benefit that he participates.

All this can be true even if the social insurance scheme has predictable redistributive effects. For example, consider a subgroup of the participants in a developed economy, made up of people who at, some given point in time, have natural talents or acquired skills which command high rates of pay. Suppose this group contains people from many different occupations, from world-class tennis players to brain surgeons, from popular singers to CEOs of large firms. These people might credibly claim that they could organize a risk-pooling scheme among themselves, with better terms for each of them than universal social insurance could provide. Nevertheless, it is in their interests that *everyone's* expectations are underwritten, and not merely their own. The redistributive effects of social insurance are a price that high earners pay for the psychological stability of the institutions within which their skills have the exchange values that they do.

To say this is not to treat rich individuals' contributions to social insurance merely as a kind of protection money.[12] Social insurance can be seen as an integral part of a system of economic organization based on mutual advantage. The underlying intuition is well expressed by Kenneth Arrow (1984):

> My own view is that in some deep sense there are increasing returns to scale.... There are significant gains to social interaction above and beyond what individuals and subgroups can achieve on their own. The owners of scarce personal assets do not have substantial private use of these assets; it is only their value in a large system which makes these assets valuable. Hence, there is a surplus created by the existence of society as such which is available for redistribution.
>
> (Arrow, 1984: 188)

Take the case of a star player in European football. According to the Forbes list of the world's highest-paid athletes in 2016, Lionel Messi ranked second with an income of $53.4 million, excluding earnings from endorsements.[13] I see no reason to doubt that this was a fair measure of the value of his extraordinary skills to his employers, FC Barcelona. But those skills would be worth only a tiny fraction of $53.4 million without the network of economic cooperation in which they are put to use. Messi needs other players to make up a team; the team needs other teams to play against; it needs a stadium in which to play and spectators who are willing to pay to watch. The uniqueness of Messi's skills give him more bargaining power than, say, a steward at the Camp Nou stadium, but Arrow is surely right to say that Messi's income is in large part a surplus created by the existence of an economically well-ordered society.

Nothing that I have said implies that the terms on which effort can be transformed into income should be the same for Messi as they are for the steward. It is brute luck that Messi's natural talents are worth so much more than the steward's, but one can recognize that fact without claiming that it must somehow be neutralized. As I have said earlier in this chapter, markets cannot be fair. Still, it is disturbing to learn that in 2016 Messi was convicted by a Spanish court of trying to evade 4.1 million euro in taxes.[14] One might have hoped that he would have thought of the taxes he was expected to pay as reciprocating the contributions that people like the steward make to the overall scheme of cooperation from which he derives such huge benefits. Looking at this from the other side, by paying those taxes, Messi would have been assuring his fellow-citizens that they could share in the surplus that his talents help to create. Adapting Mill's argument against mercantilism, redistributive taxation may be an essential component of a society in which people can see one another's prosperity with good will.

9

Intrinsic Motivation, Kindness, and Reciprocity

This book has been written to defend the liberal tradition of economics against the challenges set by behavioural findings. In previous chapters I have been concerned with the accumulated evidence against the neoclassical assumption that individuals' choices reveal integrated preferences. I have tried to show that the core ideas of the liberal tradition can be reformulated so that they do not depend on that assumption. However, as I pointed out in Section 1.3, there is also a body of behavioural evidence that challenges a different assumption that is commonly used in neoclassical economics—the assumption that individuals act on self-interested preferences.

It is sometimes suggested that this evidence poses a problem for the liberal tradition. One of the earliest appearances of this suggestion is in what is now a classic paper in behavioural economics. The grand theme of this paper is hinted at in the title, 'Fairness and the assumptions of economics'. Daniel Kahneman, Jack Knetsch, and Richard Thaler (1986) are reporting the first Dictator Game experiment. In this trivially simple game, a small sum of money is to be divided between two players. One player, the *allocator*, decides between alternative divisions of that sum. The other player, the *receiver*, has no decision to make; she simply gets whatever the allocator decides she should have. There is no communication and the game is entirely anonymous. In Kahneman et al.'s experiment, allocators had to choose between taking 90 per cent of the money and taking 50 per cent. A large majority chose the equal division.[1] Kahneman et al. interpret this result as showing that many people have a preference for 'fairness', and suggest that such findings are an 'embarrassment' to economists because their discipline is committed to the assumption that individuals are self-interested.

Kahneman et al. acknowledge that some economists treat self-interest only as an as-if assumption that works well in predicting aggregate behaviour, and that others (whom they call 'moderate true-believers') believe only that 'the economic arena, like a boxing ring or a parlour game, is an environment in which many of the rules that govern other human institutions are suspended'. But, they say, there are many 'extreme true-believers' for whom 'any appearance of concern for values of fairness or for the welfare of strangers is interpreted in terms of self-interest and strategic behavior'. Whatever nuances may be given to this 'nonfairness assumption', Kahneman et al. (in a passage I quoted in Chapter 1) present it as expressing

> a resistance to explanations of economic actions in moral terms that has deep roots in the history of the discipline. The central insight that gave rise to modern economics is that the common good is well served by the free actions of self-interested agents in a market.   (Kahneman et al., 1986: S286)

It is indeed a central insight of classical and neoclassical economics that the achievement of mutual benefit is generally well served by the free actions of self-interested agents in competitive markets. This insight is encapsulated in one of the most famous passages in *The Wealth of Nations*, where Adam Smith (1776/1976: 26–7) remarks that it is not from the benevolence of the butcher, the brewer, or the baker, that we expect our dinner, but from their regard to their own interest. One might question whether the observation of generosity in a Dictator Game experiment has anything much to do with that insight. If, as Kahneman et al.'s moderate true-believers maintain, the market is an institution in which self-interested behaviour has a special licence, it is not clear that the Dictator Game is a suitable environment for testing hypotheses about market behaviour—any more than it would be suitable for testing hypotheses about how people play games of Monopoly on family holidays. My guess is that what Kahneman et al. want to attribute to economists is the hypothesis that individuals act on preferences that are self-interested *and context-independent*. That is a hypothesis that can legitimately be tested in a Dictator Game.

Although Smith did not maintain the hypothesis of context-independent self-interest, many later economists have certainly done so.[2] But no serious economist would claim that the free actions of self-interested individuals invariably promote the common good. Economists of all persuasions recognize that there are situations—the provision of public goods is the most obvious example—in which self-interested motivations can frustrate the realization of mutually advantageous transactions. In neoclassical economics, however, such collective action problems are normally seen as calling for government intervention. The idea that individuals might solve these problems for themselves by acting contrary to self-interest has not usually been taken seriously. There would be a more substantial challenge to neoclassical economics if experimental environments could be found in which (contrary to what is the case in the Dictator Game) opportunities for mutual benefit are available, self-interested agents would fail to realize those opportunities, but ordinary human beings succeed.

In fact, such environments *have* been found. The Trust Game, which I described in Section 1.3, is a case in point. In Sections 9.3 to 9.5, I revisit this example, describe some others, and discuss how behavioural economists have interpreted them. This body of evidence undoubtedly shows that, in some situations in which there are opportunities for mutual benefit, significant numbers of individuals act contrary to self-interest in ways that allow those opportunities to be realized. But how far this evidence poses a challenge for the liberal tradition depends on what form this pro-social motivation takes. (I will use the generic term 'pro-social' as a shorthand to describe any motivation that leads an individual to act contrary to his immediate self-interest in a way that promotes the common good of some group of which he is a member.) We need to ask whether the kinds of pro-sociality that allow people to solve collective action problems are antithetical to the motivations by which people realize mutual benefit in markets.

In behavioural economics, pro-sociality is usually modelled using concepts that do not apply easily to ordinary market transactions—concepts such as fairness and unfairness, kindness and unkindness, deservingness and unde-servingness, reward and punishment. These ways of understanding pro-sociality lead naturally to the thought that the motivations that underlie behaviour in markets—or at least, that underlie the kind of market behaviour that neoclassical economic theory represents—are fundamentally *asocial*. This is perhaps what Kahneman et al. have in mind when they say that economics as a discipline has been resistant to explanations of economic actions in moral terms.

This way of thinking about the behavioural evidence has some fit with an older and more fundamental criticism of the liberal tradition of economics. This is the argument from virtue ethics (touched on in Section 7.7) that, because the workings of markets depend on asocial motivations, markets tend to corrode genuine sociality. Thus, it is said, it is important to recognize the 'moral limits' of markets, and to prevent markets from contaminating domains of life in which human flourishing depends on pro-social motivations. The behavioural and virtue-ethical literatures have a point of contact in the 'crowding-out' hypothesis. According to this hypothesis, if a given type of behaviour can be produced both by self-interested and by pro-social motivations, people tend to attribute that behaviour (whether by others or, more surprisingly, by themselves) to self-interest. In such cases, pro-social motivations are not reinforced by social approval or self-approval, and so are gradually displaced. I will discuss these ideas in Sections 9.1 and 9.2.

Underlying these lines of thought in behavioural economics and virtue ethics is the idea of a fundamental opposition between the attitudes that are expressed in market relationships and those that are expressed in genuinely social relationships. In Section 9.6, I will suggest that this idea is mistaken, and that it may be possible to think of market relationships as expressing coopera- tive attitudes that are complementary with kinds of pro-sociality that can help individuals to solve collective action problems.

9.1 The Virtue-ethical Critique of the Market

The virtue-ethical critique of the market has ancient roots: the founding text of virtue ethics is often said to be Aristotle's *Nicomachean Ethics* (*c.* 350 BC/ 1980).[3] For philosophers in the Aristotelian tradition, the central concern of virtue ethics is with *moral character*—with what sort of person one is and should be. Virtues are acquired character-traits or dispositions that are judged to be good. Crucially, virtues are not judged to be good *because* they tend to induce actions which, for other moral reasons, are good or right. In virtue ethics, actions are judged to be good because they are in character for a virtuous person. A morally well-constituted individual cultivates virtues not as rules of thumb for moral action, but because these virtues are characteristic of the kind of person she is or wants to be.

Aristotle's account of virtue begins from the idea that within any 'practice' or domain of life, goodness is understood in relation to the *telos* (literally, 'end' or 'purpose') of that domain—'that for whose sake everything is done'. For example, Aristotle (Book 1, section 1) treats medicine as a domain whose *telos* is 'health' and military strategy as a domain whose *telos* is 'victory'. In relation to a given domain, an acquired character trait is a virtue to the extent that the person who possesses it is thereby better able to contribute to the *telos* of that domain. The underlying idea is that human happiness or flour- ishing (*eudaimonia*) requires that people are oriented towards their various activities in ways that respect the intrinsic ends of the domains to which those activities belong.

How is the *telos* of a domain determined? Aristotle seems to think of the *telos* as a natural fact that can be ascertained by intuition, but many modern virtue ethicists favour a communitarian approach. This approach, espoused by Alasdair MacIntyre (1984), Elizabeth Anderson (1993), and Michael Sandel (2009), understands the concept of flourishing as internal to specific commu- nities and cultural traditions. Thus, to identify the *telos* of a practice, one must discover the meaning of that practice within the community of practitioners (Anderson 1993:143; Sandel, 2009: 184–92, 203–7).

In virtue ethicists' critiques of the market and of economics, a recurring theme is that markets rely on extrinsic and thereby non-virtuous motiva- tions. This idea can also be traced back to Aristotle, who wrote: 'The life of money-making is one undertaken under compulsion, and wealth is evidently not the good we are seeking; for it is merely useful and for the sake of something else' (*c*. 350 BC/1980: Book 1, §5). This sentence makes two claims that are echoed in modern virtue ethics. The first claim is that when individuals participate in markets, they show a lack of autonomy—they act *under compulsion*. The suggestion seems to be that a truly autonomous person would not need to seek wealth (perhaps because he would already have as much as he needed without having to seek for it).[4] The second claim is that the motivation for economic activity is extrinsic and thereby of an inferior kind—the things that economic activity can achieve are *merely useful and for the sake of something else*.

These ideas appear in more modern guise in the work of Anderson and Sandel. These writers recognize, at times reluctantly, that markets are a necessary part of social organization. But they argue that the instrumental logic of markets is liable to corrupt virtues that are proper to other domains of social life, and that it is therefore appropriate for citizens collectively to impose limits on the scope of markets.

Anderson (1993: 12) proposes a 'pluralist theory of value' in which different kinds of goods ought to be valued in different ways. She tries to delimit the proper scope of the market by identifying the norms that are characteristic of market relations, and the corresponding class of goods that are properly valued in terms of those norms. For Anderson, the ideal type of an economic good is a 'pure commodity'. The mode of valuation appropriate to pure commodities is 'use':

> Use is a lower, impersonal, and exclusive mode of valuation. It is contrasted with higher modes of valuation, such as respect. To merely use something is to subordinate it to one's own ends, without regard for its intrinsic value.
>
> (Anderson, 1993: 144)

This definition immediately introduces the Aristotelian ranking of intrinsic value over instrumental value. Anderson is presenting market norms as a kind of second-rate morality: the market's mode of valuation is *lower* than that of other domains of life; it is *merely* use; it has *no regard for* intrinsic value. In this account, market norms are impersonal and egoistic. Impersonality is the idea that market transactions are viewed instrumentally: each party to a transaction considers it only as a means to the satisfaction of his own ends. Egoism is the idea that those ends are defined in terms of self-interest.

Anderson acknowledges that market norms embody a moral ideal of 'economic freedom'. However, this ideal is presented in negative terms—as freedom from the kinds of moral constraints that one would face if one recognized the intrinsic value of goods, the obligations of personal relationships, and the potential validity of other people's judgements about value (1993: 144–6).

Indeed, Anderson seems comfortable with the ideal of economic freedom only in the context of inessential but harmless consumer products. Accepting (if condescendingly) that 'the market . . . also has its proper place in human life', her examples of goods that properly belong to the domain of economic freedom are 'the conveniences, luxuries, delights, gadgets, and services found in most stores' (1993: 166–7). There is no mention of the role of the market in supplying goods like food, clothing, fuel, and shelter, on which we all depend for our survival.

Anderson develops her critique of the instrumentality of the market by considering the intrinsic value of the goods and services provided by professional workers such as doctors, academics, athletes, and artists. She argues that for such workers, the norms of the market can conflict with 'the norms of excellence internal to their professional roles'. The result is that, when professionals sell their services, intrinsically valuable goods are 'partially commodified' (1993: 147–50). She does not claim that commodification is wholly undesirable, but the thrust of her argument is that the internal goals of professional practices must be partially insulated from the extrinsic motivations that are fostered by markets.

Sandel (2009) develops a different but complementary critique of the market, focusing on the virtue ethics of justice.[5] Sandel's concern is less with the cultivation of proper attitudes towards goods and practices, and more with how individuals are honoured and rewarded for showing appropriate virtues. Justice, for Sandel, is about 'giving people what they deserve'. That requires judgements about 'what virtues are worthy of honor and reward, and what way of life a good society should promote' (2009: 9). Sandel begins his book by describing some recent issues of public debate in America, intended to support his claim that virtue ethics is alive and well in ordinary political discourse. Two of these issues concern what Sandel sees as the ethical limitations of the market. Sandel's views on one of these, 'price gouging' by firms after Hurricane Charley, were considered in Section 8.4. The second issue is the remuneration of senior corporate executives. Sandel asks whether the chief executive officers of large American corporations deserved the payments they received in the years leading up to 2008, when their firms were generating large profits. He suggests that effort and talent are qualities that are worthy of reward in business, but that when the market rewards executives for profits that are *not* attributable to effort or talent, a principle of justice is being violated (2009: 12–18). The message from both examples, developed over the course of Sandel's book, is that the market generates incomes that are not properly aligned with the virtues of the people who receive them.

In their accounts of virtue, Anderson and Sandel seem to be expressing a sense of moral alienation from the reality of everyday economic life. Anderson's dismissive attitude to 'use' and her choice of academic research, athletics, and the arts as examples of occupations with 'norms of excellence' suggest that she may be having difficulty in seeing moral significance in the ordinary useful jobs by which most people earn their livings. Sandel seems to find it hard to come to terms with the unavoidable fact that market rewards depend on luck as well as on talent and effort. More fundamentally, the idea that economic activities, or the goods that they realize, ought to be seen as ends *in themselves* is inconsistent with the market principle of producing goods and services with the aim of exchanging them for other things. I would like to think, and in Chapters 10 and 11 will try to show, that people can find moral significance in simply being useful to one another.

9.2 Intrinsic Motivation and Crowding-out

There is much common ground between Aristotelian virtue ethics, with its emphasis on the intrinsic value of practices, and those strands of modern 'positive psychology' that emphasize the importance of intrinsic motivation for human happiness, in particular the *self-determination theory* of Edward Deci and Richard Ryan (1985). In this theory, the analogue of flourishing is a concept of psychological health or well-being. The core hypothesis is that individual autonomy is a source of psychological well-being, and thus that human flourishing is linked with authenticity and self-realization.

In Ryan and Deci's (2000) taxonomy of motivation, there is a continuum from 'amotivation', through increasingly autonomous forms of 'extrinsic motivation', to the full autonomy of 'intrinsic motivation'. A person who is extrinsically motivated performs an activity 'in order to obtain some separable outcome'. Extrinsic motivations can become more 'internal' (and thereby more autonomous) to the extent that the individual has a sense of having chosen the objective on which he acts and having endorsed its value. But an intrinsically motivated person performs an activity 'for its inherent satisfactions rather than for some separable consequence'; such a person 'is moved to act for the fun or challenge entailed rather than because of external prods, pressures, or rewards' (2000: 56–60). Notice how this definition of intrinsic motivation excludes all ordinary market activities: supplying goods or services because other people want them and are willing to pay for them would count as a concern for 'separable consequences' or 'rewards'.

An important hypothesis in this psychological literature is that external rewards can *crowd out* intrinsic motivation: people tend to perceive an activity as less intrinsically satisfying if there are external rewards for performing it (Deci, 1971; Lepper and Greene, 1978). One of the underlying psychological mechanisms is *self-perception*. In the absence of strong emotional cues, people are liable to construct their attitudes by observing their own behaviour and inferring the attitude that could have caused it (Bem, 1967). Thus, a person's knowledge that he has chosen to perform a task for which there is a monetary payment can induce the belief that the payment is his reason for performing it, crowding out the thought that the task is intrinsically satisfying. A parallel hypothesis in relation to social policy is due to Richard Titmuss (1970). Titmuss's famous example is the effect of introducing financial incentives for blood donors. In a regime in which donors are entirely unpaid, blood donation is motivated by altruism, reciprocity, or public spirit. If financial incentives are introduced into such a setting, this may prompt the thought that people who supply blood may be self-interested sellers rather than altruistic donors. Titmuss argues that this can undermine the would-be donors' sense that giving blood is a morally significant and socially valued act, and so lead to a reduction in the supply of blood. A similar interpretation is now often given for the much-quoted finding that fines for lateness in collecting children from a day-care centre led to an increase in the incidence of lateness (Gneezy and Rustichini, 2000a).[6]

The economic implications of the hypothesis of motivational crowding-out were first explored by Bruno Frey (1994, 1997). There is now a large literature in behavioural economics that builds on ideas from positive psychology and echoes Anderson's argument about the importance of insulating intrinsic motivation from contamination by the market (see, for example, Gneezy, Meier, and Rey-Biel, 2011). It should be no surprise that the economic literature on intrinsic motivation has been seen as supporting the virtue-ethical critique of markets (e.g. Sandel, 2012: 64–5, 113–20).

Economists have begun to be interested in the question of how intrinsic motivation can be shielded from market forces. One approach is summarized in the slogan 'getting more by paying less'. Suppose there is some occupation in which workers are better able to provide the services that their employers value if they are intrinsically motivated to pursue the internal ends of that occupation—if, in Ryan and Deci's taxonomy, they are attracted by its 'inherent satisfactions' and 'challenges' rather than by its material rewards. Viewed in the standard conceptual framework of economics, a person with such a motivation for a particular type of work (say, nursing) has a lower reservation wage for working as a nurse than for working in other occupations. So employers may be able to separate the better workers from the worse by offering *low* wages—they can get more by paying less (Brennan, 1996; Katz and Handy, 1998; Heyes, 2005). When a person accepts the low wages of an employer who is looking for intrinsic motivation, she signals to herself and to others that she is intrinsically motivated. So there need be no crowding-out effect.

Writing from a feminist position, Julie Nelson (2005) points to some uncomfortable implications of this method of protecting intrinsic motivation in a market economy. Low wages will tend to screen out, not only people with extrinsic motivations, but also intrinsically motivated individuals who need to support themselves and their families. Thus, access to intrinsically rewarding occupations may be restricted to people with private incomes or well-off partners or parents. And when social norms treat self-sacrifice as a characteristic virtue of 'caring' occupations such as nursing, they can act as a cover for, and an incitement to, exploitation. (Compare John Stuart Mill's views on 'self-abnegation' as an ideal of feminine character, discussed in Section 1.1.)

Nancy Folbre and Nelson (2000) suggest a different response to the crowding-out problem. This is to separate the payment of intrinsically motivated workers from the specific services they provide, so that payment can be construed as an *acknowledgement* of intrinsic motivation rather than as one side of a market exchange. The implication seems to be that authentic caring is compromised if carers and cared see their relationship as that of seller and buyer. There is another echo here of the Aristotelian idea that market relationships are instrumental and thereby non-virtuous. Folbre and Nelson's proposal is designed to transform a relationship of explicit exchange into one with the appearance of two-sided giving. It seems that the care worker is supposed to act on her intrinsic motivation, just as if she did not expect any financial return from providing care rather than not, but in the confidence that she will in fact receive a regular income. And it seems that the employer is supposed to maintain the illusion that care is not being exchanged for money by providing this income as if making a free gift, while being confident that the care worker will in fact do the work that he wants to have done. I will say more about the problems of this account of reciprocity in Section 9.4.

This example illustrates some of the difficulties of shielding intrinsic motivation from the supposedly corrosive effects of exchange relationships. The fundamental problem is this: It is inherent in the concept of intrinsic motivation that an individual's autonomy and authenticity are compromised whenever he enters into exchange relationships, but exchange relationships are fundamental to the workings of any economy that relies on comparative advantage and the division of labour. The literature of intrinsic motivation invites us to aspire to the profoundly unrealistic ideal of an economy in which everyone's actions and efforts are coordinated to realize gains from trade, but in which no one is actually motivated to seek those gains. If we are to reconcile the ideas of virtue and authenticity with real economic life, we need a way of understanding economic relationships that acknowledges that gains from trade are not realized by accident: they are realized because individuals seek them out. And so we must be able to show how people can find virtue and authenticity in their participation in mutually beneficial practices. One of the aims of the present book is to show that that requires a particular understanding of what it means to be motivated by reciprocity—an understanding that is fundamentally different from the one that is now current in behavioural economics.

9.3 Reciprocity: The Experimental Evidence

Behavioural economists have proposed a range of hypotheses about how individuals act on non-self-interested 'social preferences'. One of the most important of these hypotheses is that individuals have preferences for reciprocity. In this section, I describe some of the experimental evidence that has led to the formation of this hypothesis. I begin with the Trust Game.

This is now one of the paradigm games of the literature on social preferences. In its modern manifestation as an experimental design, it is due to Joyce Berg, John Dickhaut, and Kevin McCabe (1995), but (as I pointed out in Sections 1.3 and 3.1), it can be traced back to Thomas Hobbes's (1651/1962) discussion of the prisoner of war who is released in return for a promise to pay a ransom. The game tree for the stripped-down version I will discuss here is shown in Figure 9.1.

Of course, the whole idea of representing an interaction between individuals as a game in the formal sense of game theory attributes more rationality to those individuals than I needed to attribute to consumers in Chapters 6 and 7. But in this section, and in the rest of this chapter, I am concerned with how behavioural economists have understood pro-social behaviour. For this purpose, I need to use modelling frameworks that are standard in behavioural economics. My own model of pro-social behaviour, which I will present in Chapter 10, rests on less demanding assumptions about rationality.

The numbers shown in Figure 9.1 represent the possible payoffs of the game to the two players, A (listed first) and B (listed second). Payoffs are to be interpreted as normalized measures of the values of the relevant outcomes to the individual players, these 'values' being understood in terms of the players' own interests, as they perceive them at the time the game is being played. To aid intuition, I will assume that payoffs are also measures of the material outcomes of the game, expressed as increments of some good (say, money) that both players value. I do *not* assume that each player necessarily acts so as

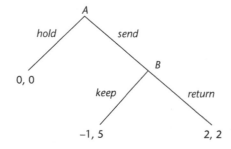

Figure 9.1. The Trust Game.

to maximize his or her expected payoff. Thus, the formal description of the game does not predetermine what each player will (or rationally ought to) do.

A moves first, choosing between *hold* and *send*. If he chooses *hold*, the game ends, with a baseline payoff of zero for each player. *A*'s choice of *send* can be interpreted as the action of investing one unit of material payoff in an activity which will generate a gross return of five units. If *A* chooses *send*, *B* then chooses between two alternative distributions of the costs and benefits of this activity. If she chooses *keep*, *A* loses the cost of his investment and *B* gains all the gross returns. If *B* chooses *return*, the cost of *A*'s investment is returned to him and the net surplus of four units is divided equally between the two players.

If both players act on self-interest and if each knows that this is true of the other, the outcome is (0, 0). (If *A* were to *send*, *B* would *keep*; knowing this, *A* chooses *hold*.) However, it is a matter of common experience that in situations of this general kind, individuals in *A*'s position sometimes (but not always) choose *send*, and individuals in *B*'s position sometimes (but not always) respond by choosing *return*. Relative to the baseline of self-interested behaviour, the combination of *send* and *return* benefits both players. This pattern of behaviour has been observed in experiments with many variants of the Trust Game, even when games are played only once and even when players do not know one another's identities. In anonymous experiments, perhaps disappointingly, *B*-players typically do not choose *return* quite often enough (or, in versions in which *B*-players can choose how much to return, do not return quite enough) to make *send* a beneficial strategy for an *A*-player to use when facing an unknown *B*. It is natural to conjecture that *A*-players in experiments are drawing on their experience of non-anonymous interactions in everyday social life and so are overestimating the willingness of *B*-players to return when everything is anonymous. In any event, experimental Trust Games show that a significant proportion of people succeed in achieving mutual benefit in situations in which self-interested individuals would fail.

It might seem that, in trying to explain this success, the only real problem is to explain why *B* chooses *return*, since if *A* expects this, it is in his self-interest to choose *send*. One possibility is to invoke a theory of social preferences in which each player's utility is a function of the profile of material payoffs to the two players. Then *return* would be individually rational for *B* if her utility from the payoff profile (2, 2) was greater than her utility from (−1, 5), which would be the case if she were sufficiently altruistic or if, as in the theories of inequality-averse social preferences proposed by Ernst Fehr and Klaus Schmidt (1999) and Gary Bolton and Axel Ockenfels (2000), she were sufficiently averse to being on the advantageous side of inequality. But if that were the correct explanation of *return*, the tendency for *B*-players in experiments to choose (2, 2) rather than (−1, 5) would be independent of any previous choices by A-players. It turns out that if A-players have no opportunity to make any choice and if B-players face the same choice as they would in a Trust Game in which their co-player had chosen *send*, the (2, 2) choice is much less common (McCabe et al., 2003). This suggests that some intention of reciprocity is involved in B's choice of *return* in the Trust Game.

George Akerlof (1982) has used a variant of the Trust Game as a theoretical model of how some labour contracts involve 'partial gift exchange'. Akerlof's idea is that an employer (corresponding with player A in the Trust Game) can choose to pay more than the minimum wage necessary to attract the labour she needs. A worker (corresponding with player B) who is paid this higher wage can choose to work harder than self-interest would dictate, given the limited ability of the employer to monitor individual effort. In Akerlof's model, workers come to have 'sentiment' for the firm that employs them, and this sentiment leads them to supply more-than-minimum effort in response to more-than-minimum wages. Thus, through a mechanism of reciprocity, employers and employees are able to realize mutual benefits that would be unobtainable if everyone acted on self-interest. (The downside of this mechanism is that if all firms try to pay wages above the level necessary to secure a supply of labour, equilibrium is possible only if there is a permanent pool of involuntarily unemployed workers.)

Another paradigm game that provides evidence about reciprocity is the Public Good Game. In the classic version of this game, there are n players (with $n \geq 2$). Each player has the same endowment of 'tokens'. Simultaneously, each player chooses what proportion of his tokens to put into a 'public account', which is shared by all players; the remainder goes into his own 'private account'. Tokens have a face value in money. Tokens placed in private accounts keep their face value, but the value of tokens in the public account is multiplied by some factor m, where $1 < m < n$. At the end of the game, each player receives the value of the tokens in his private account, plus an equal share of the value of all the tokens in the public account. Thus, each token that a player puts in the public account yields him a private return of m/n (in token units), while each token put in his private account yields him a private return of 1. If all players put the same number of tokens in the public account, each player receives a return of m for each of the tokens that *he* puts in that account. Since $m > 1$, the best symmetrical strategy for the players collectively is for them to put all their tokens in the public account. However, since $m/n < 1$, the dominant strategy for a self-interested player is to put all his tokens in his private account. So, like the Trust Game, the Public Good Game is a setting in which individuals have opportunities for mutual benefit that cannot be realized through individual self-interest. It can be interpreted as a model of a situation in which a public good can be supplied only through individuals' voluntary contributions.

Experimental research on this game has led to three main conclusions. First, if m/n is not too close to zero, a significant proportion of players make significant positive contributions, contrary to the assumption of self-interest. Second, if the game is played repeatedly, or if players make their contribution decisions sequentially rather than simultaneously, each player's contribution tends to be positively correlated with the previous contributions of her co-players. Third, as the game is repeated, contributions to the public account decline. The best explanation of these findings seems to be that they result from interactions between two types of players—free-riders (who never contribute) and conditional reciprocators (who contribute if and only if others' contributions are sufficiently large). Because of the presence of the free-riders and because of the ungenerous terms on which many conditional reciprocators are willing to reciprocate, the conditional reciprocators progressively withdraw from cooperation (Bardsley and Moffatt, 2007; Fischbacher and Gächter, 2010). It seems that, as in the Trust Game (and perhaps for the same reasons), experimental subjects initially over-estimate one another's cooperativeness.

Fehr and Simon Gächter (2000) initiated a new line of research into the supply of public goods by establishing that the tendency for contributions to decline can be eliminated if, after each repetition of a Public Good Game, each subject is able to choose whether to impose costly punishments on individual others. For this mechanism to work, there must be some subjects with a pro-social preference for punishing free-riders, but Fehr and Gächter show theoretically that there can be high and stable rates of contributions even if the proportion of such individuals is quite small and even if their preferences for punishing are quite weak. There is now a large body of experimental evidence showing that, if the cost of punishing is low relative to the cost of being punished and if (which is rarely the case in ordinary life) individuals who are punished do not have any opportunity to retaliate, high rates of contributions can be sustained.[7]

Taken all round, the evidence from Trust and Public Good Games suggests that many people are motivated to reciprocate other people's cooperative behaviour. The idea of reciprocity is now so commonly used in behavioural economics that it may be difficult for a reader to understand how counter-intuitive it seemed to neoclassical economists only a few decades ago. But consider some good on which you spend only a small proportion of your income—say, your favourite breakfast cereal. Suppose that, as part of a special promotion, the manufacturers give you free tokens that can be redeemed at any supermarket for (and only for) packets of the cereal. These tokens are equivalent to 10 per cent of your current rate of consumption of the cereal. What would be the change in your purchases of cereal—that is, in the quantity of cereal that you actually pay for? Neoclassical theory predicts that your purchases would fall by almost 10 per cent, because the tokens are perfect substitutes for purchases. (The 'almost' is because the money value of the tokens is an addition to your income. If cereal is a 'normal' good, this will induce a miniscule increase in your total consumption of cereal.) A behavioural economist might want to add qualifications about mental accounting, but the neoclassical prediction seems quite intuitive. Now consider a different example. Replace 'purchases of breakfast cereal' with 'voluntary contributions towards the provision of a public good from which you benefit'. Suppose that you devote a small proportion of your income to these contributions. Now suppose that the sum of other people's contributions increases by an amount equal to 10 per cent of your current contribution. How would your contribution change? In traditional neoclassical theory, a person's preferences for the services he derives from public goods are modelled in the same way as his preferences for breakfast cereals. Thus, that theory predicts that your contributions to the public good would *fall* by almost 10 per cent—an effect that is diametrically opposite to reciprocity.

Up to the 1980s, what I have described as the traditional neoclassical theory was generally accepted as appropriate for modelling voluntary contributions to public goods and to philanthropic activities. (It was conventional to model charitable activities as public goods for which potential donors have altruistic preferences.) The implication of counter-reciprocity in contributions was accepted too (see, for example, Becker, 1974). In two of my first contributions to behavioural economics, I showed that the magnitude of the counter-reciprocal effect implied by this model was contrary to econometric evidence about philanthropy, and indeed completely implausible. I proposed an alternative model in which contributors were motivated by reciprocity (Sugden, 1982, 1984).[8]

A third paradigm game in the research programme of social preferences has been seen as providing evidence of *negative reciprocity* (returning harm for harm, rather than benefit for benefit). This is the Ultimatum Game, first investigated by Werner Güth, Rolf Schmittberger, and Bernd Schwarze (1982). A stripped-down version of this game is shown in Figure 9.2. It can be interpreted as a situation in which two players A and B are jointly endowed with ten units of a valuable resource. Neither of them can access this resource unless they both agree on how to divide it between them. A moves first, choosing either *equal* (proposing a 5:5 division) or *unequal* (proposing an 8:2 division in his favour). After learning what A has chosen, B chooses *accept* (accepting the division proposed by A) or *reject* (with the result that neither player gets anything). If both players act on self-interest and if each knows that this is true of the other, the outcome is (8, 2): B will accept either proposal, and so A makes the proposal that is more favourable to him. In

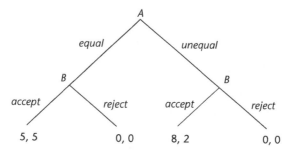

Figure 9.2. The Ultimatum Game.

experiments, however, significant proportions of A-players make proposals that are not the most favourable to themselves, and significant proportions of B-players reject proposals that would give them significantly less than an equal share.

As in the Trust Game, it might seem that B-players who choose *reject* are motivated by aversion to unequal outcomes—or at least, to unequal outcomes that do not favour them—and that A-players who choose *equal* anticipate this and act on self-interest. But if that was the correct explanation of *reject*, B-players' choices would depend only on the payoff profiles corresponding to *accept* and *reject* (in the current version of the game, only on the profiles (8, 2) and (0, 0)). Payoffs associated with other offers that A could have made would be irrelevant. But in fact, B-players' choices *do* depend on what their co-players could have done, but chose not to do. Thus, a typical B-player would be more likely to accept an (8, 2) proposal if the only alternative for her co-player had been to propose (9, 1) than if the only alternative had been (5, 5) (Falk, Fehr, and Fischbacher, 2003). In the literature of social preference, this pattern of behaviour is often interpreted in terms of B's judgements about A's intentions. If, in B's judgement, A has revealed an intention to benefit unfairly at her expense, she responds in a way that harms both of them. This response is seen as expressing negative reciprocity or (to put it slightly differently) as an act of costly punishment.

Although the idea that people can be motivated by reciprocity is now generally accepted in economics, there is less agreement about how this motivation is best understood. Different understandings support different conceptions of the relationship between market interaction and non-market social life. In the following two sections, I will consider how reciprocity is represented in the current literature of behavioural economics. This discussion will set the scene for Chapter 10, in which I will present a very different account of reciprocity, more closely related to the model I proposed in 1984.

9.4 Reciprocity and Social Preferences

Consider the stripped-down version of the Trust Game, as shown in Figure 9.1. Suppose that player A chooses *send* and that player B responds by choosing *return*. It seems natural to say that the strategy combination (*send, return*) is a practice of trust. In choosing to send, A trusts B to return; in choosing to return, B reveals herself as trustworthy by repaying A's trust. But what exactly does it mean to say that *send* is an act of trust, and how does its being such an act motivate A to choose it? And what does it mean to say that *return* is a repayment of trust, and how does that motivate B to choose it? Clearly, the idea of *repaying* trust involves reciprocity and, as I have explained, the consensus among behavioural economists is that some form of reciprocity is implicated in the combination of *send* and *return*. But how should we understand this reciprocity?

The idea of repaying trust presupposes a concept of trust itself, and that must refer to A's action. One way of representing the idea that A is trusting B is in terms of A's beliefs about what B will do. It is natural to say that A's choice of *send* is evidence that he believes that B is likely to respond by choosing *return*. We might hypothesize that if (in B's belief) A believes that B will act in a way that will benefit A, B has a preference for confirming that expectation—or, which comes to the same thing, has a preference for avoiding the sense of guilt associated with disconfirming it (Sugden, 1998b; Pelligra, 2005; Bacharach, Guerra, and Zizzo, 2007; Battigalli and Dufwenberg, 2007). This kind of *trust responsiveness* would allow us to explain B's *return* as a response to A's *send*, rather than as an unconditional act of altruism.

But consider the Confidence Game, shown in Figure 9.3. (As an example of a situation that might be modelled by this game, suppose you are B, visiting a crowded tourist site on a hot day. A is a street seller with a stock of cans of iced Coke. He makes eye contact with you and says that you must need a drink. You do not like Coke, but before you have time to say anything, he opens a can, passes it towards you, and asks you to pay the conventional price. If you

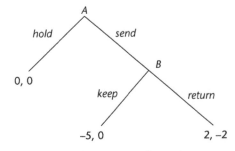

Figure 9.3. The Confidence Game.

refuse, the seller will be left with a worthless opened can.) In this game, too, *A*'s choice of *send* is naturally interpreted as signalling his belief that *B* will choose *return*; and *B*'s choice of *return* would clearly benefit *A*. But, even if *B* had pro-social motivations, would she want to confirm this belief? In the Trust Game, (*send*, *return*) benefits both players, but in the Confidence Game it benefits *A* at *B*'s expense. *B* might reasonably think that *A*'s expectation of *return* in the Confidence Game is gratuitous, and that to confirm that expectation would show, not trustworthiness, but susceptibility to a confidence trick. Trustworthiness is surely something more than an unconditional preference for confirming other people's expectations of benefit from you. Or, expressing the same idea from the viewpoint of a trustor, merely signalling that you are expecting someone else to benefit you may not be enough to activate their desire to do so.

Vittorio Pelligra (2005) suggests that trust responsiveness is induced only when the trustor's action expresses confidence in some *praiseworthy* attribute of the trustee, and not when what is being signalled is confidence in her gullibility. That thought seems right, but it leaves open the question of what makes trust responsiveness praiseworthy in some contexts but not in others. Another idea, for which Florian Ederer and Alexander Stremitzer (2016) find some experimental support, is that trust responsiveness occurs when the trustor's expectation about the trustee's behaviour is a reasonable inference from a deliberately chosen act of the trustee, such as an explicit promise.[9] A third idea, represented in the model of 'normative expectations' presented in my 1998 paper, is that *B*'s desire to confirm *A*'s expectation about her (*B*'s) behaviour is conditional on that expectation being grounded on common experience about the typical behaviour of people in *B*'s position. The latter two ideas feature in the concept of 'intending mutual benefit' that I will present in Chapter 10.

A different way of understanding the feature of *A*'s choice of *send* that induces reciprocation is to ask what this action signals about *A*'s preferences or intentions. The idea that people care about other people's intentions is a common theme in the literature of social preferences. In this literature, it is a standard modelling strategy to follow Matthew Rabin (1993) in characterizing intentions as *kind* or *unkind*. Each player's intentions are defined in terms of the payoff profiles that his actions can be expected to induce, given his beliefs about the other player's actions. (To keep things simple, I will present Rabin's ideas in relation to two-player games.) Developing this idea in general raises some difficult problems, but the essential concept of kindness is closely related to altruism or benevolence, in the sense that Smith uses that word when he says that we do not rely on the baker's benevolence to provide us with bread for our dinners. The greater the degree to which one player benefits the other by forgoing his own payoffs, the kinder he is. Rabin's hypothesis is that individuals derive utility from their own payoffs, from being kind towards people who are being kind to them, and from being unkind towards people who are being unkind to them.[10]

Strictly, Rabin's theory applies only to normal-form games (that is, games in which each player makes only one choice, and these choices are effectively simultaneous). Viewed as a general problem, extending the theory to games in which players move sequentially is not straightforward.[11] But it seems that any reasonable extension of Rabin's theory will have the following implication for the Trust Game: It cannot be the case that A plays *send*, expecting B to play *return* with probability 1, and that B, knowing that A has played *send*, plays *return*.

To see why not, suppose that A chooses *send*, believing that B will choose *return* with probability 1. Then B's choice is between *return*, which induces the payoff combination (2, 2), and *keep*, which induces (–1, 5). Reasons of self-interest point towards the latter, but we need to take account of B's judgments about A's intentions. Given that A expected B to return, his choice was between (0, 0) and (2, 2). According to Rabin's definitions, choosing (2, 2) from this menu was neither kind nor unkind. Given the intuitions on which the theory is built, this conclusion seems unavoidable: A has not faced any trade-off between his payoffs and B's, and so has not had the opportunity to display kindness or unkindness.[12] Rabin recognizes that his theory has this implication. Discussing a simultaneous-move version of a Trust Game, he suggests that, contrary to the implications of his model, 'it seems plausible that cooperation would take place'. His response to this problem is to say, reasonably enough, that his model is not intended to represent all psychological factors that can affect behaviour in games; theorists may need to consider modelling 'additional emotions'. Still, what Rabin is saying is that the particular kind of reciprocity that appears in his model does not provide an adequate explanation of trust. Significantly, the additional emotion he has in mind is a desire 'to reward trust' (1993: 1296–7). Since Rabin often describes positive reciprocity as 'rewarding' kind behaviour (and describes negative reciprocity as 'punishing' unkind behaviour), the idea seems to be that B's choice of *return* is her way of rewarding A for the goodness of *send*. But if A's action was self-interested, it is not clear why it deserves reward.

It may seem paradoxical that, in a theory in which individuals are motivated by reciprocity, two individuals cannot have common knowledge that they will both participate in a practice of trust. Nevertheless, this conclusion reflects the fundamental logic of a modelling strategy in which pro-social motivations are represented as preferences that are acted on by individually rational agents. It is an essential feature of (*send, return*), understood as a practice of trust, that both players benefit from both players' adherence to the practice. If A plays his part in the practice, expecting B to play hers, he must believe and intend that his action will lead to an outcome that will in fact benefit both of them. Thus, if pro-sociality is interpreted as kindness—as a willingness to forgo one's own interests to benefit others—A's choice of *send* cannot signal pro-social intentions, and so cannot induce reciprocal kindness from B. I will call this the Paradox of Trust.

9.5 Reciprocity and Social Norms

The theories of pro-social behaviour that I discussed in Section 9.4 share an important common feature: they explain that behaviour as expressing 'social preferences'. A person's social preferences, like her preferences among ordinary consumption goods, are understood as reasonably stable dispositions towards choice and as expressions of that person's own subjective tastes and judgements. Notice that a social preference is a property of an individual agent. It is not a property *of* society; it is an individual's attitude *to* society. Just as an individual's preferences may express her willingness to give up money in return for some consumption good, so they may express her willingness to give up personal consumption to bring about a fairer distribution of resources between herself and another person, to reward another person for his kindness, or to punish him for his unkindness. In behavioural economics, the most common way of explaining pro-social behaviour is by postulating particular kinds of social preferences. However, another explanatory strategy is beginning to gain ground. In this strategy, the fundamental explanatory concept is that of a *social norm*, understood as an interlocking network of preferences, beliefs, and expectations within a society. In this section, I will investigate this way of understanding reciprocity. But I will approach the topic obliquely.

In the light of other findings of behavioural economics, it should be no surprise that individuals' social preferences, as revealed in their actual choices, often turn out to be highly context-dependent. For example, consider people's responses to charitable collections. Two ingenious field experiments, half a century apart, have investigated how American shoppers respond to Salvation Army collectors at store entrances. In the earlier experiment, James Bryan and Mary Ann Test (1967) employed a confederate to walk past a collector every 60 seconds and put a coin in the 'Red Kettle' collection box. They found that donations were significantly more frequent in the 20-second time windows immediately after the confederate's action than in the 20-second windows immediately before it.

In the later experiment, James Andreoni, Justin Rao, and Hannah Trachtman (2017) used a store with two entrances close together, both easily visible to shoppers approaching from the parking lot. The experimenters crossed two treatments in a 2×2 design. In *one door* treatments, there was a collector at only one entrance; in *two doors* treatments, there were collectors at both. In *opportunity* treatments, the collector rang a bell to indicate her presence but made no attempt to interact with potential donors; in *ask* treatments, she also tried to make eye contact while saying 'Hi, how are you? Merry Christmas, please give today'. From an analysis of their data, Andreoni et al. estimate that this minimal form of asking increased the frequency of donations by about 50 per cent. In the opportunity treatments, shoppers' decisions about which entrance to use were unaffected by the presence or absence of collectors. In the one-door asking treatments, in contrast, a relatively small proportion of shoppers deliberately chose to make a detour to use the collector's entrance and then made a donation; a much larger minority deliberately chose the opposite detour and so avoided passing the collector. Most of the latter were people who would not have given if asked (2017: 645–6, 651).

If one starts from the assumption that charitable donations are motivated by stable social preferences, it is difficult to explain why decisions to donate are so strongly influenced by seeing one unknown person do so or by encountering a formulaic request for a contribution. The Salvation Army is a large and well-known charity, and their Christmas appeal is a familiar event. If people had settled preferences about charitable actions, one might expect a shopper in the weeks before Christmas to know her own preferences about giving to a Salvation Army collection. It seems more plausible to interpret these influences as psychological cues that activate short-lived positive attitudes towards the act of giving. Andreoni et al.'s evidence suggests that many people can predict their own responses to these cues. It seems that the shoppers who (as Andreoni et al. put it) 'avoided the ask' were able to foresee that ignoring a direct request to give would induce some emotional discomfort—perhaps guilt, shame, or embarrassment. Presumably, too, the shoppers who went out of their way to give in response to an ask, but who would not have done so merely to give to a passive bell-ringer, were able to foresee some emotional reward from responding to being asked.

Andreoni et al.'s explanation of their findings relies on the familiar device (familiar, that is, to readers of behavioural economics) of a dual-self model. Drawing an explicit analogy with dual-self models of dieting, Andreoni et al. postulate that each shopper has a 'planning self' and a 'short-run self'. In the parking lot, the shopper is in an emotional 'cold state', acting under the control of his planning self. The planning self knows that if the shopper were to face the collector's ask, a 'hot state' of wanting to give would be activated and the short-run self would take control (2017: 634). According to Andreoni et al.'s account, the shoppers who go out of their way to avoid being asked to give must in fact be altruists: if they were purely selfish, they would not find it painful to say no. But they are *sophisticated* altruists:

> Psychologists posit that giving is initiated by a stimulus that elevates sympathy or empathy in the mind of the potential giver, much like the smell of freshly baked bread can pique appetite.... [S]omeone with (implicit or explicit) knowledge of their vulnerability to such stimuli can, by controlling the input of that stimuli, control both their emotions and the actions that result. Just as we should not eat our favorite dessert at every opportunity, we also cannot give at every opportunity, even though we might wish we could do both. Just as a sophisticated eater will avoid exposure to the chocolate cake, a sophisticated altruist can avoid being asked.
>
> (Andreoni et al., 2017: 627)

Yet again, we are being offered a model of an inner rational agent that is vulnerable to the impulses of its psychological shell, and which constrains its own future opportunities as a means of maintaining self-control. (Compare the models discussed in Sections 3.4, 4.8, and 7.3.) In explaining the rationale of this model, Andreoni et al. seem to be particularly concerned to explain the behaviour of 'giving-avoiders'—the relatively small proportion of shoppers who would have given if they had been asked but who deliberately avoided getting into that situation.[13] If one thinks of a person's giving or not giving as revealing his preferences for kindness relative to acting on self-interest, a giving-avoider is someone who, in the cold state of the parking lot, chooses to prevent himself from acting on the preferences that he would in fact want to act on, were he to be asked to give. Interpreted in this way, giving-avoidance does indeed seem like a sophisticated response to a self-control problem. But this understanding of giving-avoidance ignores the possibility that not giving when asked induces social embarrassment, even for people who have no altruistic desire to give.

One does not need to have a divided self to want to avoid experiences of social embarrassment, any more than one does to want to avoid the taste of broccoli. (I am thinking of the first President Bush, famously ruling that broccoli should not be served on Air Force One. His justification—that he had never liked broccoli since he was a little kid and his mother had made him eat it—seems entirely adequate.) If not giving when asked causes emotional discomfort, a desire to avoid that discomfort might explain both why some people give only if they are asked and why some people deliberately avoid being asked.

An alternative explanation of the behaviour of Andreoni et al.'s shoppers is that they were responding to social norms. Perhaps what their behaviour revealed was not that their preferences were context-dependent, but rather that they had consistent preferences for not violating social norms, and that *the norms themselves* were context-dependent. It is surely a social norm that if someone makes eye contact with you and says 'Hi, how are you?' in a friendly manner, you should give some kind of friendly acknowledgement. It is also a social norm (if perhaps one that is decaying) that if a stranger asks you to do something for them, you ought to give some consideration to that request, not dismiss it out of hand. And, I take it, there is some degree of common understanding in America that the Salvation Army is a worthy cause that can reasonably ask Christmas shoppers for small donations. Thus, it is difficult to walk past a Salvation Army collector who says 'Please give today' without giving anything and yet without violating a social norm. But if it is not a norm that you should seek out people who will say 'Hi' to you and then ask you to do things for them, the shoppers who avoided the ask were not violating any norm. If a person has a preference for conforming to norms rather than violating them and also for not giving rather than giving, taking a detour to avoid passing a collector might be the action that best satisfies her preferences.

One of the fullest accounts of social norms in relation to behavioural economics is that of Cristina Bicchieri (2006). Bicchieri is concerned with 'rules of behaviour'. A rule of behaviour R applies to some game-like situation S that is faced recurrently by the members of some population P. This concept of a rule is to be read as including formally codified legal rules, rules of morality, and recurrent patterns of behaviour that have no normative status at all. Bicchieri distinguishes social norms from these other kinds of rules. According to her definition, a rule of behaviour R is a social norm if, for each member i of a sufficiently large subset of the population, i has a *conditional preference* for conforming to R. A person i is defined to have such a preference if he prefers to conform to R, conditional on his believing that the following two properties hold for each other member j of a sufficiently large subset of the population. First, j in fact conforms to R. (The belief that j in fact conforms is an *empirical expectation* held by i.) Second, j has a *normative expectation* that i conforms to R (2006: 11).

Explaining the concept of a normative expectation, Bicchieri says that 'people... think that everyone "ought to" conform to R'. She puts the quotation marks around 'ought to' to signify that the 'ought' might be merely prudential (everyone ought to be careful when handling fragile glassware), but she immediately goes on to say that she is not concerned with such cases: in the cases she wants to analyse, the 'ought' is a statement about 'obligation' (2006: 14). Bicchieri's definition allows but does not require that normative expectations may be backed up by informal social sanctions against individuals who fail to meet their obligations. It seems that what Bicchieri intends is that i prefers to conform to R, conditional on it being the case that sufficiently many members of the population both conform to R and believe that people in general have some kind of obligation to conform.

In Bicchieri's definition, the conditionality of 'conditional preference' is worded slightly ambiguously. I take her to mean that conditionality is part of the content of i's preference, and not just a condition under which the preference happens to be held. Thus, what i prefers is the whole of the following: that she conforms to R, conditional on certain properties of other people's actual behaviour and beliefs. (Given that i acts on this preference, whether she in fact conforms to R will depend on whether she *believes* these properties to hold; but the preference itself is conditioned on the fact, not the belief.)

Conditionality in this sense is essential for Bicchieri's distinction between social norms and morality. According to Bicchieri:

> [B]y their very nature, moral norms demand (at least in principle) an unconditional commitment.... [E]xpectations of other people's conformity to a moral rule are not a good *reason* to obey it. Nor is it a good reason that others expect me to follow it. If I find their expectations reasonable, it is because I find the moral norm reasonable; so the reason to obey it must reside in the norm itself.
>
> (Bicchieri, 2006: 20–1)

Suppose we accept this account of what moral norms 'demand'. There is still a gap between nominally endorsing a norm and actually acting on it, and it is surely a fact of human social life that a typical individual is more likely to act on a given moral norm if other people act on it and expect him to do so. The distinctive feature of *social* norms must be that conditionality is not just a contingent fact about people's propensity to conform to them, but is built into the preference for conforming.

It is an implication of Bicchieri's theory that, in situations in which an individual's conditional preference for following a norm is sufficiently strong, that preference may lead him to act contrary to his self-interest. For example, consider Andreoni et al.'s experiment in the treatment in which a shopper has no option but to meet a collector who will ask for a donation. A shopper who has no desire to support the Salvation Army may make a donation because giving to charity collectors who ask is a social norm. Although the Salvation Army benefits from the shopper's action, that benefit is no part of his intention: his intention is simply *to conform to a social norm.*

In principle, the same argument might be applied to the Trust Game. Suppose it is a social norm that acts of trust should be reciprocated, and that this is understood as implying that if a person in the role of A chooses *send*, the player in the role of B should choose *return*. Then if, in a specific game, player A chooses *send*, player B might choose *return* simply with the intention of conforming to a norm. B's action would benefit A, but that benefit would be no part of B's intention. If *return* could be explained in this way, the problem that I wrestled with in Section 9.4 would no longer arise. That problem was to understand what it means for *B* to choose *return* with the intention of reciprocating *A*'s choice of *send*. But, according to the theory I am now considering, *B* has no such intention. Attitudes to trust and trustworthiness are being understood in the same way as attitudes to workplace dress codes.

Suppose that in my workplace, male workers always wear ties. There has been no explicit requirement of tie-wearing from our managers, but there is an unspoken understanding that this is how we should dress at work. In wearing a tie, I am not expressing any specific attitude *towards ties*, but I may be expressing an attitude towards conforming to workplace dress codes. (Even in this case, it must be said, something more than conformism might be in play: following a workplace dress code can be a way of showing respect to the seriousness of the work being done.) Similarly, one might claim, *B*'s choice of *return* does not express any specific attitude to trust and trustworthiness, or kindness and unkindness: it expresses an attitude towards conforming to social norms.

But can this be all there is to practices of trust? I do not think so, and on my reading of Bicchieri (2006), neither does she. In Section 3.2, I discussed David Hume's theory of justice, and argued that its structure was contractarian. Bicchieri discusses the same theory, and argues that, by her definition, Hume's principles of justice are social norms. Recall that it is part of that definition that each person *i* prefers to conform to the relevant rule *R*, conditional on sufficiently many other people conforming to *R* and on their having the normative expectation that *i* will conform. According to Bicchieri:

> What distinguishes norms of justice from other social norms is that many of us would have a conditional preference for abiding by such norms because we acknowledge that the normative expectations [about conformity with these norms] are *legitimate* and should therefore be satisfied. Their legitimacy may stem from recognizing how important it is for the good functioning of our society to have such norms, but of course their ongoing value depends on widespread conformity. (Bicchieri, 2006: 21; italics in original)

In other words, when a person acts on Hume's principles of justice—say, by not taking advantage of an opportunity to steal someone else's property—his *intention* may not be properly described as 'conforming to a social norm', even if Bicchieri is right to say that, *extensionally*, stealing is contrary to a social norm. This person's intention may be to respect other people's legitimate property rights. To recognize this is to recognize that an explanation of why people conform to social norms may require an explanation of how and why the expectations they embody are perceived as legitimate.[14]

It seems that Bicchieri is having difficulty incorporating the concept of legitimacy into her definition of a social norm. The source of the problem, I think, is her attempt to draw a sharp distinction between social norms and moral rules. Even if one accepts that this distinction is meaningful and useful at the conceptual level, many rules that would naturally be classified as 'moral' have conventional aspects. Take the case of reciprocity. It is a general principle of reciprocity that when other people go out of their way to benefit you, you ought to make some kind of return. You might uphold this as a moral principle in Bicchieri's sense: your commitment to it is not conditional on other people's normative expectations. But what kind of return you give for what kind of benefit may still be governed by social conventions. In an American restaurant, you return courteous and helpful service by leaving a tip of significantly more than 15 per cent. In a British department store, you return courteous and helpful service by smiles and sincere words of thanks. Something similar can be true of dress codes. By following certain dress codes at a funeral, you show respect for the memory of the person who has died. You can have an unconditional commitment to showing respect to the dead while recognizing that the way in which respect is expressed is a matter of convention.

For the purposes of the current chapter, the crucial problem is to understand practices of reciprocity. In Section 9.4, I argued that existing theories of social preferences fail to explain how, in a context in which people can reliably be expected to be trustworthy, returning trust can express intentions of reciprocity. A theory of social norms, of the kind proposed by Bicchieri, can avoid this problem only if it assumes that trustworthiness is merely an arbitrary social norm, like wearing ties at work. As soon as we introduce the idea that trustworthiness is a response to *legitimate* expectations, we face the problem of identifying the properties of trustworthiness by virtue of which people feel entitled to expect others to be trustworthy. And that takes us back to the Paradox of Trust.

9.6 Escaping from the Paradox of Trust

The escape route from the Paradox of Trust is to recognize that mutually beneficial cooperation between two individuals is not the same thing as the coincidence of two acts of kindness. When A chooses *send* in the Trust Game, his intention is not to be kind to B: it is to play his part in a mutually beneficial scheme of cooperation, defined by the *joint* action (*send, return*). A's action will in fact be part of this intended cooperative scheme only if B chooses to play her part too. Thus, B's choice of *return* reciprocates A's cooperative intention.[15] If A is completely confident that B will reciprocate, and if that confidence is in fact justified, A's choice of *send* is in his own interests, while B's choice of *return* is not in hers. Nevertheless, both players can understand their interaction as a mutually beneficial cooperative scheme in which each is playing his or her part.

This way of thinking about cooperation has implications for the commonly held view (discussed in Sections 9.1 and 9.2) that market transactions are inherently asocial. Consider the Market Game, shown in Figure 9.4. The only difference between this and the Trust Game is that B's payoff from (*send*, *keep*) is −1 rather than 5. The implication is that if A chooses *send*, it is in B's interest as well as A's that B chooses *return*. So if both players act on self-interest and if each knows that this is true of the other, A will choose *send* and B will choose *return*. This combination of actions is mutually beneficial, just as it is in the Trust Game.

Why do I call this the 'Market Game'? Suppose that A is Adam Smith's baker and that B is a customer, wanting bread for her dinner. The baker has displayed various loaves of bread, with labels showing their prices. The customer asks for a particular loaf. The baker wraps it and hands it over the counter to the customer. She takes it and then hands over coins equal in value to the price. We might model the final stages of this interaction as a game in which A chooses whether to hand over the bread (*send*) or not (*hold*), and if A chooses the former, B chooses whether to hand over the money (*return*) or to run out of the shop without paying (*keep*). In normal circumstances, the rankings of payoffs for each player will be as in the Market Game. Relative to the baseline of not trading, the exchange of the bread for the money is mutually beneficial. If the customer tries to avoid paying, the baker will certainly be inconvenienced, but it is very unlikely that the expected benefits to the customer will exceed the expected costs. (She might be caught and punished; the baker will probably refuse to deal with her again; her action might be observed by third parties whose trust she may later want to rely on.)

The point of this story is that everyday market transactions often have the structure of the Market Game. Of course, one can imagine variants of this story in which the interaction between potential trading partners is better modelled

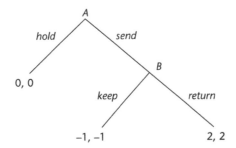

Figure 9.4. The Market Game.

by the Trust Game: Akerlof's account of partial gift exchange is an example. Economics needs to be able to explain *both* the prevalence of mutually beneficial behaviour in interactions like the Market Game *and* the fact that such behaviour is at least sometimes found in interactions like the Trust Game.

Theorists of social preferences sometimes comment on the fact that behaviour in market environments, unlike behaviour in Trust and Public Good Games, does not seem to reveal the preferences for equality, fairness and reciprocity that their models are designed to represent. The explanation usually offered is that people have social preferences in all economic interactions, but the rules of the market are such that individuals with such preferences have no way of bringing about the fair outcomes that they really desire. Thus, discussing a market experiment in which many sellers compete to trade with a single buyer, David Levine (1998) explains the apparently unfair outcome (the buyer appropriates almost the whole surplus) by saying:

> In a relatively competitive environment, players can have a significant effect on their own utility, but it is difficult for them to transfer utility to or from other players. Consequently, we might expect that spite or altruism would play a very small role in such environments. (Levine, 1998: 605–6)

Referring to the same experiment, Fehr and Schmidt (1999: 830) say of a representative seller: 'There will be inequality anyway, but by winning the competition, [a seller] can increase his own monetary payoff, and he can turn the inequality to his advantage'. And Armin Falk and Urs Fischbacher (2006: 307) say: 'The intuition is that in a competitive market a proposer [i.e. someone who announces the price at which he is willing to trade] has no chance to achieve a "fair" outcome'. Notice the parallel between this line of thought and the virtue-ethical critique of the market as fundamentally asocial.

But perhaps the truth is the other way round. Could it be that behaviour in markets expresses the same intentions for reciprocity as are expressed in Trust and Public Good Games, but that these intentions are misrepresented in theories of social preference? Recall that in the Trust Game, (*send, return*) is a mutually beneficial practice with the property that if *A* is confident that *B* will play her part in that practice, it is in *A*'s self-interest to play his. I argued that, even if *A* has this confidence, his choice of *send* can express a cooperative intention. In the Market Game too, (*send, return*) is a mutually beneficial practice. If *A* is confident that *B* will play her part in that practice, it is in *A*'s self-interest to play his. The Market Game has an additional feature: given that *A* has already played his part in the practice, it is in *B*'s self-interest to play hers. If *A*'s objectively self-interested behaviour in the Trust Game can express a cooperative intention, cannot the same be true of both players' behaviour in the Market Game? In Chapter 10, I will argue that it can.

10

Cooperative Intentions

In Chapter 9, I described a tendency in both behavioural economics and virtue ethics to contrast market relationships with relationships that are genuinely social. In this chapter, I will argue that market transactions are not fundamentally different from cooperative activities in many other spheres of social life. When people participate in markets, just as when they engage in other schemes of social cooperation, they do not necessarily act on self-interest: they can act with the intention of achieving mutual benefit.

In arguing this, I will draw on ideas from a strand of literature at the interface of philosophy and economics. In this literature, concepts such as preference, belief, intention, and choice can be attributed to groups of individuals, a group being treated as if it were a single agent. My starting point will be one of the theories in this literature—the theory of *team reasoning*, as originally proposed by Michael Bacharach and by me. Building on ideas from this theory, I will develop an analysis of how cooperative interactions can be guided by intentions for mutual benefit, and apply this analysis to the games discussed in Chapter 9.[1]

10.1 Team Reasoning

The underlying principle of team reasoning was first proposed by David Hodgson (1967) to demonstrate a fundamental difference between *act utilitarianism* (in which the utilitarian criterion of maximizing the sum of happiness is applied to individual acts) and *rule utilitarianism* (in which it is applied to general rules of action). This principle was presented by Hodgson as the distinguishing feature of rule utilitarianism. His argument was developed more fully by Donald Regan (1980) as a theory of 'cooperative utilitarianism'. Independently, John Harsanyi (1980) presented a game-theoretic analysis of rule utilitarianism as a theory of moral behaviour. Building on the work of Hodgson and Regan, I proposed a concept of 'team reasoning' which was later developed more formally by Michael Bacharach (Sugden, 1991, 1993b; Bacharach, 1999, 2006).[2]

The core idea of team reasoning is that when two or more individuals, understanding themselves as constituting a single unit of agency or 'team', engage in team reasoning, each of them asks 'What should *we* do?', and not (as in conventional game theory) 'What should *I* do, given my beliefs about what the others will do?' An individual who is rational in the sense of team reasoning considers the possible *profiles* of actions (one action for each team member) that might be chosen by the team. She assesses these profiles in terms of their consequences for the team members *together*, finds the profile that is in the common or collective interest of the team, and then chooses her component of that profile.

It is important to recognize that 'What should we do?' and 'What should I do?' remain distinct questions even if the person who asks 'What should I do?' has preferences that take account of others' payoffs. Indeed, it remains true even if all the people who ask 'What should I do?' have *the same* preferences over relevant outcomes. To see this, imagine a football coach addressing a meeting of all the players in his team before a match. He describes a situation that might arise in the course of play, outlines a combination of moves by players A and B that will lead to a shot on goal, and tells them they should be prepared to act on this plan. Let us call the moves m_A and m_B. This is not the only way in which A and B could sensibly coordinate their actions in the situation that is being planned for, but the coach shows them that it is the way that is most likely to produce a goal. Imagine the following exchange between one of the players and the coach:

PLAYER A: But why should I play m_A?

COACH: Because if you play m_A and B plays m_B, that maximizes the probability that our team scores a goal. Don't you want that?

PLAYER A: Of course I do, but how do I know that by playing m_A I maximize the probability of a goal being scored? That depends on what B does.

COACH: But B is here too. I'm speaking to both of you.

PLAYER A: I know that, but you haven't given him a reason to play m_B, just as you haven't given me a reason to play m_A.

Viewed in the perspective of classical game theory, A's objection to the coach's argument is entirely legitimate. A's preferences are fully aligned with the team's collective interest in scoring a goal, but he is asking to be shown that m_A is the best move *for him*, given those preferences and given well-grounded beliefs about what B will do. The coach has not shown this. But seen from outside that perspective, A's objection is obtuse.

It is obtuse because it fails to understand what a coaching session for a team is all about. The coach is not addressing A and B as separate individuals; he is addressing them collectively, as members of a team. The logic of his recommendation can be put like this: Given that the team's objective is to maximize the probability that a goal is scored, the best combination of moves *by the team* is that A chooses m_A and B chooses m_B. Therefore, A should choose m_A and B should choose m_B. The 'therefore' is self-explanatory to anyone who understands what it is to be a member of a team: if this combination of moves is best for the team, then this is what the team should do.

The core idea of team reasoning can be developed in different ways. To date, the fullest game-theoretic development is that by Bacharach (1999, 2006). Bacharach's theory is an extension of classical game theory in which groups (or 'teams') of individuals can be treated as single players. Groups have utility functions in much the same way that individuals do in the classical theory. If an individual 'identifies' with a particular group of which he is a member, he looks for a profile of strategies which, if followed by all individuals who identify with that group, and given the expected behaviour of everyone who does not, would maximize the expected value of the group's utility. If there is only one such profile, the individual then plays his component of that profile. Bacharach's solution concept is an extension of the concept of Nash equilibrium, in which each group's joint decision is optimal for it, given the decisions of other groups. This is a sophisticated theoretical construction, and formalizes some of the ideas that I presented more intuitively in my 1991 and 1993 papers. However, it may not be the best way to think about how, in most everyday contexts, ordinary people actually cooperate, or (taking a contractarian perspective) to think about how ordinary people might best be advised to cooperate.

Viewed in relation to the objectives of the present book, Bacharach's approach has two limitations. The first is that, like the classical game theory on which it builds, it is a theory of ideally rational decision-making, rationality being understood as acting on integrated preferences. The novel feature is that groups, as well as individuals, can behave as (or as if they were) rational agents. The assumption that a group has well-articulated preferences that can be represented by a single utility function is very restrictive, given what is known about the volatility and context-dependence of individuals' preferences. The further assumption that team members *independently* identify the optimal profile for their team makes heavy demands on individuals' knowledge about the game, their knowledge of the team utility function (if it exists at all), and their powers of reasoning. In some very simple games, these assumptions are indeed plausible and lead to predictions that are consistent with experimental evidence. In particular, they have proved useful in helping to explain how players coordinate on 'focal points' in pure coordination games of the kind first described by Thomas Schelling (1960).[3] But in most real-world interactions, successful cooperation involves conforming to ongoing practices that, at best, are satisfactory rather than optimal. And the whole point of the present book is to develop a kind of normative economics that does not depend on any strong assumptions about rationality.

The second limitation of Bacharach's approach is that, by representing team reasoning in terms of the maximization of a function that describes the overall utility or welfare of a group of individuals, it is taking what in Chapter 2 I called a view from nowhere. Bacharach (2006: 87–8) argues that it is reasonable to assume that team utility is an increasing function of individual payoffs, and suggests that additional properties of this function might include the 'utilitarian' addition of individual payoffs or 'principles of fairness such as those of Nash's axiomatic bargaining theory'. Any function that assigns a utility value to every strategy profile (and whose application is not restricted to a very narrow class of games) must incorporate interpersonal comparisons between the payoffs of different team members. Thus, team reasoning as modelled by Bacharach can involve trade-offs between members' interests: achieving the best outcome for the team may require that some members bear losses so that others achieve greater gains.

This way of thinking about the good of the team does not fit well with the idea of intentional cooperation for mutual benefit that I have suggested is at the heart of practices of trust. Of course, given the assumption that team utility is increasing in individual payoffs, any profile of actions that benefits all the members of a team (relative to some given benchmark) will also increase the utility of the team that comprises those players. Nevertheless, intending that each player benefits is not the same thing as intending the benefit of the team of players, considered as a single entity. The former intention is cooperative in a sense that is not necessarily true of the latter. In a contractarian theory of team reasoning, the members of a team should be concerned with achieving mutual benefit rather than with maximizing the overall good of the team, as judged from some neutral viewpoint.

In the rest of this chapter, I will describe a form of team reasoning in which each team member aims to play his part in the creation of mutual benefit. In previous chapters, I have said a lot about mutual benefit, but I have tried to avoid using preference-based measures of benefit. My analysis has been concerned with individuals' opportunities to make voluntary transactions. Provided that those opportunities are ones that the relevant individuals might plausibly want to take advantage of, I have treated them as opportunities to realize mutual benefit. To put this another way, I have identified mutual benefit with voluntariness. I follow the same strategy in this chapter.

10.2 Practices

My aim is to provide a way of understanding of how each member of a group of individuals can act with the intention of playing his part in a practice that is mutually beneficial for those members together. I begin by explaining how I will use the concept of a 'practice'.

First, a very simple example. In rural parts of Britain, drivers repeatedly have to deal with situations in which two vehicles are approaching one another on a road that is only just wide enough to allow them to pass. Almost always, this problem is solved without any communication and with very little inconvenience: each driver keeps to the left. Just about every driver on the British road system knows that this is what other drivers almost always do. Knowing this, each driver chooses to keep left. For this class of recurrent interactions, keeping left is the practice among British drivers.

This pattern of behaviour is clearly a convention in the sense defined by David Hume (1739–40/1978: 490) in the passage that I quoted in Section 3.2, and in the sense that this term has been used in game-theoretic analysis since David Lewis's path-breaking book *Convention* (1969). However, I have a reason for calling it by a different name. In game theory, a convention is a particular kind of Nash equilibrium, and is therefore defined in relation to the optimizing behaviour of individuals who act on integrated preferences: in a Nash equilibrium, each player's strategy is a best response to the strategies of other players. Of course, in any sensible game-theoretic model of the problem faced by the drivers, keeping left *would* be a Nash equilibrium. But I want a concept of 'practice' that does not presuppose any kind of optimization. For my purposes, what is significant about the example is simply that there is a regularity of behaviour in the population of British drivers, and that each person chooses to conform to that regularity in the knowledge that other people can reliably be expected to conform too.

Consider another example. In American cities, taxi-users normally pay their drivers a tip on top of the metered fare—or so foreigners like me are led to understand. Here is a typical item of internet guidance:

> Tipping a taxi or limo driver in New York City is customary. Tip the driver 10 per cent to 20 per cent of the total fare, depending on how large a bill it is and how good the service was.... If you choose to not give a tip to a cab driver, be prepared to defend your choice and you may also receive a tirade of insults as New York cabbies are not known for being shrinking violets.[4]

If this information is correct, giving tips of at least 10 per cent is a regularity of behaviour among New York taxi-users. New York taxi-users conform to this regularity in the knowledge that most other taxi-users can be expected to conform too. In other words, this is the practice in New York. This practice has a feature, not shared by the practice of keeping left on British roads, which will be important in the argument of this chapter. In a sense that I will define more formally later, interactions between taxi-drivers and customers are *voluntary*: an interaction between a specific driver and a specific customer is initiated only if both individuals so choose.

It is an open question whether the practice of tipping should be thought of as a Nash equilibrium. If we were to presuppose the validity of a model in which each individual's behaviour is governed by her own well-articulated preferences, we might infer from the behaviour of taxi-users that they prefer tipping to not tipping—whether because of pro-social motivations, desires to conform with social norms, or fear of being insulted—and then conclude that tipping is a Nash equilibrium strategy. But whether such a model provides a satisfactory explanation of pro-social behaviour is one of the questions that the present chapter is trying to answer.

The idea of following a practice should not be interpreted as necessarily implying conformity to a rigid rule. Take a famous example of Hume's. Immediately after his definition of 'convention', Hume says: 'Two men, who pull the oars of a boat, do it by an agreement or convention, though they have never given promises to each other' (1739–40/1978: 490). I take it that what Hume has in mind is the second-by-second coordination of movements by two rowers that enables their boat to move smoothly through the water. The suggestion is that experienced rowers, even if previously unknown to one another, can coordinate their actions without explicit communication. Each rower is guided by his previous experience of rowing with other people, but when two people are rowing together, they tacitly adapt their actions to one another's capabilities and to the specific circumstances they confront. Similar examples are often used in the literature of collective intentions. Michael Bratman (1993) has given particular attention to this kind of coordination, achieved by a continuous process of *mutual responsiveness*; his illustrations include the coordination involved in singing a duet together, painting a house together, and taking a trip together. My concept of a 'practice' is intended to encompass such cases, even though the more subtle aspects of mutual responsiveness will not appear in the simple models I use. Take the problem faced by the two drivers approaching one another. If the road is very narrow, there may be a lot of mutual responsiveness in the drivers' manoeuvres as they pass one another, but it may still be illuminating to use a model in which each driver simply chooses between 'keep left' and 'keep right'.

I will represent practices as regularities of behaviour in recurrent interactions. Formally, I model an *interaction* as a game (strictly, a 'game form') for n *players*, where $n \geq 2$.[5] It is defined in relation to a *population M* of potential players of the game, where M is a set that contains at least (but typically many more than) n individuals. For example, an encounter between a specific taxi-driver and a specific customer on a specific occasion is a single interaction; interactions of this general kind recur within a much larger population of taxi-drivers and customers. The description of an interaction can be separated into three components.

The first component is its *tree structure*. (I have already used these structures informally, in Figures 9.1 to 9.4 of Chapter 9.) In specifying a tree structure, I treat the 'players' $1, \ldots, n$ as roles in the game rather than as specific individuals. (Compare the roles of 'White' and 'Black' in Chess.) The tree structure specifies every sequence of moves that is possible for the players collectively. It is made up of *decision nodes* (representing points in the game at which moves are made) and *terminal nodes* (representing possible endpoints of the game). Nodes are connected by *directed links* (representing possible moves in the game). One decision node, the *initial node*, has no predecessors; this represents the starting point of the game. Every other node has exactly one immediate predecessor. At each decision node, a specified player has a choice between alternative moves; each of these moves is represented by a distinct directed link which leads either to another decision node or to a terminal node. Cases in which two or more players move simultaneously are represented by using information sets. (An information set is a set of decision nodes for a specific player such that, if any node in this set is reached, that player does not know which of them has been reached.) To avoid unnecessary complications, I exclude the possibility that chance plays a role in the game, but it would be straightforward to generalize the definition of a tree structure by including 'chance nodes' at which what happens is determined by a 'move of nature'. Any complete sequence of decision nodes that could be reached as a result of the players' decisions is a *path* through the game. In any specific instance of the game, the actual behaviour of the players can be described by the particular path that is *followed*—that is, by the sequence of nodes, starting at the initial node and ending at some terminal node, that are in fact reached.

The second component is an assignment of consequences to paths (or, equivalently, to terminal nodes). This can be represented by a function which assigns a *consequence* $c(i, p)$ to each pair of a player role i and a path p. This consequence describes what happens to i as a result of p being followed. Each consequence is to be understood as an element of some set C of possible consequences, specified without reference to particular individuals. For example, one might want to define C as the set of real numbers, interpreted as increments of one-dimensional 'material payoff', as in many game-theoretic models of social preferences (and as in the games I discussed in Chapter 9). In general, however, I impose no particular structure on C. In the modelling framework that I am using, the specification of a game does not include any reference to individuals' preferences over consequences.

The final component is an assignment of particular individuals to the n roles. Formally, this assignment can be represented by a function which assigns a distinct person $m(i)$ to each player role i, each $m(i)$ being a member of the population M. Taken together, the three components specify a well-defined game to be played by n specific individuals.

In the spirit of Lewis's analysis of conventions, I consider games that are played recurrently within some large population of potential players.[6] In the formal analysis that I present in this chapter, I assume that play is entirely anonymous. That is, when an individual participates in a specific interaction, she has no knowledge about how any of her specific co-participants has behaved in previous interactions. However, her expectations about her co-participants' behaviour may be influenced by her general experience of similar interactions in the past.

In reality, of course, few types of recurrent interaction are completely anonymous. How much individuals know about the previous behaviour of the people with whom they interact is a matter of degree, and can vary greatly between otherwise similar interactions. What is important for my account of practices is that, when individuals engage in specific interactions, population-level regularities of behaviour provide salient benchmarks for those individuals' expectations about one another. For example, I have patronized the same hairdresser for over thirty years. Over that time, we have conversed about many topics, but tipping has never been mentioned. My sense that a hairdresser might expect to be tipped by a regular customer, and about what size of tip a hairdresser might expect, do not derive from my personal relationship with my hairdresser; they derive from general knowledge about tipping practices in Britain. The anonymity assumption represents this idea in an extreme form. In Chapter 11, I will consider some of the implications of relaxing this assumption. For my present purposes, however, there are some advantages in analysing an extreme case. I am trying to explain how intentions directed at mutual benefit might lead a person to act contrary to his self-interest. This problem is made sharper if self-interested motivations to build reputations are screened out by assuming anonymity.

To express the idea of recurrent play more formally, I define a concept of similarity. A *similarity class S* is a set of games that are regarded as similar to one another by the members of the relevant population of potential players; the games in this set will be called *instances* of S. To keep things simple, I assume that all the games in a given similarity class have the same number of player roles and the same tree structure. Thus, for any two such games, there are one-to-one correspondences between players in one game and players in the other, and between paths in one game and paths in the other. This allows me to use the same notation for all games in a similarity class, and to talk meaningfully about some single path being followed in all those games.

I now need a way of describing regularities of behaviour within a similarity class of games. Consider a similarity class S of games that are played recurrently within a population M. Each instance of S is an interaction that can be described by a specific assignment of n distinct individuals (all of whom are members of M) to the game's n player roles, and a specific assignment of consequence profiles to its paths. Consider any path p for that class of games. In a specific instance of S, a player i will be said to *conform to p* if the following is true: if any decision node for i on path p is in fact reached, then i's move at that node keeps the game on that path. Thus, if every player conforms to p, p is the path that is in fact followed. Conversely, if a node is reached at which actual play deviates from p, the condition of 'conformity to p' has no bite from that point on, since no subsequent node is that path.[7]

I will say that a path p^* for interactions in similarity class S is *the practice* in population M if, in instances of S in that population, players almost always conform to p^*. I will assume that no game belongs to more than one similarity class and that, for a given similarity class and a given population, there is no more than one practice at any one time (although there may be none). Beyond this, it is not necessary to be precise about what is meant by 'almost always'. It is sufficient to say that, if p^* is the practice for games in similarity class S, each player in any such interaction has a defeasible expectation that each of his co-players will conform to p^*. This expectation is founded on each player's experience of previous instances of S in which other players have almost always behaved in this way.

Notice that the concept of a practice is defined without any reference to *why* it is followed. Some people may follow a practice for one reason, some for another. There is no presumption that following a practice is in any individual's self-interest, given the expected behaviour of her co-players. However, it is crucial to the concept of a practice that (almost) every member of the population (almost always) chooses to conform to it, knowing that (almost) every other member (almost always) chooses to do the same. Whatever individuals' motivations for conforming may be, those motivations are sustained when others conform.

10.3 Voluntariness in a Simple Model

My concern is with interactions that are mutually beneficial. Whether the concept of mutual benefit is understood in terms of the satisfaction of individuals' preferences or (as in my analysis) in terms of voluntary choice, we immediately confront the problem that mutual benefit has to be defined relative to some baseline. If, as I have suggested, the pursuit of mutual benefit is to be thought of as cooperation, the baseline must be non-cooperation. But what does that mean?

Theorists of team reasoning sometimes suggest that the non-cooperative baseline should represent rationally self-interested behaviour by each individual (in the same sense that 'defection' by both players in the Prisoner's Dilemma is usually seen as the opposite of 'cooperation'). For example, when Bacharach (2006: 84–6) sketches a psychological theory of how individuals come to identify with groups of which they are members, he proposes the hypothesis that group identification is more likely in games in which there is some strategy profile whose outcome is strictly Pareto-superior to at least one Nash equilibrium of the game. The intuition is that team reasoning is activated when individual reasoning might lead to collectively undesired consequences. Relatedly, Jurgis Karpus and Mantas Radzvillas (2018) propose a measure of mutual advantage in which each individual's baseline level of utility is the lowest that is possible for her in the relevant game, subject to the constraint that each player chooses a rationalizable strategy (that is, a strategy choice that is consistent with the assumption that all players are individually rational maximizers of expected utility, and that this is common knowledge). The problem with these baselines is that they do not allow us to say something that seems obviously true: that individuals' self-interested actions can sometimes combine to generate mutual benefit.

In a previous attempt to define mutual benefit in a game, I have suggested that each individual's baseline level of utility should be her *maximin* payoff—that is, the highest payoff that she can guarantee herself, irrespective of the other players' strategy choices (Sugden, 2015d). This definition of the baseline requires that each player's payoffs from different outcomes can be ranked, which is not compatible with the approach I am taking in this book, of not using the concept of preference. But quite apart from that problem, the maximin definition has the implication that the sale of 'protection' services by a criminal gang can count as mutually beneficial: the sellers benefit from the payments they receive, and the buyers avoid the worse outcomes that would otherwise be imposed on them.[8]

It is perhaps more natural to think of the non-cooperative baseline as non-interaction.[9] Roughly speaking, the idea is that individuals take part in a cooperative practice by interacting with one another in such a way that each of them benefits overall, relative to what she would have achieved *had they not interacted at all*. A baseline of non-interaction would allow us to say that a practice in which some or all individuals act in accordance with self-interest can be mutually beneficial. It would also allow us to say that a protection racket is *not* a mutually beneficial interaction, since the racketeers' threat is not to disengage from interaction altogether, but rather to engage in an unwanted kind of interaction with their would-be customers.

A non-interaction baseline is useful only in a model of a 'small world'—that is, in a model that considers a small-scale problem in isolation from a larger, unmodelled background. A whole world of non-interacting individuals would be an extravagant fiction, perhaps something like Jean-Jacques Rousseau's (1755/1988) account of the state of nature. But, while recognizing that everyone is embedded in a background network of economic and social interaction, it can make sense to describe *specific* groups of individuals and *specific* kinds of interaction within those groups in such a way that interaction and non-interaction are credible alternatives. As a way of trying to make progress in understanding intentions for mutual benefit, I offer a model of this kind of small world. I believe that this model, despite its simplicity, elucidates some fundamental properties of cooperative activity.

In using a small-world model of an interaction that takes place within a specific group of individuals, I effectively ignore any effects that decisions made within that interaction may have on people outside the group. Here it is important to remember that my analysis is ultimately concerned with opportunity and not with preference-satisfaction. I do not assume that decisions made within an interaction have no effect on the degree to which outsiders' preferences are satisfied. What I assume is that those decisions have no effect on outsiders' *opportunities*—as individuals, to use their own endowments as they see fit, or collectively, to transact with one another by mutual agreement. For example, consider an interaction in which Annie and Bill negotiate about the terms on which Bill might buy Annie's car. A small-world model of this interaction might contain only Annie and Bill. Suppose there is a third person, Charlie, who would like to own Annie's car, but is not willing to pay as much for it as Bill is. The outcome of Annie and Bill's interaction may impinge on Charlie's preference-satisfaction (he would prefer that Bill did not buy the car) and on his opportunities to transact with Annie (if she sells her car to Bill, she cannot sell it to Charlie). But his opportunities to use his own endowments are not affected. Nor are the collective opportunities of Charlie and (say) Delia to trade between themselves on mutually agreeable terms. Generalizing from this example in the light of the Strong Market Opportunity Theorem (presented in Section 6.6), interactions between potential buyers and sellers of private goods in competitive markets can legitimately be modelled as small worlds in the sense that I have explained.

I begin with the simplest case, that of a situation in which two individuals have an opportunity to engage with one another in some specific interaction, no other interaction between them being possible. Intuitively, such an interaction is voluntary if it is preceded by some procedure in which each player can declare whether or not she is willing to participate in that interaction, and such that the interaction takes place only if both players declare willingness, and fails to take place only if at least one player declares unwillingness. Take the case of an interaction between a taxi-driver and a potential customer. The driver has an empty taxi and is cruising along a city street; the customer is standing at the kerbside. In the pre-interaction procedure, the customer flags down the taxi, indicating her willingness to interact with the driver. In stopping to pick her up, the taxi-driver indicates his willingness to interact with her. The interaction itself begins if and only if these signals of willingness have been made.

I will model a pre-play procedure as a particular type of game. Consider any two-player interaction between players 1 and 2. Formally, an *initiation game* for this interaction is a game for the same two players. This game has a tree structure (as defined in Section 10.2) and an assignment of consequences to ⟨player, path⟩ pairs. Irrespective of which path through the game is followed, there are only two possible consequences for each player. For player 1, the consequence is *either* that he participates in the interaction in his assigned role (denoted by the consequence I_1) *or* that he does not participate in it (the consequence O_1). Similarly, the consequence for player 2 is *either* participation in her assigned role (I_2) *or* non-participation (O_2). Thus, at each terminal node, the profile of consequences for the two players is *either* (I_1, I_2), that is, the interaction takes place, *or* (O_1, O_2), that is, it does not take place. O_1 and O_2 are the players' respective *outside options*. Each O_i can be interpreted as an opportunity set of alternative outcomes for player i, each of which i can reach without participating in the interaction, and between which i is free to choose. Notice the implicit assumption that, if the interaction does not take place, each player's subsequent choices have no effect on the other player. Thus, (O_1, O_2) is a baseline of non-interaction.

An initiation game has the additional feature that it can contain decision nodes of the following special type. A *declaration node* for player i is a decision node at which i chooses between exactly two moves, *in* and *out*. Intuitively, *in* is a declaration of willingness to participate in the interaction; *out* is a declaration of unwillingness to participate. It is an assumption of the model that the players understand the meanings of these moves as declarations of willingness and unwillingness. However, the definition of an initiation game leaves open whether these declarations have any actual effect on the outcome of the game. The idea that an interaction is voluntary can be represented by imposing additional restrictions on its initiation game. Consider the following conditions that a two-player initiation game might satisfy:

Irrevocability.   For each path through the game and for each player: there is no more than one declaration node for that player on that path.

Opting In.   For each path through the game that has the consequence pair (I_1, I_2): that path includes both a declaration node for player 1 at which he chooses *in* and a declaration node for player 2 at which she chooses *in*.

Opting Out. For each path through the game that has the consequence pair (O_1, O_2): that path includes *either* a declaration node for player 1 at which he chooses *out*, or a declaration node for player 2 at which she chooses *out*.

Irrevocability expresses the idea that declarations, once made, cannot be taken back. Opting In states that the interaction is initiated only if both players declare their willingness to participate. Opting Out states that the interaction fails to be initiated only if at least one player declares her unwillingness to participate. If an initiation game has these three properties, moves chosen at declaration nodes can be interpreted as binding decisions about whether or not to participate in the interaction. I will say that a two-person interaction is *voluntary* if it is preceded by an initiation game that satisfies Irrevocability, Opting In, and Opting Out.

Now consider any similarity class S of voluntary two-person interactions that recur in some population M and for which some practice p^* exists. (That is, in instances of S in that population, players almost always conform to p^*.) Any individual who declares her willingness to participate in an instance of S can expect that, if the interaction takes place and if she conforms to p^*, the person with whom she interacts will (very probably) conform too. Thus, if she enters the interaction with the intention of conforming to p^*, she is effectively choosing to participate, not merely in the interaction, but also in that practice. In this sense, her participation *in the practice* can be said to be voluntary.

10.4 Voluntariness Generalized

In my model of a voluntary interaction between two individuals, that interaction is the *only* route by which either individual's actions can affect the opportunities available to the other. (Recall that this is an implication of the definition of players' outside options.) It is straightforward to generalize this model to apply to any situation in which there are n individuals but only one possible interaction, an interaction in which all n individuals are players. (Think of a productive activity that requires the complementary skills of three individuals, or a task that can be carried out only by the combined actions of three volunteers when only three people are in a position to volunteer.) In such a case, it is easy to generalize the Irrevocability, Opting In, and Opting Out properties of two-player initiation games so that the relevant interaction is initiated only if all n players declare their willingness to participate in it, and fails to be initiated only if at least one player declares her unwillingness to participate.

Things are more complicated if, within the small world that is being modelled, there are two or more possible ways in which individuals can interact, and if these have overlapping sets of players. For example, suppose that Tom, Dick, and Harry are academics who are thinking about initiating a research collaboration. The topic for investigation does not arise out of any particular discoveries that these individuals have already made, individually or collectively; it just requires sustained work from a team of suitably skilled people. Within the small world of the three individuals, there are two (and only two) teams with the necessary mix of skills: {Tom, Dick, Harry} and {Tom, Dick}. There are therefore two possible and mutually exclusive interactions—one involving all three individuals (interaction I) and one involving only Tom and Dick (interaction J). Assume that, for each of Tom, Dick, and Harry respectively, there is a well-defined outside option, O_T, O_D, or O_H, that this individual will get if he does not participate in either interaction. (Notice that this assumption implies that if interaction J takes place, what Tom and Dick do within it has no effect on Harry's opportunities.) However, there is still a problem in defining a non-interaction baseline for either interaction *considered separately*.

To illustrate this problem, suppose that, relative to their outside options, all three individuals would benefit from participating in I. However, Tom and Dick would both benefit more from participating in J than from participating in I. Should I be considered mutually beneficial? Arguably not. To say that some arrangement is *mutually* beneficial is to say, not only that each party benefits from that arrangement, but also that each party contributes something to the benefits that the others enjoy. But, if account is taken of the existence of J as a feasible alternative to I, Harry's participation in I does not benefit Tom or Dick. In this sense, Harry's role in I is that of a free-rider.

Because my method of analysis identifies mutual benefit with voluntariness, I need to represent voluntariness in a way that allows the exclusion of free-riders.[10] The essential idea behind the generalized model I now develop is that, when two or more interactions are mutually exclusive, any one of them can count as voluntary only if (generalized versions of) the Opting In and Opting Out conditions hold for *all* of them. In terms of the example: in order for interaction I to be considered voluntary, it is not sufficient that all three individuals choose to participate in it; it is also necessary that Tom and Dick collectively have (but choose not to exercise) the opportunity to participate in J instead.

Consider any situation involving a group of n individuals and a finite set I of possible interactions, in each of which two or more of those individuals are players. Each individual has a fixed outside option, which he gets if he does not participate in any interaction. If two interactions have one or more player in common, they will be said to *overlap*. I stipulate that (as in the case of interactions *I* and *J* for Tom, Dick, and Harry) such interactions are mutually exclusive: each individual can participate in no more than one interaction. I need to generalize the concept of an initiation game so that a single *n*-player game determines which (if any) of the interactions in I take place.

In such a game, the profile of consequences at each terminal node must specify, for each individual, which (if any) interaction he participates in. Take the case of Tom, Dick, and Harry. For Tom, the initiation game has three possible consequences: I_T (he participates in interaction *I*), J_T (he participates in interaction *J*), and O_T (he participates in neither). Similarly, the possible consequences for Dick are I_D, J_D, and O_D, and those for Harry are I_H and O_H. Thus, at each terminal node, the profile of consequences for the three players is *either* (I_T, I_D, I_H), that is, *I* takes place, *or* (J_T, J_D, O_H), that is, *J* takes place, *or* (O_T, O_D, O_H), that is, neither interaction takes place.

A declaration node must now refer not only to a specific individual (the individual who makes the declaration) but also to a specific interaction in which that individual is a player (the interaction about which the declaration is made). For example, at a declaration node for Tom with respect to inter-action *I*, *in* is a declaration of Tom's willingness to participate in *I*; *out* is a declaration of his unwillingness to participate in *I*. More generally, let *i* denote any individual (Tom, Dick, or Harry in the example) and let *k* denote any interaction in which *i* is a player (*I* or *J* in the example). Then an (i, k) declaration node is one at which *i* chooses *in* or *out* with respect to *k*.

The conditions of Irrevocability, Opting In, and Opting Out can be generalized to:

Generalized Irrevocability. For each path *p* through the initiation game, for each interaction *k*, and for each individual *i* who is a player in *k*: *p* includes no more than one (i, k) declaration node.

Generalized Opting In. For each path *p* through the initiation game, for each interaction *k*, and for each individual *i* who is a player in *k*: if *p* leads to *k* taking place, then *p* includes an (i, k) declaration node at which *i* chooses *in*.

Generalized Opting Out. For each path *p* through the initiation game, for each interaction *k*: if *p* leads to *k* not taking place, then *either* (a) for some individual *i* who is a player in *k*, *p* includes an (i, k) declaration node at which *i* chooses *out*, *or* (b) for some interaction *k'* that overlaps with *k*, *p* leads to *k'* taking place.

Generalized Irrevocability expresses the idea that declarations cannot be taken back. Generalized Opting In states that any given interaction is initiated only if each of its participants declares her willingness for this to happen. Given that Generalized Opting In is satisfied, Generalized Opting Out implies that any given interaction fails to be initiated only if at least one of its participants vetoes it, either by declaring his unwillingness to participate in it, or by being a willing participant in some other interaction which in fact takes place. Thus, these properties imply that for each possible interaction I, the individuals who are players in I have the collective opportunity to ensure that I takes place. (I will certainly take place if each of its players uses every opportunity to declare her willingness to participate in it and to declare her unwillingness to participate in other interactions.) I will say that an interaction is *voluntary* if it is preceded by an initiation game that satisfies Generalized Irrevocability, Generalized Opting In, and Generalized Opting Out.

Can we be sure that, for any set of n individuals and any set I of possible interactions, there is an initiation game that satisfies all three properties? To see that the answer is 'Yes', consider the following general procedure for determining which interactions will be initiated. List the possible interactions in any order. Begin with the first interaction on the list, denoted I^1. Require each of the players in I^1 to make a simultaneous declaration of *in* or *out* with respect to that interaction. If all those players declare *in*, record I^1 as 'to be initiated'; otherwise, record it as 'not to be initiated'. Now move to the second interaction on the list, I^2. If I^2 overlaps with any interaction that has already been recorded as 'to be initiated', record I^2 as 'not to be initiated'. Otherwise, require all the players in I^2 to make a simultaneous declaration of *in* or *out*. And so on. It is easy to check that this procedure, represented as an initiation game, satisfies Generalized Irrevocability, Generalized Opting In, and Generalized Opting Out.

For any given set of n individuals and any given set I of possible interactions, there may be many different initiation games that satisfy the three voluntariness conditions. Some individuals' interests might be better served by one such game, others' interests by another. For example, consider a variant of the case of Tom, Dick, and Harry in which Tom benefits more from I than from J, but the opposite is true for Dick. (As before, participating in I is better than the outside option for all three individuals, and participating in J is better than the outside option for both Tom and Dick.) If each individual expects the others to make rational decisions, it is in Tom's interest that he is able to veto J before Dick is able to veto I; it is in Dick's interest that the opposite is the case. A whole research programme in game theory, initiated by David Gale and Lloyd Shapley (1962), investigates the efficiency, distributional, and stability properties of different procedures for making matches between players—for example, between potential husbands and potential wives, or between college applicants and colleges. But my aim is not to design ideal initiation games; it is simply to identify conditions under which interactions can be understood as voluntary. As an analogy, compare the traditional procedure by which potential husbands propose to potential wives with the opposite procedure in which women propose to men. One implication of Gale and Shapley's analysis is that the traditional procedure tends to benefit men relative to women. But that surely does not imply that marriages that result from proposals by willing men and acceptances by willing women are other than voluntary.

The conclusion of Section 10.3 can now be stated more generally. Consider any similarity class S of voluntary n-person interactions that recur in some population M and for which some practice p^* exists. If, for some interaction in this class, an individual enters that interaction with the intention of conforming to p^*, she can be said to be choosing to participate in that practice. This idea underlies the following definition: any practice that applies to a similarity class of voluntary interactions is a *voluntary practice*. A voluntary practice provides opportunities for mutual benefit in something like the same way as does the price system of a competitive economy, as analysed in Chapter 6. By conforming to a voluntary practice, individuals not only realize mutual benefit directly; they also help to sustain the expectations on which that practice depends, and so to sustain an institution that provides everyone with opportunities to realize mutual benefit.

Notice, however, that none of this implies that, if a voluntary practice exists, it is in each individual's interest to conform to it. In a world in which other people can be relied on to conform to a certain voluntary practice p^*, it might be in your interest to enter an interaction to which p^* applies but then to deviate from that practice, taking advantage of the other participants' expectations about your behaviour. We must therefore ask whether individuals can be motivated to conform to voluntary practices even when doing so is contrary to self-interest.

10.5 Intending Mutual Benefit

Extensionally, anyone who conforms to a voluntary practice is engaging with others in a way that is productive of mutual benefit. But that does not mean that mutual benefit is necessarily part of his intention. I now ask what it means to *intend* mutual benefit in a voluntary interaction.

As a preliminary step, I need to introduce the concept of 'public observation'. A state of the world w is *publicly observed* by a group of individuals if its occurrence reveals itself in such a way that each member of the group is in a position to infer all of the following: that w is the case; that each other member is in a position to infer that w is the case; that each other member is in a position to infer that each other member is in a position to infer that w is the case; and so on. For example, suppose that the group is the set of passengers in an aircraft cabin, and the captain makes an announcement on the public address system. The fact that the announcement has been made is publicly observed by the passengers. Notice that the concept of public observation does not presuppose that individuals engage in sophisticated reasoning. Each passenger can recognize that the announcement is publicly observed without making any *actual* inferences about what any other passenger believes or infers. Similarly, British drivers' repeated experience of conformity to the practice of keeping left by different drivers on different roads shows them that this practice is publicly observed.[11]

I now present a schema of practical reasoning that might be used by an individual *i* who is participating in an interaction *I*. *N* is the set of players in that interaction, *S* is the similarity class to which the interaction belongs, *M* is the population of potential players of interactions in that class, and p^* is a path for that class of games. P1 to P3 are premises that *i* believes to be true, and C is the conclusion to be drawn from these premises. An intention is expressed by the formula 'Let me . . . '. Notice that, by definition, a voluntary interaction can take place only as a consequence of an initiation game that satisfies Generalized Irrevocability, Generalized Opting In, and Generalized Opting Out. Thus, given that *i* is participating in *I*, the proposition '*I* is voluntary' implies that every member of *N*, including *i*, has chosen to participate in *I*. Here is the schema:

Intending Mutual Benefit
(P1)   That *I* belongs to similarity class *S* is publicly observed by *N*.
(P2)   That p^* is the practice in *M* for interactions in similarity class *S* is publicly observed by *N*.
(P3)   That *I* is voluntary is publicly observed by *N*.
So (C)   Let me conform to p^*.

If *i* reasons according to the schema of Intending Mutual Benefit, he is reasoning *as a member of a group*, namely the group *N* of people who are participating in interaction *I*. In accepting P1 and P2, *i* is able to say: '*We* (the members of *N*) came to the interaction recognizing it be of a type such that, if all players choose to participate in it, they can expect one another to conform to the practice p^*'. In accepting P3, he is also able to say: '*We* recognize that, in the light of that expectation, *we* chose to participate'. In accepting the conclusion of the schema, *i* is able to say of p^*: 'This is the practice that *we* chose to follow, so now I will play my part in implementing that choice, in the expectation that the others will play theirs'. In these respects, Intending Mutual Benefit is a schema of team reasoning.[12]

I will say that an individual *i* *endorses* a schema of practical reasoning if, however its variables are filled in, he accepts the validity of drawing the stated conclusion from the stated premises, and is disposed to act on the intentions that this reasoning produces. Thus, if *i* endorses the schema of Intending Mutual Benefit, he stands ready to use it for any specification of the variables

I, *N*, *S*, *M*, and *p**, including specifications in which it leads him to act contrary to self-interest. Whenever he uses the schema, he forms an intention to play his part in implementing a choice that has been made voluntarily by a group of which he is a member. I must stress that I am not claiming that, as a matter of empirical fact, most people endorse the schema of Intending Mutual Benefit. Nor (or at least, not yet) am I arguing that people *ought* to endorse it. As far as the present chapter is concerned, my claim is merely that this is an intelligible mode of reasoning, which (to some degree of approximation) people sometimes use and act on.

Intending Mutual Benefit expresses a conception of team reasoning that is significantly different from the one developed by Bacharach (1999, 2006), described in Section 10.1. One difference is that there is no concept of group utility that players jointly try to maximize; the players are concerned with mutual benefit rather than with the overall good of the group. In endorsing the schema of Intending Mutual Benefit, an individual is committing herself to conform to voluntary practices only in interactions in which she has chosen to participate: if, for whatever reason, she does not expect to benefit from some interaction, she remains free to opt out of it and thereby out of the domain of team reasoning. A second difference is that the players do not try to identify a combination of actions that is uniquely best (whether 'best' is assessed in terms of group utility or the extent of mutual benefit). Having chosen to participate in an interaction, they take the existing practice as given and conform to it. Thus, they do not need to know one another's preferences. A third difference is that reasoning according to the schema will not lead a player to conform to any given rule of behaviour unless that rule is the practice in the relevant population—a condition that gives that player reason to expect that the other players will conform too. And if, contrary to that expectation, any other player fails to conform, the schema will cease to require anything of her.

I have said that, in using the schema, an individual forms an intention to play her part in implementing a choice that has been made voluntarily by a group of which she is a member. Speaking about such a group, she can therefore say: '*I* intend to play my part in our realizing mutual benefit'. But can she also say: '*We* intend that we realize mutual benefit'?

Notice that there is no premise in the schema that refers to the other players' *reasons* for conforming to *p**. Suppose that it is in the self-interest of each of the other players to conform to *p**, and that *i* believes that each of those players' reason for conforming is self-interest. In this case, *i* does not believe that the other players *intend* mutual benefit even though, extensionally, what each of them intends is his component of what he has reason to believe is a mutually beneficial practice. Or suppose that *p** is a practice that requires all the players to act contrary to self-interest, and that *i* believes that each other player j conforms to p^* because he wants to be kind, in the sense that this word is used in Matthew Rabin's (1993) model of reciprocity, discussed in Section 9.4. That is, each j intends to benefit other players at some cost to himself. Again, but for opposite reasons, i does not believe that the other players intend mutual benefit: each of the others intends self-sacrifice, and mutual benefit is an unintended outcome of their combined actions.

Thus, the schema of Intending Mutual Benefit does not produce *collective* intentions for mutual benefit. In contrast, consider the schema of *Collectively Intending Mutual Benefit*. This is the same as Intending Mutual Benefit except that it has an additional premise P4: 'That each member of N has endorsed the schema of Collectively Intending Mutual Benefit is publicly observed by N'. Notice the recursive structure of this schema: its premises include a proposition about players' endorsement of that very schema.[13] This is not circular: what is being said is that a person who endorses the schema stands ready to use it when interacting with other people who have endorsed it too. (Compare the commitment that is made in a wedding ceremony by the first person who says 'I do': this is an unconditional commitment, but it is not activated unless and until the second person says the same words.) The intentions that are represented by Intending Mutual Benefit are perhaps not as philosophically profound as ones that can be expressed by 'We intend...'. Nevertheless, as I will explain in Section 11.5, my model gains robustness by not requiring, as a precondition for a player's intending to participate in the production of mutual benefit, that she believes that the other players intend mutual benefit too.

The intentions created by the schema of Intending Mutual Benefit are in many ways similar to intentions to keep agreements. (Indeed, as I will argue in the next paragraph, the schema can create intentions to keep agreements.) Recall Hume's definition of 'convention' (quoted in Section 3.2). Hume says that when the members of a society regulate their conduct by rules that they acknowledge as serving their common interests, and when each person follows those rules on the supposition that the others will do the same, this feature of social life may properly enough be called a convention or agreement. A practice governing a class of voluntary interactions is a set of rules by which the members of some population regulate their conduct. If the premises of the schema are true, the fact that these rules allow the members to further their common interests is publicly observed. So too is the fact that the rules are generally followed. Each member follows these rules on the supposition that other members will do the same. In Hume's sense, such a practice is very like an agreement. Notice, however, that the concept of agreement that is implicit in the schema is not that of a hypothetical agreement between ideally rational individuals.[14] Individuals who reason according to the schema do not try to simulate the outcome of a process of rational bargaining; they merely conform to ongoing practices that allow them to realize mutual benefit.

Hume's definition of 'convention' begins with the example of 'stability of possession' (that is, those regularities of behaviour that sustain *de facto* property rights). Referring to this example, he says: 'This convention is not of the nature of a *promise*: For even promises themselves, as we shall see afterwards, arise from human conventions' (1739–40/1978: 490). As I explained in Section 3.2, Hume sees the concept of convention as more fundamental than that of an exchange of explicit promises: promise-keeping is just one (very important) example of a convention. I see Intending Mutual Benefit in a similar way. Situations in which promises can be exchanged can be modelled as voluntary interactions. In a population of people who can be relied on to keep their promises, promise-keeping is a voluntary practice. Intending Mutual Benefit is a schema of reasoning that can lead people to conform to, and so to sustain, the practice of promise-keeping.

10.6 Four Examples

In this section, I reconsider four games that I discussed in Sections 9.3, 9.4, and 9.6. I will redescribe each of these, sometimes in a stripped-down form, as a voluntary interaction for two players *A* and *B*. Thus, it is implicit in the description of each interaction that it is preceded by an initiation game that satisfies Generalized Irrevocability, Generalized Opting In, and Generalized Opting Out. In each case, I will assume that the interaction belongs to a class of similar interactions that take place recurrently within some population. Because I want to compare the kind of pro-sociality that I have theorized in this chapter with the kind that is assumed in theories of social preferences, I need to present each game in a form that is compatible with both theoretical frameworks. I will therefore interpret the payoffs in these games as material consequences for the respective players, measured as increments of some commodity that they both value. I will assume that each player's outside option leads to a determinate material consequence, and use a normalization in which all these baseline consequences are zero. When referring to social preference theories, I will assume that payoffs are common knowledge, as in conventional game theory. When referring to intentions for mutual benefit, I will assume only that each player knows the consequence for himself of each strategy profile.

Example 1: Public Good Game. This interaction is a stripped-down variant of the Public Good Game described in Section 9.3. *A* and *B* move simultaneously, each choosing *work* (contributing to a public good) or *shirk* (not contributing). If neither chooses *work*, the outcome is (0, 0). If either player chooses *work*, that player incurs a cost of 3, and creates a benefit of 4 which is shared equally by both players. Let p^* be the path on which both players choose *work*. This path leads to the outcome (1, 1): both players benefit relative to their non-participation baselines. However, *work* is a strictly dominated strategy in the participation subgame. Thus it would not be consistent with self-interested play for each player to conform to p^*, expecting the other player to conform too.[15]

But suppose that, in recurrent play of voluntary interactions from the relevant similarity class, participants almost always conform to p^*. In other words, p^* is the voluntary practice in the population. How might this fact be explained? This is a case in which cooperation might express intentions to reciprocate kindness, as in Rabin's (1993) model of reciprocity. That is, in choosing to behave as he does, each player might act on the conditional intention of being kind to those who are kind to him. Expecting *B* to choose *work*, *A* interprets this expected action as showing kindness to him, and so he chooses *work* to be kind to *B* in return; and conversely. But another possibility seems at least equally plausible: each player acts on the intention of conforming to a voluntary practice in which both players choose *work* and, in consequence, both players benefit. Each expects that the other will conform too. Neither intends kindness to the other, in the sense of intending to benefit that person at a personal cost. Each intends that the other person will benefit, but as part of a practice in which he or she will benefit too.

Example 2: Trust Game. This interaction is as shown in Figure 9.1 of Section 9.3. *A* moves first, choosing *hold* or *send*. If he chooses *hold*, the game ends with the outcome (0, 0). If *A* chooses *send*, *B* chooses between *keep*, which gives (–1, 5), and *return*, which gives (2, 2). Let p^* be the path on which *A* chooses *send* and *B* chooses *return*. If both players conform to p^*, both benefit relative to their non-participation baselines. But this is not consistent with self-interested play. Given *B*'s conformity to p^*, *A*'s choice of *send* is payoff-maximizing for him; but *B*'s payoff-maximizing response to *send* is not *return* but *keep*.

Suppose that, nevertheless, p^* is the voluntary practice in the population. It seems natural to say that the two players are cooperating with one another, and that *B*'s move reciprocates some feature of *A*'s. But, given that p^* is the voluntary practice, *A* can expect *B* to conform to it, and so to play *return* in response to *send*. Given this expectation, *B*'s move cannot be a reciprocation of kindness, since *A* does not incur any cost to benefit *B*. However, *send* and *return* can still express cooperative intentions by both players. Each can understand his or her move as a part of a practice that will benefit both of them, expecting the other to play her or his part too. If this is how the players think of their actions, their intentions are fundamentally reciprocal even though, given their expectations about the other, A's move is individually payoff-maximizing and B's is not.

Example 3: Ultimatum Game. This interaction is as shown in Figure 9.2 of Section 9.3. A moves first, choosing *equal* or *unequal*. Knowing what A has chosen, B chooses *accept* or *reject*. If A chooses *equal* and B chooses *accept*, the outcome is (5, 5). If A chooses *unequal* and B chooses *accept*, the outcome is (8, 2). Otherwise, the outcome is (0, 0). Let p^* be the path on which A chooses *equal* and B chooses *accept*. If both players conform to p^*, both benefit relative to their non-participation baselines. But this is not consistent with self-interested play, because B's payoff-maximizing response to *unequal* is *accept*. If A expected this response, it would be payoff-maximizing for him to play *unequal* rather than *equal*.

Suppose that p^* is the voluntary practice in the population and that, were A unexpectedly to choose *unequal*, B would choose *reject*, contrary to her self-interest. (Recall that behaviour of this kind is often observed in Ultimatum Game experiments.) It would be in the spirit of a genre of social preference theory to suggest that, in this event, B's intention would be to punish A for deviating from his expected course of action in a way that is unfair to her. Indeed, when Rabin (1993: 1284) uses his model of reciprocity to explain why people act against self-interest by rejecting 'unfair' offers, he describes this behaviour as showing that people 'are willing to punish unfair offers by rejecting them'; throughout his paper, he refers to negative reciprocity as 'punishment'. And recall Ernst Fehr and Simon Gächter's (2000) theory of how punishment can sustain cooperation, discussed in Section 9.3. But if one thinks in terms of cooperation rather than kindness, one may recognize another possibility: B may see her choice of *reject* as a way of undoing her earlier choice of *in*.

Suppose that when B chooses *in*, she does so with the intention of playing her part in a practice in which A chooses *equal* and she chooses *accept*. If she discovers that, contrary to her prior expectation, A has not played his part in this practice, that intention becomes void. Were she to accept A's unequal proposal, she would be accepting a disadvantageous change in the normal terms of cooperation, imposed unilaterally by A. Rather than play the role of sucker, she might choose to break off the relationship with A.

If this is how B understands *reject*, is her intention to *punish* A? In choosing *reject* in response to *unequal*, B knowingly acts contrary to A's interests. But her intention, as I have described it, is to walk away from a relationship whose terms she is not willing to accept; the effect on A is collateral damage. In contrast, punishment is the intentional infliction of harm. Even if the ultimate objective of punishment is to deter future failures of cooperation, the harm it inflicts is the means by which that objective is to be achieved. This distinction is not trivial. Moral rules often distinguish between harm as a foreseen but unintended side-effect and harm as an intended means to a chosen end. In warfare, for example, it may be deemed permissible to attack a military target even if civilians will unavoidably be killed, but not to kill civilians as a means of undermining enemy morale.[16]

Example 4: Market Game. This interaction is as shown in Figure 9.4 of Section 9.6. It is the same as Example 2, except that if *A* chooses *send* and *B* chooses *keep*, the outcome is (–1, –1) instead of (–1, 5). Let p^* be the path on which *A* chooses *send* and *B* chooses *return*. If both players conform to p^*, both benefit relative to their non-participation baselines. However, unlike the paths considered in the other examples, conformity to p^* *is* consistent with self-interested play. In this game, *B*'s payoff-maximizing response to *send* is *return*. If *A* expects this response, his payoff-maximizing move is *send*.

Suppose that p^* is the voluntary practice in the population. One possible explanation is that each player acts on self-interested intentions and that mutual benefit occurs as an unintended outcome. But, just as in the other examples, each player's intention might be to play his or her part in a mutually beneficial practice, expecting the other to do the same. I have already argued that *one* player (the first mover in the Trust Game) can act on such an intention, even if his action serves his self-interest. In philosophical language: an action that is *extensionally* self-interested need not be *intensionally* self-interested. The Market Game shows how this can be true for both players in a two-person game.

11

The Principle of Mutual Benefit

In behavioural social science, the tendency for people to follow social norms is often treated in much the same way as the tendency for people to choose default options—that is, as a psychological bias that social planners can use to steer people towards choices that promote social welfare, or that are supposed to be in accord with those people's latent preferences. For example, Cristina Bicchieri (2006: 63) is explicit about the usefulness of a scientific study of norms: 'Norms of beneficence, promise-keeping, and reciprocity, to name but a few, are critical in maintaining social order and stability. . . . Knowing how to make them focal may render obsolete more costly and dubiously effective policies of social control'. Richard Thaler and Cass Sunstein (2008: 182) are more subtle, but their proposals for nudging are often based on a similarly instrumental view of social norms. A typical example is their praise for a State of Illinois website that promotes organ donation, using messages about the proportion of Illinois adults who think that registering as an organ donor is 'the right thing to do' and about the proportion who have already registered. This website is held up as 'an excellent example of good nudging' because of the skill with which it 'enlist[s] existing norms in the direction of lifesaving choices'.

But if one takes a contractarian approach, normative economics is not addressed to social planners. Its recommendations are addressed *to individuals together*, showing them how they can coordinate their behaviour to achieve mutual benefit. The content of such a recommendation—the thing that it is everyone's interest to agree to—can be a putative social norm or code of morality. To put this another way, norms can be the objects of collective choice. In this final chapter, I will try to persuade my readers of the advantages of living in a society that upholds a morality of mutual benefit.

11.1 Morality and Norms

Some readers may think that I am making a category mistake in claiming that individuals collectively can *choose* which rules they will treat as morally obligatory and that, if a collective decision is being made about matters of morality, each individual is entitled to consult her own interests. Don't we *discover* our moral obligations through moral reasoning, rather than *choose* them to suit our interests? A more conciliatory critic might suggest the need for a distinction between moral rules and social norms. Perhaps social norms can be the object of collective choice, the critic might say, but not moral rules. In this section, I explain why I will not use this distinction.

The idea that moral rules are discovered by reason takes its purest form in the philosophy of Immanuel Kant. For Kant, there is a 'moral law', accessible to human reason, that is independent of all facts of experience and all properties of human psychology. In what is probably his most famous sentence, Kant says: 'Two things fill the mind with ever new and increasing admiration and awe, the oftener and the more steadily we reflect on them: *the starry heavens above and the moral law within*'. The point of the contrast is that the starry heavens above inspire awe by showing us our insignificance in the universe, while our inner perception of the moral law 'infinitely elevates' our worth as intelligent beings by revealing 'a life independent of animality and even of the whole sensible world' (1788/2004: 199). To allow mere feelings to influence our moral judgements would be to violate the purity of morality:

> But now the moral law in its purity and genuineness . . . is to be sought nowhere else than in a pure philosophy; hence this (metaphysics) must go first, and without it there can be no moral philosophy at all; that which mixes those pure principles among empirical ones does not even deserve the name of a 'philosophy' . . . , still less of a 'moral philosophy', because precisely through this mixture it violates the purity of morals and proceeds contrary to its own end.
>
> (Kant, 1785/2002: 6)

Although few modern philosophers would make such an extreme separation between morality and psychology as Kant does, the idea of an autonomous domain of moral truth retains some hold in moral philosophy. Some philosophers argue for 'moral realism'—the theory that moral judgements have a special kind of objectivity. According to Russ Shafer-Landau (2003: 2), who defends such a theory, moral judgements 'when true, are so independently of what any human being, anywhere, in any circumstance whatever, thinks of them'.

I have to say that my sympathies are with a diametrically opposite position in meta-ethics—the position taken by David Hume. Hume argues that the human sense of morality is not a perception of any property of the external world (whether that world is understood empirically or as a domain of pure rational thought). He asks his readers to consider a case, say of murder, that everyone can agree is morally wrong:

> Examine it in all lights, and see if you can find that matter of fact, or real existence, which you call *vice*. In whichever way you take it, you find only

certain passions, motives, volitions and thoughts. There is no other matter of fact in the case.... So that when you pronounce any action or character to be vicious, you mean nothing, but that from the constitution of your nature you have a feeling or sentiment of blame from the contemplation of it.

(Hume, 1739–40/1978: 468–9)

According to Hume, the sense of moral obligation—the sense of *oughtness*—is a particular kind of feeling, and nothing more.

But whether or not Hume is right to say that our sense of morality is *only* a kind of feeling—that it has no reference to anything outside our minds that can be true or false—there is no avoiding the fact that a sense of morality *is* a kind of feeling. In Chapter 4, I argued that rational choice is not self-explanatory: if there are circumstances in which human beings behave in accordance with the theory of rational choice, that behaviour still requires a psychological explanation. It is equally true to say that moral judgement is not self-explanatory. If human beings have a sense of morality, that too is a fact that calls for psychological explanation. Even if moral truths somehow exist independently of what any human being thinks about them, the existence of those truths by itself does nothing to explain the actual moral thinking of human beings. John Stuart Mill reaches much the same conclusion when he poses the question of how any moral standard comes to be thought of as obligatory. He replies that, ultimately, the perception that a moral principle is binding on us is nothing more than a 'subjective feeling in our own minds':

Its binding force ... consists in the existence of a mass of feeling which must be broken through in order to do what violates our standard of right.... Whatever theory we have of the origin or nature of conscience, this is what essentially constitutes it.   (Mill, 1861/1972: 26)

Any plausible explanation of this subjective feeling must allow (as Hume's and Mill's theories do allow) some role for hard-wired properties of human psychology and some role for social learning. It is obvious too that beliefs about principles of morality differ between societies and over time. Social learning is not just an interactive mechanism by which people learn a set of culture-independent moral rules; at least part of what each person learns is the particular morality of the society in which the learning takes place. If this is right, there cannot be a categorical distinction between moral rules and social norms, understood empirically.

This claim may seem to run contrary to the findings of the psychological literature on the *moral/conventional distinction task*. This is a well-established experimental protocol for testing whether a subject (usually but not always a child) can recognize the distinction between moral and conventional rules. Moral rules are perceived as objectively valid, independently of particular social practices and sources of authority. Conventional rules are perceived as socially contingent; the wrongness of violating them is removed if people in authority give their permission, or if one moves to a social environment in which they are not operative. Normal children can recognize the moral/ conventional distinction from about the age of three or four, but people with psychopathic tendencies or antisocial personality disorders give anomalous responses to the task, even as adults.[1]

There is strong evidence that, from a very young age, normal children acquire *the subjective perception that* some of the rules of behaviour that they learn are universally moral, while others are socially contingent, or contingent on the commands of authority (typically parents or teachers). The fact that children can distinguish between these two categories is evidence that they are developing a concept of moral obligation that is not merely a reproduction of commands from adults. But this is not to say that the rules that children classify as universally moral really are independent of social contingencies.

Some writers on the moral/conventional distinction claim that the two types of rule are fundamentally different in content. For example, Judith Smetana (1993: 112–13) argues that moral rules 'pertain to issues such as others' welfare (or harm), trust, or the fair distribution of resources', while conventional rules refer to 'arbitrary and consensually agreed-upon behavioural uniformities that structure social interactions within social systems'. However, there is a substantial body of evidence showing that whether a given rule is in fact classified as moral or conventional can be socially and historically contingent. For example, Jonathan Haidt, Silvia Koller, and Maria Dias (1993) find that actions that evoke disgust tend to be perceived as universally prohibited. Some of the hypothetical actions that are perceived in this way (such as sexual intercourse with dead animals) might be universally disgusting, but the disgust evoked by others (such as cutting up the American flag and using the pieces as rags to clean the toilet) is clearly socially contingent.[2]

Disgust, along with fear and sadness, is known to be particularly susceptible to emotional contagion. (I will say more about this in Section 11.6.) The fact that actions that evoke disgust tend to be given the same moral classification as ones that directly harm other people suggests that emotional contagion might be implicated in the emergence and reproduction of (what people perceive as) moral rules. If codes of morality are socially contingent and transmitted through social interaction, there is no oddity in supposing that moral rules might be matters of collective choice.

11.2 A Contractarian Perspective on Morality

One does not have to be a contractarian to recognize that a group of people might make a collective decision about which norms should apply to their interactions with one another. Most forms of social interaction are structured by rules of behaviour to which individuals would sometimes prefer not to have to conform. In some cases, these rules are codified as explicit laws or regulations, enforced by formal systems of reward and punishment; in others, they are merely common understandings, enforced by informal mechanisms of social approval and disapproval. There is no sharp divide between those rules that are better enforced in one way and those that are better enforced in the other. In a democratic society, one might expect both kinds of rule to be potential objects of collective choice. For example, think of the rules governing mutually respectful behaviour between co-workers in a well-functioning office. In the grey area between comradely humour and outright bullying and harassment, there are norms of appropriate behaviour, violations of which meet with disapproval from fellow-workers. Suppose disagreements start to arise: what some people see as humour, others see as bullying. It would be entirely reasonable for the workers to try to reach a collective agreement about what, in their office, is to count as mutual respect. And, having agreed about this, it would be reasonable for each of them to censure others for what, by virtue of a collective decision, has *become* disrespectful behaviour.[3]

In contractarian theories, the idea that moral principles can be created by agreement takes centre stage. Indeed, one significant contractarian theory is *called* 'morals by agreement' (Gauthier, 1986). In Chapter 8, I discussed John Rawls's concept of psychological stability, and his argument that a theory of justice has to take account of the strains of commitment. When he first proposes his theory, Rawls (1971) presents its principles of 'justice as fairness' as ones that would be agreed by rational persons, concerned to advance their individual interests in an imagined initial state of equality. He requires that each individual makes this agreement in good faith, expecting to be able to honour it in all contingencies. Economists who use Rawls's ideas often overlook the significance of this requirement, because they treat his theory as if it were a particular specification of a social welfare function— that is, as if it were simply a way of ranking alternative states of society. If, as welfare economists typically do, one thinks of a social welfare function as giving recommendations to a benevolent and unconstrained government, the idea of an individual citizen honouring or not honouring it does not arise. But, crucially, Rawls's contracting parties are not agreeing principles on which their government will act: they are agreeing moral principles that *they themselves* will uphold:

> Justice as fairness is an example of what I have called a contract theory.... [T]he content of the relevant agreement is not to enter a given society or to adopt a given form of government, but to accept certain moral principles. (Rawls, 1971: 16)

Notice that Rawls is taking it as given that individuals, consulting only their own interests, can collectively agree about what, for them, is to count as moral.

In later work, Rawls (1985) argues that justice as fairness is not a 'meta-physical' theory about moral truth. Rather, it is (or perhaps: it should be re-interpreted as) a 'political conception of justice'. Such a conception 'is, of course, a moral conception', but it is intended to apply only to the political, social, and economic institutions of a constitutional democracy. It is not derived from any general or (to use a term later favoured by Rawls) *comprehensive* moral doctrine. To the contrary, it is intended to be compatible with, and acceptable to the adherents of, the widest possible range of comprehensive doctrines:

> We hope that this political conception of justice may at least be supported by what we may call an 'overlapping consensus', that is, by a consensus that includes all the opposing philosophical and religious doctrines likely to persist and to gain adherents in a more or less just constitutional democratic society.
>
> (Rawls, 1985: 223–6)

The guiding idea throughout Rawls's work is that a well-ordered society is 'a cooperative venture for mutual advantage' (1971: 84). Individuals who subscribe to different moral doctrines have a common interest in participating in this venture. Rawls's political conception of justice is proposed as a restricted form of morality that can underpin social cooperation without requiring that individuals agree about morality in general.

If I am reading him correctly, the later Rawls is presenting his principles of justice as ones that *actual* people in an *actual* constitutional democratic society can agree to uphold. The argument that those principles would be agreed by hypothetical contracting parties in a hypothetical original position of perfect equality is intended to help explain why, if actual people agree to uphold them, the content of that agreement can be understood as a conception *of morality* and not 'a mere modus vivendi' (Rawls, 1993: 147). (Let me interject here that I am uneasy about attaching the adjective 'mere' to any modus vivendi—any way in which people can live together while agreeing to differ. In the world as it really is—a world in which people do not easily agree with one another on moral questions, and in which failures to agree can all too quickly escalate into conflicts from which everyone loses—there are many worse things than a modus vivendi.) But, crucially, the actual people in Rawls's account are not acknowledging a pre-existing metaphysical truth about morality: they are looking at a menu of alternative *conceptions of* morality and agreeing about which of these they will uphold together.

What I have in mind is less grand in scope than Rawls's theory, but similar in spirit. Within the limited domain of economics, I am looking for arrangements that will provide opportunities for individuals to realize mutual benefit. It is essential to the contractarian approach that each person's benefit is defined in terms of what he or she wants to achieve, rather than in terms of some unified conception of human well-being that is supposed to apply to everyone. (Recall the contrast, discussed in Chapters 2 and 3, between the contractarian viewpoint and the view from nowhere.) A well-ordered economy is to be understood as a cooperative venture among people who may have different ideas about the constituents of well-being. However, that venture may be more productive of mutual benefit if those people uphold certain moral principles—principles, one might say, of an *economic* conception of morality. If those principles do not presuppose the truth of any particular theory of well-being and if they can be shown to be psychologically stable, a contractarian economist might be able to recommend them.

11.3 The Principle of Mutual Benefit

I will now present a contractarian argument in favour of a particular principle of economic morality. My argument is addressed to citizens together, considered as potential parties to an agreement. It recommends that they all agree that each of them will uphold that principle. That is, each will use her best endeavours to conform to the principle, to support each of the others in conforming to it, and to censure each of the others if they fail to conform. I do not claim that this is the *only* principle of economic morality—still less, the only principle of morality in general—that a contractarian can recommend. But I will try to show its value in guiding economic cooperation in voluntary interactions.

Here is the principle:

Principle of Mutual Benefit. When participating with others in a voluntary interaction, and for as long as others' behaviour in that interaction is consistent with this very principle, behave in such a way that the other participants are able to satisfy normal expectations about the consequences of the interaction for them.

This formula is deliberately expressed without using the full formal structure of the model of voluntary interactions that I developed in Chapter 10. In the present chapter, I am addressing my real fellow-citizens, not the imaginary individuals of a theoretical model. However, the formula is meant to correspond as closely as possible with the reasoning schema of Intending Mutual

Benefit, presented in Section 10.5. Like that schema, it is intended to be applied only in situations that can be thought of as self-contained small worlds, in the sense explained in Section 10.3. Within my theoretical model of voluntary interactions, a person who reasons according to that schema and who acts on the intentions it generates will thereby conform to the Principle of Mutual Benefit.[4]

I must now explain how this principle can be recommended as a norm. The first and most important step is to show that, if everyone acts on the principle, their actions taken together will provide everyone with opportunities to realize mutual benefit. Here I repeat an argument that I advanced in Section 10.4. The Principle of Mutual Benefit tells people to conform to voluntary practices. Recall that such a practice is a regularity of behaviour in a voluntary interaction, such that each participant can reliably expect other participants to conform to it. When specific individuals, participating together in some specific interaction, conform to a voluntary practice, those individuals realize mutual benefit among themselves. The cumulative effect of such conformity by individuals in general is to maintain the practice. The existence of such practices provides individuals with opportunities to make transactions that, for whatever reason, each party wants to make at the time he makes them. In this contractarian sense, everyone's acting on the Principle of Mutual Benefit secures everyone's opportunities to realize mutual benefit.

These opportunities include, but are more extensive than, the opportunities that are made available to self-interested individuals by competitive markets. They are more extensive because they can include mutually beneficial practices that require some or all participants to act contrary to individual self-interest. The Public Good, Trust, and Ultimatum Games discussed in Section 10.6 provide stylized models of such practices. As I have said before, in an economy in which all goods are private and in which property rights are fully enforced, a competitive market gives each individual the opportunity to have whatever he wants and is willing to pay for. If individuals act on the Principle of Mutual Benefit, there can also be opportunities of this kind in some cases in which goods are not private (as illustrated by the Public Good Game) or in which property rights are imperfectly enforced (as illustrated by the Trust Game).

However, as I explained in Chapter 8, the extent of each individual's opportunities in a competitive market depends on other people's decisions about how to use theirs. For this reason, the ability of a market system to provide opportunities for mutually beneficial transactions does not necessarily imply that everyone can expect to benefit from its continued operation. I argued that an opportunity-based contractarian justification of the market has force only if, relative to her economic position at any given time, everyone has a realistic expectation of sharing in the benefits generated by the future workings of the market. Conversely, if one wants it to be the case that the market can be justified to everyone, one must be willing to countenance schemes of social insurance that can underwrite those expectations. The same arguments extend to a contractarian recommendation of the Principle of Mutual Benefit. In what follows, it should be taken as read that I am recommending that principle to people who can rely on some such scheme of social insurance.

11.4 How the Principle of Mutual Benefit can be Self-sustaining

It might seem that there is a circularity in my recommendation of the Principle of Mutual Benefit. This principle tells people to honour agreements. (Recall the argument in Section 10.5 that people who reason according to the schema of Intending Mutual Benefit will form intentions that support the practice of promise-keeping.) But what is the point of recommending that everyone agrees to uphold a certain norm unless each party to that agreement can be expected to honour it? And so doesn't a contractarian recommendation presuppose that its addressees accept that each of them has a moral obligation to keep her promises, at least when these have been made in exchange for the promises of others?

This potential circularity is one of the reasons why the concept of psychological stability is so important in contractarian argument. A moral norm is psychologically stable to the extent that, as Rawls (1971: 177) puts it, it 'generates its own support'. That is, a norm is psychologically stable to the extent that, through the workings of natural human psychology, the general practice of upholding the norm tends to reproduce a general willingness to conform to it, and a general belief that each person ought to conform to it. In this sense, a collective choice between alternative psychologically stable norms is analogous with a choice between self-enforcing traffic rules. On 3 September 1967, for example, Sweden switched from the rule of driving on the left-hand side of the road to the rule of driving on the right. That was the result of a controversial act of national choice, but once the switch had been made, the new rule generated its own support, just as the old one had done. In driving on the right from then on, individual Swedes did not need to think of themselves as honouring a collective choice: given the behaviour of other Swedes, it was not in their interest to do anything else.

I will argue that the Principle of Mutual Benefit has many features that tend to give it psychological stability. In this section, I focus on the *behaviour* that that principle prescribes. I consider the psychological costs and rewards to each individual of conforming to the Principle of Mutual Benefit, and of sanctioning those who fail to conform to it, in an economy in which most people can in fact be expected to conform. In Section 11.6, I will consider a deeper kind of psychological stability: I will ask whether *desires* for mutual benefit can be self-sustaining.

Reputation. In the formal model that I presented in Chapter 10, interactions are completely anonymous, and so no one can acquire a reputation for his behaviour as a specific individual. As I explained in Section 10.2, this assumption is useful as a modelling device to isolate mechanisms that can lead individuals to act contrary to self-interest; but it should not be taken too literally. In thinking about whether the Principle of Mutual Benefit can be recommended to real people, we need to take account of reputation as a source of psychological stability.

In the recurrent interactions of the real world, people often have opportunities to track the behaviour of particular individuals with whom they might want to interact. In many cases, people can rely on memories of face-to-face contacts and on personal recommendations. The growth of internet commerce has reduced the importance of these mechanisms in economic life, but there has been a compensating growth of web-based information-sharing platforms. The existence of these various sources of information allows individuals to acquire reputations for behaving (or not behaving) according to particular principles.

In an economy in which there is a general tendency for people to act on the Principle of Mutual Benefit, it is in each person's interest that other people expect him to act on that principle. To see why this is so, it is important to recognize that the Principle of Mutual Benefit does not require trust, but only trustworthiness. More precisely, it does not require anyone to enter a relationship of trust, but only to honour the implicit terms of such a relationship *if she chooses to enter it*. In choosing whether or not to enter a trust relationship, each individual is free to judge for herself whether or not that will be to her benefit, taking account of the possibility that other participants may be untrustworthy. To the extent that some person, say Joe, can be expected to act on the Principle of Mutual Benefit, he can be seen by others, and sought out by them, as a potential partner in mutually beneficial interactions that those others are free to enter or not enter, as they choose. Thus, Joe's being seen in this way allows him to access opportunities for benefit that would be closed off if his potential partners expected him always to act on self-interest. Notice that not all normative principles have this stability-supporting property. Suppose that Jane can be expected to act on a norm of benevolence. She will be seen by others, and sought out by them, as a potential partner in interactions in which she gives and others receive. It might be in her interest that her benevolence was *not* expected.

The idea that practices of trustworthiness can be maintained by the value of reputation has deep roots in economic and social thought. It can be found in Thomas Hobbes's (1651/1962) justifications of his third and fourth laws of nature—respectively 'that men perform their covenants made' and the law of 'gratitude'—discussed in Section 3.1. These laws are ancestors of the Principle of Mutual Benefit. Adam Smith (1763/1978: 538–9) argues that in economies in which people are continually making contracts with one another, self-interest induces them to maintain reputations for 'probity'—hence, he claims, the greater trustworthiness of the Dutch of his time than the English, and of the English than the Scots.

I do not want to claim that conforming to the Principle of Mutual Benefit is *always* in a person's interest. It is sufficient for my argument that, because of the value of reputation, conformity to that principle is *often* rewarded. Hume (1777/1975: 280–3) strikes a nice balance in his discussion of the 'sensible knave' (a relative of the 'fool' who features in Hobbes's account of his third law of nature: see Section 3.1). Hume is trying to show that it is in the 'true interest' of each individual to fulfil his moral duties. He acknowledges that his argument runs into difficulty

> ...in the case of justice, where a man, taking things in a certain light, may often seem to be a loser by his integrity. And though it is allowed that, without a regard to property, no society could subsist; yet according to the imperfect way in which human affairs are conducted, a sensible knave, in particular instances, may think that an act of iniquity or infidelity will make a considerable addition to his fortune, without causing any considerable breach in the social union and confederacy. That *honesty is the best policy*, may be a good general rule, but is liable to many exceptions; and he, it may perhaps be thought, conducts himself with most wisdom, who observes the general rule, and takes advantage of all the exceptions.
> (Hume, 1777/1975: 283)

Hume's first response to this difficulty is to argue that an honest man will be able to enjoy the pleasure of reflecting on the praiseworthiness of his own conduct, even if there are no observers around to praise it. But I am more interested in what Hume goes on to say about the honest man:

> Such a one has, besides, the frequent satisfaction of seeing knaves, with all their pretended cunning and abilities, betrayed by their own maxims; and while they purpose to cheat with moderation and secrecy, a tempting incident occurs, nature is frail, and they give into the snare; whence they can never extricate themselves, without a total loss of reputation, and the forfeiture of all future trust and confidence with mankind.   (Hume, 1777/1975: 283)

Hume is pointing out that, because of the value of reputation, the knave's strategy is risky and is vulnerable to over-confidence. But notice that Hume does not actually assert that honesty *is* the best policy. What he is saying is that, for people who pursue the policy of honesty, the satisfaction of seeing knaves discomfited is psychologically reinforcing. Whatever the exact balance of the costs and benefits of knavery, that satisfaction is a force that helps to stabilize practices of trustworthiness.

Translucency. Even if interactions are entirely anonymous, there may be some positive correlation between the actual behaviour of a participant and his co-participants' expectations about that behaviour. It is known that human beings have some ability to read one another's emotional states. (I will say more about this in Section 11.6.) Thus, one participant may be able to predict another participant's behaviour by reading the latter's emotional state. Some evidence of this ability is provided by an experiment reported by Robert Frank, Thomas Gilovich, and Dennis Regan (1993), in which participants who were initially unknown to one another engaged in unstructured, face-to-face interaction before playing one-shot Prisoner's Dilemma games. The games and payoffs were organized in such a way that participants could not discover how particular others had behaved. Before playing the games, participants were asked to predict one another's behaviour. It turned out that they were quite successful in predicting which of their co-participants would cooperate and which would defect. The implication is that, to use an expression coined by David Gauthier (1986), individuals' dispositions or intentions towards trustworthiness are *translucent*.[5] Thus, having a disposition to act on the Principle of Mutual Benefit may make it more likely that other people expect you to act in this way. Since it is to each person's advantage that other people have such an expectation, translucency of dispositions contributes to the psychological stability of the principle.

Psychological costs of conforming to the principle. Suppose you are a member of a population in which the Principle of Mutual Benefit is generally followed. Consider any situation in which that principle requires you to act contrary to what you see as your self-interest. You have chosen to participate with other people in some voluntary interaction. There is some voluntary practice that grounds participants' normal expectations about each other's behaviour in this interaction. You chose to participate, knowing this to be the practice. Since the time at which you and the others chose to participate, none of the others has deviated from the practice. However, you have reached a point in the interaction at which *you* can deviate in a way that will benefit you, but will prevent at least one of the other participants from achieving something that, when she chose to participate, she would have expected to be able to achieve. If you choose not to deviate, how painful is the thought of the benefit you have forgone?

A partial anaesthetic is provided by the fact that the Principle of Mutual Benefit does not require you to do anything that is not normal behaviour for people in your position. Thus, you have 'social proof', in the sense first analysed by Robert Cialdini (1984), of the appropriateness of following the practice rather than deviating from it. You may dislike the thought that you are forgoing a benefit, but you are not taking on the socially humiliating role of a sucker. And there is a further anaesthetic. You do not *have* to think of yourself as forgoing anything, as sacrificing your own interests for the benefit of someone else. You can think of your action as an integral part of a practice in which you and the other person have chosen to participate, and that creates benefits for both of you.

Mutual sanctioning. One of the ways in which a norm is enforced is through informal social sanctions against people who fail to conform to it. A norm therefore gains stability from the reliability and effectiveness of the associated sanctioning. Sanctioning is more likely to be reliable, the less scope there is for different interpretations of what the norm requires. Viewed in this light, the fact that the Principle of Mutual Benefit requires only trustworthiness and not trust is a merit. Recall that this principle makes no reference to the preferences or beliefs of the participants in a voluntary interaction. Whether it is in any participant's interest to enter such an interaction is for her to decide on whatever grounds she thinks fit; the Principle of Mutual Benefit requires only that, after entry, her behaviour is in accordance with the existing practice, whatever that may be. To identify violations of the principle, there is no need for anyone to try to reconstruct other people's preferences or beliefs.

To the extent that there are psychological costs in expressing disapproval of violations of a norm, this works against the stability of that norm. How significant are such costs? Geoffrey Brennan and Philip Pettit (2000) have suggested that, since a person's disapproval can be known without its ever being expressed, sanctioning can be costless: because people generally care about whether others think well of them, '[w]e may reward and punish one another just by being there and registering the character of one another's behaviour' (Brennan and Pettit, 2000: 78). I think this is too optimistic. Moral disapproval is not just a rational matter of information transmission: it depends for its force on common awareness of a dissonance of feeling between the person who disapproves and the person who is the object of disapproval. If disapproval is effective in enforcing a norm, that is because that dissonance is painful. But if Joe is painfully conscious of being the object of Jane's disapproval, he is liable to feel resentment and anger towards Jane as the cause of that pain. Being the target of this response will be psychologically costly for Jane—and perhaps costly in more material ways too. Anticipating these costs, Jane may pretend acquiescence in Joe's behaviour, or she may take care *not* to be 'just there' when Joe behaves as he does. In either case, his behaviour will not be sanctioned.

However, a countervailing force is brought into play if Joe's violation of the norm directly provokes resentment in Jane. Then Jane may feel a desire (or perhaps be unable to control an impulse) to express this emotion. Joe's consciousness of being the target of Jane's resentment may then be psychologically costly for him. Since resentment is a natural psychological response to being harmed by another person's unexpected and deliberate action, and since unease or fear is a natural psychological response to being the target of another person's resentment, norms against the imposition of unexpected harm by identifiable individuals on identifiable individuals are particularly susceptible to enforcement by disapproval.[6] Understood as social norms, the rules of behaviour implied by the Principle of Mutual Benefit have exactly this property.

Norm avoidance. Compare the Principle of Mutual Benefit with the norm of benevolence, discussed in Section 9.5, that tells you to give to worthy charities when their collectors look you in the eye and ask you to contribute. Suppose that, as in the case of the supermarket with two entrances and with a collector at only one of them, the interaction between you and the collector is voluntary. If you walk past her without giving, you can expect to be the object of her disapproval; your consciousness of this disapproval will cause a painful feeling of embarrassment. But if you do not derive any benefit from giving, you can avoid the disapproval by not participating in the interaction: you can use the other entrance. In contrast, the Principle of Mutual Benefit is not vulnerable to norm avoidance, because it applies only to interactions in which people *want* to participate.

11.5 A Question too Far

To say that the Principle of Mutual Benefit is psychologically stable is to say that actions that conform to it tend to generate psychological reinforcement. Many of these rewards, it might be said, are separable from the moral quality of the principle itself. When a person conforms to the principle, his ultimate intention (conscious or unconscious) might be something other than, and perhaps less worthy than, that of participating in the creation of mutual benefit. Merely for reasons of self-interest, he might be trying to maintain a reputation as a trustworthy trading partner. Or he might be conforming out of fear of the consequences of being the focus of other people's resentment. Or (as Hume suggests) he might be anticipating the pleasure of seeing other people's untrustworthiness being exposed, secure in the knowledge that this cannot happen to him.

If one takes a Kantian view of morality, actions that are motivated by such considerations are not truly moral. Indeed, Kant says exactly this about honesty in economic transactions.[7] Here is his leading example of the difference between an action that merely 'conform[s] to the moral law' and one that is performed 'for the sake of' that law:

> [I]t is indeed in conformity with duty that the merchant should not overcharge his inexperienced customers, and where there is much commercial traffic, the prudent merchant also does not do this, but rather holds a firm general price for everyone, so that a child buys just as cheaply from him as anyone else. Thus one is *honestly* served; yet that is by no means sufficient for us to believe that the merchant has proceeded thus from duty and from principles of honesty; his advantage required it; but here it is not to be assumed that besides this, he was also supposed to have an immediate inclination toward the customers, so that out of love, as it were, he gave no one an advantage over another in his prices. Thus the action was done neither from duty nor from immediate inclination, but merely from a self-serving aim.
>
> (Kant, 1785/2002: 13)

But if one thinks in contractarian terms, asking about individuals' true motivations is a question too far. Suppose that I, addressing citizens together, can recommend that they all agree that each of them will uphold the Principle of Mutual Benefit. In support of this recommendation, I can show that if they all behave in conformity to this principle, they can all expect to benefit. I can also show that if conformity to the principle were to become a general practice, each of them could expect that each of the others would normally be motivated to conform. What good is served by asking whether this motivation would derive from a wholly pure sense of moral duty? In terms of Kant's example: if you can rely on the honesty of a merchant with whom it is in your interest to trade, what good is served by asking what truly motivates him to be honest?

One of the merits of the Principle of Mutual Benefit is that what it requires of any given person is independent of the motivations of the people with whom she interacts. Suppose that Joe and Jane have the opportunity to participate in an interaction in which Joe may or may not send some good to Jane, and if he sends the good, she may or may not send him a specified amount of money in return. Each is free to choose not to participate, but both prefer the exchange to the status quo. If they both choose to participate, their interaction will have the structure of a Trust Game in which Joe moves first. Suppose that, in interactions of this kind, it is the practice that the first mover chooses *send* and the second mover chooses *return*. Jane reliably conforms to the Principle of Mutual Benefit, and Joe knows enough about her past behaviour and her current emotional state to be confident that she will do so in her interaction with him. Joe participates in the expectation that Jane will choose *return* in response to *send*; Jane participates because non-participation is weakly dominated. (Recall that decisions about whether or not to participate in given interactions are outside the scope of the Principle of Mutual Benefit.) Joe chooses *send*, in conformity with the Principle of Mutual Benefit. That principle then tells Jane to choose *return*, contrary to her immediate self-interest. This prescription is not conditional on Joe's reason for choosing *send*. In particular, it is not conditional on Joe's having made this choice *for the sake of* the Principle of Mutual Benefit. Nor is it conditional on the expectation that, in other circumstances, Joe would act in accordance with the principle. Jane might believe that Joe's decision was motivated only by self-interest. Still, she chose to participate in the interaction, knowing that the practice was (*send, return*). For whatever reason, Joe has conformed to the practice. Now Jane should conform too.

At least, that is what the Principle of Mutual Benefit requires. Does this example cast doubt on the contractarian recommendation of that principle? I think not. Suppose Jane has acted on the principle. Joe's and Jane's interaction has benefited them both. It took place only because Joe expected Jane to act on the principle. So, thinking about the interaction as a whole, Jane has no reason to regret her endorsement of the principle. Jane's belief about Joe's motivation might lead her to prefer to avoid certain other kinds of interaction with him (for example, Trust Games in which she is the first mover and he is the second), but the Principle of Mutual Benefit leaves her free to act on that preference.

A reader who is familiar with the literature of social preferences might be surprised that mutual scrutiny of intentions has played no part in my argument. As I have pointed out in previous chapters, a common theme in that literature is that people have preferences for punishing others who act on 'unkind' or 'unfair' intentions, and for rewarding intentions that are 'kind' or 'fair' (see Sections 9.4 and 10.6). In contrast, the Principle of Mutual Benefit never requires anyone to make judgements about another person's intentions. In the situations of voluntary interaction to which the principle applies, this feature should be seen as a merit.

It is in each person's interest to be able to pursue mutual benefit with as many other people as possible. In a world in which different people subscribe to different moral principles and with different degrees of commitment, it is a poor policy to be willing to cooperate only with people whose principles are exactly the same as your own. It is a still poorer policy to probe into the deeper motivations of people who are willing to cooperate with you, and to assume responsibility for punishing them if you judge their intentions to be morally deficient. And this is particularly unwise if those others have as much power to harm you as you have to harm them.[8] You are much more likely to benefit if your maxim is to try to cooperate at any time with anyone who, at that time and for whatever reason, is willing to cooperate with you in the realization of mutual benefit.

All this would be true even if the concept of a person's underlying intentions was well-defined, and even if those intentions could be accurately detected. In many cases, however, a disposition to act according to a certain principle (such as honesty in Kant's example) is *both* moral *and* prudent. To tease the two motivations apart, if that were possible at all, one might need to know how the relevant person would behave in unlikely counterfactual situations. But the idea that each individual has an integrated system of 'true' intentions that can in principle be discovered by setting up carefully specified decision problems is yet another manifestation of the model of the inner rational agent. In reality, human beings act on a mixture of motivations, the relative strengths of which can depend on context and attention. For citizens who are trying to agree about norms that they will enforce through decentralized processes of mutual sanctioning, it is surely good advice to look for principles that regulate observable behaviour rather than hidden intentions.

In Section 5.6, I presented a concept of responsibility that cohered with my analysis of opportunity. A responsible agent, I said, has no need to explain his decisions to anyone else. The claims he makes on others are not conditioned on his preferences. He claims certain opportunities, acknowledging the corresponding claims of other people; what he then chooses from those opportunities is up to him. A related idea of responsibility is embedded in the Principle of Mutual Benefit. According to that principle, each person should behave in such a way that other people's opportunities to realize mutual benefit are sustained. But beyond that, no one is accountable to anyone else for his preferences, intentions, or decisions. Individuals relate to one another, not as one another's benefactors, guardians, or moral judges, but as potential partners in the achievement of their common interests.

11.6 Correspondence of Sentiments

I have argued that the Principle of Mutual Benefit gains robustness from its blindness to individuals' underlying intentions—from its toleration of any intentions which, in a given interaction, lead to behaviour in conformity with its prescriptions.[9] One might say that it is a principle that accepts fellow-travellers. Nevertheless, a person who endorses the principle adopts a particular kind of intention in relation to voluntary interactions: in the sense of the schema I presented in Section 10.5, she intends mutual benefit. It is natural to ask whether there is any psychological mechanism that could support such an intention. Is it plausible to hypothesize that people desire that benefits to themselves should be accompanied by benefits to others?

In Chapter 10, I presented intentions for mutual benefit in contrast to intentions of altruism or 'kindness'. When economists discuss altruistic preferences, they often suggest that the psychological substrate of those preferences is *sympathy*. It is a time-honoured rhetorical device for economists to bring in Adam Smith at this point, and to quote the opening sentence of *The*

Theory of Moral Sentiments: 'How selfish soever man may be supposed, there are evidently some principles in his nature, which interest him in the fortune of others, and render their happiness necessary to him, though he derives nothing from it except the pleasure of seeing it' (Smith, 1759/1976: 9). For a modern economist, the idea that one person derives happiness from the happiness of others immediately suggests a model of altruistic preferences. But this is not what Smith has in mind. The sentiments that Smith analyses might be better understood as the psychological substrate of desires for mutual benefit.

In understanding Smith's theory, it is important to recognize that it is a theory about *sentiments*—that is, emotions or affective states—and not about preferences or choices. In modern economics, sentiments are rarely considered explicitly; in most economic models, the only mental states that appear are preferences and beliefs. Although sympathy for another person is clearly an affective state, it is normally represented in economics as a preference for increases in that person's well-being. Since preference is a comparative concept, the implication is that if Joe sympathizes with Jane, Joe is willing to forgo other things that he values in order to increase Jane's well-being. Thus, sympathy is represented as a preference for a certain kind of self-sacrifice. But this is not Smith's conception of sympathy.

What Smith calls sympathy or *fellow-feeling* is what psychologists now recognize as *emotional contagion*. This is the process by which one person's vivid consciousness of some affective state of someone else causes the first person to feel a mental state with similar affective qualities. In Smith's words:

> For as to be in pain or distress of any kind excites the most excessive sorrow, so to conceive or to imagine that we are in it, excites some degree of the same emotion, in proportion to the vivacity or dullness of the conception.... When we see a stroke aimed and just ready to fall upon the leg or arm of another person, we naturally shrink and draw back our own leg or our own arm; and when it does fall, we feel it in some measure, and are hurt by it as well as the sufferer.
>
> (Smith, 1759/1976: 9–10)

The existence of this mechanism, particularly for states of fear, sadness, and disgust, is now well-established, and its neural correlates are beginning to be understood.[10] Given what we now know (but Smith did not) about the way our brains are organized, the prevalence of emotional contagion should not be surprising. In a system made up of a dense network of inter-connections, we should expect that perceptions that have significant common features will be processed in overlapping ways, and thus have some tendency to activate similar affective states.

In its evolutionary origins, emotional contagion may have had nothing to do with altruism. Stephanie Preston and Frans de Waal (2002) suggest that, among animals that live in groups, one individual's reproductive success is often served by matching the actions of other members of the group. The direct perception of some phenomenon (the approach of a predator, the distinctive taste of potentially poisonous food) and the indirect perception that another individual has perceived it often call for the same action (running away, not eating); it is natural to expect that corresponding direct and indirect perceptions will activate similar representations in the nervous system. If this combination of perception and action is also linked to an emotional response such as fear or disgust, we have a rudimentary mechanism of fellow-feeling.

The most distinctive feature of Smith's account of fellow-feeling emerges in his discussion of 'the pleasure of mutual sympathy'. He proposes that human beings derive pleasure from all forms of fellow-feeling. Suppose that Jane experiences some pleasure or pain, and that Joe has fellow-feeling for this. Joe's fellow-feeling consists in a qualitatively similar, but perhaps much weaker, imaginatively experienced pleasure or pain. But, according to Smith, an additional psychological mechanism comes into play, which gives pleasure both to Joe and to Jane, *irrespective of whether Jane's original feeling was pleasure or pain*. Jane's consciousness of Joe's fellow-feeling for her is a source of pleasure to her; and Joe's consciousness of his own fellow-feeling for Jane is a source of pleasure to him.

From a theoretical point of view, this mechanism may seem surprising. It might seem more natural to model fellow-feeling as nothing more than a kind of *reflection* of feeling. That would lead to the implication that if Jane's original feeling was one of pain, Joe's fellow-feeling for it would be painful for him, and Jane's consciousness of Joe's painful fellow-feeling would be painful for her. The conventional rational-choice model of altruism implies the same kind of reflection, but in the domain of preferences rather than feelings.

Indeed, in a depressingly straight-faced paper about altruism within families and romantic relationships, Douglas Bernheim and Oded Stark (1988) use just this kind of model to argue that 'nice guys finish last': people who derive relatively little happiness (or 'felicity') from consumption and who are themselves altruistic will prefer to have partners who are not altruistic towards them. Thus, the authors claim, nice guys may be rejected as potential partners because they are too altruistic. They say: 'The explanation is quite simple. An altruistic type A [i.e. man] would be depressed by his partner's low level of felicity. Since the type B [i.e. woman] cares about her partner, she would in turn be disturbed by the fact that she has made him unhappy'. In other words: if you are unhappy, other people's sympathy with your unhappiness is an additional cause of unhappiness for you. This may be a logical implication of a standard economic model, but it is not compatible with human psychology as we all know it. When young children are in distress, they *demand* to be comforted (as indeed, and in very similar ways, do chimpanzees); any self-aware adult will recognize that the urge to solicit comfort in distress does not disappear with age, even if we learn to suppress its more blatant expressions.[11]

Smith considers using a model of reflected feelings, but immediately sees its unrealism:

> The sympathy, which my friends express with my joy, might, indeed, give me pleasure by enlivening that joy: but that which they express with my grief could give me none, if it served only to enliven that grief. Sympathy, however, enlivens joy and alleviates grief. It enlivens joy by presenting another source of satisfaction; and it alleviates grief by insinuating into the heart almost the only agreeable sensation which it is at that time capable of receiving.   (Smith, 1759/1976: 14)

This other source of satisfaction is *correspondence of sentiments*: 'this correspondence of the sentiments of others with our own appears to be a cause of pleasure, and the want of it a cause of pain, which cannot be accounted for [by a theory of reflected feelings]' (Smith, 1759/1976: 14).

Here, I think, Smith is showing a better understanding of friendship and family life than are Bernheim and Stark.[12] One of the characteristic features of friendship is that friends engage in activities together. These are often activities which, on the face of it, might equally well be pursued individually, such as eating meals, watching movies or going for walks. (If a husband and wife had the preferences postulated by Bernheim and Stark, they could celebrate their wedding anniversary by each eating alone at his or her favourite restaurant, happy in their mutual knowledge of one another's enjoyment of their solitary meals.) So how is added value created by doing things *together*? What I take to be Smith's answer, that this value arises from the lively consciousness of fellow-feeling, strikes me as convincing. For example, two hikers may gain pleasure from walking together—experiencing the same challenges, enjoying the same views, enduring the same discomforts—even though their apparent interaction is minimal. Friendships and family relationships are cultivated by finding activities that the partners in those relationships can enjoy together. In fact, just as Smith's theory suggests, relationships can be cultivated through joint engagement in activities that are *not* enjoyed. Domestic chores, repetitive workplace tasks, coping with unforeseen problems are all activities which, although not intrinsically pleasant, are made less burdensome by being done together by people who are conscious of their fellow-feeling. What is important is that the activities are ones that tend to produce *correspondences* of emotional responses, whether the emotions themselves are pleasurable or not.

One might say that Bernheim and Stark's mental picture of a couple is of two people who are preoccupied with their feelings for one another, while Smith's theory suggests a picture of two people side by side, facing life together. The second picture is more in accord with John Stuart Mill's (1869/1988: 32–52) ideal, discussed in Section 1.1, of marriage as a cooperative partnership between equals. (Recall Mill's suggestion that treating self-sacrifice as a virtue of family life can be a cover for the exploitation of wives and daughters.) I side with Mill.

Discussions of team reasoning and related concepts of 'we-thinking' have tended to focus on the attribution of *cognitive* attitudes to groups of people— attitudes such as preference, belief, intention, responsibility, and agency. Smith's analysis suggests that *emotions* might be attributed to groups too— that just as each member of a group can sometimes say 'we (together) prefer . . .' or 'we (together) intend . . .', they can say 'we (together) feel . . .'. Two people might be said to feel an emotion together if they both feel it, are mutually conscious of each other's feeling it, and are mutually conscious of the pleasure that each derives from this correspondence of their feelings.

By its nature, participation in mutually beneficial practices tends to induce this kind of 'feeling together'. Take the case of the transaction between Smith's baker and his customer, discussed in Chapter 9. The customer feels pleasure in the prospect of having bread for her dinner. The baker feels pleasure in being paid for his work. If the baker and the customer recognize that these pleasures derive from their respective roles in a single joint activity, they will be mutually conscious of a correspondence of sentiments, which they may experience as a pleasurable feeling of mutual goodwill. The baker shares in the customer's pleasure in having the bread; the customer shares in the baker's pleasure in being paid for his work. Neither the baker nor the customer is making any sacrifice for the other's benefit; they are simply taking pleasure together in the mutuality of their benefit. The key to their accessing these pleasures is their perception that mutual benefit is not (as the passage in Smith's *Wealth of Nations* perhaps suggests it is) an unintended consequence of self-interested intentions on each side of the transaction: *it is what they intended.*[13]

I do not want to claim that, in the markets of the real world, buyers and sellers always act on intentions for mutual benefit. The truth, I believe, is that many buyers and sellers *do* intend mutual benefit, but it is obvious that many do not. The picture of a market in which all transactions are carried out with intentions for mutual benefit is not a description of the world as it is; it is an expression of a liberal ideal of market ethics. But if the market is a domain of life in which unethical behaviour can often be found, in which domains is this not the case?

Compare the ideals that virtue ethicists such as Elizabeth Anderson (1993) and Michael Sandel (2009) attribute to other areas of life (see Section 9.1). In science, there are ideals of excellence and of intellectual honesty, but we all know that many scientists deviate from these in pursuit of career interests or prospects of fame. In athletics, there are ideals of fair competition that many athletes fail to live up to. In religious life, there are ideals of piety and pastoral care that ministers of religion do not always uphold. It is true that, as Anderson (1993: 147–50) points out, such deviations sometimes result from conflicts between norms that are internal to specific non-market domains and the norms of the market. (Take the case of an artist who compromises on what she judges to be the artistic merit of her work in order to make it more saleable. Taking account of the tastes of one's customers is one aspect of the general principle of seeking opportunities for mutual benefit—a principle that is intrinsic to how markets work.[14]) But unethical behaviour in science, athletics, art, or religion can have many other motivations. Material gain is a common enough motivation for such behaviour, but you do not need to have been exposed to markets to be attracted by prospects of personal wealth. Other common motivations, such as desires for fame, power, social approval, or sexual gratification, have even less connection with the practices of the market. There is no obvious reason to suppose that the market is more hostile to moral sentiments than are other domains of human life.

11.7 The Community of Advantage

In April 1784, at the age of sixty, Immanuel Kant was supervising building work on a house that he had recently bought, after many years of living in rented rooms.[15] The house was rather grand (one of the building works was to create a lecture hall); its total cost was about six times Kant's annual salary as Professor of Logic and Metaphysics at the University of Königsberg. Kant's comfortable financial position was probably the result of his friendship with Joseph Green, an English merchant based in Königsberg. Green and Kant met every afternoon to discuss philosophy, in which Green had a keen interest; Kant invested his savings in Green's business and benefited from its success. It would be surprising if the two friends did not share an interest in the ethics of markets.

While the building work was going on, Kant was beginning to write one of his most important books, *Groundwork for the Metaphysics of Morals*. One of the central ideas in this book is the 'practical imperative', which Kant presents as a dictate of reason: 'Act so that you use humanity, as much in your own person as in the person of every other, always at the same time as end and never merely as means' (1785/2002). It seems that Kant asked himself whether his engagement with the market was consistent with this imperative. Was he using the builders merely as means to his own ends? At the end of April 1784, he gave the first of a series of lectures on natural right. Here is how he begins:

> All of nature, as far as it is within the reach of his power, is subjected to the will of man, with the exception of other men and reasonable beings. From the point of

view of reason, the things in nature can only be regarded as means to ends, but man alone can himself be regarded as an end.... Animals, as well [as unreasonable things], have no value in themselves, since they have no consciousness of their existence—man is the purpose of creation; nevertheless, he can also be used as a means by other reasonable beings. However, man is never merely a means; rather he is at the same time an end. *For example: If a mason serves me as a means to building a house, I serve him, in turn, as a means to acquire money....* The world, as a system of ends, finally has to contain a purpose, and this is the reasonable being. If there existed no end, the means would serve no purpose and would have no value.— Man is an end. It is therefore contradictory that he should be a mere means.—If I am making a contract with a servant, he has to be an end as well, just as I am, and not merely a means.   (Kant, 1784/2003: 2; italics added)

I do not want to endorse Kant's rationalistic metaphysics. (The idea that rational beings are the purpose of the universe strikes me as humanistic presumption. I would prefer to say that the intelligence of *Homo sapiens* is just a particular aptitude of our species for making its way in the world, as eyesight is for hawks or sonar navigation is for bats.[16]) But Kant's analysis of his relationship with his builders says something important that many virtue-ethical critics of markets have failed to recognize. In the literatures of virtue ethics and intrinsic motivation, as I pointed out in Chapter 9, market relationships are often represented as instrumental and, in consequence, as morally impoverished. The same idea of instrumentality, although without the moral criticism, is expressed in Smith's account of the relationship between the baker and the customer. In contrast, Kant offers an account of moral duty in market relationships in which intentions are neither self-interested nor benevolent. In employing the builders, Kant (if acting morally) intends *both* that he uses them as a means to his end (the building of the house) *and* that he serves as a means to their end (getting money). In other words: he intends that his relationship with the builders is mutually beneficial.

Applying the same analysis to the other side of the transaction, the builders (if acting morally) intend that their relationship with Kant is mutually beneficial. Each builder intends *both* that he benefits by getting money *and* that Kant benefits by having his house built. This understanding of what is involved in selling one's labour is significantly different from those often presented by writers on virtue ethics and intrinsic motivation. According to what I take to be Kant's account, the builder's primary motivation is not intrinsic. He may take pride in exercising his craft, but he is not working merely for the fun or challenge of laying bricks, or in the pursuit of excellence in bricklaying.[17] Nor is he motivated by any prior concern for the welfare of the beneficiary of his work, as he might be if, say, he were working unpaid to repair his aged mother's house. But, although the builder would not be working for Kant if he were not being paid, his motivation is not wholly extrinsic. Having agreed to participate in a transaction from which he expects to benefit, he intends that Kant benefits too. In Section 9.1, I commented on the difficulty that virtue ethicists and positive psychologists often seem to have in finding moral significance and authenticity in ordinary ways of earning a living. Part of the solution to this difficulty, I suggest, is to recognize that the parties to a market transaction can intend to be useful to one another, and can find satisfaction in being so.

But what exactly does 'being useful' mean in the context of a market relationship? Suppose that in eighteenth-century Königsberg there was a competitive market for the services of builders. If Kant's builders had not contracted to work for him, they could have earned similar incomes working for someone else. If Kant had not employed these particular builders, he could have employed similarly efficient workers at a similar rate of pay. Under these assumptions, Kant's marginal contribution to the builders' welfare is very small, as are the builders' marginal contributions to Kant's welfare. Does this undermine the conception of the employment relationship as one in which the parties are useful to one another? According to the Principle of Mutual Benefit, it does not: what matters is that the participants in an interaction have entered it voluntarily, not how much benefit they expected to derive from it. But is that a flaw in my formulation of the principle? If reciprocity were understood as gift exchange, as in George Akerlof's (1982) model of 'sentiment' in labour markets, transactions in perfectly competitive markets might be deemed not to involve reciprocity. Recall that, in Akerlof's model, the firm's gift to the worker is a payment *in excess of her reservation wage*; such gifts are not possible in equilibrium unless there is involuntary unemployment (see Section 9.3). Still, I stand by my formulation. The intentions expressed in an action cannot always be defined in terms of that action's marginal consequences.

Consider an analogy. Suppose you are walking down a city street and an elderly man near you collapses, apparently suffering a heart attack. You rush to help. You are the first to reach him, but another potential helper arrives a few moments later. One of you needs to phone for an ambulance and to stay until it arrives. Both of you are willing and able to do this, but you take on the task. What is the intention of your action? Its marginal effect is to save a few minutes of the time of the other would-be helper. But you might still properly describe your intention as giving assistance to the victim of a heart attack. You might also say (as the would-be helper might say of herself too) that you were playing your part in a social practice of mutual aid. Similarly, if one of Kant's builders is asked what he is doing, he can say that he is playing his part in a building project which, taken as a whole, will be beneficial to Kant. He can also say that the time he spends on this project is part of his working week in an occupation which, taken as a whole, benefits him. Looking at things in a wider view, he can say that he is playing his part in an economy of mutual benefit. All this is true, even if it is also true that, had he not taken on the work, someone else would have been employed instead. And it is true even if, had Kant not employed him, he would have worked the same hours for someone else for the same pay.

Generalizing from the story of the builders, Kant seems to be claiming that intending mutual benefit in market relationships is a moral duty. But his underlying insight might also be expressed within the conceptual framework of virtue ethics. In that framework, virtues are understood in relation to 'practices' or domains of life. To say that some acquired character trait is a virtue within some domain is to say that a person who possesses it is thereby better able to contribute to the *telos* of that domain (see Section 9.1). Thus, one might say, bravery is a virtue in military life, and curiosity is a virtue in the life of scientific research. Luigino Bruni and I (2013) have argued that virtue ethicists should recognize that the market is a domain of life too, and so might have its own *telos* and its own virtues.

If (as Aristotle claims) health is the *telos* of medicine and victory is the *telos* of military strategy, what is the *telos* of the market? Bruni and I invited our readers to set aside philosophical sophistication, and to translate this question into common-sense terms, such as: How would you describe, in the simplest and most general terms, what markets do that is valuable? Or: What is the characteristic end or purpose or *raison d'être* of the market? Or: If you had to write a mission statement for the market, what would it say? We argued that the liberal tradition of economics offers an answer to such questions. That answer is implicit in the passage from John Stuart Mill that gave the present book its title: the *telos* of the market is mutual benefit—the realization of gains from trade through voluntary transactions. As one small test of the credibility of this claim, consider what answer an economist might give if asked to nominate one simple diagrammatic representation of what a market does. The Edgeworth Box would surely be one of the commonest choices, and the point of that diagram is to understand markets as networks of mutually beneficial transactions.

It might be objected that, in at least one strand of liberal economics, the idea that the market has a purpose is seen as a contradiction in terms. In a passage that I quoted in Section 1.4, James Buchanan (1964: 219) says that the market is not a means to the accomplishment of anything; it is 'the institutional embodiment of the voluntary exchange processes that are entered into by individuals in their several capacities. That is all there is to it.' But here Buchanan is opposing a view from nowhere—the idea that normative economics is about the maximization of some single objective function that represents the welfare of a whole society, considered impartially. I think he would still want to say that what the market characteristically does is to facilitate voluntary exchanges. If the *telos* of the market is mutual benefit, the virtues of market life must be those character traits that equip people to play their parts in the realization of mutual benefit. A disposition to intend mutual benefit in market relationships, and to find satisfaction in being useful to people who are being useful to you, is surely one such virtue.[18]

Enough of my attempts to enlist Kantian deontologists and Aristotelian virtue ethicists as fellow travellers in my reconstruction of normative economics. Let me end where I began, with the liberal tradition itself, and with John Stuart Mill. Kant's representation of his relationship with his builders is a microcosm of the understanding of the market that is encapsulated in Mill's description of it as a *community of advantage*. As I explained in Chapter 1, Mill sees a market as a network of relationships of mutually beneficial cooperation. He does not claim that when people actually engage in those relationships, they in fact always recognize them as, or intend them to be, mutually beneficial. He acknowledges that many of his contemporaries still think of economic life as a mercantilist competition for positional advantage. But he is trying to convince his readers of the value to them, individually and collectively, of coming to share his understanding of the market. My book has been written with a similar aim.

I am an economist, and I have focused on mutual benefit in economic life. But I share Mill's conviction that cooperation for mutual benefit is the fundamental organizing principle of a well-ordered society. The market is not, or should not be, an arena of non-moral, instrumental motivation from which practices that are more genuinely social or more intrinsically valuable need to be insulated. Market transactions are a crucial part of the network of cooperative relations that make up civil society.

Endnotes

1 The Liberal Tradition and the Challenge from Behavioural Economics

1. A version of the First Fundamental Theorem was first proved by Pareto (1909/ 1971). The subsequent development of the fundamental theorems is surveyed by Blaug (2007).
2. In some of my previous writing I have said that such choices reveal 'incoherent preferences', but that term does not quite capture the idea I want to express. To find *incoherence* in the person's preferences, one must first assume that her choices ought to reveal components of a single system of preferences. I do not want to presuppose that.
3. This section includes material from Infante et al. (2016).
4. Many classic contributions to behavioural economics are collected in a volume edited by Kahneman and Tversky (2000). Kahneman (2011) gives a more informal survey of the field.
5. In the case of the Allais Paradox, some such explanations have been put forward, for example by Allais (1953) himself and by Loomes and Sugden (1982). Whether the axioms of expected utility theory are compelling as principles of rationality remains controversial.
6. Theories of this kind have been proposed by, for example, Harsanyi (1955), Vickrey (1960), Pattanaik (1968), and Binmore (1994, 1998).

2 The View from Nowhere

1. Sections 2.1 and 2.2 include material from Sugden (2013).
2. This sentence skates over some difficult questions about exactly how neoclassical welfare economists interpret the concept of preference, and how they justify the preference-satisfaction criterion. Different economists take different positions on these issues. Since this book is not about neoclassical welfare economics, I do not need to explore all these subtleties. Hausman (2012) reviews what economists do, and what they say about what they do, and tries to reconstruct a single defensible interpretation of welfare economics. I will say more about his reconstruction in Sections 4.5, 5.5, and 7.7.
3. Some readers may think, as Rawls (1971: 184–5, 263–4) seems to do, that this conception of the impartially benevolent spectator is the one used by Smith in his *Theory of Moral Sentiments* (1759/1976). But Smith's impartial spectator is a representative human being, whose sympathies for other people are governed by

the mechanisms of real human psychology and so incorporate those mechanisms' natural biases. Smith is not taking a view from nowhere; he is proposing a naturalistic theory of the moral sentiments that people in fact feel. I say more about this in Section 11.6 and in Sugden (2002).

4. Buchanan attributes this critique to the earlier writings of Wicksell (1896/1958). Hayek (1948) expresses a related idea when he argues that his contemporaries are interpreting general equilibrium theory from the viewpoint of an omniscient social planner. I have argued that the many paradoxes that social choice theorists have confronted in trying to formulate principles of respect for liberty occur because the theoretical framework they are using represents the moral viewpoint of a benevolent autocrat (Sugden, 1985). The original 'paradox of the Paretian liberal' is due to Sen (1970).

5. The idea that many political philosophers treat politics as a 'generalization of the jury' is a recurring theme in the work of Buchanan (e.g. 1986: 65). Sen (2009: 110–11) reads Buchanan (1954, 1986) as *approving* this conception of politics, but I think this is a misunderstanding. Buchanan has consistently advocated a contractarian conception of politics as a 'generalization of the market' (1986: 65) and has opposed the idea of political discourse as a search for truth as a 'Platonic faith' held by writers who 'play at being God' (1975: 1–2). List and Pettit (2011) offer an explicit defence of the jury model as a basis for political philosophy.

3 The Contractarian Perspective

1. This section includes material from Sugden (2009b). For a criticism of my characterization of Hume's analysis as contractarian, see De Jasay (2010).
2. This section includes material from Sugden (2013).
3. At the time of writing, the British government's Foreign and Commonwealth Office website includes the following advice to travellers to Uzbekistan: 'Vehicles approaching a roundabout have the right of way over vehicles already on the roundabout' (https://www.gov.uk/foreign-travel-advice/uzbekistan/safety-and-security, accessed 18 April 2017). Thanks to my son Joe Sugden for directing me to this intriguing information.
4. The term 'veil of uncertainty' is not used explicitly by Buchanan and Tullock (1962). Buchanan uses it in later work when referring to this idea, to draw attention to analogies and disanalogies with the 'veil of ignorance' in Rawls's (1971) theory of justice (e.g. Brennan and Buchanan, 1985: 28–31).
5. This section includes material from Sugden (2013) and Sugden (2017a).
6. Wicksteed (1910/1933) discusses these effects on pp. 93, 118, 122, and 33 respectively. The first three of these effects will be familiar to most readers of behavioural economics. Bad-deal aversion is a form of reference-dependence in preferences, considered by Thaler (1985) and analysed more formally by Isoni (2011). The behavioural elements of Wicksteed's economics are discussed by Sugden (2009a).
7. The idea of 'regulation as delegation' is discussed by Oren Bar-Gill and Sunstein (2015). However, Bar-Gill and Sunstein's interpretation of this concept sometimes goes beyond the limits imposed by contractarianism (and indeed beyond the

normal meaning of 'delegation'), as when they suggest that it may be desirable to 'impose' delegation on 'naïve individuals who are unaware of their imperfect rationality' (2015: 10).

8. I cannot resist saying that (*d*) is not as unreasonable as it might seem. A massive meta-analysis, published in a leading medical journal, found that individuals with 'overweight' (but not 'obese') body mass indices were 6 per cent *less* likely to die in a given period than individuals of 'normal weight' (Flegal et al., 2013).

9. This bald claim needs some qualification in respect of children and the mentally incompetent (such as people with advanced Alzheimer's disease). If we are to use a normative framework based on voluntary contract, we must recognize that at least some of the interests of children and the mentally incompetent have to be looked after by agents who act in the role of guardian or trustee. In these cases, contractarian recommendations *can* properly be addressed to guardians. How to draw the line between the domains of responsible choice and guardianship is an important problem for normative economics, and particularly so for its contractarian form, but I will not try to tackle it in this book. I will take it as given that the domain of guardianship does not include the economic decisions of ordinary adults, even when those decisions fail to measure up to the standards of rationality postulated by neoclassical theory.

4 The Inner Rational Agent

1. Sections 4.1–4.3 and 4.5–4.7 derive from Infante et al. (2016).
2. In this chapter, to avoid cumbersome expressions, I will refer to all three publications as the work of 'Sunstein and Thaler'.
3. The term 'latent' is borrowed from Kahneman's (1996) critique of Plott's (1996) 'discovered preference hypothesis'. Kahneman characterizes Plott's approach as attributing latent rationality to economic agents whose behaviour contravenes neoclassical theory.
4. This section includes material from Sugden (2015a).
5. Bordalo et al. actually say: 'Quality and price are measured in dollars and known to the consumer' (2013: 807). Despite the literal meaning of this sentence, I think my interpretation is faithful to their intentions. It is only because quality and price are measured in different units that the consumer faces a non-trivial choice problem.
6. Some readers may be tempted to think that this requirement could be justified by a 'money pump' (or 'Dutch book') argument, but that thought would be mistaken. Invulnerability to money pumps does *not* imply that choices are determined by preferences. (For a general demonstration of the truth of this claim, see Cubitt and Sugden, 2001.) As a simple counter-example, consider an agent who acts on the decision heuristic of never making exchanges, whatever her initial endowment and whatever options are available to her. This heuristic implies a pattern of choice that cannot be rationalized by any (reference-independent) preference relation, but which is clearly invulnerable to money pumps.
7. The implicit claim that the original and revised versions of the problems are equivalent to one another is open to question, but it is an implication of Savage's axioms.

5 Opportunity

1. There is a large literature in economics and philosophy dealing with the question of how to rank opportunity sets in terms of the 'quantity' or 'value' of opportunity they provide. There is general agreement that if there are two sets O and O such that O' is a strict superset of O, O' should be ranked as at least as highly as O; but there is no consensus about how to rank other pairs of sets. At various times I have made proposals about how this might be done (e.g. Jones and Sugden, 1982; Sugden, 1998a), but these are not used in the contractarian criteria I present in this book.

2. There is a related distinction in neuroscience between 'wanting' (desire) and 'liking' (pleasure). The effects of addictive drugs are sometimes modelled as directly attaching 'incentive salience' (the perception of being wanted) to mental representations of events associated with drug-taking, short-circuiting the normal process of reinforcement learning by which an experience of pleasure induces a desire to repeat the action that caused it (Robinson and Berridge, 1993).

3. I have an ulterior motive in raising the issue of the account that parents should take of their children's preferences. In Section 3.4 I explained 'why a contractarian cannot be a paternalist', but added a footnote recognizing that some of the interests of children have to be looked after by guardians or trustees. Supporters of paternalism sometimes argue that, if one recognizes that parents can properly act as guardians of their children, it is dogmatic to deny that there can be analogous circumstances in which governments can properly act as guardians of citizens. It is at least a partial answer to this objection to say that even parents should not always be paternalistic: contractarianism is sometimes appropriate for parents. Compare John Stuart Mill's ideas about the moral rules that mankind should practise in the family, discussed in Section 1.1.

4. For my reading of Hume's decision theory, and my reasons for agreeing with its main features, see Sugden (2006a, 2008).

5. This section includes material from Sugden (2006b).

6. In effect, I am assuming that Jane can freely dispose of any money that is surplus to her requirements. Thus, any spending plan that is compatible with Z is also compatible with X.

7. Because the symbols X, Y, and Z represent *sets* of options that might be faced in period 3, each of these symbols is nested within *two* pairs of brackets (i.e. two pairs fewer than the number of periods). An equivalent representation of Jane's problem in period 1 would write out the contents of these sets explicitly, replacing X, Y, and Z by $\{x_1, x_2, \ldots\}, \{y_1, y_2, \ldots\}$, and $\{z_1, z_2, \ldots\}$ respectively. Then each option that might be experienced in period 4 would be nested within *three* pairs of brackets.

8. The idea of multiple selves as a modelling technique can be traced back to Strotz (1955–56), that of metarankings to Frankfurt (1971) and Sen (1977).

9. Schubert (2015) is one of several readers of my previous work who have criticized me for seeming to suggest that imposing constraints on one's own future opportunities is irresponsible in the everyday sense of that word. I do not want to say that. Although I believe that economists and philosophers often over-state the

extent to which people want to constrain themselves, I accept that there are exceptional cases in which choosing self-constraint is a sign of responsibility. A classic case is the driver in the pub who, knowing that alcohol affects both his ability to drive safely and his ability to judge that ability, gives his car keys to a friend with the instruction not to return them if he drinks more than some limit. I will say more about such cases in Section 7.3.

10. The applicability of this quotation to my account of responsibility was first noticed by Schubert (2015). The quotation is recorded in the *Oxford Dictionary of Political Quotations* (Second edition, 2001: 115).

6 The Invisible Hand

1. Sections 6.2–6.6 derive from Sugden (2017b). The analysis of the Interactive Opportunity Criterion was first presented in McQuillin and Sugden (2012).

2. If modelled in this way, 'contextual features' would have some similarities with Bernheim and Rangel's (2007, 2009) concept of 'ancillary conditions' and with Salant and Rubinstein's (2008) concept of 'frames': see Section 4.1. Since contextual features are treated as fixed properties of the economy, they must be defined independently of consumers' opportunities and choices.

3. The assumption that *individual* behaviour is uniquely determined simplifies the analysis I present in this chapter, but is not strictly necessary. Actual choices made by consumers enter the analysis only through the concept of 'joint feasibility', defined in the following paragraph. Since joint feasibility is a property of the aggregated choices of all consumers, it is sufficient to assume that consumers' aggregate behaviour is predictable.

4. This criterion is presented in McQuillin and Sugden (2012), where it is called the 'Opportunity Criterion'. I have added the word 'interactive' to distinguish this from the Individual Opportunity Criterion, presented in Chapter 5. A slightly different version of the (Interactive) Opportunity Criterion is presented in Sugden (2004a). The differences between the two versions are explained in the later paper.

5. In Sugden (2004a) I present a model of an exchange economy in which profit-seeking traders interact with consumers who are price-sensitive. No other substantive assumptions are made about the behaviour of individual consumers. I show that in every Nash equilibrium of the game played by traders, the Law of One Price and the Law of Supply and Demand are satisfied.

6. Strictly speaking, and given that consumers have not been assumed to be rational, this conclusion depends on an assumption about the continuity of consumers' aggregate responses to prices. For more on this, see Sugden (2004a).

7. A final question will come to mind for some economic theorists: Can we be sure that there exists a price vector such that all markets clear? Proofs of the existence of competitive equilibrium (such as the famous proof by Arrow and Debreu, 1954) usually involve some neoclassical assumptions about individuals' preferences. But the existence of equilibrium in my model can be proved by assuming only that excess demand for each commodity, aggregated over all individuals and with

context held constant, is a continuous function of prices and (roughly speaking) that individuals' desire for money is never satiated. The proof is in Sugden (2017b).

8. It is natural to ask whether the converse of this theorem is also true—that is, whether every opportunity profile that satisfies the Strong Interactive Opportunity Criterion is a competitive equilibrium. The answer is 'No'. However, there is a sense in which the converse theorem is 'almost true' for sufficiently large economies, roughly analogous with the sense in which, as first conjectured by Edgeworth (1881/1967) and formalized by Debreu and Scarf (1963), the core of an exchange economy shrinks towards competitive equilibrium as the economy increases in size. For more on this, see Sugden (2017b).

9. These restrictions are encapsulated in the Strong Axiom of Revealed Preference, first formulated by Houthakker (1950).

10. Arrow and Debreu (1954: 267) assume non-increasing returns to scale. Formally, this is less restrictive than the assumption of constant returns to scale which I will use in this section, but it has much the same economic significance. Arrow and Debreu also allow the possibility that a production process has more than one output.

11. The analysis in Sections 6.8 and 6.9 was first presented in McQuillin and Sugden (2012).

12. In this model, claims are not 'dated', as they are in general equilibrium models in the tradition of Arrow and Debreu (1954). That is, a claim is not an entitlement to consume a specified quantity of a specified commodity *in a specified period*. Roughly, it is an entitlement to consume a specified quantity of a specified commodity in whatever period the (then) holder of that claim chooses, subject to any constraints imposed by the holder's opportunity set in each period.

13. In a more realistic model, traders would own 'working capital' out of which arbitrage losses (within the limits of that capital) could be financed. One function of market regulation, briefly discussed in Section 7.1, is to ensure that arbitrageurs have sufficient assets to cover likely losses.

7 Regulation

1. Cap-and-trade regimes are designed to induce economic efficiency for *given* total emissions. Choosing the level of total emissions is a separate problem, which requires implicit or explicit valuation of environmental goods and bads. But, at least in the context of the most serious environmental issue of our time, the problem of climate change, economics is more likely to be immediately useful in showing how to achieve efficiency within a given emissions ceiling than in saying what the ceiling should be. Setting overall limits at the world level and dividing these between nations are multi-dimensional problems, involving contestable judgements about natural science, contestable ethical judgements and, ultimately, horse-trading between nations and between interest groups.

2. This section and Section 7.4 include material from Mehta and Sugden (2013).

3. See the meta-analysis of choice overload experiments reported by Scheibehenne, Griefeneder, and Todd (2010).

4. The evidence summarized in this paragraph is reviewed by Botti and Iyengar (2006).

5. The quote is from a discussion piece entitled 'Choice and its enemies', dated 19 April 2005, by Pejman Yousefzadeh, published on the website of *TCS Daily* at http://www.tcsdaily.com/article.aspx?id=041905D, accessed 16 January 2006.

6. This statement is deliberately imprecise, because of theoretical issues associated with fixed costs and economies of scale. I will discuss these issues in Section 7.5.

7. My information is taken from the StickK website, http://www.stickk.com, accessed 4 October 2017. Information about fees is in paragraph 6.5.4 of 'Terms and Conditions of Commitment Contract'.

8. Schubert (2015) uses this argument in opposition to my use of opportunity as a normative criterion. I reply to this criticism in Sugden (2015b).

9. This item, written by Michael Bow, appeared in *The Independent* on 23 March 2016 and at the web address http://www.independent.co.uk/news/uk/home-news/-william-hill-betting-firm-complains-panic-button-allowing-gamblers-to-take-break-is-hurting-profits-a6948766.html, accessed 4 January 2018.

10. This information is taken from http://www.stickk.com, accessed 4 October 2017.

11. This evidence is reviewed by Crossley et al. (2012).

12. The classic papers on this topic are by Scitovsky (1950) and Salop and Stiglitz (1977).

13. These pricing strategies are described in more detail in Office of Fair Trading (2011), a report which summarizes the academic literature on obfuscation. Ellison and Ellison (2009) discuss examples of drip pricing in internet trading. Armstrong and Zhou (2016) discuss exploding offers.

14. These pricing strategies are discussed by Ellison (2005) and Gabaix and Laibson (2006).

15. Ellison and Ellison (2009: 434–5) describe a case of this kind, involving an internet platform for the sale of computer parts. Observing that many sellers were imposing excessive shipping charges at the checkout point, the platform required all firms to offer a standard form of ground shipping with prescribed maximum charges.

16. This 'common standard' effect is analysed by Gaudeul and Sugden (2012).

17. I say more about this aspect of Dupuit's work in Sugden (2015c).

18. Walras (1874/1954: 443), one of the founders of neoclassical economics, dismissed Dupuit's analysis of utility as an 'egregious error'. Most historians of economic ideas have seen this criticism as ungenerous but broadly correct. See, for example, Ekelund and Hébert (1985). I defend Dupuit's analysis in Sugden (2015c).

19. For example, two major meta-analyses have shown that the disparity between willingness-to-pay and willingness-to-accept valuations is much greater for non-marketed than for marketed goods (Horowitz and McConnell, 2002; Tuncel and Hammitt, 2014).

20. Isoni et al. (2016) present experimental evidence of the tendency for individuals' valuations of goods to be 'shaped' by irrelevant price information.

21. In Sugden (1990), I discuss some of the merits and demerits of mechanisms of this kind.

8 Psychological Stability

1. Sugden and Teng (2016) discuss this concept of stability in more detail, in relation to the 'polices for happiness' proposed by Layard (2005).

2. This section and Section 8.2 derive from Sugden (2004b).

3. When Dworkin considers how this ideal arrangement might be approximated in a real-world economy, he ends up proposing a more practical and more conventional system of graduated income taxation. In such a system, transfers are determined by individuals' actual earnings rather than by their earning opportunities. However, Dworkin still relies on the supposed possibility of calculations of the kind performed by the islanders' computer to determine fair tax rates (1981: 314–23).

4. Dworkin (1981: 310) says that his theory is concerned with 'equality of resources devoted to whole lives'. Roemer (1998: 43–53) holds individuals within a given 'type' responsible for differences in medical costs that result from different decisions about smoking. The lag between taking up smoking and suffering a serious smoking-related illness is often measured in decades.

5. The invisible hand makes a third appearance when Smith writes about the history of astronomy: see Macfie (1971).

6. This is exactly what would happen in a very simple model with identical landowners and a Cobb–Douglas production function for grain. Let N be the fixed total supply of labour and R the fixed total supply of land. Assume that total output of grain is given by $Q = L^\alpha R^\beta I^\gamma$, where $L \leq N$ is labour used in grain production and I is a measure of land improvement; α, β, and γ are positive parameters that sum to 1. Think of 'luxury' simply as the purchase of non-agricultural labour (say as domestic servants). Profit-maximizing behaviour by landowners implies that, in equilibrium, the wage rate (in units of grain, and assumed equal for all workers) is given by $w = \partial Q/\partial L$. If profits (the excess of grain production over wages paid to agricultural workers) are spent entirely on the purchase of non-agricultural labour, we have $Q - wL = w(N - L)$, i.e. $Q = wN$. It is then a simple mathematical exercise to show that $L/N = \alpha$. Thus, changes in I have no effect on the distribution of labour between sectors: even if improvements were costless, landowners would not benefit from them.

7. Let w be the initial price of labour and let q be the initial total quantity traded. Let Δq be the (proportionately very small) additional quantity of labour bought by our landowner as a result of his improvements, and let Δw be the resulting small increase in price. If the supply of labour is fixed, this increase in price must be just sufficient to reduce the quantity demanded by other buyers by Δq. It follows that the absolute value of the ratio of $q\Delta w$ (the sum of losses to other buyers of labour and the equal and opposite sum of gains to sellers) to $w\Delta q$ (our landowner's additional outlay on labour) is equal to the reciprocal of the absolute value of the elasticity of demand for labour.

8. That the latter claim is true of an exchange economy in competitive equilibrium is an implication of the Strong Market Opportunity Theorem (see Section 6.6).

9. Dworkin (1981: 310–11) explicitly rejects this metaphor, denying that he is proposing a 'starting-gate theory' and suggesting that such a theory is suitable

only for a game of Monopoly. He claims that his model of hypothetical computer-generated insurance does not equalize resources at an arbitrary starting point, but instead allows the distribution of resources at any particular moment to be 'ambition-sensitive' while neutralizing differences in talent. It seems to me that, if Dworkin's insurance scheme can be given a coherent economic interpretation, it *is* a device to ensure a kind of starting-gate equality.

10. I defend this contractarian reading of Hayek's defence of the market in Sugden (1993a).

11. I develop this argument more fully in Sugden (1986).

12. 'Merely' is significant here. Arguably, the first steps towards the creation of welfare states in Germany and Britain occurred in response to changes in the economic and political balance of power between classes that were becoming obvious in late nineteenth-century Europe with the rise of socialism and the extension of the franchise.

13. See http://www.forbes.com/athletes/list/#tab:overall, accessed 11 January 2018.

14. Reported by *The Guardian*, 6 July 2016: https://www.theguardian.com/football/2016/jul/06/lionel-messi-barcelona-prison-21-months-tax-fraud, accessed 4 January 2018.

9 Intrinsic Motivation, Kindness, and Reciprocity

1. Subsequent Dictator Game experiments have found less generosity than this result suggests. When allocators are free to choose any division of the sum of money, the modal proportion given to recipients is around 20 per cent (e.g. Forsythe et al., 1994). Even this degree of apparent generosity may be an artefact of an experimental design which, by allowing allocators to give but not to take, signals to subjects that some giving is expected. See Bardsley (2008) for experimental evidence of this 'experimenter demand effect'.

2. One of the main purposes of Smith's *Theory of Moral Sentiments* (1759/1976) is to show how psychological mechanisms of fellow-feeling lead people to take an interest in other people's well-being. In explaining *economic* behaviour, however, Smith normally assumes that individuals are motivated by 'self-love'. He recognizes the importance of trust in business, but explains practices of trust among merchants as responses to the market value of reputations for trustworthiness (Smith, 1763/1978: 538–9).

3. This section and Section 9.2 derive from Bruni and Sugden (2013).

4. In a witty account of the history of Western intellectuals' criticisms of capitalism, Alan Kahan (2010: 31) presents the 'Three Don'ts' of anti-capitalism. The first is 'Don't make money (just have it)'.

5. In a more recent book, Sandel (2012) presents an argument about the 'moral limits of markets'. As he acknowledges (2012: 208, note 18), this argument is similar to that of Anderson (1993).

6. It is only very recently that economists have taken this hypothesis seriously. Titmuss's work was well-known to economists in the 1970s, but his crowding-out argument was viewed sceptically (see, e.g., Arrow, 1972). Gneezy and Rustichini (2000a, 2000b) discussed motivational crowding-out as a possible explanation of

their findings, but favoured a more conventional economic interpretation in terms of incomplete contracts.

7. If there are opportunities for retaliation, punishment is much less effective in sustaining contributions. See, for example, Nikiforakis (2008).

8. One of my proudest moments as a young economist was when, in 1983, I received a letter from Kenneth Arrow saying that my arguments had persuaded him that there was a flaw in the received theory of voluntary contributions to public goods.

9. Charness and Dufwenberg (2006) present a model of a Trust Game in which B has a unilateral opportunity to send a message to A before the game is played. If B is motivated by trust responsiveness and if A knows this, there can be an equilibrium of the following kind: B sends a message promising to choose *return*; interpreting this action as indicating that B will in fact chose *return*, A chooses *send*; B's desire to conform to A's expectations then leads her to choose *return*. Charness and Dufwenberg report experimental evidence showing that the opportunity for B to make 'cheap talk' promises increases both trust and trustworthiness.

10. Levine (1998) presents a somewhat similar hypothesis, formulated in terms of preferences instead of intentions. In Levine's theory, individuals can derive positive utility ('altruism') or negative utility ('spite') from other people's material payoffs. An individual who is motivated by reciprocity is more altruistic towards any given other person, the more altruistic that person is towards people in general. Since kindness in Rabin's sense is a signal of altruism in Levine's sense, the two theories have similar implications. Levine's theory allows a (*send*, *return*) equilibrium in the Trust Game, but only as a result of unconditional (as opposed to reciprocal) altruism on the part of B. The same conclusion follows from the theory of reciprocity proposed by Charness and Rabin (2002). Yet another related theory, proposed by Falk and Fischbacher (2006), combines elements of reciprocity, inequality aversion, and trust responsiveness. In this theory, A is kind to B if B's expected material payoff is greater than A's, and the kindness is greater if this inequality results from A's intentional choice. In my version of the Trust Game, A and B get equal payoffs from (*send*, *return*), and so *send* is not kind. Thus, (*send*, *return*) is not an equilibrium.

11. One possible generalization is proposed by Dufwenberg and Kirchsteiger (2004).

12. In their generalization of Rabin's theory, Dufwenberg and Kirchsteiger (2004) take a different view. According to their definitions, A's choice of *send* is kind even if he believes that B will choose return with probability 1. If A has this belief, Rabin's theory treats *hold* as a Pareto-dominated action (it necessarily leads to (0, 0), while *send* leads to (2, 2) with probability 1), and therefore as not relevant in assessing the kindness of *send*. In contrast, Dufwenberg and Kirchsteiger argue that *hold* is not dominated in the set of *possible* outcomes, because (*send*, *keep*) is possible and leads to (–1, 5). By treating *hold* as an eligible action for A, Dufwenberg and Kirchsteiger are able to claim that choosing *send* instead of *hold* is kind. Oddly, if the payoffs to (*send*, *keep*) were changed to (1, –1), *send* would still count as kind, even though A would benefit from this action irrespective of what B did. But if they were changed to (1, 1), *both* players would benefit from *send* irrespective of

what *B* did, and yet *send* would no longer be kind. It seems to me that Rabin's concept of kindness has greater internal coherence.

13. Andreoni et al. (2017) estimate that, in their experiment, giving-avoiders made up only a 'small fraction' of potential givers, but refer to other experiments that have found behaviour similar to giving-avoiding. For example, in a Dictator Game experiment, Lazear et al. (2012) estimate that approximately one-third of their subjects were 'reluctant sharers'. These are subjects who, if placed in the role of allocator in a Dictator Game with a $10 endowment to divide with an anonymous co-player, would not take it all for themselves. Given a choice, however, they would accept a fixed payment of $10 rather than play that role, even though the would-be co-player would then not play the game at all.

14. The final sentence of the quotation from Bicchieri is her summary of Hume's (1739–40/1978) own explanation of the perceived legitimacy of rules of property. My understanding of that explanation was presented in Section 3.2.

15. In the paper which introduced the Trust Game to behavioural economics, Berg, Dickhaut, and McCabe (1995: 124) suggest exactly this kind of reciprocity: 'If [B] interprets [A's] decision to send money as an attempt to improve the outcome for both parties, then [B] is more likely to reciprocate'. But the main line of development in the theory of social preferences has used concepts of kindness, fairness, and reward rather than mutual benefit.

10 Cooperative Intentions

1. The model I develop is loosely based on an analysis presented in Sugden (2015d), but differs by describing team reasoning in terms of opportunities rather than in terms of measures of individuals' preferences or interests, and by using a different baseline for defining mutual benefit.

2. There are close connections between team reasoning and other 'we' notions used in the literature of social ontology, particularly the concepts of plural subjects (Gilbert, 1989), collective intentionality (Tuomela and Miller, 1988; Searle, 1990; Bratman, 1993; Bardsley, 2007) and group agency (List and Pettit, 2011). Natalie Gold and I have suggested that collective intentions can be characterized as intentions that are supported by team reasoning (Gold and Sugden, 2007).

3. See, for example, the theoretical analyses of Bacharach (1993, 2006), Sugden (1995), Casajus (2001), and Janssen (2001) and the experimental evidence reported by Bacharach and Bernasconi (1997) and Bardsley et al. (2010).

4. This is from the 'New York City Tipping Guide' offered by New York Show Tickets Inc. at http://www.nytix.com/NewYorkCity/articles/tipping.html, accessed 17 February 2017. The internet guidance about tipping taxi drivers in Britain is more diverse, reflecting greater ambivalence in Britain about the practice of tipping.

5. A game, as usually defined, is specified to include each player's payoff from each possible combination of strategies; payoffs are measured in units of utility and represent the players' preferences. In keeping with the approach that I have used throughout this book, I will not specify players' preferences over outcomes.

6. Following Lewis (1969), many other writers have developed related models of the emergence and reproduction of conventions and norms. See, for example, Ullman-Margalit (1977), Sugden (1986), Binmore (1994, 1998), Skyrms (1996), Young (1998), and Bicchieri (2006). Lewis was a philosopher, writing at a time when game theory did not have the tools to represent games that were played recurrently within populations of potential players. In order to analyse conventions, he developed a distinctive (and still largely unappreciated) form of game theory, inspired by the work of Schelling (1960). On Lewis's contribution to game theory, see Cubitt and Sugden (2003).

7. If the definition of a game is generalized to allow chance nodes, conformity has to be defined in terms of 'branching sets' of paths. Intuitively, a branching set of paths uniquely specifies how every player behaves, conditional on each possible combination of moves of nature. A player i conforms to a branching set P of paths if, at any decision node for i on any path in P, i chooses the move that keeps the game on some path or paths in P.

8. In my 2015 paper (Sugden, 2015d), I avoid this implication by restricting my analysis to games in which every strategy is 'normatively legitimate' in the sense that it can be chosen 'without violating any other player's entitlements'. But introducing the concept of moral entitlements at this point is an awkward manoeuvre.

9. A related idea is used by Gauthier (1986: 200–8) to define a baseline for contractarian reasoning. Gauthier's baseline is one in which no one 'better[s her] situation through interaction that worsens the situation of another'; bettering and worsening 'are judged by comparing what I actually do with what would have occurred, *ceteris paribus*, in my absence'. But, as Gauthier acknowledges, it is not always clear how this *ceteris paribus* clause should be interpreted.

10. In Sugden (2015d) I offer an analysis of mutual benefit and free-riding within a more conventional theoretical framework in which games have well-defined payoffs.

11. The concept of a publicly observed fact is essentially the same as Lewis's (1969) concept of a 'basis for common knowledge'. On this, see Cubitt and Sugden (2003).

12. It might be objected that, on a literal reading, this schema can lead to pointless conformity. For example, suppose I am a member of a reading group. Our activities are structured by various informal rules, governing when and where we meet, how we decide which books to discuss, and so on. We understand these rules as defining a practice to which each of us, as long as he or she remains a member, has some obligation to conform. But there may be other predictable regularities in our behaviour that no one cares about. Suppose that, at our meetings, people almost always dress casually, but that no one would be inconvenienced if I were to turn up in a business suit. It seems wrong to say that, by virtue of intending mutual benefit, I ought to dress like everyone else. If this problem is to be resolved, the schema may need to be refined so that it refers to common understandings about acceptable deviations from empirically expected behaviour. For my present purposes, it is not necessary to pursue this complication.

13. Gold and Sugden (2007) and Sugden (2015d) discuss recursive reasoning schemas that are similar to Collectively Intending Mutual Benefit. This recursive pattern also appears in Bardsley's (2007) analysis of collective intentionality.

14. The idea that individuals cooperate by jointly implementing profiles of actions on which they would rationally have agreed, had they been able to make binding contracts, is implicit in Gauthier's (1986, 2013) theory of *constrained maximisation* and its later formulation as *rational cooperation*. I discuss the relationship between constrained maximisation and team reasoning in Sugden (2016). Related ideas, but without the assumption that the hypothetical bargainers are able to make enforceable agreements, are developed in Binmore's (1994, 1998) theory of *social contract* and in Misyak and Chater's (2014) theory of *virtual bargaining*.

15. Throughout this section, I will say that a participation path is 'consistent with self-interested play' if it is a path in a subgame-perfect Nash equilibrium defined with respect to material payoffs. However, it is sufficient for my purposes to appeal to intuitive ideas about rational self-interest. My analysis is concerned with intentions for mutual benefit, defined without reference to individuals' preferences. Self-interest serves only as a point of comparison in my discussion of how these games would be analysed in theories of social preference.

16. This distinction is codified in the doctrine of double effect, which originated in the teaching of Thomas Aquinas (1265–74, Part II.II, Question 64, Article 7). More recently, it has been discussed through the medium of 'trolley problems' (Foot, 1967; Thomson, 1985). Experiments have found that the moral judgements of ordinary people often conform to this doctrine (e.g. Gold et al., 2013).

11 The Principle of Mutual Benefit

1. My knowledge about this area of psychology is gleaned from Turiel et al. (1987), Smetana (1993), Nucci (2001), and Blair et al. (2005).

2. For further evidence, see Edwards (1987), Shweder et al. (1987) and Kelly et al. (2007). I discuss the significance of this evidence in Sugden (2010).

3. I have taken the idea of 'counting as' from Searle's (1995) analysis of 'institutional facts'.

4. By formulating the Principle of Mutual Benefit in terms of other people's expectations about 'the consequences for them of that interaction' rather than about other players' behaviour in its entirety, I am trying to deal with a problem I mentioned but did not resolve in Section 10.5—that of allowing 'acceptable' deviations from a voluntary practice.

5. For more on this hypothesis and its implications, see Gauthier (1986), Frank (1988), and Winter (2014).

6. For more on this concept of resentment and its relationship to morality, see Sugden (2004c: 218–23). Guala (2012) reviews evidence of the enforcement of norms in small-scale societies of hunter-gatherers, horticulturalists, and nomadic pastoralists. He concludes that individual acts of punishment (perhaps better described as revenge) are usually not 'third-party punishment' of behaviour that is impersonally anti-social; they are responses to harmful behaviour that was specifically directed at the person who takes the revenge.

7. As an aside, it is interesting that Kant seems to regard price discrimination as an inherently dishonest trading practice. I think he is wrong about this: see Section 7.5.

8. Experiments show that many people are willing to engage in costly 'counter-punishment' of other people who have punished them for anti-social behaviour. These acts of retaliation tend to destabilize cooperative practices in which free-riders are deterred by the threat of 'altruistic punishment' meted out by cooperators. For more on this, see Cinyabuguma et al. (2006), Denant-Boemont et al. (2007), Herrmann et al. (2008), and Nikiforakis (2008).

9. This section derives from Sugden (2005).

10. See Rizzolatti et al. (2001) and Chaminade and Decety (2003).

11. On the chimpanzees, see de Waal (1996: 53–62).

12. I say 'here' because when, briefly and in rather rose-tinted terms, Smith (1759/1976: 38–40) discusses family life, he pictures it in terms of the 'amiable passions' of 'mutual love and esteem' rather than in terms of cooperation and the correspondences of sentiments that cooperation can induce. Smith makes a sharp (and sometimes gendered) distinction between 'justice' on the one hand and 'beneficence' and 'humanity' on the other. Justice is the principal virtue of economic and political life; beneficience and humanity are virtues of family and friendship. On this, see Bruni and Sugden (2008).

13. For more on this understanding of 'fraternal' goodwill between buyers and sellers, see Bruni and Sugden (2008).

14. That respecting the tastes of one's customers is a virtue in the domain of markets is argued by Bruni and Sugden (2013).

15. My information about this episode is derived from Kuehn (2001) and Willaschek (2017). I was directed to it by Christian Schubert, who recognized its connection with my account of intentions for mutual benefit.

16. For me, one of the most attractive features of Hume's philosophy is his rejection of the idea that rationality gives our species a special place in the universe. On this, see Sugden (2008).

17. In a rather unworldly virtue-ethical critique of the market, MacIntyre (1984: 187) uses bricklaying as an example of a kind of work that lacks the internal standards of excellence that would allow it to count as a 'practice' with its own *telos*. I disagree.

18. For more on this and other market virtues, see Bruni and Sugden (2013).

References

Entries in square brackets after a reference identify the pages of *The Community of Advantage* at which that reference is used or cited. An asterisk denotes the use of material from the cited publication (see Sources of Material).

Akerlof, George (1982). Labor contracts as partial gift exchange. *Quarterly Journal of Economics* 97: 543–69. [216, 231, 279]

Allais, Maurice (1953). Le comportement de l'homme rationnel devant le risque: critique des postulats et axiomes de l'ecole Americaine. *Econometrica* 21: 503–46. [9]

Anderson, Elizabeth (1993). *Value in Ethics and Economics.* Cambridge, MA: Harvard University Press. [169, 208, 276]

Andreoni, James, Justin Rao, and Hannah Trachtman (2017). Avoiding the ask: a field experiment on altruism, empathy, and charitable giving. *Journal of Political Economy* 125: 625–53. [223]

Aquinas, Thomas (1265–74). *Summa Theologica.* Available at http://www.documenta-catholicaomnia.eu/03d/1225-1274,_Thomas_Aquinas,_Summa_Theologiae_%5B1%5D,_EN.pdf, accessed 11 January 2018. [317]

Ariely, Dan, George Loewenstein, and Drazen Prelec (2003). Coherent arbitrariness: stable demand curves without stable preferences. *Quarterly Journal of Economics* 118: 73–105. [71]

Aristotle (*c.* 350 BC/1980). *The Nicomachean Ethics.* Translated by David Ross. Oxford: Oxford University Press. [208]

Armstrong, Mark and Jidong Zhou (2016). Search deterrence. *Review of Economic Studies* 83: 26–57. [289]

Arneson, Richard (1989). Equality of opportunity for welfare. *Philosophical Studies* 56: 77–93. [89]

Arrow, Kenneth (1972). Gifts and exchanges. *Philosophy and Public Affairs* 1: 343–62. [291]

Arrow, Kenneth (1984). *Collected Papers of Kenneth J. Arrow. Volume 1: Social Choice and Justice.* Oxford: Basil Blackwell. [204]

Arrow, Kenneth and Gérard Debreu (1954). Existence of an equilibrium for a competitive economy. *Econometrica* 22: 265–90. [146, 287]

Atkinson, Anthony, Thomas Piketty, and Emmanuel Saez (2011). Top incomes in the long run of history. *Journal of Economic Literature* 49: 3–71. [200]

Bacharach, Michael (1987). A theory of rational decision in games. *Erkenntnis* 27: 17–55. [122]

Bacharach, Michael (1993). Variable universe games. In Ken Binmore, Alan Kirman, and Piero Tani (eds), *Frontiers of Game Theory*, pp. 255–76. Cambridge, MA: MIT Press. [293]

Bacharach, Michael (1999). Interactive team reasoning: a contribution to the theory of cooperation. *Research in Economics* 53: 117–47. [233, 250]

Bacharach, Michael (2006). *Beyond Individual Choice*. Princeton, NJ: Princeton University Press. [233, 250, 293]

Bacharach, Michael and Michele Bernasconi (1997). The variable frame theory of focal points: an experimental study. *Games and Economic Behavior* 19: 1–45. [293]

Bacharach, Michael, Gerardo Guerra, and Daniel Zizzo (2007). The self-fulfilling property of trust: an experimental study. *Theory and Decision* 63: 349–88. [270]

Bardsley, Nicholas (2007). On collective intentions: collective action in economics and philosophy. *Synthese* 157: 141–59. [293, 295]

Bardsley, Nicholas (2008). Dictator game giving: altruism or artefact? *Experimental Economics* 11: 122–33. [291]

Bardsley, Nicholas, Judith Mehta, Chris Starmer, and Robert Sugden (2010). Explaining focal points: cognitive hierarchy theory *versus* team reasoning. *Economic Journal* 120: 40–79. [293]

Bardsley, Nicholas and Peter Moffatt (2007). The experimetrics of public goods: inferring motivations from contributions. *Theory and Decision* 62: 161–93. [217]

Bar-Gill, Oren and Cass Sunstein (2015). Regulation as delegation. *Journal of Legal Analysis* 7: 1–36. [284]

Battigalli, Pierpaolo and Martin Dufwenberg (2007). Guilt in games. *American Economic Review: Papers and Proceedings* 97: 171–6. [220]

Bebchuk, Lucian and Jesse Fried (2003). Executive compensation as an agency problem. *Journal of Economic Perspectives* 17(3): 71–92. [201]

Becker, Gary (1974). A theory of social interactions. *Journal of Political Economy* 82: 1063–93. [218]

Bem, Daryl (1967). Self-perception: an alternative interpretation of cognitive dissonance phenomena. *Psychological Review* 74: 183–200. [212]

Berg, Joyce, John Dickhaut, and Kevin McCabe (1995). Trust, reciprocity, and social history. *Games and Economic Behavior* 10: 122–42. [10, 214, 293]

Berg, Nathan and Gerd Gigerenzer (2010). As-if behavioral economics: neoclassical economics in disguise? *History of Economic Ideas* 18: 133–66. [66]

Bernheim, Douglas (2016). The good, the bad, and the ugly: a unified approach to behavioural welfare economics. *Journal of Benefit–Cost Analysis*. Available on CJO 2016 doi:10.1017/bca.2016.5. [57]

Bernheim, Douglas and Antonio Rangel (2007). Toward choice-theoretic foundations for behavioral welfare economics. *American Economic Review: Papers and Proceedings* 97: 464–70. [18, 21, 57, 62, 287]

Bernheim, Douglas and Antonio Rangel (2009). Beyond revealed preference: choice-theoretic foundations for behavioral welfare economics. *Quarterly Journal of Economics* 124: 51–104. [18, 21, 57, 62, 287]

Bernheim, Douglas and Oded Stark (1988). Altruism within the family reconsidered: do nice guys finish last? *American Economic Review* 78: 1034–45. [274]

Bershears, John, James Choi, David Laibson, and Brigitte Madrian (2008). How are preferences revealed? *Journal of Public Economics* 92: 1787–94. [60]

Bicchieri, Cristina (2006). *The Grammar of Society: The Nature and Dynamics of Social Norms*. Cambridge: Cambridge University Press. [226, 256, 294]

Binmore, Ken (1994). *Game Theory and the Social Contract, Volume 1: Playing Fair*. Cambridge, MA: MIT Press. [283, 294, 295]

Binmore, Ken (1998). *Game Theory and the Social Contract, Volume 2: Just Playing*. Cambridge, MA: MIT Press. [283, 294, 295]

Blair, James, Derek Mitchell, and Karina Blair (2005). *The Psychopath: Emotion and the Brain*. Oxford: Blackwell. [295]

Blaug, Mark (2007). The fundamental theorems of modern welfare economics, historically contemplated. *History of Political Economy* 39: 185–207. [283]

Bleichrodt, Han, Jose-Luis Pinto-Prades, and Peter Wakker (2001). Making descriptive use of prospect theory to improve the prescriptive use of expected utility. *Management Science* 47: 1498–514. [58, 77]

Bolton, Gary and Axel Ockenfels (2000). ERC: A theory of equity, reciprocity and competition. *American Economic Review* 90: 166–93. [215]

Bordalo, Pedro, Nicola Gennaioli, and Andrei Shleifer (2013). Salience and consumer choice. *Journal of Political Economy* 121: 803–43. [69, 114]

Botti, Simona and Sheena Iyengar (2006). The dark side of choice: when choice impairs social welfare. *Journal of Public Policy and Marketing*, 25: 24–38. [289]

Bown, Nicola, Daniel Read, and Barbara Summers (2003). The lure of choice. *Journal of Behavioral Decision Making* 16: 297–308. [143]

Bratman, Michael (1993). Shared intention. *Ethics* 104: 97–113. [237, 293]

Brennan, Geoffrey (1996). Selection and the currency of reward. In Robert Goodin (ed.), *The Theory of Institutional Design*, pp. 256–75. Cambridge: Cambridge University Press. [212]

Brennan, Geoffrey and James Buchanan (1985). *The Reason of Rules*. Cambridge: Cambridge University Press. [284]

Brennan, Geoffrey and Philip Pettit (2000). The hidden economy of esteem. *Economics and Philosophy* 16: 77–98. [268]

Bruni, Luigino and Robert Sugden (2008). Fraternity: why the market need not be a morally free zone. *Economics and Philosophy* 24: 35–64. [296]

Bruni, Luigino and Robert Sugden (2013). Reclaiming virtue ethics for economics. *Journal of Economic Perspectives* 27: 141–64. [208–11*, 211–13*, 296]

Bryan, James and Mary Ann Test (1967). Models and helping: naturalistic studies in aiding behaviour. *Journal of Personality and Social Psychology* 6: 400–7. [223]

Buchanan, James (1954). Individual choice in voting and the market. *Journal of Political Economy* 62: 334–43. [284]

Buchanan, James (1964). What should economists do? *Southern Economic Journal* 30: 213–22. [14, 280]

Buchanan, James (1968). *The Demand and Supply of Public Goods*. Chicago: Rand McNally. [165]

Buchanan, James (1975). *The Limits of Liberty*. Chicago: University of Chicago Press. [38, 174]

Buchanan, James (1986). *Liberty, Market and State*. Brighton: Wheatsheaf. [21, 29, 283]

Buchanan, James (1987). The constitution of economic policy. *American Economic Review* 77: 243–50. [21]

Buchanan, James and Gordon Tullock (1962). *The Calculus of Consent*. Ann Arbor, MI: University of Michigan Press. [40, 284]

Camerer, Colin, Samuel Issacharoff, George Loewenstein, Ted O'Donaghue, and Matthew Rabin (2003). Regulation for conservatives: behavioral economics and the case for 'asymmetric paternalism'. *University of Pennsylvania Law Review* 151: 1211–54. [18, 56, 166]

Casajus, André (2001). *Focal Points in Framed Games: Breaking the Symmetry*. Berlin: Springer-Verlag. [293]

Chaminade, Thierry and Jean Decety (2003). Neural correlates of feeling sympathy. *Neuropsychologia* 41: 127–38. [296]

Charness, Gary and Martin Dufwenberg (2006). Promises and partnership. *Econometrica* 74: 1579–601. [292]

Charness, Gary and Matthew Rabin (2002). Understanding social preferences with simple tests. *Quarterly Journal of Economics* 117: 817–69. [292]

Cialdini, Robert (1984). *Influence: The Psychology of Persuasion*. New York: Quill Press. [268]

Cinyabuguma, Matthias, Talbot Page, and Louis Putterman (2006). Can second-order punishment deter perverse punishment? *Experimental Economics* 9: 265–79. [296]

Cohen, Gerald (1989). On the currency of egalitarian justice. *Ethics* 99: 906–44. [177]

Core, John, Robert Holthausen, and David Larcker (1999). Corporate governance, chief executive officer compensation, and firm performance. *Journal of Financial Economics* 51: 371–406. [201]

Crossley, Thomas, Carl Emmerson, and Andrew Leicester (2012). *Raising Household Saving*. Report by Institute for Fiscal Studies and British Academy Policy Centre. [289]

Cubitt, Robin and Robert Sugden (2001). On money pumps. *Games and Economic Behavior* 37: 121–60. [285]

Cubitt, Robin and Robert Sugden (2003). Common knowledge, salience and convention: a reconstruction of David Lewis's game theory. *Economics and Philosophy* 19: 175–210. [294]

Debreu, Gerard and Herbert Scarf (1963). A limit theorem on the core of an economy. *International Economic Review* 4: 235–46. [288]

Deci, Edward (1971). Effects of externally mediated rewards on intrinsic motivation. *Journal of Personality and Social Psychology* 18: 105–15. [211]

Deci, Edward and Richard Ryan (1985). *Intrinsic Motivation and Self-determination in Human Behavior*. New York: Plenum. [211]

De Jasay, Anthony (2010). Ordered anarchy and contractarianism. *Philosophy* 85: 399–403. [284]

DellaVigna, Stefano and Ulrike Malmendier (2004). Contract design and self-control. *Quarterly Journal of Economics* 119: 353–402. [152]

DellaVigna, Stefano and Ulrike Malmendier (2006). Paying not to go to the gym. *American Economic Review* 96: 694–719. [152]

Denant-Boemont, Laurent, David Masclet, and Charles Noussair (2007). Punishment, counter-punishment and sanction enforcement in a social dilemma experiment. *Economic Theory* 33: 145–67. [296]

de Waal, Frans (1996). *Good Natured: The Origins of Right and Wrong in Humans and Other Animals*. Cambridge, MA: Harvard University Press. [248–52]

Dufwenberg, Martin and Georg Kirchsteiger (2004). A theory of sequential reciprocity. *Games and Economic Behavior* 47: 268–98. [292]

Dupuit, Jules (1844/1952). On the measurement of the utility of public works. *International Economic Papers* 2 (1952): 83–110. Translated by R. H. Barback. (Page references to reprint in *Cost–Benefit Analysis*, edited by Richard Layard. London: Penguin, 1973.) [160, 199]

Dworkin, Ronald (1981). What is equality? Part 2: Equality of resources. *Philosophy and Public Affairs* 10: 283–345. [175, 193]

Ederer, Florian and Alexander Stremitzer (2016). Promises and expectations. Cowles Foundation Discussion Paper no. 1931. Yale University, New Haven, CT. [221]

Edgeworth, Francis Ysidro (1881/1967). *Mathematical Psychics: An Essay on the Application of Mathematics to the Moral Sciences*. New York: Kelley. [288]

Edwards, Carolyn (1987). Culture and the construction of moral values: a comparative ethnography of moral encounters in two cultural settings. In Jerome Kagan and Sharon Lamb, *The Emergence of Morality in Young Children*, pp.125–51. Chicago: University of Chicago Press. [295]

Ekelund, Robert and Robert Hébert (1985). Consumer surplus: the first hundred years. *History of Political Economy* 17: 419–54. [289]

Ellison, Glenn (2005). A model of add-on pricing. *Quarterly Journal of Economics* 120: 585–637. [289]

Ellison, Glenn and Sara Fisher Ellison (2009). Search, obfuscation, and price elasticities on the Internet. *Econometrica* 77: 427–52. [289]

Falk, Armin, Ernst Fehr, and Urs Fischbacher (2003). On the nature of fair behavior. *Economic Inquiry* 41(1): 20–6. [219]

Falk, Armin and Urs Fischbacher (2006). A theory of reciprocity. *Games and Economic Behavior* 54: 293–315. [231, 292]

Fehr, Ernst and Simon Gächter (2000). Cooperation and punishment in public goods experiments. *American Economic Review* 90: 980–94. [217, 254]

Fehr, Ernst and Klaus Schmidt (1999). A theory of fairness, competition and cooperation. *Quarterly Journal of Economics* 114: 817–68. [215, 231]

Fischbacher, Urs and Simon Gächter (2010). Social preferences, beliefs, and the dynamics of free riding in public goods experiments. *American Economic Review* 100: 541–56. [217]

Flegal, Katherine, Brian Kit, Heather Orpana, and Barry Graubard (2013). Association of all-cause mortality with overweight and obesity using standard body mass index categories: a systematic review and meta-analysis. *Journal of the American Medical Association (JAMA)* 309(1): 71–82. [285]

Folbre, Nancy and Julie Nelson (2000). For love or money—or both? *Journal of Economic Perspectives* 14: 123–40. [213]

Foot, Philippa (1967). The problem of abortion and the doctrine of the double effect. *Oxford Review* 5: 5–15. [295]

Forsythe, Robert, Joel Horowitz, Nathan Savin, and Martin Sefton (1994). Fairness in simple bargaining experiments. *Games and Economic Behavior* 6: 347–69. [291]

References

Frank, Robert (1988). *Passions within Reason: The Strategic Role of the Emotions*. New York: Norton. [295]

Frank, Robert and Philip Cook (1995). *The Winner-Take-All Society*. New York: Free Press. [201]

Frank, Robert, Thomas Gilovich, and Dennis Regan (1993). The evolution of one-shot cooperation: an experiment. *Ethology and Sociobiology* 14: 247–56. [267]

Frankfurt, Harry (1971). Freedom of the will and the concept of a person. *Journal of Philosophy* 68: 5–20. [286]

Frey, Bruno (1994). How intrinsic motivation is crowded in and out. *Rationality and Society* 6: 334–52. [212]

Frey, Bruno (1997). *Not Just for the Money: An Economic Theory of Personal Motivation*. Cheltenham: Edward Elgar. [212]

Fudenberg, Drew and David Levine (2006). A dual-self model of impulse control. *American Economic Review* 96: 1449–76. [151]

Gabaix, Xavier and David Laibson (2006). Shrouded attributes, consumer myopia, and information suppression in competitive markets. *Quarterly Journal of Economics* 12: 505–40. [289]

Gale, David and Lloyd Shapley (1962). College admissions and the stability of marriage. *American Mathematical Monthly* 69: 9–15. [247]

Gaudeul, Alexia and Robert Sugden (2012). Spurious complexity and common standards in markets for consumer goods. *Economica* 79: 209–25. [289]

Gauthier, David (1986). *Morals by Agreement*. Oxford: Oxford University Press. [39, 89, 260, 294, 295]

Gauthier, David (2013). Twenty-five on. *Ethics* 123: 601–24. [295]

George, Henry (1879). *Progress and Poverty*. New York: Appleton. [199]

Gilbert, Margaret (1989): *On Social Facts*. London: Routledge. [293]

Gneezy, Uri and Aldo Rustichini (2000a). A fine is a price. *Journal of Legal Studies* 29: 1–17. [212, 291]

Gneezy, Uri and Aldo Rustichini (2000b). Pay enough or don't pay at all. *Quarterly Journal of Economics* 115: 791–810. [291]

Gneezy, Uri, Stephan Meier, and Pedro Rey-Biel (2011). When and why incentives (don't) work to modify behavior. *Journal of Economic Perspectives* 25(4): 191–210. [212]

Gold, Natalie, Briony Pulford, and Andrew Colman (2013). Your money or your life: comparing judgments in trolley problems involving economic and emotional harms, injury and death. *Economics and Philosophy* 29: 213–33. [295]

Gold, Natalie and Robert Sugden (2007). Collective intentions and team agency. *Journal of Philosophy* 104: 109–37. [293, 295]

Griffin, James (1986). *Well-being: Its Meaning, Measurement and Moral Importance*. Oxford: Oxford University Press. [89]

Guala, Francesco (2012). Reciprocity: weak or strong? What punishment experiments do (and do not) demonstrate. *Behavioral and Brain Sciences* 35: 1–59. [295]

Güth, Werner, Rolf Schmittberger, and Bernd Schwarze (1982). An experimental analysis of ultimatum bargaining. *Journal of Economic Behavior and Organization* 3: 367–88. [218]

Habermas, Jürgen (1995). Reconciliation through the public use of reason: remarks on John Rawls's political liberalism. *Journal of Philosophy* 92: 109–31. [26]

Haidt, Jonathan, Silvia Koller, and Maria Dias (1993). Affect, culture and morality, or is it wrong to eat your dog? *Journal of Personality and Social Psychology* 65: 613–28. [259]

Harsanyi, John (1955). Cardinal welfare, individualistic ethics and interpersonal comparisons of utility. *Journal of Political Economy* 63: 309–21. [283]

Harsanyi, John (1980). Rule utilitarianism, rights, obligations and the theory of rational behavior. *Theory and Decision* 12: 115–33. [232]

Hausman, Daniel (2012). *Preference, Value, Choice, and Welfare*. New York: Cambridge University Press. [55, 74, 90, 189, 283]

Hausman, Daniel and Brynn Welch (2010). Debate: to nudge or not to nudge. *Journal of Political Philosophy* 18: 123–36. [63]

Hayek, Friedrich von (1948). *Individualism and Economic Order*. Chicago: University of Chicago Press. [179, 284]

Hayek, Friedrich von (1960). *The Constitution of Liberty*. London: Routledge. [196]

Hayek, Friedrich von (1976). *Law, Legislation and Liberty. Volume 2: The Mirage of Social Justice*. Chicago: University of Chicago Press. [195]

Herrmann, Benedikt, Christian Thöni, and Simon Gächter (2008). Antisocial punishment across societies. *Science* 319: 1362–7. [296]

Heyes, Anthony (2005). The economics of vocation, or 'Why is a badly-paid nurse a good nurse?' *Journal of Health Economics* 24: 561–9. [212]

Hobbes, Thomas (1651/1962). *Leviathan*. London: Macmillan. [10, 30, 214, 266]

Hodgson, David (1967). *Consequences of Utilitarianism*. Oxford: Clarendon Press. [232]

Horowitz, John and Kenneth McConnell (2002). A review of WTP/WTA studies. *Journal of Environmental Economics and Management* 44: 426–47. [289]

Houthakker, Hendrik (1950). Revealed preference and the utility function. *Economica* 17: 59–174. [288]

Hume, David (1739–40/1978). *A Treatise of Human Nature*. Oxford: Oxford University Press. [10, 30, 33, 95, 196, 236, 252, 293]

Hume, David (1748/1985). Of the original contract. In *Essays, Moral, Political and Literary*, pp. 465–87. Indianapolis: Liberty Fund. [34]

Hume, David (1777/1975). *Enquiries concerning Human Understanding and concerning the Principles of Morals*. Oxford: Oxford University Press. [266]

Infante, Gerardo, Guilhem Lecouteux, and Robert Sugden (2016). Preference purification and the inner rational agent: a critique of the conventional wisdom of behavioural welfare economics. *Journal of Economic Methodology* 23: 1–25. [7–12*, 53–68*, 72–78*]

Isoni, Andrea (2011). The willingness-to-accept/willingness-to-pay disparity in repeated markets: loss aversion or 'bad-deal' aversion? *Theory and Decision* 71: 409–70. [114, 284]

Isoni, Andrea, Peter Brooks, Graham Loomes, and Robert Sugden (2016). Do markets reveal preferences or shape them? *Journal of Economic Behavior and Organization* 122: 1–16 [289]

Iyengar, Sheena and Mark Lepper (2000). When choice is demotivating: can one desire too much of a good thing? *Journal of Personality and Social Psychology* 79: 995–1006. [144]

References

Janssen, Maarten (2001). Rationalising focal points. *Theory and Decision* 50: 119–48. [293]

Jevons, William Stanley (1871/1970). *The Theory of Political Economy*. London: Penguin. [5]

Johnson, Eric and David Schkade (1989). Bias in utility assessments: further evidence and explanations. *Management Science* 35: 406–24. [71]

Jones, Peter and Robert Sugden (1982). Evaluating choice. *International Review of Law and Economics* 2: 47–65. [286]

Kahan, Alan (2010). *Mind vs. Money: The War Between Intellectuals and Capitalism*. Piscataway, NJ: Transaction Publishers. [291]

Kahneman, Daniel (1996). Comment [on Plott (1996)]. In Kenneth Arrow, Enrico Colombatto, Mark Perlman, and Christian Schmidt (eds), *The Rational Foundations of Economic Behaviour*, pp. 251–4. Basingstoke: Macmillan and International Economic Association. [67, 285]

Kahneman, Daniel. (2003). A perspective on judgment and choice: mapping bounded rationality. *American Psychologist* 58: 697–720. [67]

Kahneman, Daniel (2011). *Thinking, Fast and Slow*. New York: Farrar, Straus and Giroux. [67, 153, 283]

Kahneman, Daniel, Jack Knetsch, and Richard Thaler (1986). Fairness and the assumptions of economics. *Journal of Business* 59: S285–S300. [12, 205]

Kahneman, Daniel, Jack Knetsch, and Richard Thaler (1990). Experimental tests of the endowment effect and the Coase Theorem. *Journal of Political Economy* 98: 1325–48. [7]

Kahneman, Daniel and Amos Tversky (1979). Prospect theory: an analysis of decision under risk. *Econometrica* 47: 263–91. [9]

Kahneman, Daniel and Amos Tversky (eds) (2000). *Choices, Values, and Frames*, Cambridge: Cambridge University Press and Russell Sage Foundation. [283]

Kant, Immanuel (1784/2003). *Natural Right*. Lecture notes taken by Gottfried Feyerabend, translated by Lars Vinx. http://www.academia.edu/5541693/English_Translation_of_the_Naturrecht_Feyerabend (accessed 16 April 2017). [278]

Kant, Immanuel (1785/2002). *Groundwork for the Metaphysics of Morals*. Translated by Allen Wood. New Haven, CT: Yale University Press. [257, 270]

Kant, Immanuel (1788/2004). *Critique of Practical Reason*. Translated by Thomas Kingsmill. Mineola, NY: Dover. [257]

Karpus, Jurgis and Mantas Radzvillas (2017). Team reasoning and a measure of mutual advantage in games. *Economics and Philosophy* 34: 1–30. [241]

Katz, Eliakim and Femida Handy (1998). The wage differential between non-profit institutions and corporations: getting more by paying less? *Journal of Comparative Economics* 26: 246–61. [212]

Kelly, Daniel, Stephen Stich, Serena Eng, and Daniel Fessler (2007). Harm, affect, and the moral/conventional distinction. *Mind and Language* 22: 117–31. [295]

Kőszegi, Botond and Matthew Rabin (2007). Mistakes in choice-based welfare analysis. *American Economic Review* 97: 477–81. [59]

Kőszegi, Botond and Matthew Rabin (2008). Choices, situations, and happiness. *Journal of Public Economics* 92: 1821–32. [59]

Kuehn, Manfred (2001). *Kant: A Biography*. Cambridge: Cambridge University Press. [296]

Lange, Oskar and Fred Taylor (1938). *On the Economic Theory of Socialism*. Minneapolis: University of Minnesota Press. [179]

Layard, Richard (2005). *Happiness: Lessons from a New Science*. London: Allen Lane. [137, 290]

Lazear, Edward, Ulrike Malmendier, and Roberto Weber (2012). Sorting in experiments with application to social preferences. *American Economic Journal: Applied Economics* 4: 136–63. [293]

Le Grand, Julian and Bill New (2015). *Government Paternalism: Nanny State or Helpful Friend?* Princeton, NJ: Princeton University Press. [46, 61]

Lepper, Mark and David Greene (eds) (1978). *The Hidden Costs of Reward: New Perspectives on the Psychology of Human Motivation*. Hillsdale, NY: Erlbaum. [211]

Levine, David (1998). Modeling altruism and spitefulness in experiments. *Review of Economic Dynamics* 1: 593–622. [231, 292]

Lewis, David (1969). *Convention: A Philosophical Study*. Cambridge, MA: Harvard University Press. [236, 239, 294]

Lindahl, Erik (1919/1958). Just taxation—a positive solution. Translated by Elizabeth Henderson. In Richard Musgrave and Alan Peacock (eds), *Classics in the Theory of Public Finance*, pp. 168–76. Basingstoke: Palgrave Macmillan. [165]

List, Christian and Philip Pettit (2011). *Group Agency: The Possibility, Design, and Status of Corporate Agents*. Oxford: Oxford University Press. [284, 293]

Locke, John (1690/1960). *Two Treatises of Government*. Cambridge: Cambridge University Press. [181]

Loewenstein, George and Peter Ubel (2008). Hedonic adaptation and the role of decision and experience utility in public policy. *Journal of Public Economics* 92: 1795–810. [18]

Loomes, Graham and Robert Sugden (1982). Regret theory: an alternative theory of rational choice under uncertainty. *Economic Journal* 92: 805–24. [283]

McCabe, Kevin, Mary Rigdon, and Vernon Smith (2003). Positive reciprocity and intentions in trust games. *Journal of Economic Behavior and Organization* 52: 267–75. [216]

Macfie, Alec (1971). The invisible hand of Jupiter. *Journal of the History of Ideas* 32: 595–9. [290]

MacIntyre, Alasdair (1984). *After Virtue: A Study in Moral Theory*, second edition. Notre Dame, IN: University of Notre Dame Press. First edition 1981. [296]

McQuillin, Ben and Robert Sugden (2012). How the market responds to dynamically inconsistent preferences. *Social Choice and Welfare* 38: 617–34. [126, 133, 287, 288]

Manzini, Paola and Marco Mariotti (2012). Categorize then choose: boundedly rational choice and welfare. *Journal of the European Economic Association* 10: 939–1213. [58]

Manzini, Paola and Marco Mariotti (2014). Welfare economics and bounded rationality: the case for model-based approaches. *Journal of Economic Methodology* 21: 342–60. [58]

Mehta, Judith and Robert Sugden (2013). Making sense of complex choice situations. In Judith Mehta (ed.), *Behavioural Economics in Competition and Consumer Policy*, pp. 41–8. Norwich: Centre for Competition Policy. [140–7*, 156–9*, 288]

Menger, Carl (1871/1950). *Principles of Economics*. Translated by James Dingwall and Bert Hoselitz. Glencoe, IL: Free Press. [5]

References

Milanovic, Branko (2013). Global income inequality in numbers: in history and now. *Global Policy* 4(2): 198–208. [200]

Mill, John Stuart (1859/1972). *On Liberty*. London: Dent. [3]

Mill, John Stuart (1861/1972). *Utilitarianism*. London: Dent. [3, 258]

Mill, John Stuart (1869/1988). *The Subjection of Women*. Indianapolis, IN: Hackett. [2, 99, 213, 275]

Mill, John Stuart (1871/1909). *Principles of Political Economy*. London: Longmans. First edition 1848. [1, 4, 175, 190, 198]

Misyak, Jennifer and Nick Chater (2014). Virtual bargaining: a theory of social decision-making. *Philosophical Transactions of the Royal Society B* 369: 20130487. [295]

Munro, Alistair and Robert Sugden (2003). On the theory of reference-dependent preferences. *Journal of Economic Behavior and Organization* 50: 407–28. [114]

Nagel, Thomas (1986). *The View From Nowhere*. Oxford: Oxford University Press. [18, 24]

Nelson, Julie (2005). Interpersonal relations and economics: comments from a feminist perspective. In Benedetto Gui and Robert Sugden (eds), *Economics and Social Interaction: Accounting for Interpersonal Relations*, pp. 250–61. Cambridge: Cambridge University Press. [212]

Nikiforakis, Nikos (2008). Punishment and counter-punishment in public good games: can we really govern ourselves? *Journal of Public Economics* 92: 91–112. [292, 296]

Nozick, Robert (1974). *Anarchy, State, and Utopia*. New York: Basic Books. [192]

Nucci, Larry (2001). *Education in the Moral Domain*. Cambridge: Cambridge University Press. [295]

Nussbaum, Martha (2000). *Women and Human Development: The Capabilities Approach*. Cambridge: Cambridge University Press. [89]

Office of Fair Trading (2011). Consumer behavioural biases in competition: a survey. Report to Office of Fair Trading by London Economics in association with Steffen Huck and Jidong Zhou. [289]

Parducci, Allen (1965). Category judgment: a range-frequency model. *Psychological Review* 72: 407–18. [71]

Pareto, Vilfredo (1909/1971). *Manual of Political Economy*. New York: Kelley. Translated by Ann Schwier and Alfred Page. Milan: Società Editrice Libraria. [283]

Pattanaik, Prasanta (1968). Risk, impersonality and the social welfare function. *Journal of Political Economy* 76: 1152–69. [283]

Pelligra, Vittorio (2005). Under trusting eyes: the responsive nature of trust. In Benedetto Gui and Robert Sugden (eds), *Economics and Social Interaction*, pp. 195–24. Cambridge: Cambridge University Press. [220]

Pettit, Philip (2006). Preference, deliberation and satisfaction. *Philosophy*, Supplement 59 (*Preferences and Well-Being*): 131–53. [90]

Pigou, Arthur (1920). *The Economics of Welfare*. London: Macmillan. [142]

Piketty, Thomas (2014). *Capital in the Twenty-First Century*. Cambridge, MA: Harvard University Press. First published in French 2013. [200]

Piketty, Thomas and Emmanuel Saez (2003). Income inequality in the United States, 1913–1998. *Quarterly Journal of Economics* 118: 1–39. [200]

Plott, Charles (1996). Rational individual behaviour in markets and social choice processes: the discovered preference hypothesis. In Kenneth Arrow, Enrico Colombatto, Mark Perlman, and Christian Schmidt (eds), *The Rational Foundations of Economic Behaviour*, pp. 225–50. Basingstoke: Macmillan and International Economic Association. [285]

Prelec, Drazen and George Loewenstein (1998). The red and the black: mental accounting of savings and debt. *Marketing Science* 17: 4–28. [194]

Preston, Stephanie and Frans de Waal (2002). Empathy: its ultimate and proximate bases. *Behavioral and Brain Sciences* 25: 1–20. [273]

Putnam, Hillary (2004). *Ethics without Ontology*. Cambridge, MA: Harvard University Press. [26]

Rabin, Matthew (1993). Incorporating fairness into game theory and economics. *American Economic Review* 83: 1281–302. [221, 251, 253]

Rabin, Matthew (2013). Incorporating limited rationality into economics. *Journal of Economic Literature* 51: 528–43. [60]

Rawls, John (1971). *A Theory of Justice*. Cambridge, MA: Harvard University Press. [174, 194, 260, 264, 283, 284]

Rawls, John (1985). Justice as fairness: political not metaphysical. *Philosophy and Public Affairs* 14: 223–51. [261]

Rawls, John (1993). *Political Liberalism*. New York: Columbia University Press. [26]

Read, Daniel and Barbara van Leeuwen (1998). Predicting hunger: the effects of appetite and delay on choice. *Organizational Behavior and Human Decision Processes* 76: 189–205. [8]

Regan, Donald (1980). *Utilitarianism and Cooperation*. Oxford: Clarendon Press. [232]

Rizzolatti, Giacomo, Leonardo Fogassi, and Vittorio Gallese (2001). Neurophysiological mechanisms underlying action understanding and imitation. *Nature Reviews: Neuroscience* 2: 661–70. [296]

Robbins, Lionel (1935). *The Nature and Significance of Economic Science*, second edition. London: Macmillan. First edition 1932. [14]

Robinson, Terry and Kent Berridge (1993). The neural basis of drug craving: an incentive-sensitization theory of addiction. *Brain Research Reviews* 18: 247–91. [286]

Roemer, John (1998). *Equality of Opportunity*. Cambridge, MA: Harvard University Press. [177, 190]

Rousseau, Jean-Jacques (1755/1988). Discourse on the origin and foundations of inequality among men. In Alan Ritter and Julia Conaway Bondanella (eds), *Rousseau's Political Writings*, pp. 3–57. New York: Norton. [242]

Ryan, Richard and Edward Deci (2000). Intrinsic and extrinsic motivations: classic definitions and new directions. *Contemporary Educational Psychology* 25: 54–67. [211]

Salant, Yuval and Ariel Rubinstein (2008). (A, f): choice with frames. *Review of Economic Studies* 75: 1287–96. [21, 58, 287]

Salop, Steven and Joseph Stiglitz (1977). Bargains and ripoffs: a model of monopolistically competitive price dispersion. *Review of Economic Studies* 44: 493–510. [289]

Sandel, Michael (2009). *Justice: What's the Right Thing to Do?* London: Penguin. [190, 208, 276]

Sandel, Michael (2012). *What Money Can't Buy: The Moral Limits of Markets*. New York: Farrar, Straus and Giroux. [169, 291]

Savage, Leonard (1954). *The Foundations of Statistics*. New York: Wiley. [9, 70]

Scheibehenne, Benjamin, Rainer Griefeneder, and Peter M. Todd (2010). Can there ever be too many options? A meta-analytic review of choice overload. *Journal of Consumer Research* 37: 409–25. [288]

Schelling, Thomas (1960). *The Strategy of Conflict*. Cambridge, MA: Harvard University Press. [234, 294]

Schelling, Thomas (1980). The intimate contest for self-command. *The Public Interest* 60 (Summer): 94–118. [148]

Schubert, Christian (2015). Opportunity and preference learning. *Economics and Philosophy* 31: 275–95. [286, 287, 289]

Schwartz, Barry (2004). *The Paradox of Choice: Why More is Less*. New York: Harper Collins. [143]

Scitovsky, Tibor (1950). Ignorance as a source of oligopoly power. *American Economic Review* 40(2): 48–53. [289]

Searle, John (1990). Collective intentions and actions. In Philip Cohen, Jerry Morgan, and Martha Pollack (eds), *Intentions in Communication*, pp. 401–15. Cambridge, MA: MIT Press. [293]

Searle, John (1995). *The Construction of Social Reality*. New York: Free Press. [295]

Sen, Amartya (1970). The impossibility of a Paretian liberal. *Journal of Political Economy* 78: 152–7. [284]

Sen, Amartya (1977). Rational fools: a critique of the behavioral foundations of economic theory. *Philosophy and Public Affairs* 6: 317–44. [286]

Sen, Amartya (1999). *Development as Freedom*. Oxford: Oxford University Press. [24, 89]

Sen, Amartya (2009). *The Idea of Justice*. London: Allen Lane. [26]

Shafer-Landau, Russ (2003). *Moral Realism: A Defence*. Oxford: Oxford University Press. [257]

Shweder, Richard, Manamohan Mahapatra, and Joan Miller (1987). Culture and moral development. In Jerome Kagan and Sharon Lamb, *The Emergence of Morality in Young Children*, pp. 1–83. Chicago: University of Chicago Press. [295]

Skyrms, Brian (1996). *Evolution of the Social Contract*. Cambridge: Cambridge University Press. [294]

Slovic, Paul and Sarah Lichtenstein (1968). Relative importance of probabilities and payoffs in risk taking. *Journal of Experimental Psychology* 78: 1–18. [71]

Smetana, Judith (1993). Understanding of social rules. In Mark Bennett (ed.), *The Child as Psychologist: An Introduction to the Development of Social Cognition*, pp. 111–41. Harlow: Prentice-Hall. [295]

Smith, Adam (1759/1976). *The Theory of Moral Sentiments*. Oxford: Oxford University Press. [26, 186, 190, 273, 283, 291, 296]

Smith, Adam (1763/1978). *Lectures on Jurisprudence*. Oxford: Oxford University Press. [266, 291]

Smith, Adam (1776/1976). *The Wealth of Nations*. Oxford: Oxford University Press. [6, 15, 107, 137, 186, 198, 206]

Strotz, Robert (1955–56). Myopia and inconsistency in dynamic utility maximisation. *Review of Economic Studies* 23: 165–80. [286]

Sugden, Robert (1982). On the economics of philanthropy. *Economic Journal* 92: 341–50. [218]

Sugden, Robert (1984). Reciprocity: the supply of public goods through voluntary contributions. *Economic Journal* 94: 772–87. [218]

Sugden, Robert (1985). Liberty, preference and choice. *Economics and Philosophy* 1: 213–29. [284]

Sugden, Robert (1986). *The Economics of Rights, Cooperation and Welfare*. Oxford: Blackwell. [39, 291, 294]

Sugden, Robert (1990). Rules for choosing among public goods: a contractarian approach. *Constitutional Political Economy* 1: 63–82. [289]

Sugden, Robert (1991). Rational choice: a survey of contributions from economics and philosophy. *Economic Journal* 101: 751–85. [233]

Sugden, Robert (1993a). Normative judgements and spontaneous order: the contractarian element in Hayek's thought. *Constitutional Political Economy* 4: 393–424. [291]

Sugden, Robert (1993b). Thinking as a team: toward an explanation of nonselfish behavior. *Social Philosophy and Policy* 10: 69–89. [233]

Sugden, Robert (1995). A theory of focal points. *Economic Journal* 105: 533–50. [293]

Sugden, Robert (1998a). The metric of opportunity. *Economics and Philosophy* 14: 307–37. [286]

Sugden, Robert (1998b). Normative expectations: the simultaneous evolution of institutions and norms. In Avner Ben-Ner and Louis Putterman (eds), *Economics, Values, and Organization*, pp. 73–100. Cambridge: Cambridge University Press. [220]

Sugden, Robert (2002). Beyond sympathy and empathy: Adam Smith's concept of fellow-feeling. *Economics and Philosophy* 18: 63–87. [284]

Sugden, Robert (2004a). The opportunity criterion: consumer sovereignty without the assumption of coherent preferences. *American Economic Review* 94: 1014–33. [287]

Sugden, Robert (2004b). Living with unfairness: the limits of equality of opportunity in a market economy. *Social Choice and Welfare* 22: 211–36. [175–80*, 180–5*]

Sugden, Robert (2004c). *The Economics of Rights, Cooperation and Welfare*, second edition. Basingstoke: Palgrave Macmillan. First edition 1986. [295]

Sugden, Robert (2005). Fellow feeling. In Benedetto Gui and Robert Sugden (eds), *Economics and Social Interaction*, pp. 52–75. Cambridge: Cambridge University Press. [272–7*]

Sugden, Robert (2006a). Hume's non-instrumental and non-propositional decision theory. *Economics and Philosophy* 22: 365–91. [286]

Sugden, Robert (2006b). Taking unconsidered preferences seriously. *Philosophy*, Supplement 59 ('Preferences and Well-Being'): 209–32. [100–6*]

Sugden, Robert (2008). David Hume's *Treatise of Human Nature*. *Topoi* 27: 153–9. [296]

Sugden, Robert (2009a). Can economics be founded on 'indisputable facts of experience'? Lionel Robbins and the pioneers of neoclassical economics. *Economica* 76: 857–72. [284]

Sugden, Robert (2009b). Can a Humean be a contractarian? In Michael Baurmann and Bernd Lahno (eds), *Perspectives in Moral Science: Contributions from Philosophy, Economics, and Politics in Honour of Hartmut Kliemt*, pp. 11–24. Frankfurt: Frankfurt School Verlag. [33–7*]

Sugden, Robert (2010). Is there a distinction between morality and convention? In Michael Baurmann, Geoffrey Brennan, Robert Goodin, and Nicholas Southwood (eds), *Norms and Values: The Role of Social Norms as Instruments of Value Realisation*, pp. 47–65. Baden-Baden: Nomos Verlagsgesellschaft. [256–9*]

Sugden, Robert (2013). The behavioural economist and the social planner: to whom should behavioural welfare economics be addressed? *Inquiry* 56: 519–38. [17–19*, 19–24*, 37–42*, 42–50*]

Sugden, Robert (2015a). Looking for a psychology for the inner rational agent. *Social Theory and Practice* 41: 579–98. [68–72*]

Sugden, Robert (2015b). Opportunity and preference learning: a reply to Christian Schubert. *Economics and Philosophy* 31: 297–303. [289]

Sugden, Robert (2015c). Consumers' surplus when individuals lack integrated preferences: a development of some ideas from Dupuit. *European Journal of History of Economic Thought* 22: 1042–63. [289]

Sugden, Robert (2015d). Team reasoning and intentional cooperation for mutual benefit. *Journal of Social Ontology* 1: 143–66. [241, 293, 294, 295]

Sugden, Robert (2016). On David Gauthier's theories of coordination and cooperation. *Dialogue* 55: 713–37. [295]

Sugden, Robert (2017a). Do people really want to be nudged towards healthy lifestyles? *International Review of Economics* 64: 113–23. [42–50*]

Sugden, Robert (2017b). Characterising competitive equilibrium in terms of opportunity. *Social Choice and Welfare* 48: 487–503. [112–24*]

Sugden, Robert and Joshua Chen-Yuan Teng (2016). Is happiness a matter for governments? A Millian perspective on Layard's 'new science'. In Stefano Bartolino, Ennio Bilancini. Luigino Bruni, and Pier Luigi Porta (eds), *Policies for Happiness*, pp. 36–57. Oxford: Oxford University Press. [290]

Sunstein, Cass (2018). 'Better off, as judged by themselves': a comment on evaluating nudges. *International Review of Economics* 65: 1–8. [46]

Sunstein, Cass and Richard Thaler (2003a). Libertarian paternalism is not an oxymoron. *University of Chicago Law Review* 70: 1159–202. [18, 49, 53, 143, 166]

Sunstein, Cass and Richard Thaler (2003b). Libertarian paternalism. *American Economic Review, Papers and Proceedings* 93(2): 175–9. [18, 53]

Sunstein, Cass and Richard Thaler (2008). See Thaler and Sunstein (2008).

Thaler, Richard (1985). Mental accounting and consumer choice. *Marketing Science* 4: 199–214. [284]

Thaler, Richard (2015). *Misbehaving: How Economics Became Behavioural*. London: Allen Lane. [55]

Thaler, Richard and Cass Sunstein (2008). *Nudge: Improving Decisions About Health, Wealth, and Happiness*. New Haven, CT: Yale University Press. [11, 18, 20, 45, 50, 53, 80, 82, 89, 144, 154, 256]

Thomson, Judith Jarvis (1985). The trolley problem. *Yale Law Journal* 94: 1395–415. [295]

Titmuss, Richard (1970). *The Gift Relationship*. London: Allen and Unwin. [212]

Tuncel, Tuba and James Hammitt (2014). A new meta-analysis on the WTP/WTA disparity. *Journal of Environmental Economics and Management* 68: 175–87. [289]

Tuomela, Raimo and Kaarlo Miller (1988). We-intentions. *Philosophical Studies* 53: 367–89. [293]

Turiel, Elliot, Melanie Killen, and Charles Helwig (1987). Morality: its structure, functions, and vagaries. In Jerome Kagan and Sharon Lamb, *The Emergence of Morality in Young Children*, pp. 155–243. Chicago: University of Chicago Press. [295]

Tversky, Amos and Daniel Kahneman (1991). Loss aversion in riskless choice: a reference-dependent model. *Quarterly Journal of Economics* 106: 1039–61. [114]

Tversky, Amos and Daniel Kahneman (1992). Advances in prospect theory: cumulative representation of uncertainty. *Journal of Risk and Uncertainty* 5: 297–323. [59]

Ullman-Margalit, Edna (1977). *The Emergence of Norms*. Oxford: Clarendon Press. [294]

Vickrey, William (1960). Utility, strategy and social decision rules. *Quarterly Journal of Economics* 74: 507–35. [283]

Walras, Léon (1874/1954). *Elements of Pure Economics*. Translated by William Jaffé. Allen and Unwin: London. [5, 113, 179, 289]

Wason, Peter and Jonathan Evans (1975). Dual processes in reasoning? *Cognition* 3: 141–54. [67]

Weaver, Ray and Shane Frederick (2012). A reference-price theory of the endowment effect. *Journal of Marketing Research* 49: 696–707. [114]

Wicksell, Knut (1896/1958). A new principle of just taxation. Translated by James Buchanan. In Richard Musgrave and Alan Peacock (eds), *Classics in the Theory of Public Finance*, pp. 72–118. London: Macmillan. [165, 284]

Wicksteed, Philip (1910/1933). *The Common Sense of Political Economy*. London: Routledge. [43, 284]

Willaschek, Marcus (2017). Die Vulkane im Monde und das moralische Gesetz in mir. Immanuel Kant mit 60 Jahren. Forthcoming in Festschrift for Birgit Recki, edited by Stefan Waller. [296]

Winter, Eyal (2014). *Feeling Smart: Why Our Emotions Are More Rational than We Think*. New York: PublicAffairs. [295]

Young, Peyton (1998). *Individual Strategy and Social Structure*. Princeton, NJ: Princeton University Press. [294]

Index

Please note: '*f*' following a locator indicates a figure, 'n' following a locator indicates an endnote.